MECHANICSBURG PUBLIC LIBRARY

W9-CBG-128

3 0246 000794274

F
KIN   Kindt, Matt.
            Red handed : the fine art of
        strange crimes

RED HANDED

MATT KINDT

RED HANDED
THE FINE ART OF
STRANGE
CRIMES

First Second

NEW YORK

GAZ E

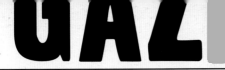

Today marks the ten year anniversary of Detective Gould's first year on the police force. Ten years ago, Gould made the first of many amazing arrests that would eventually lead to a string of high profile arrests over the years.

Since Gould's rise to crime-stopping stardom, there has yet to be one unsolved murder. In fact, the rate of unsolved crimes has plummeted since his rise to prominence.

Ironically, the rate of murder hasn't declined, but, with Detective Gould on the case the likelihood of a murder going unsolved is microscopic. When interviewing Gould regarding his unbelievable success, he credits the latest in technology, surveillance gadgets, and his fellow police officers with keeping his record perfect for so many years.

(continued on A12)

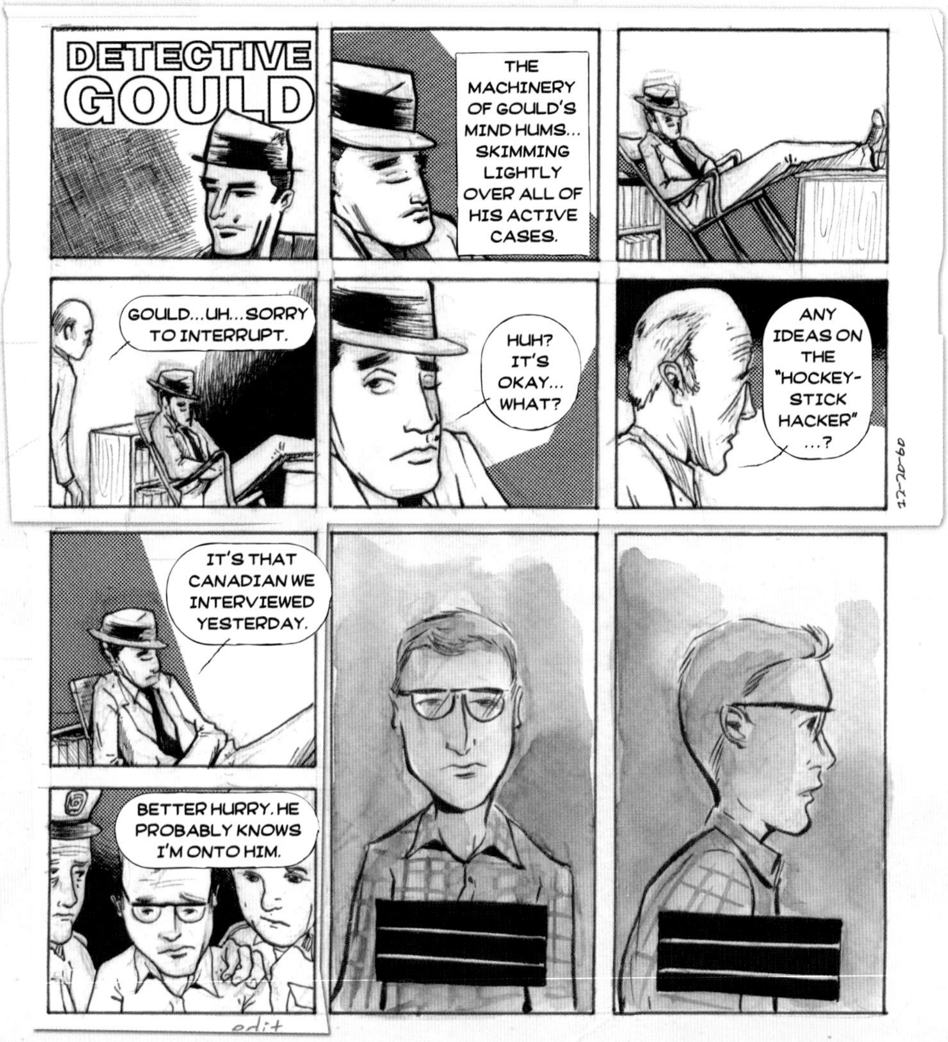
DETECTIVE GOULD
THE MACHINERY OF GOULD'S MIND HUMS... SKIMMING LIGHTLY OVER ALL OF HIS ACTIVE CASES.
GOULD...UH...SORRY TO INTERRUPT.
HUH? IT'S OKAY... WHAT?
ANY IDEAS ON THE "HOCKEY-STICK HACKER" ...?
IT'S THAT CANADIAN WE INTERVIEWED YESTERDAY.
BETTER HURRY. HE PROBABLY KNOWS I'M ONTO HIM.

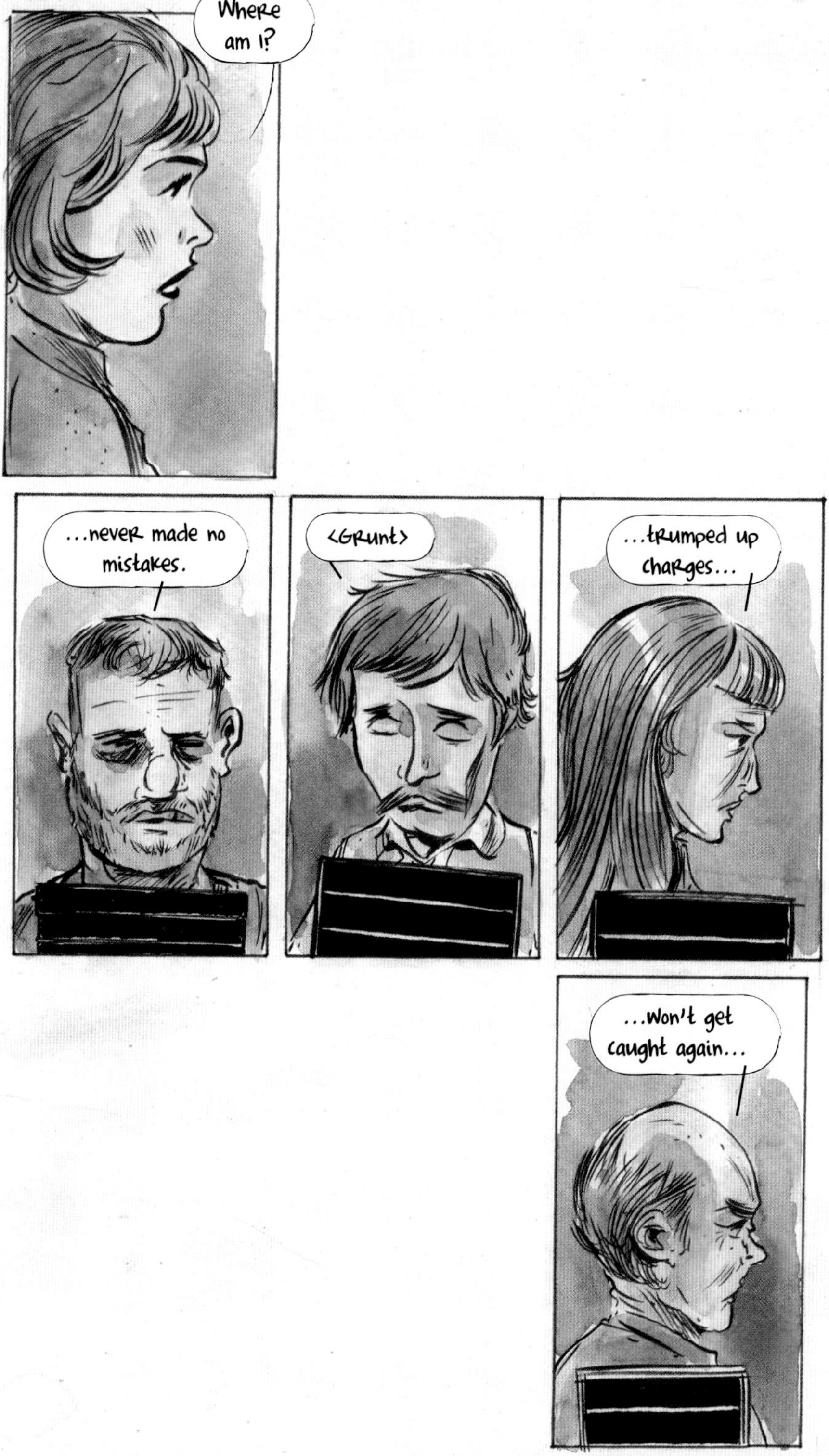
Where am I?
...never made no mistakes.
<Grunt>
...trumped up charges...
...Won't get caught again...

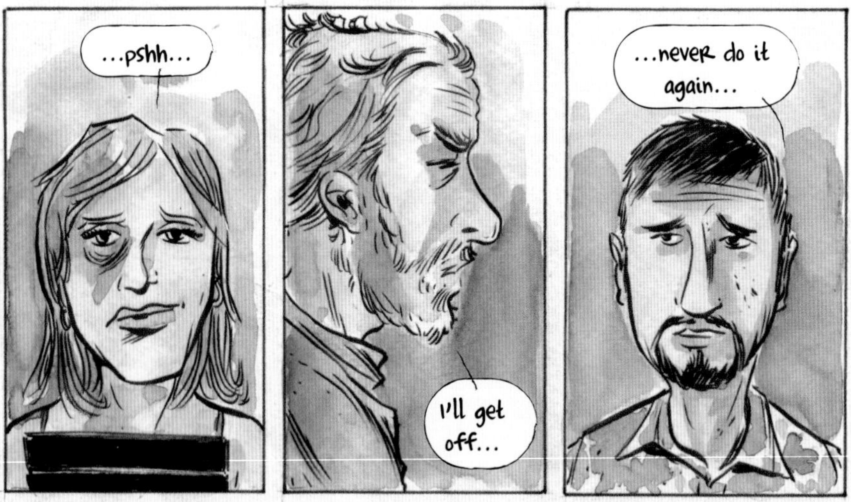
...pshh...
I'll get off...
...never do it again...

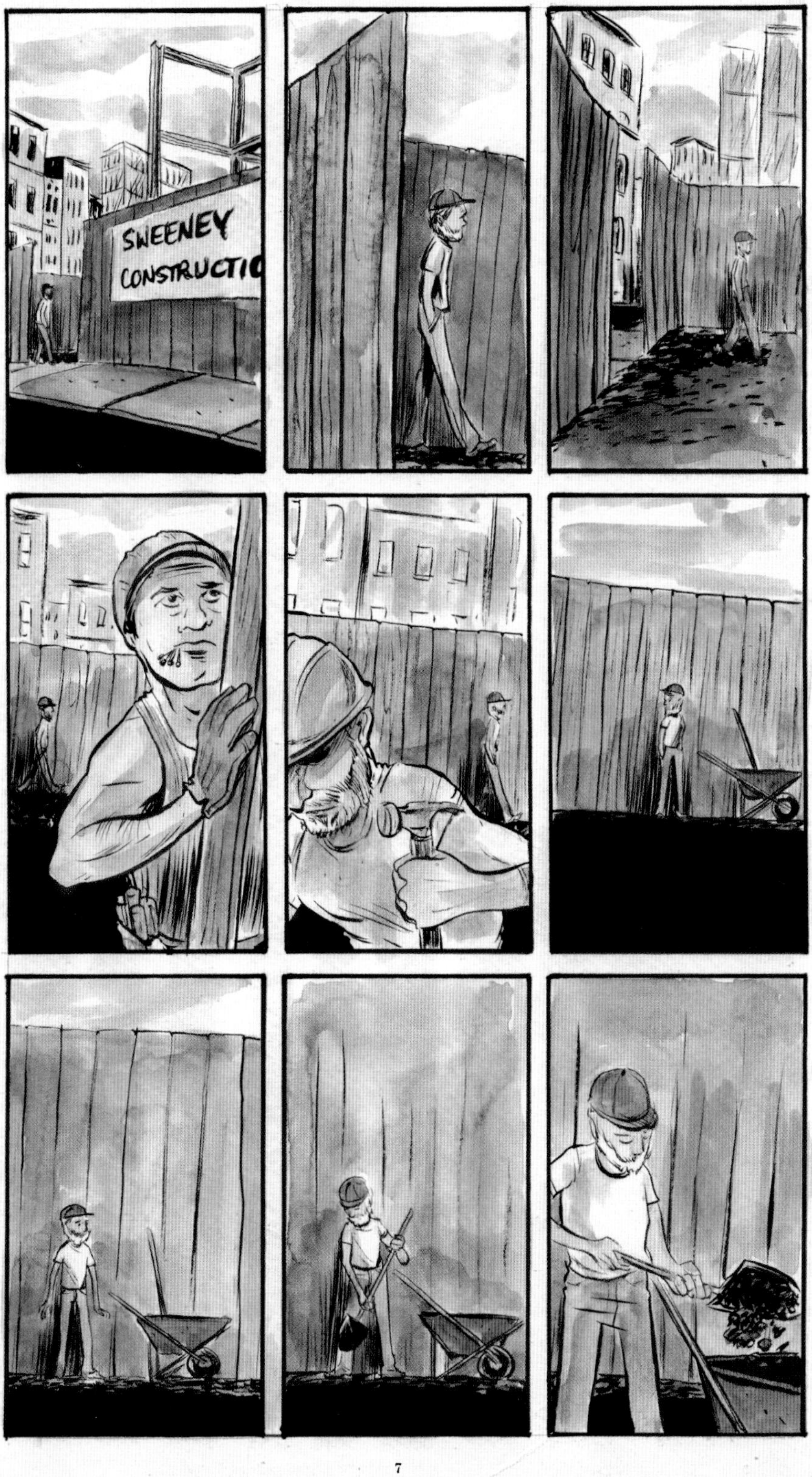
SWEENEY
CONSTRUCTIO

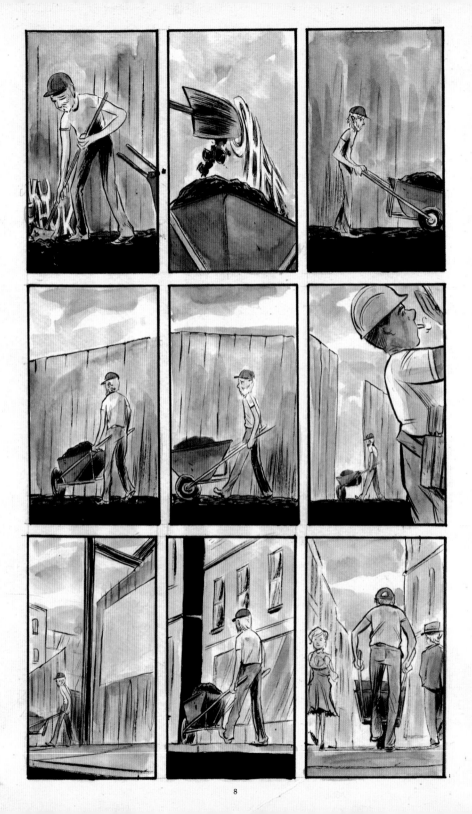

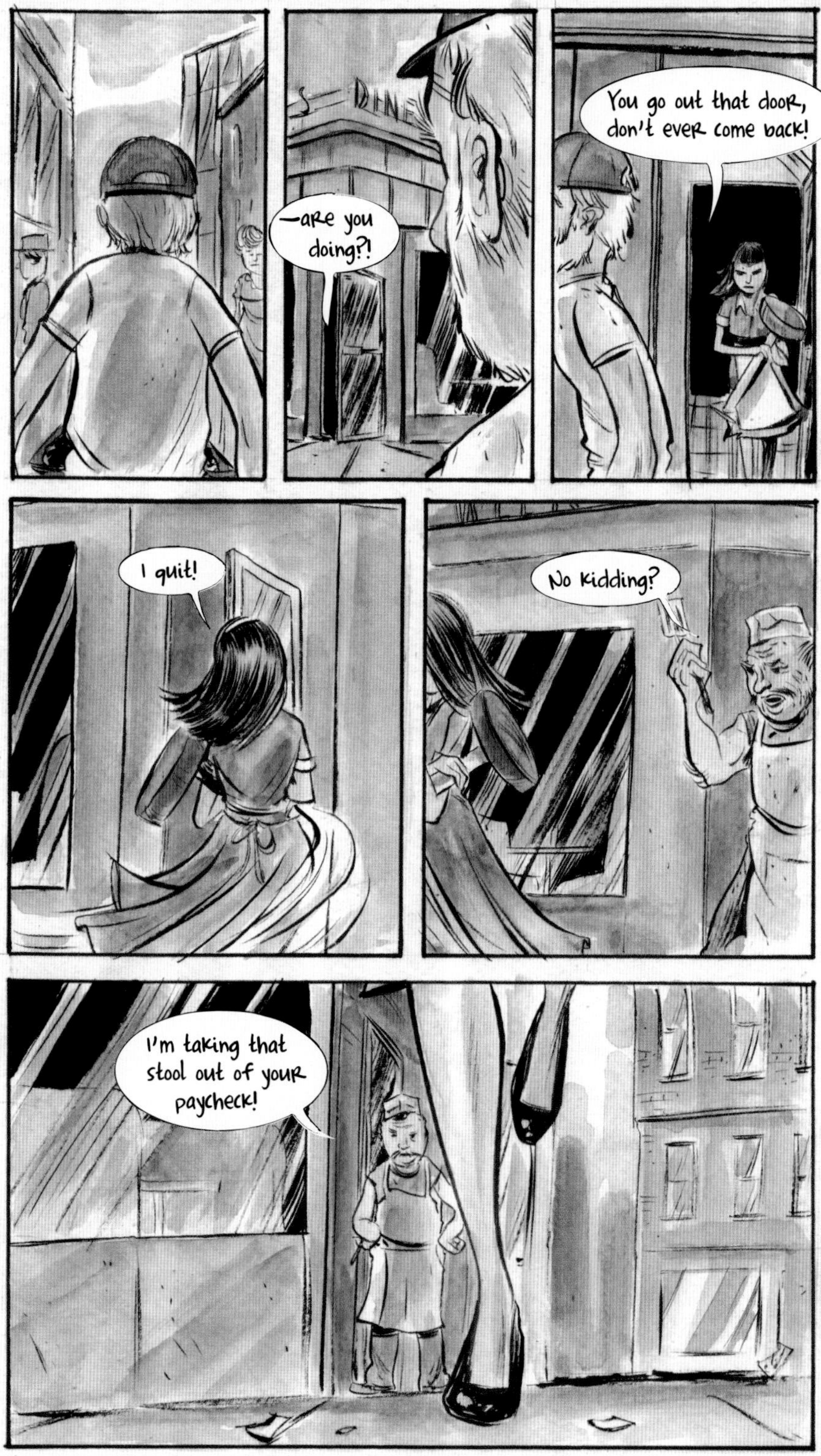
—are you
doing?!
You go out that door,
don't ever come back!
I quit!
No kidding?
I'm taking that
stool out of your
paycheck!

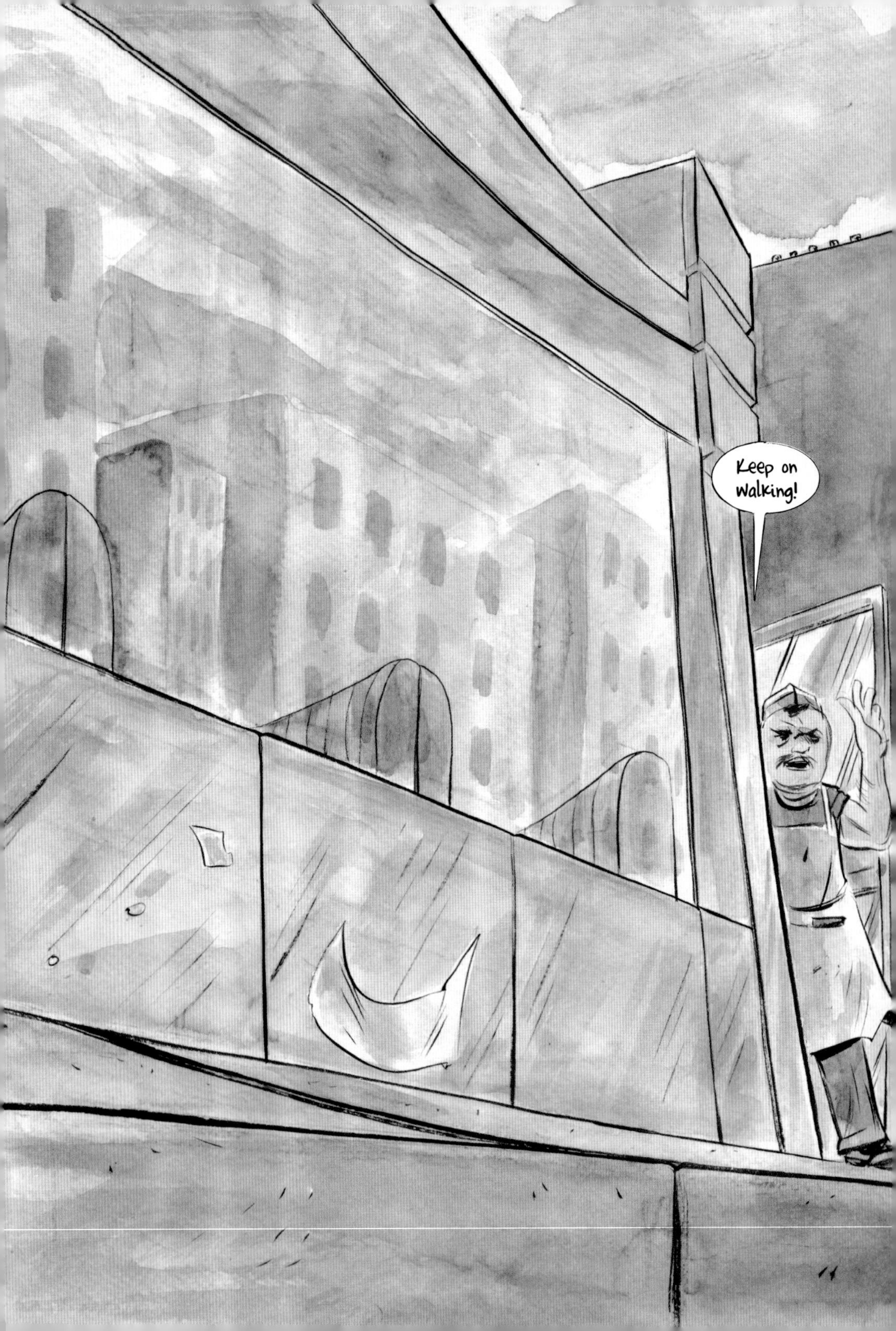
Keep on walking!

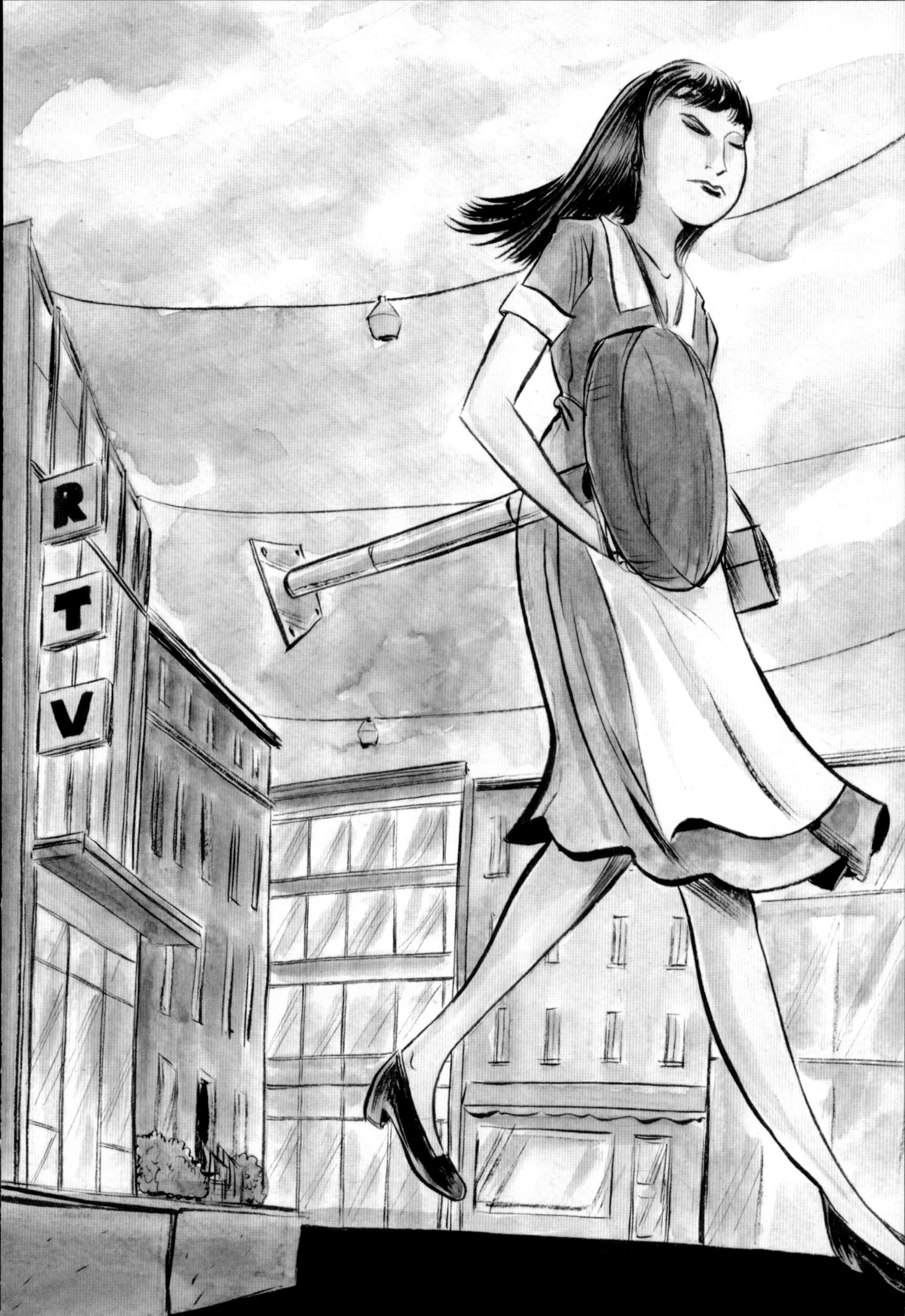
R
T
V

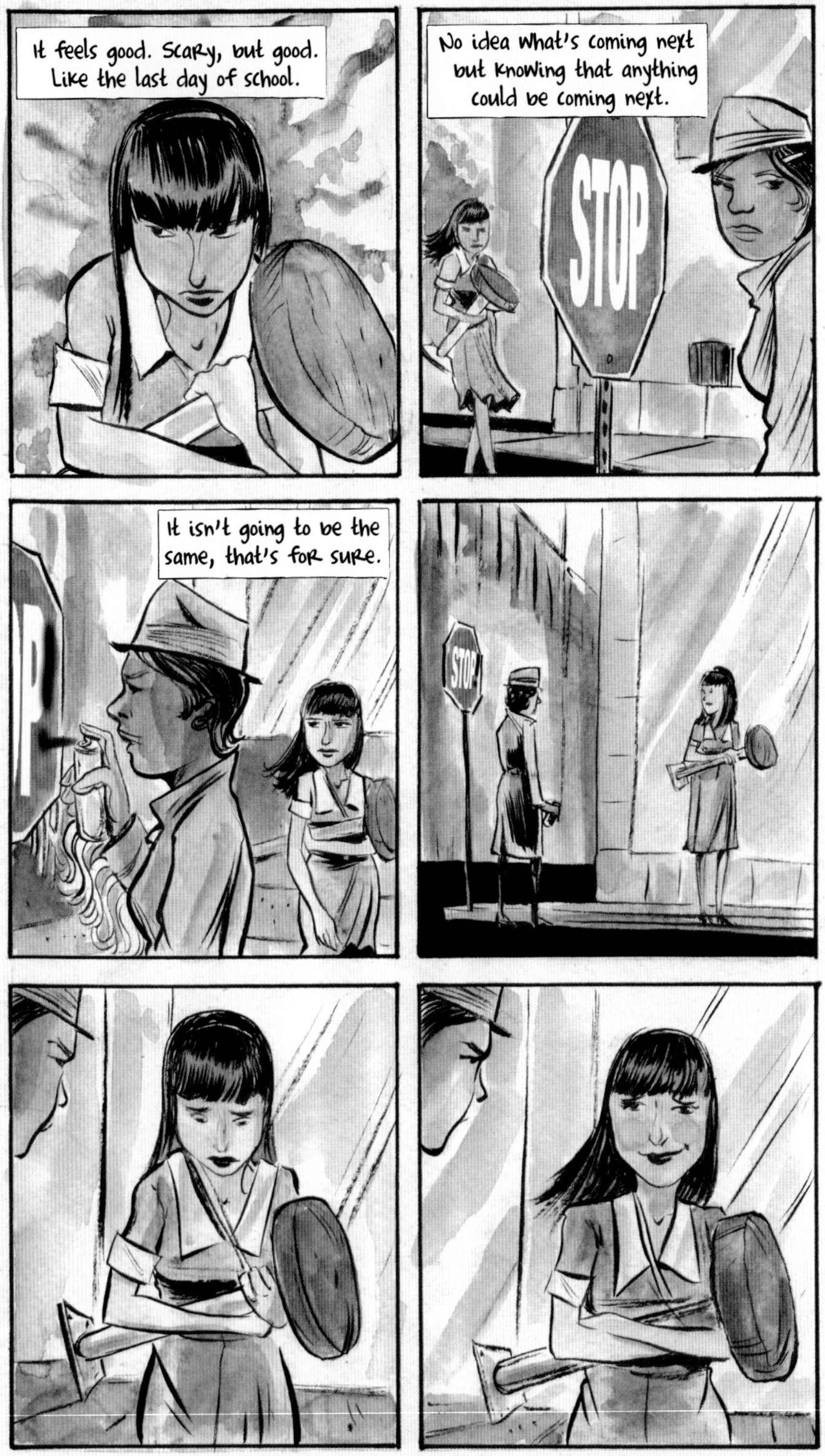
It feels good. Scary, but good. Like the last day of school.
No idea what's coming next but knowing that anything could be coming next.
STOP
It isn't going to be the same, that's for sure.
STOP

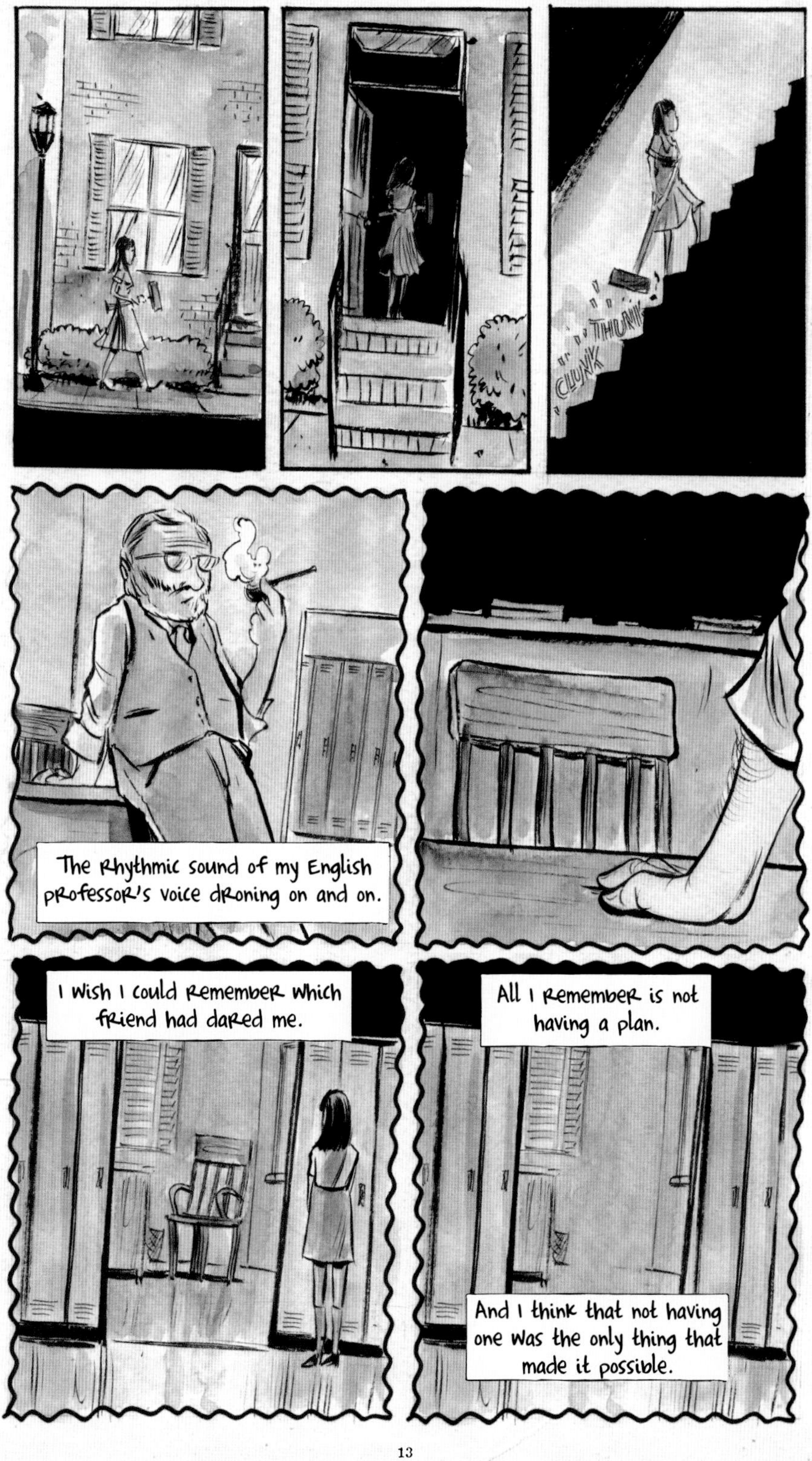
THUNK
CLUNK
The rhythmic sound of my English professor's voice droning on and on.
I wish I could remember which friend had dared me.
All I remember is not having a plan.
And I think that not having one was the only thing that made it possible.

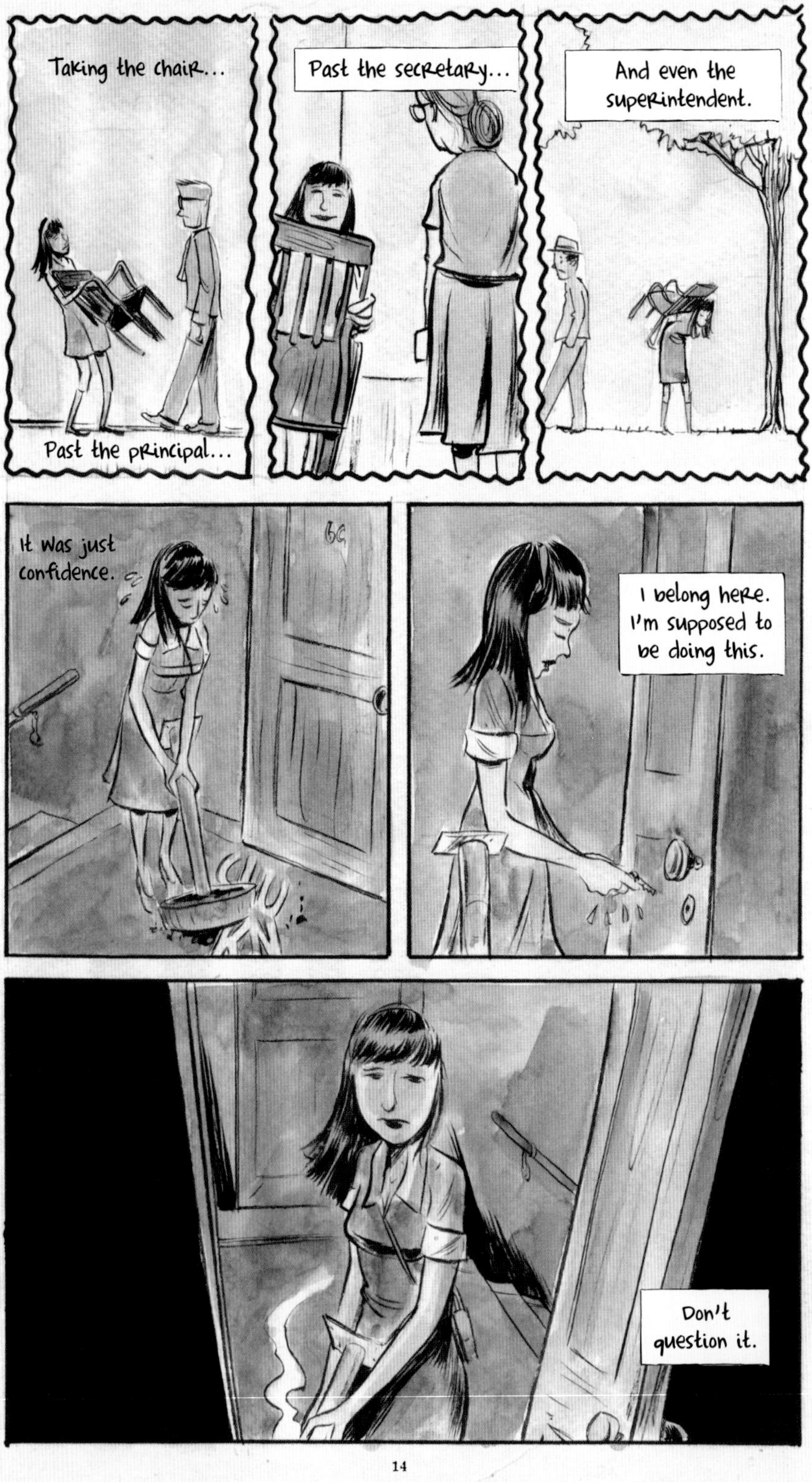
Taking the chair...
Past the principal...
Past the secretary...
And even the superintendent.
It was just confidence.
I belong here. I'm supposed to be doing this.
Don't question it.

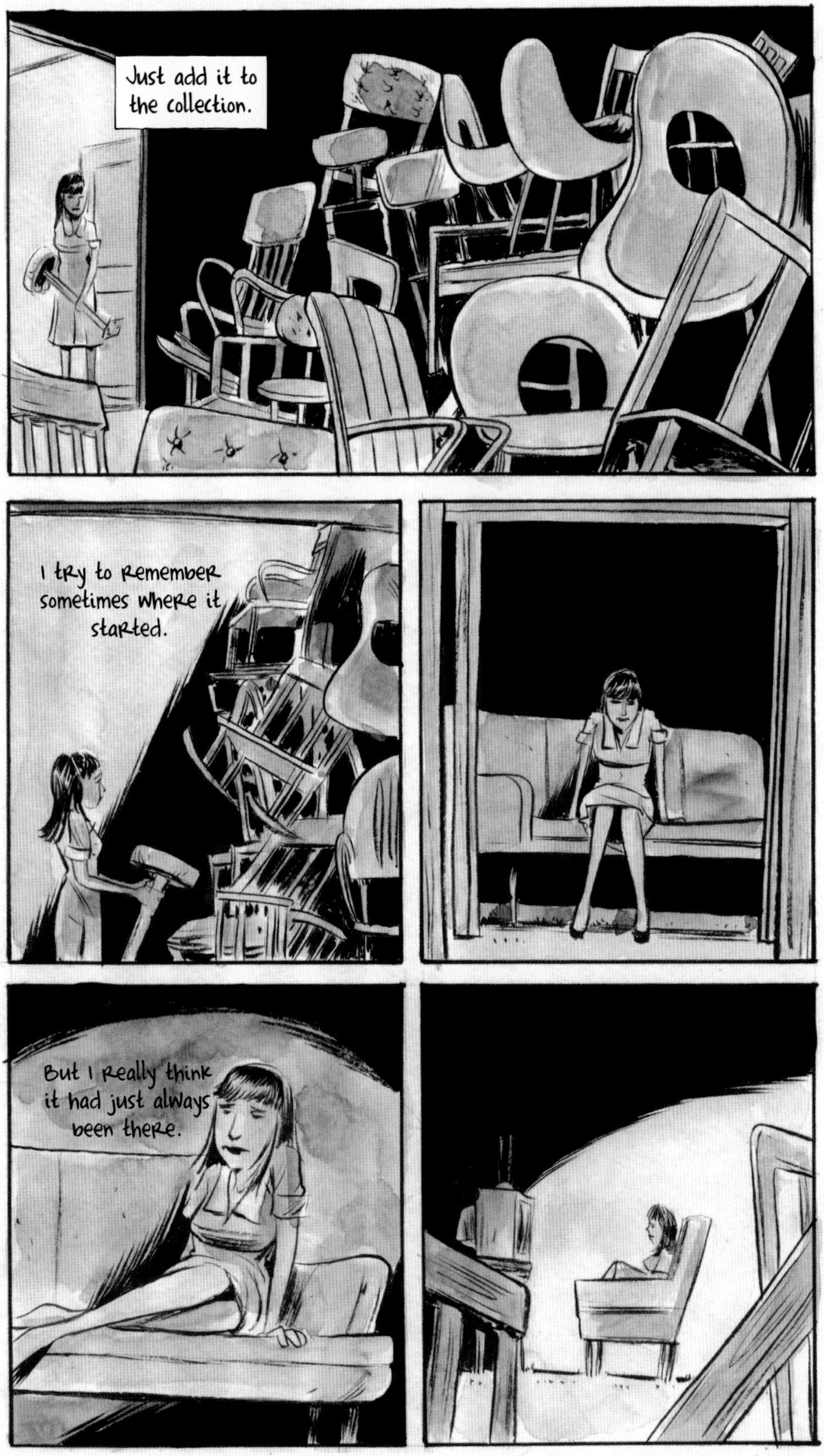
Just add it to the collection.
I try to remember sometimes where it started.
But I really think it had just always been there.

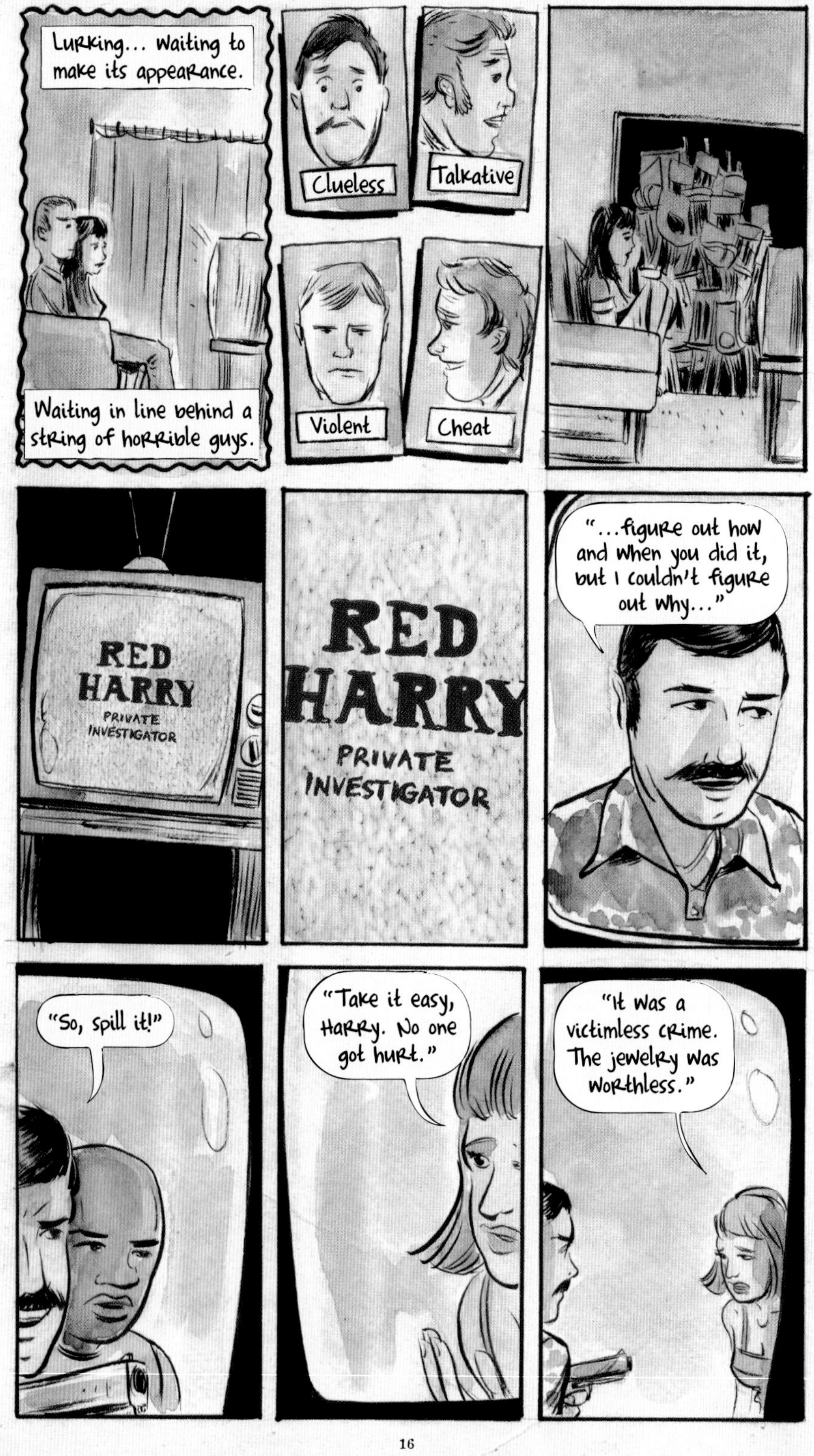

Lurking... Waiting to make its appearance.
Waiting in line behind a string of horrible guys.
Clueless
Talkative
Violent
Cheat
RED HARRY PRIVATE INVESTIGATOR
RED HARRY PRIVATE INVESTIGATOR
"...figure out how and when you did it, but I couldn't figure out why..."
"So, spill it!"
"Take it easy, Harry. No one got hurt."
"It was a victimless crime. The jewelry was worthless."

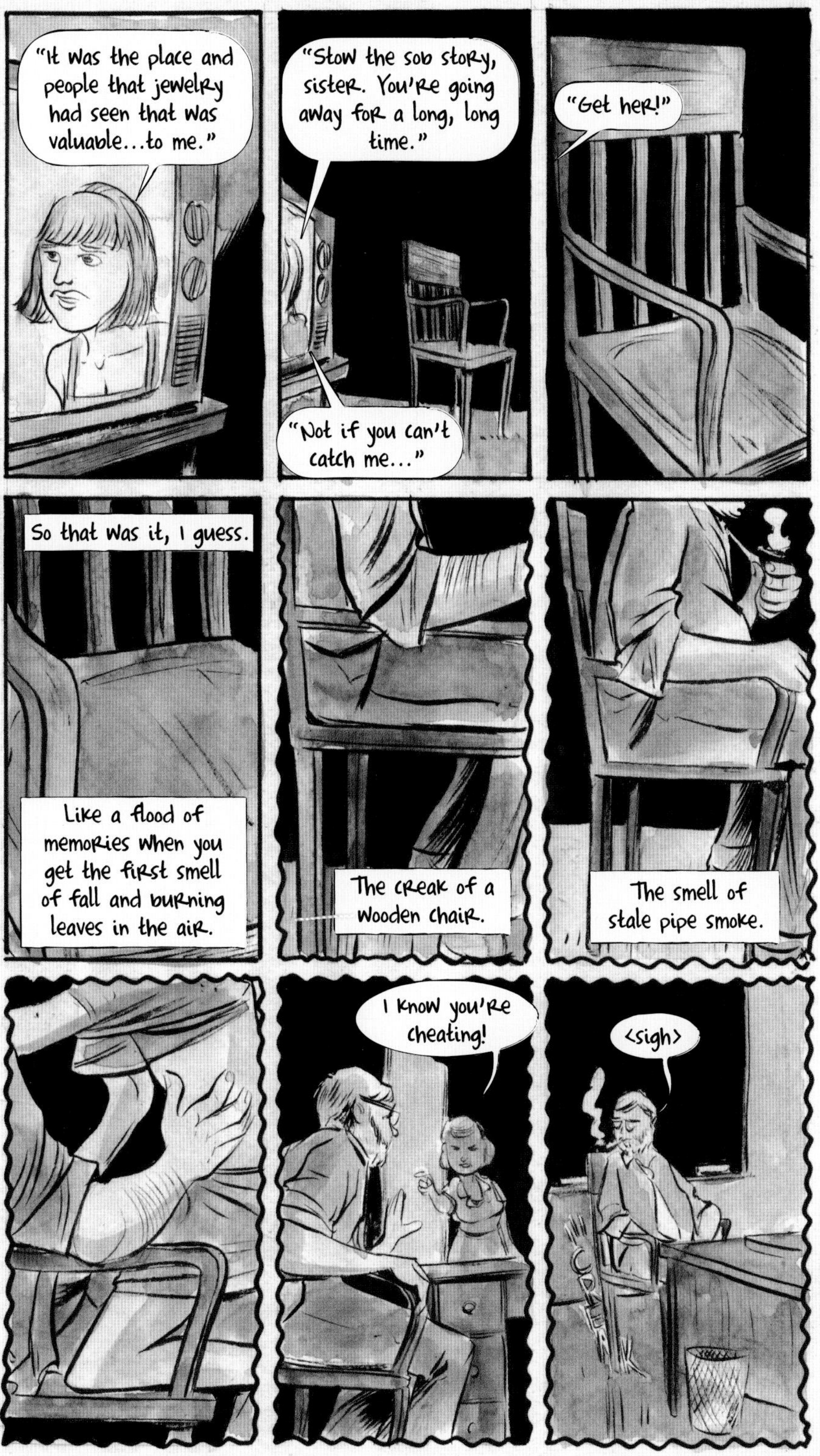
"It was the place and people that jewelry had seen that was valuable...to me."
"Stow the sob story, sister. You're going away for a long, long time."
"Not if you can't catch me..."
"Get her!"
So that was it, I guess.
Like a flood of memories when you get the first smell of fall and burning leaves in the air.
The creak of a wooden chair.
The smell of stale pipe smoke.
I know you're cheating!
<sigh>

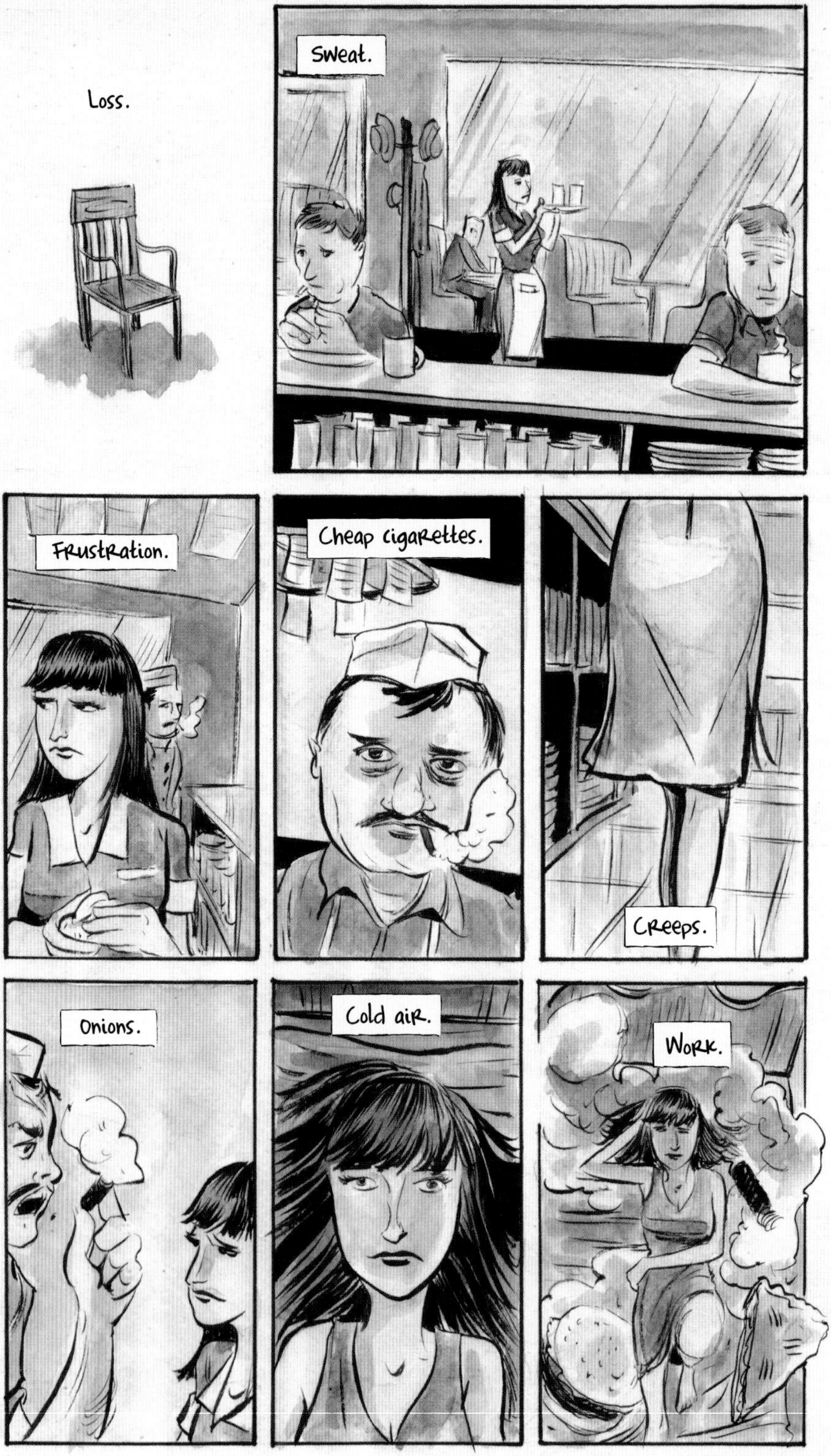
Loss.
Sweat.
Frustration.
Cheap cigarettes.
Creeps.
Onions.
Cold air.
Work.

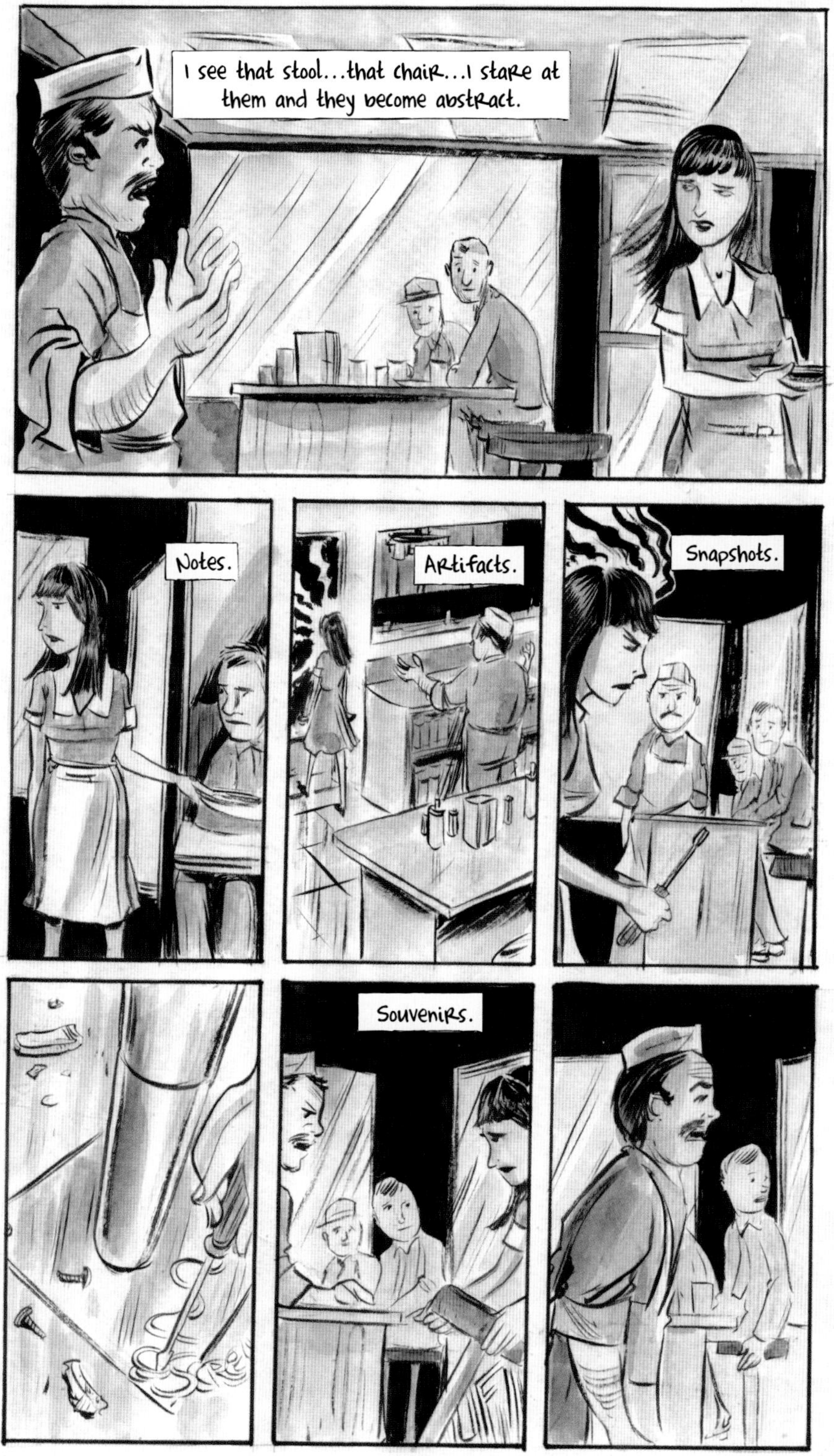
I see that stool...that chair...I stare at them and they become abstract.
Notes.
Artifacts.
Snapshots.
Souvenirs.

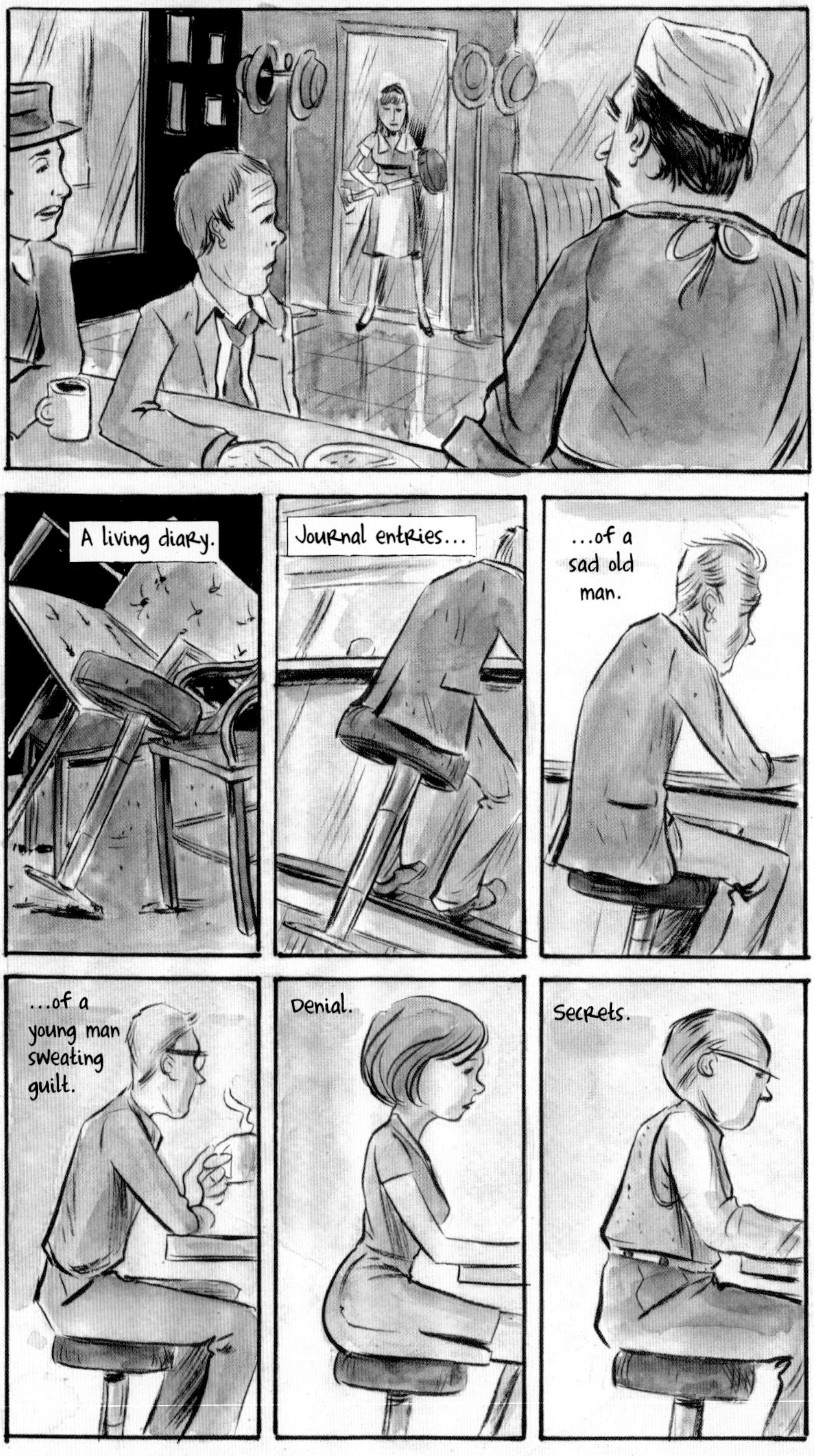
A living diary.
Journal entries...
...of a sad old man.
...of a young man sweating guilt.
Denial.
Secrets.

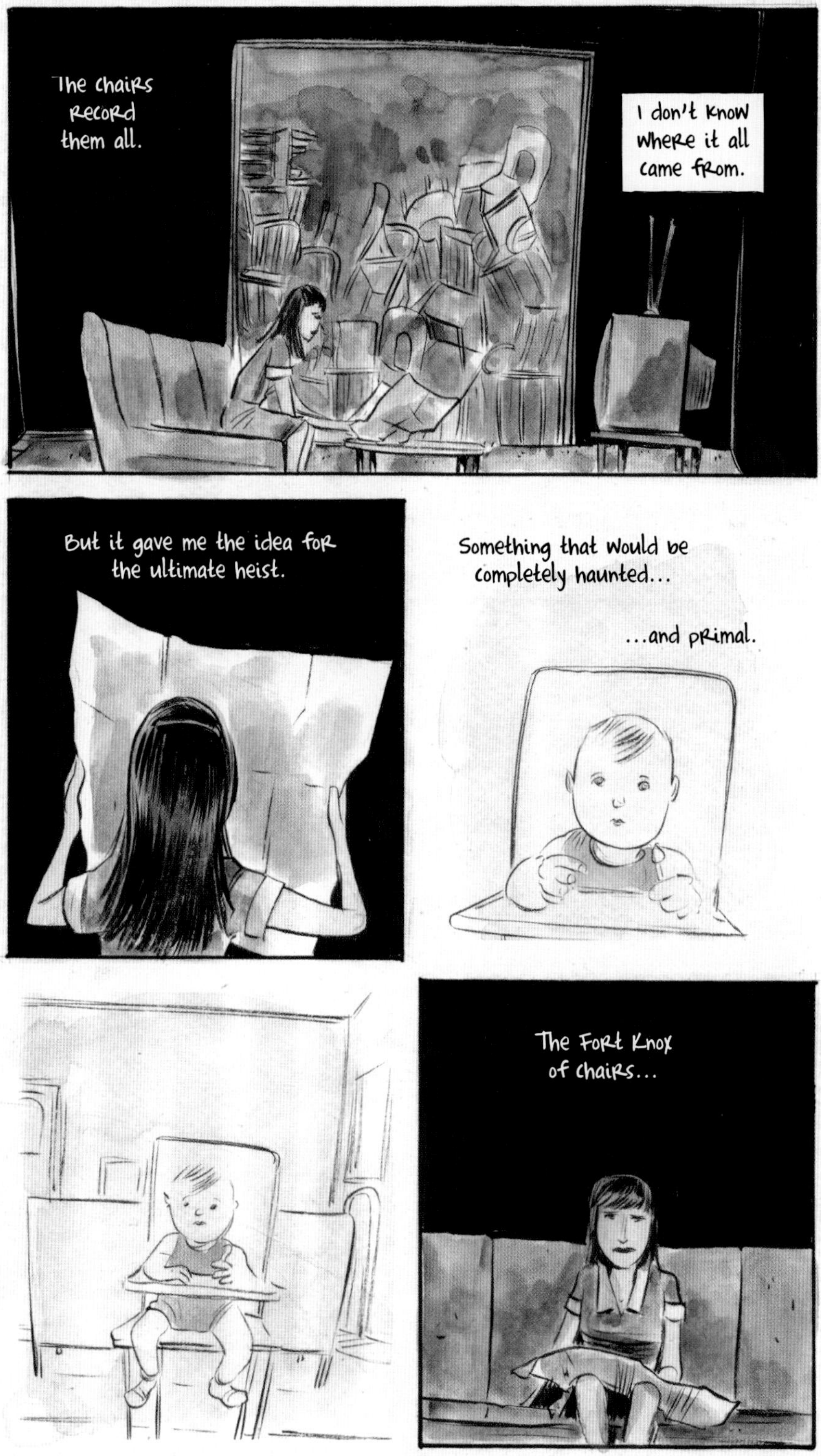
The chairs record them all.
I don't know where it all came from.
But it gave me the idea for the ultimate heist.
Something that would be completely haunted...
...and primal.
The Fort Knox of chairs...

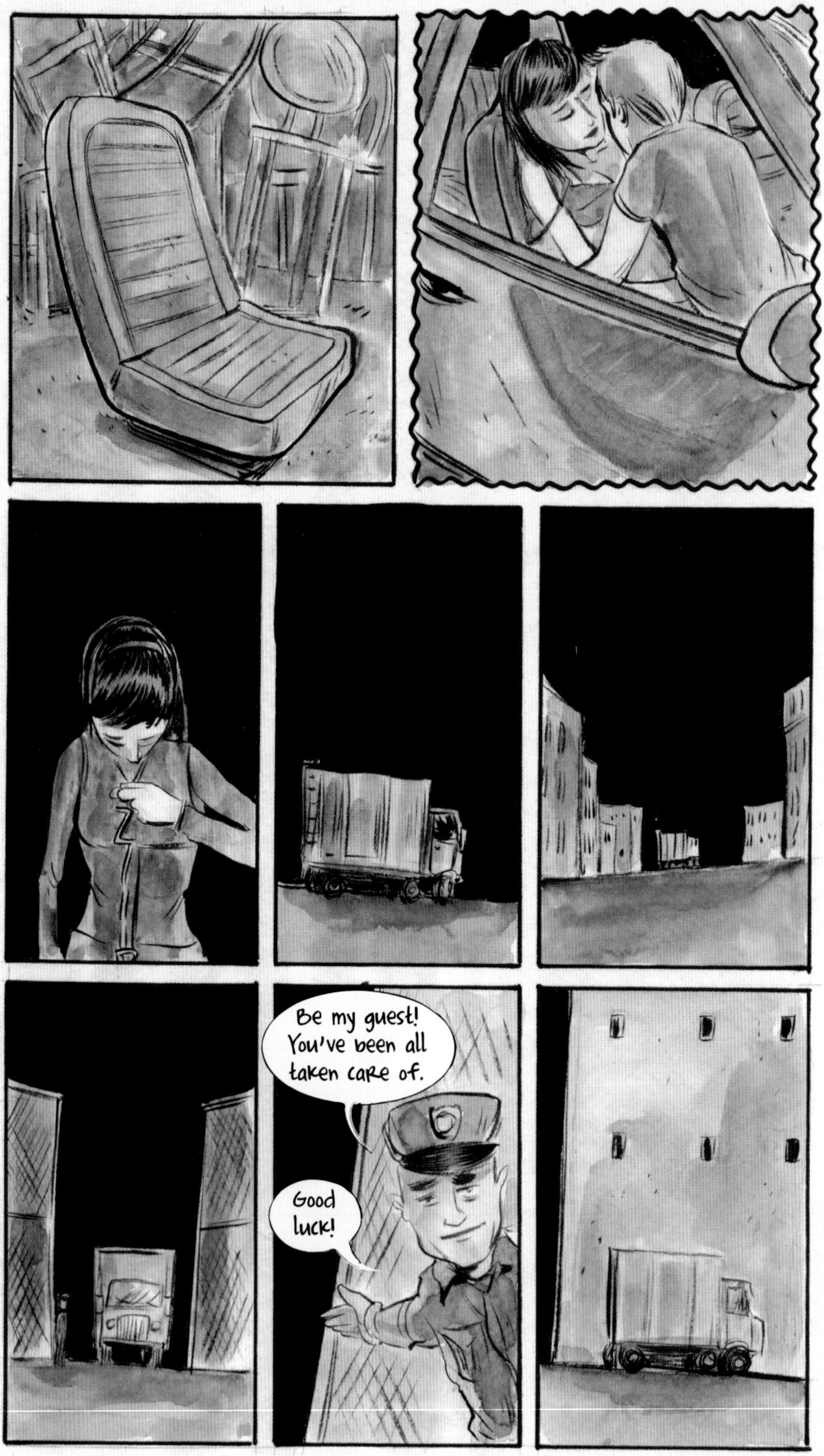
Be my guest! You've been all taken care of.
Good luck!

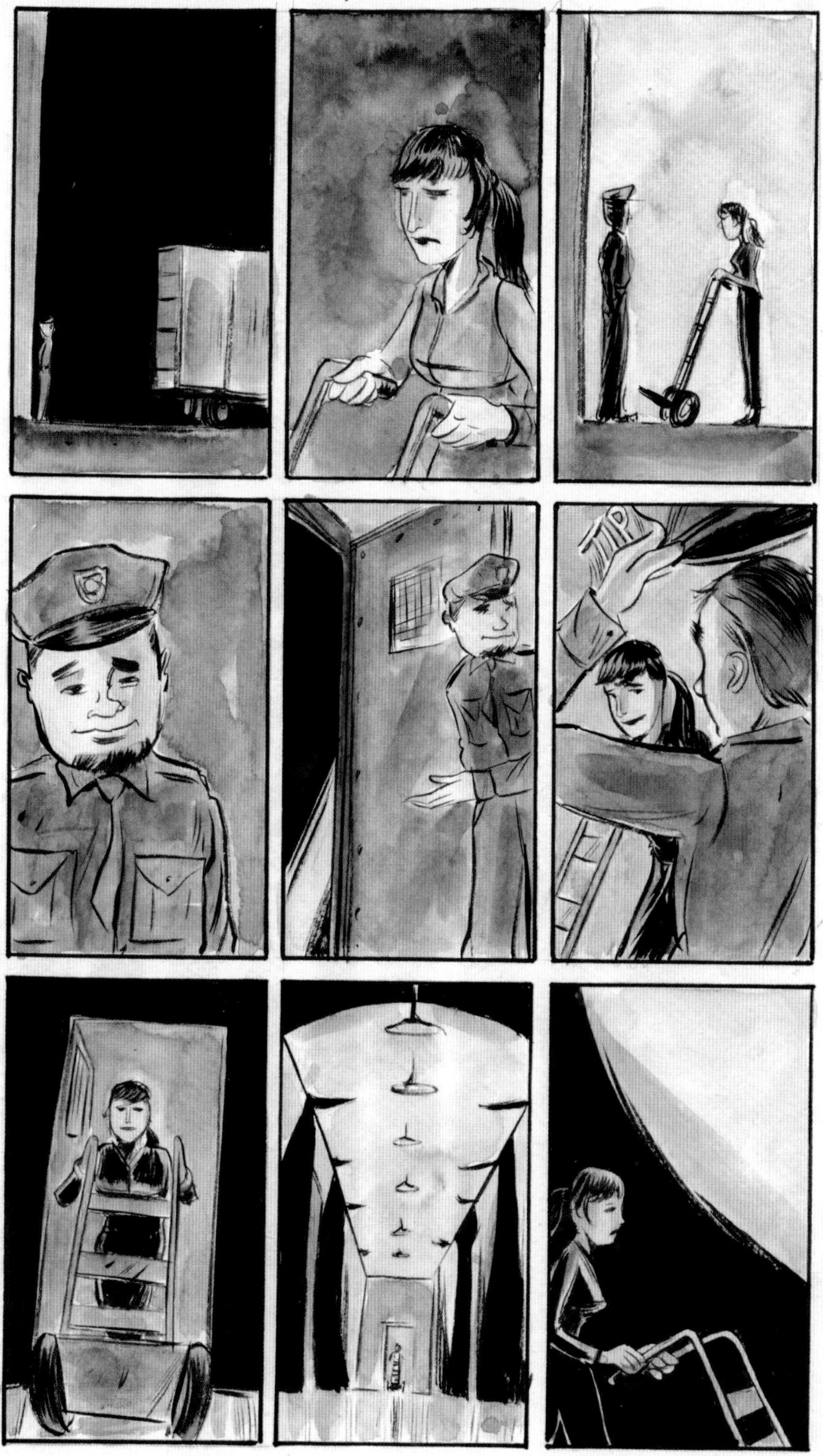
TIP

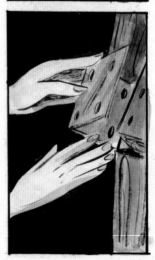

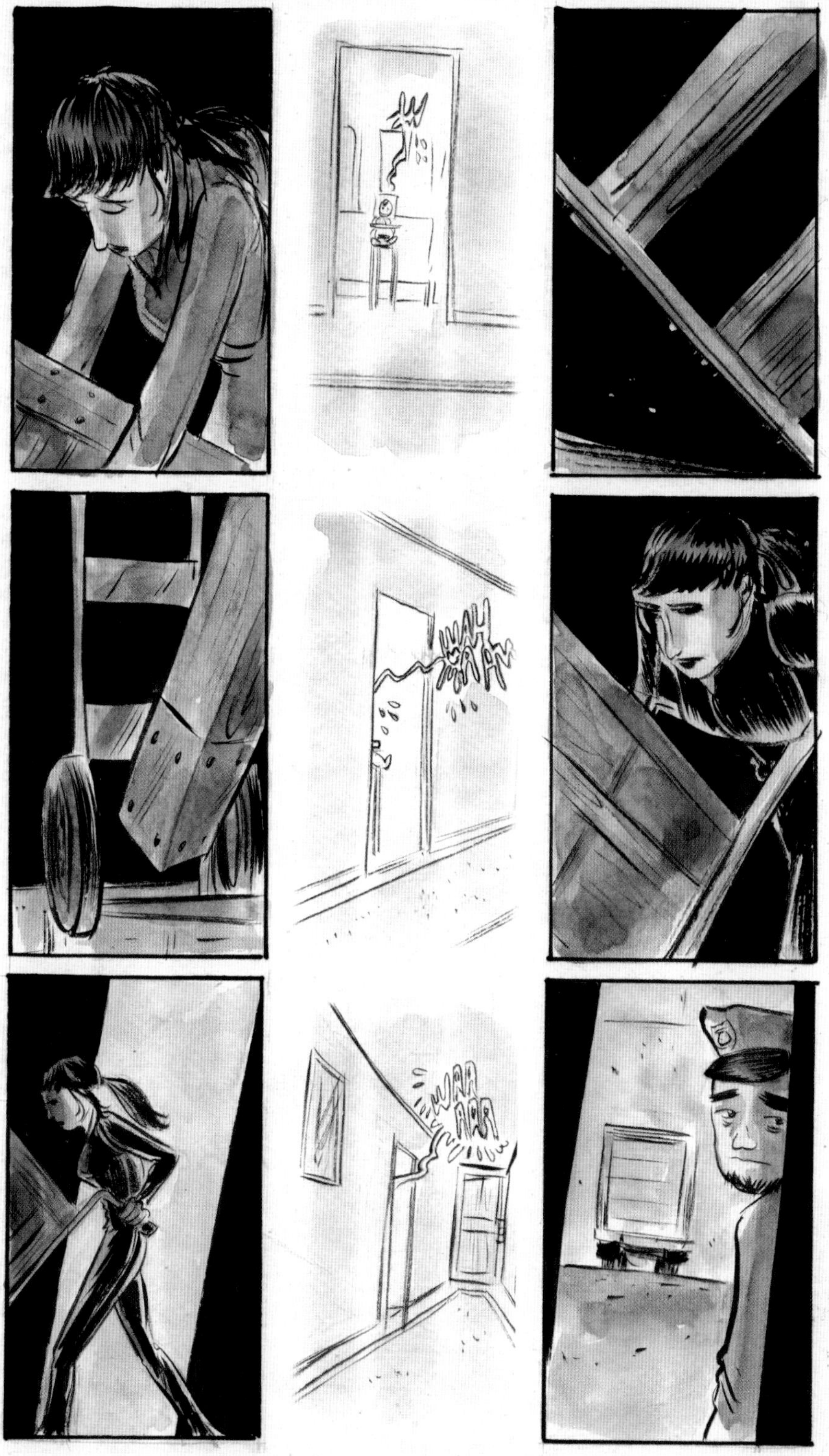
WAH
WAAH
WAA
AAA

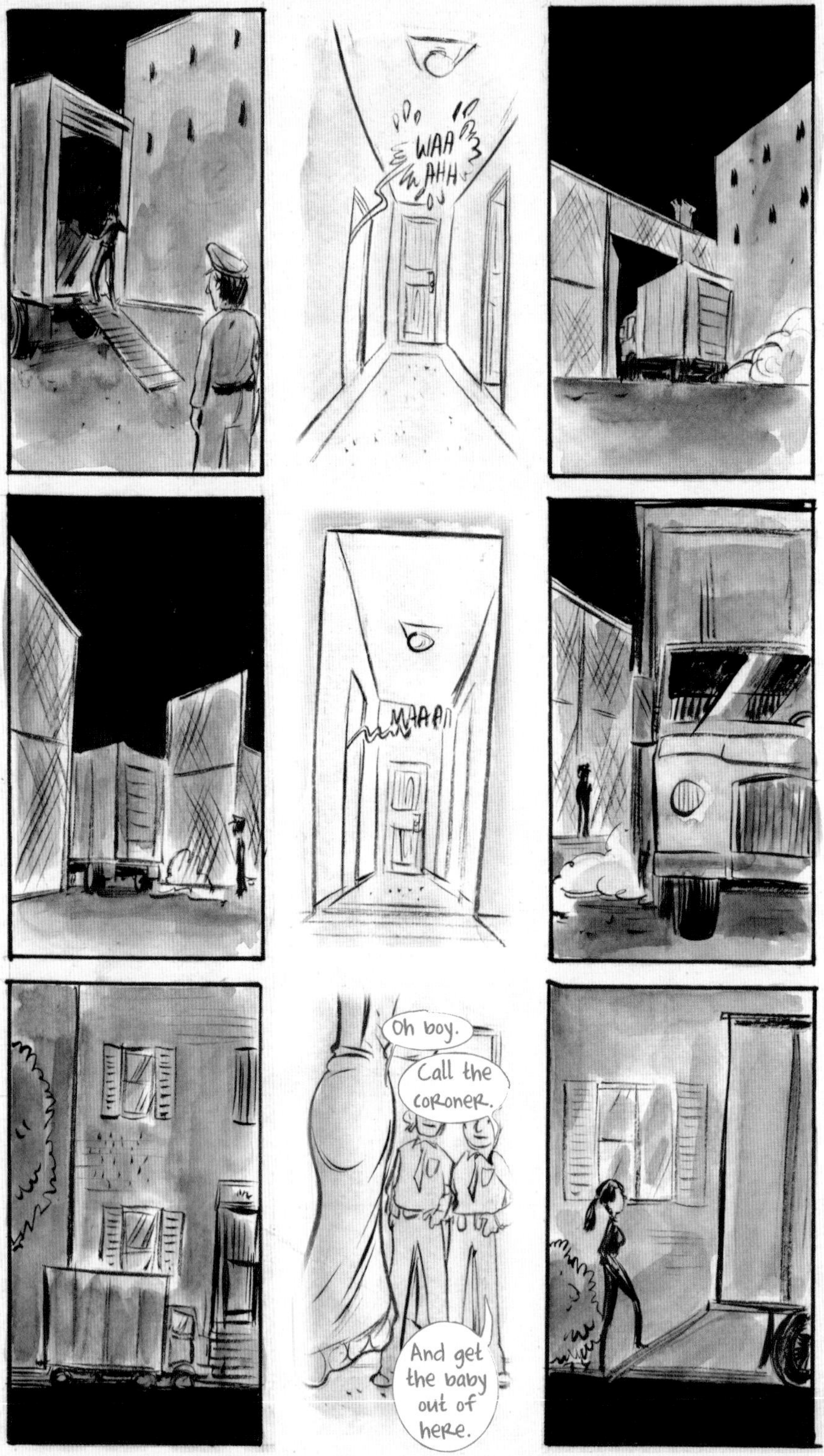
WAA AHH
WAAA
Oh boy.
Call the coroner.
And get the baby out of here.

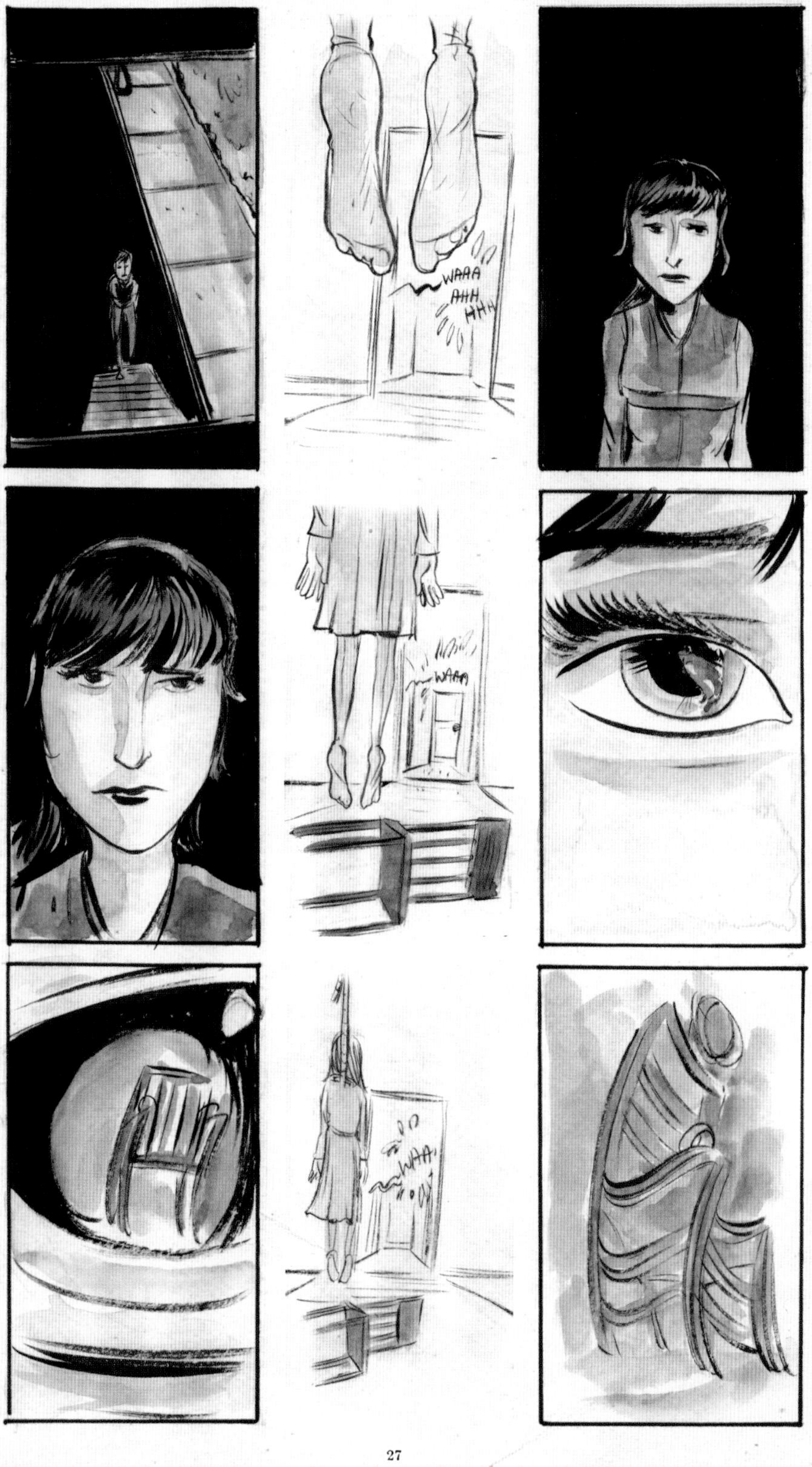
WAAA
AHH
HHH
WAAA
WAA

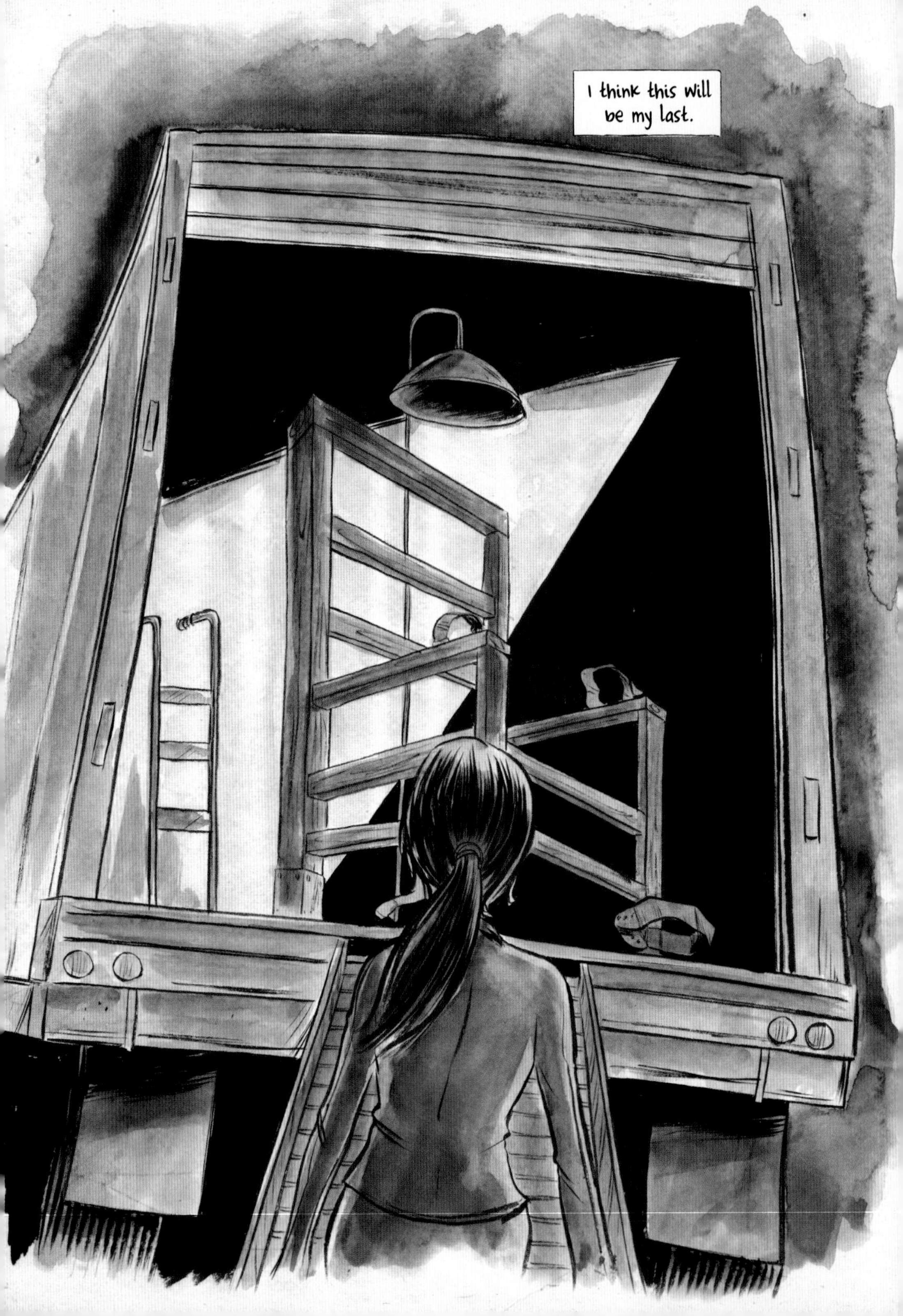
I think this will be my last.

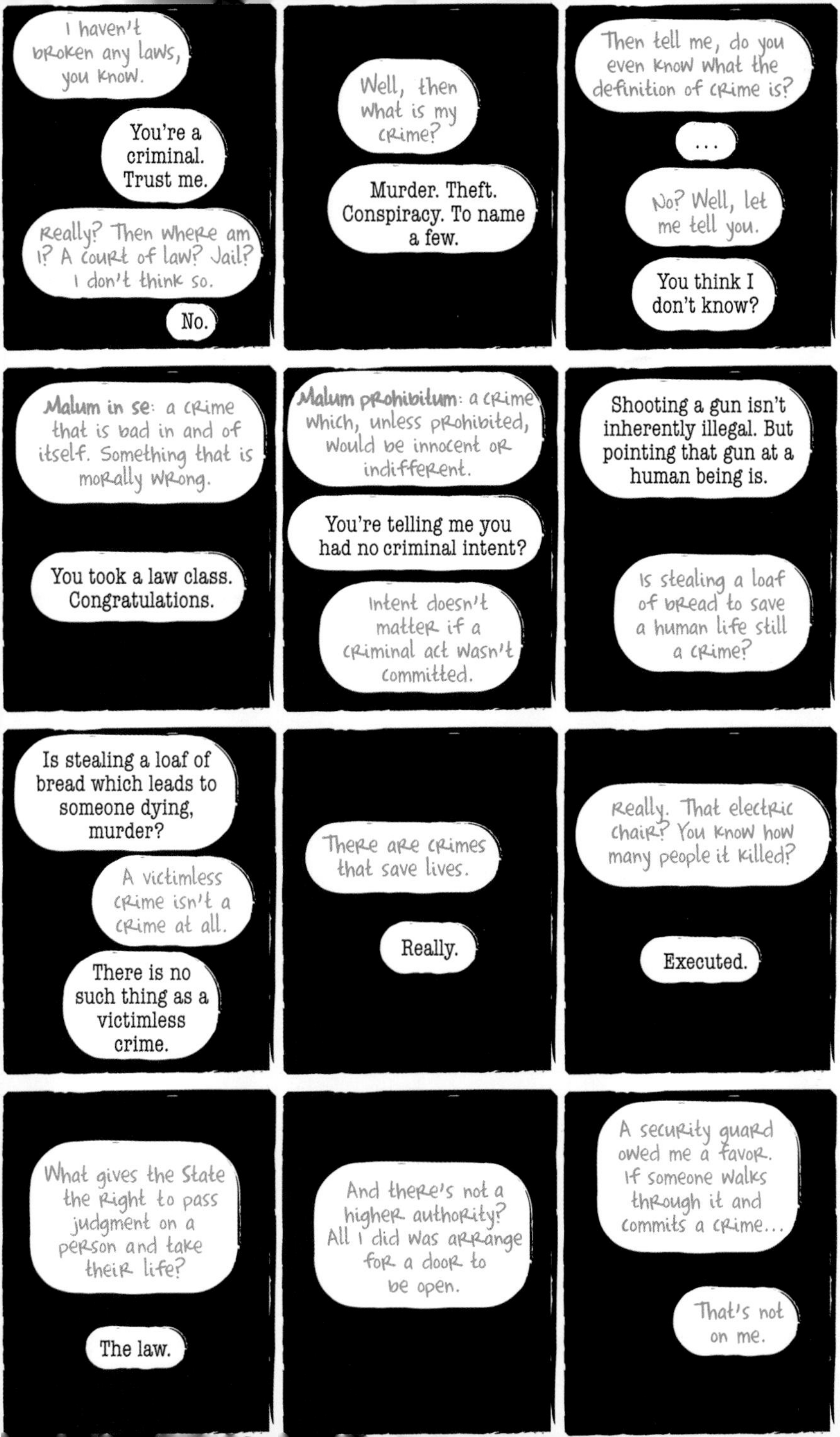

I haven't broken any laws, you know.
You're a criminal. Trust me.
Really? Then where am I? A court of law? Jail? I don't think so.
No.
Well, then what is my crime?
Murder. Theft. Conspiracy. To name a few.
Then tell me, do you even know what the definition of crime is?
...
No? Well, let me tell you.
You think I don't know?
Malum in se: a crime that is bad in and of itself. Something that is morally wrong.
You took a law class. Congratulations.
Malum prohibitum: a crime which, unless prohibited, would be innocent or indifferent.
You're telling me you had no criminal intent?
Intent doesn't matter if a criminal act wasn't committed.
Shooting a gun isn't inherently illegal. But pointing that gun at a human being is.
Is stealing a loaf of bread to save a human life still a crime?
Is stealing a loaf of bread which leads to someone dying, murder?
A victimless crime isn't a crime at all.
There is no such thing as a victimless crime.
There are crimes that save lives.
Really.
Really. That electric chair? You know how many people it killed?
Executed.
What gives the State the right to pass judgment on a person and take their life?
The law.
And there's not a higher authority? All I did was arrange for a door to be open.
A security guard owed me a favor. If someone walks through it and commits a crime...
That's not on me.

THE
JIGSAW

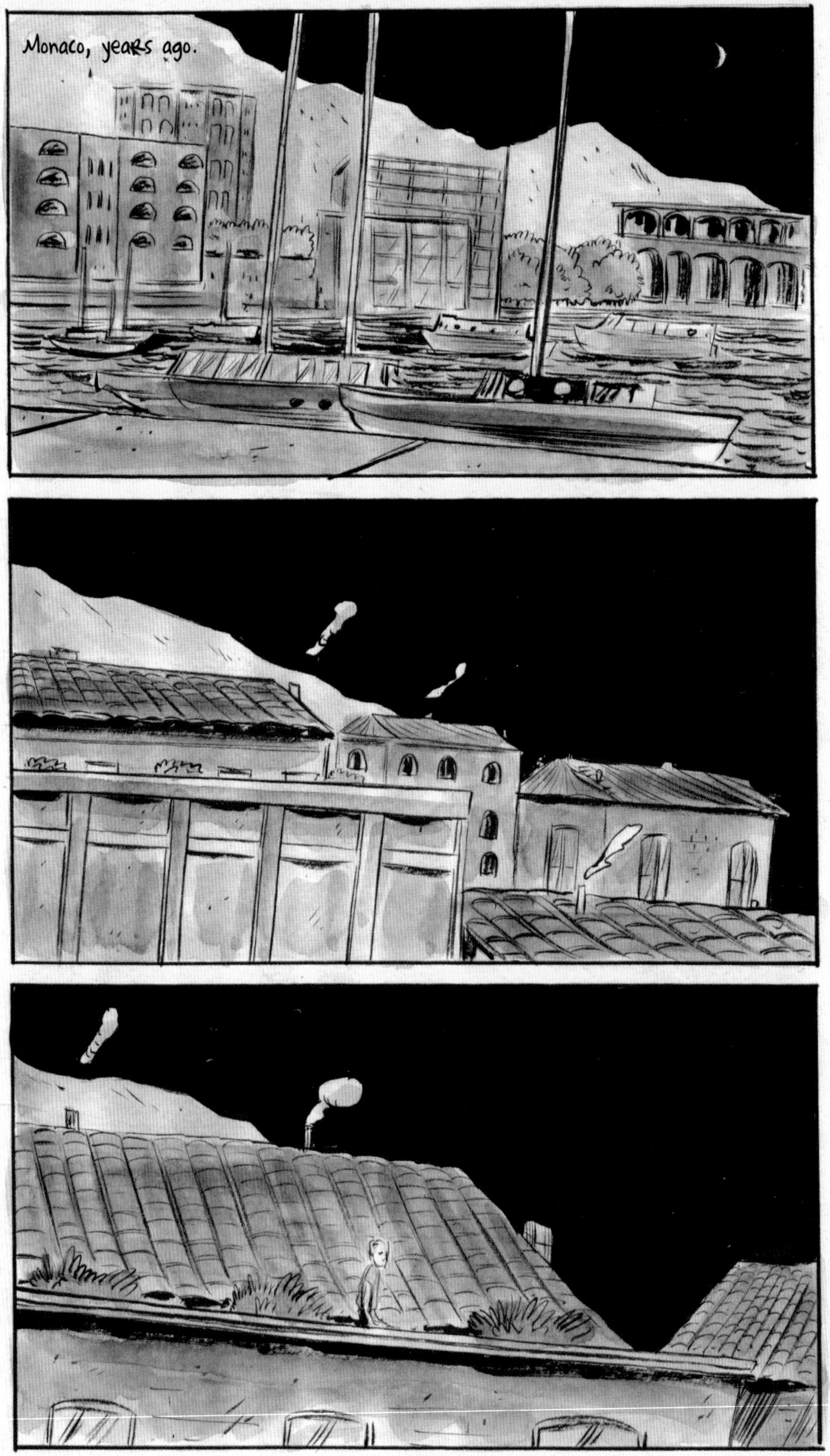
Monaco, years ago.

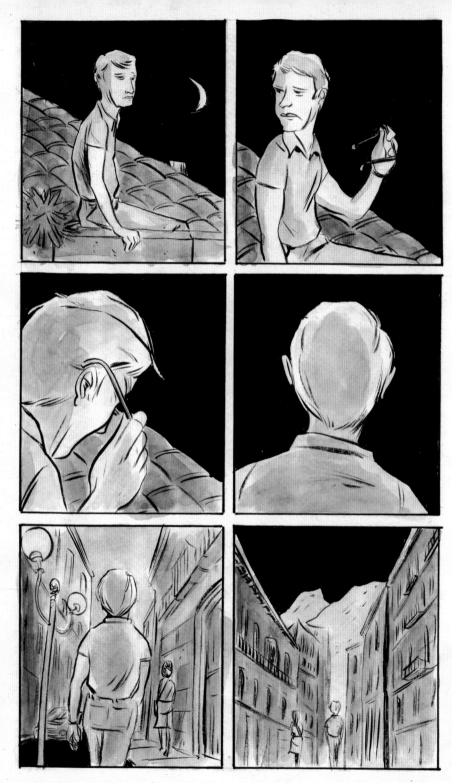

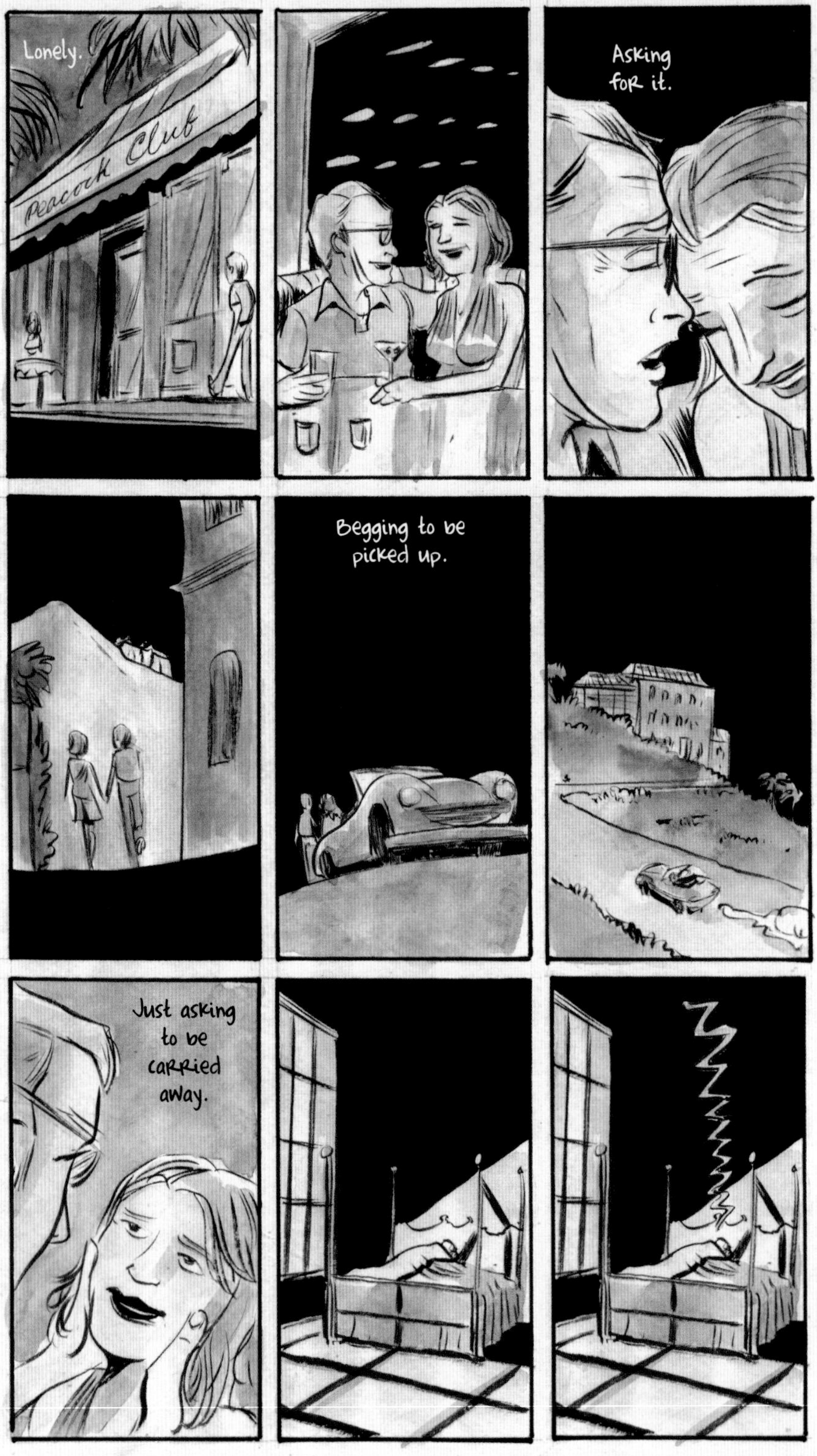
Lonely.
Peacock Club
Asking for it.
Begging to be picked up.
Just asking to be carried away.

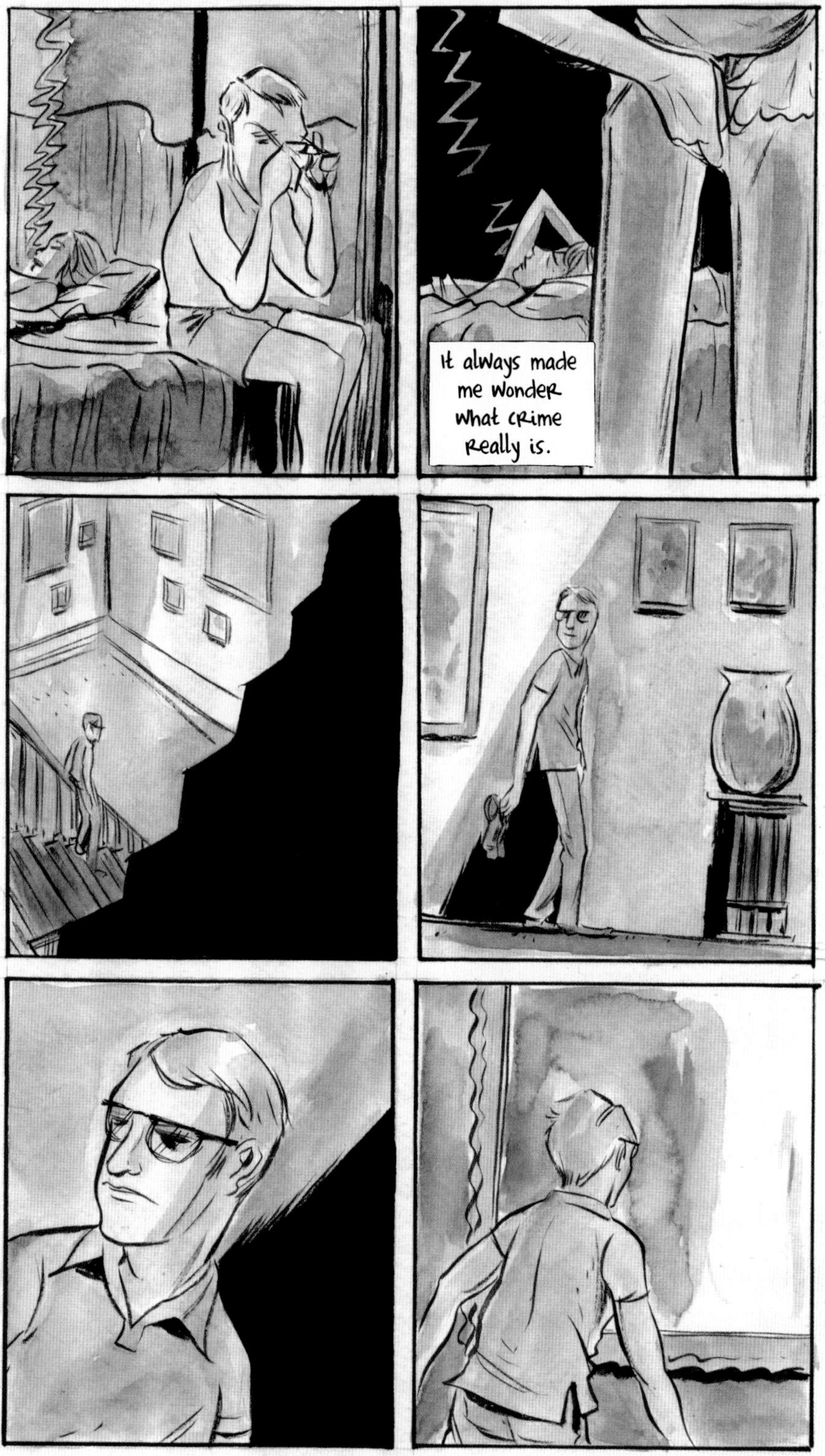
It always made me wonder what crime really is.

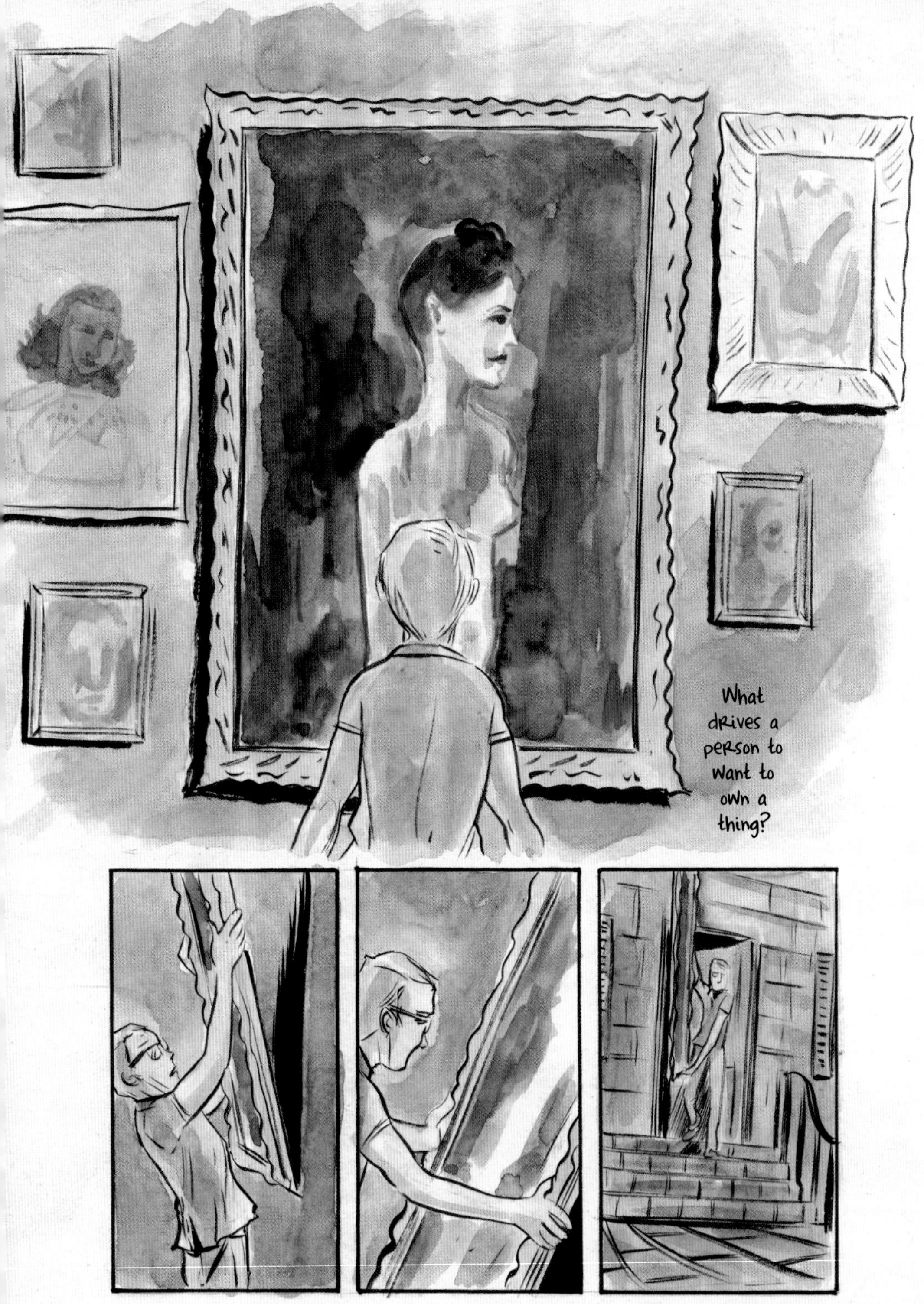
What drives a person to want to own a thing?

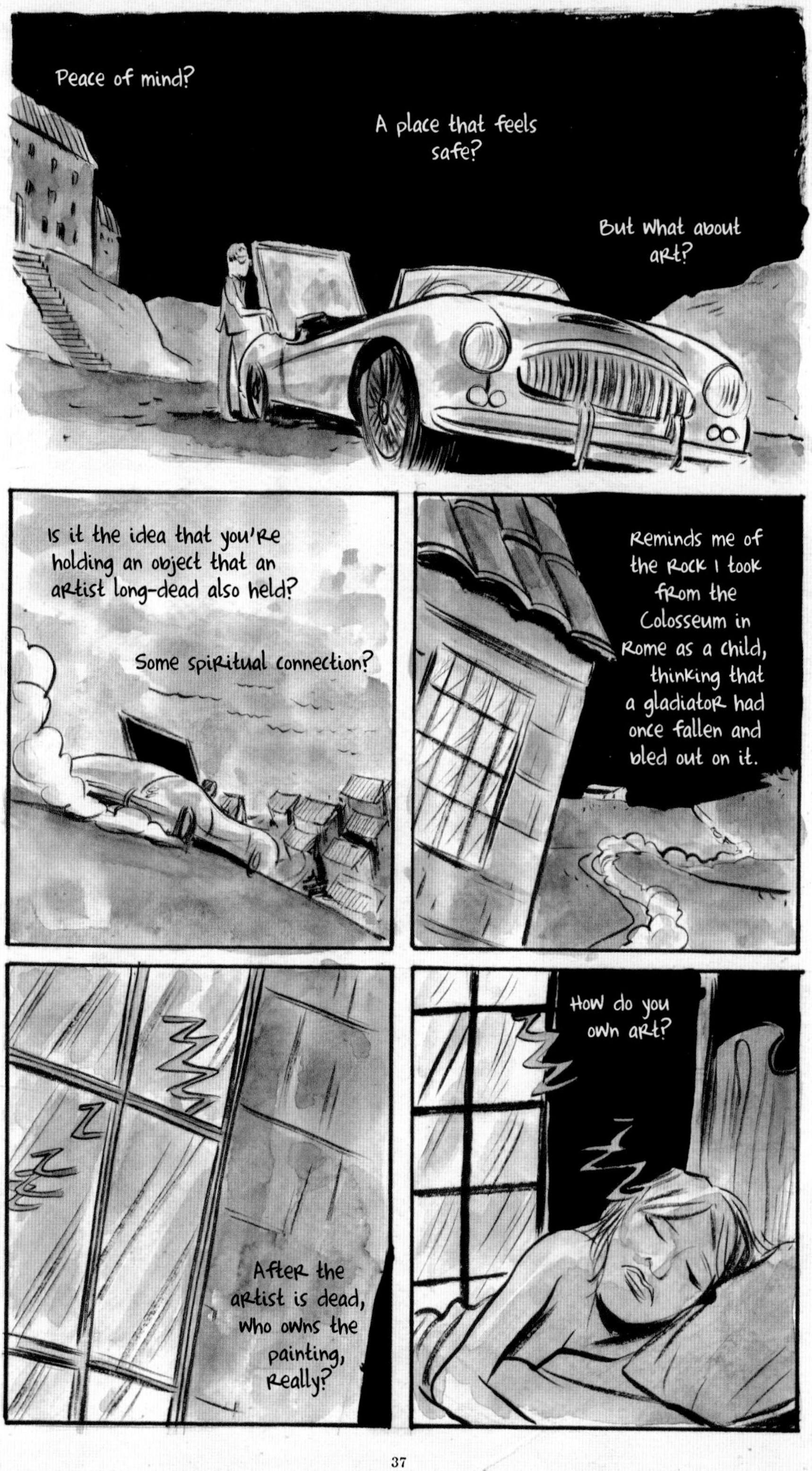
Peace of mind?
A place that feels safe?
But what about art?
Is it the idea that you're holding an object that an artist long-dead also held?
Some spiritual connection?
Reminds me of the rock I took from the Colosseum in Rome as a child, thinking that a gladiator had once fallen and bled out on it.
After the artist is dead, who owns the painting, really?
How do you own art?

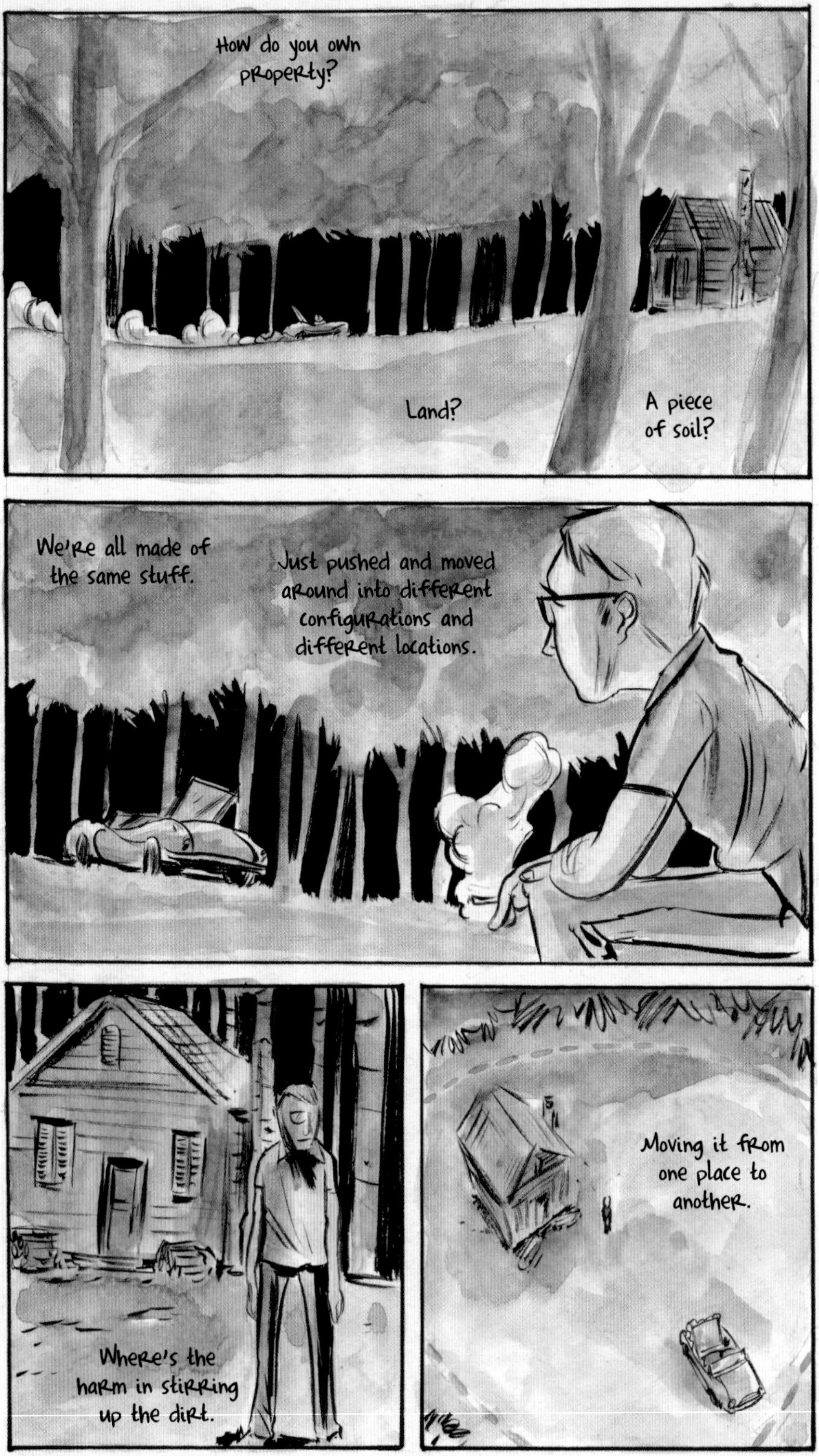
How do you own property?
Land?
A piece of soil?
We're all made of the same stuff.
Just pushed and moved around into different configurations and different locations.
Where's the harm in stirring up the dirt.
Moving it from one place to another.

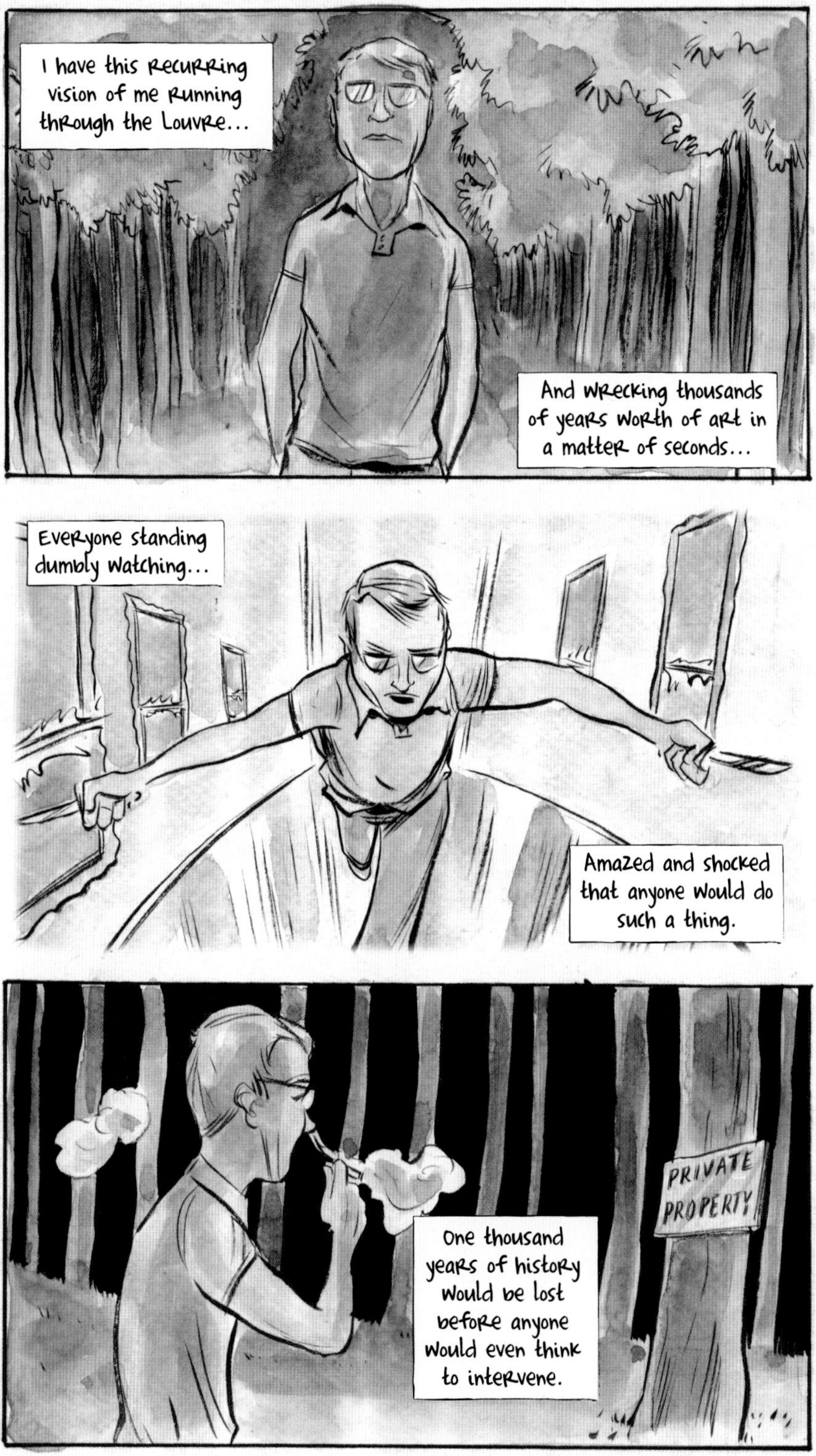
I have this recurring vision of me running through the Louvre...
And wrecking thousands of years worth of art in a matter of seconds...
Everyone standing dumbly watching...
Amazed and shocked that anyone would do such a thing.
PRIVATE PROPERTY
One thousand years of history would be lost before anyone would even think to intervene.

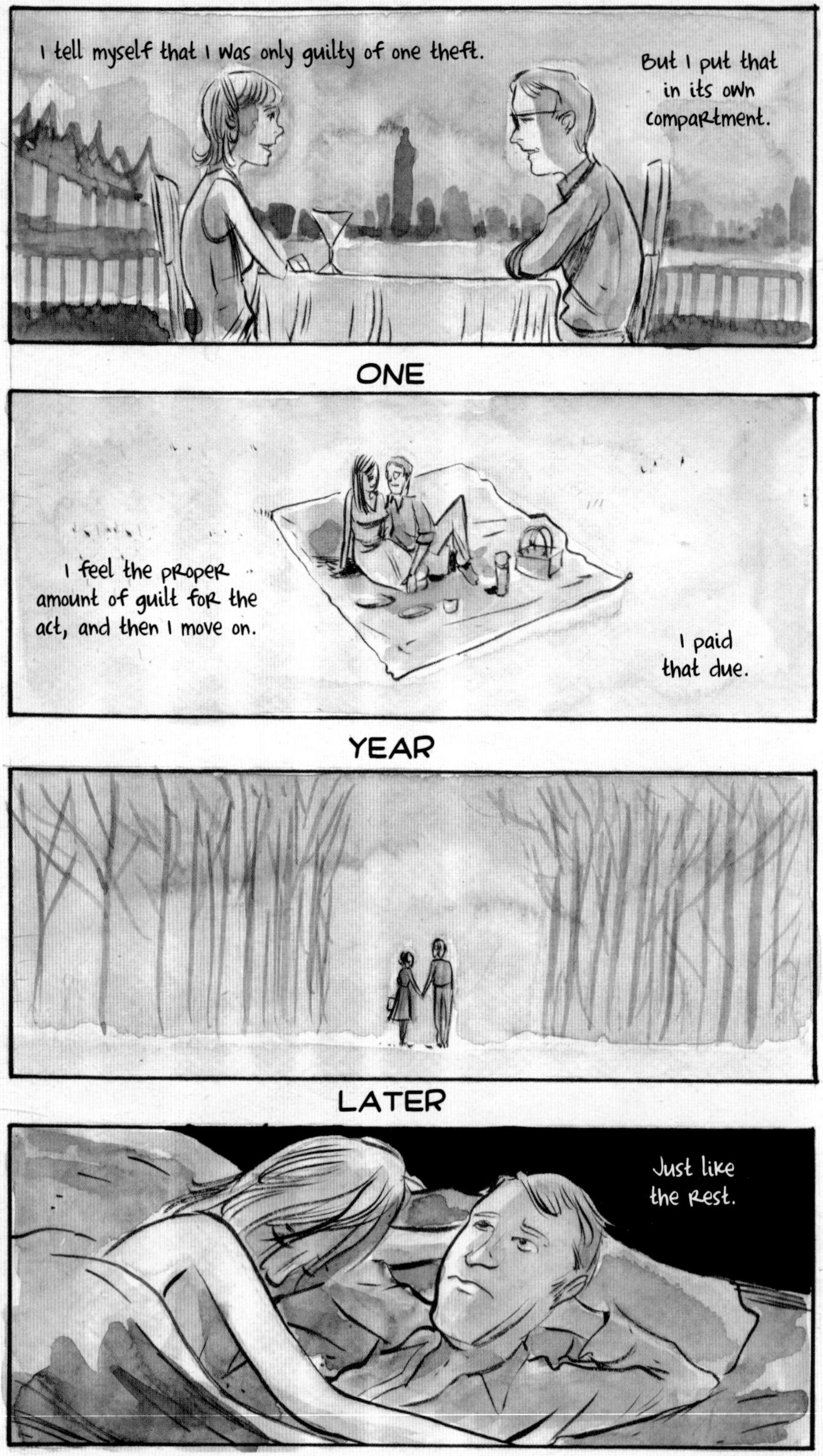
I tell myself that I was only guilty of one theft.
But I put that in its own compartment.
ONE
I feel the proper amount of guilt for the act, and then I move on.
I paid that due.
YEAR
LATER
Just like the rest.

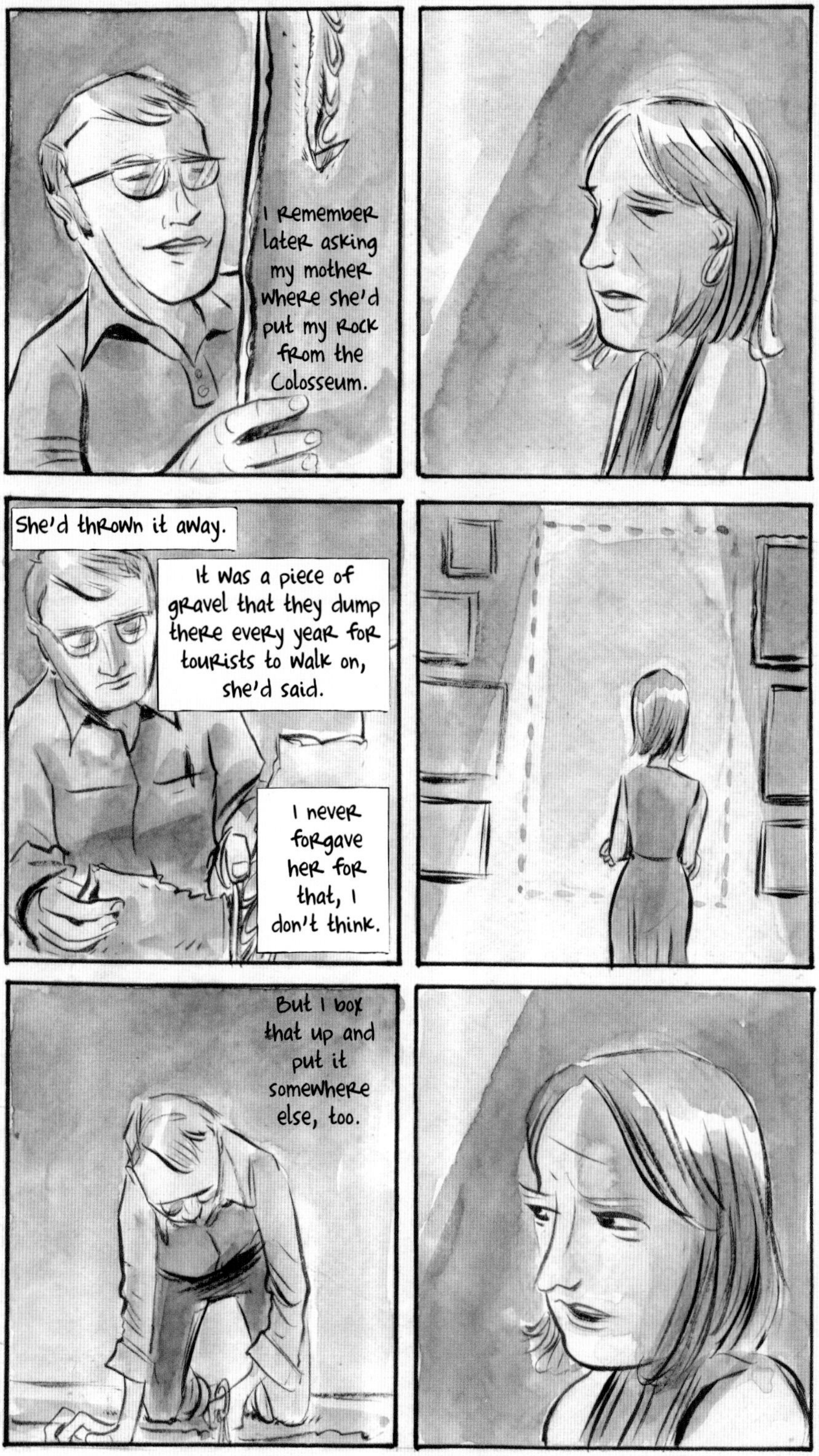
I remember later asking my mother where she'd put my rock from the Colosseum.
She'd thrown it away.
It was a piece of gravel that they dump there every year for tourists to walk on, she'd said.
I never forgave her for that, I don't think.
But I box that up and put it somewhere else, too.

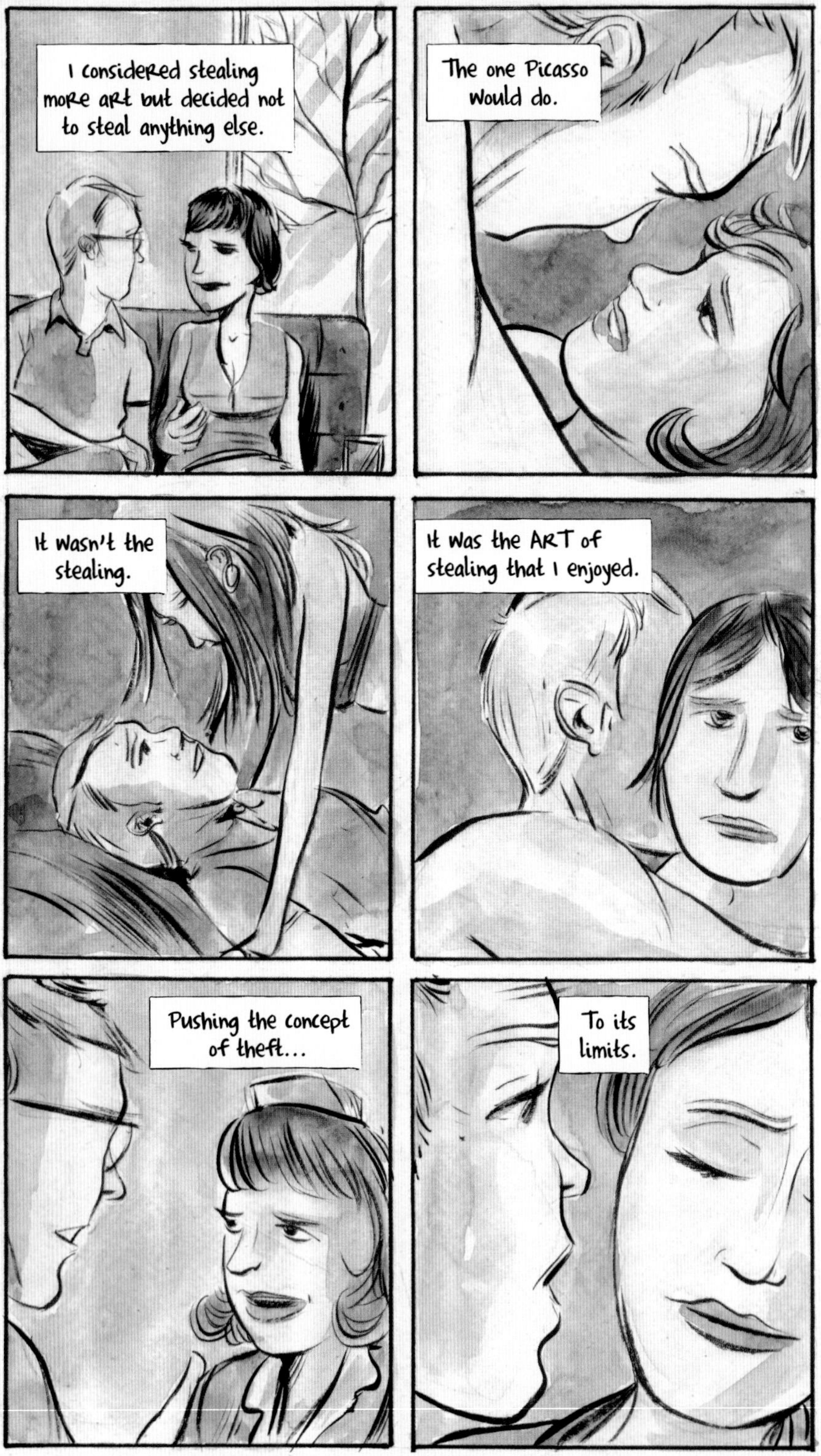
I considered stealing more art but decided not to steal anything else.
The one Picasso would do.
It wasn't the stealing.
It was the ART of stealing that I enjoyed.
Pushing the concept of theft...
To its limits.

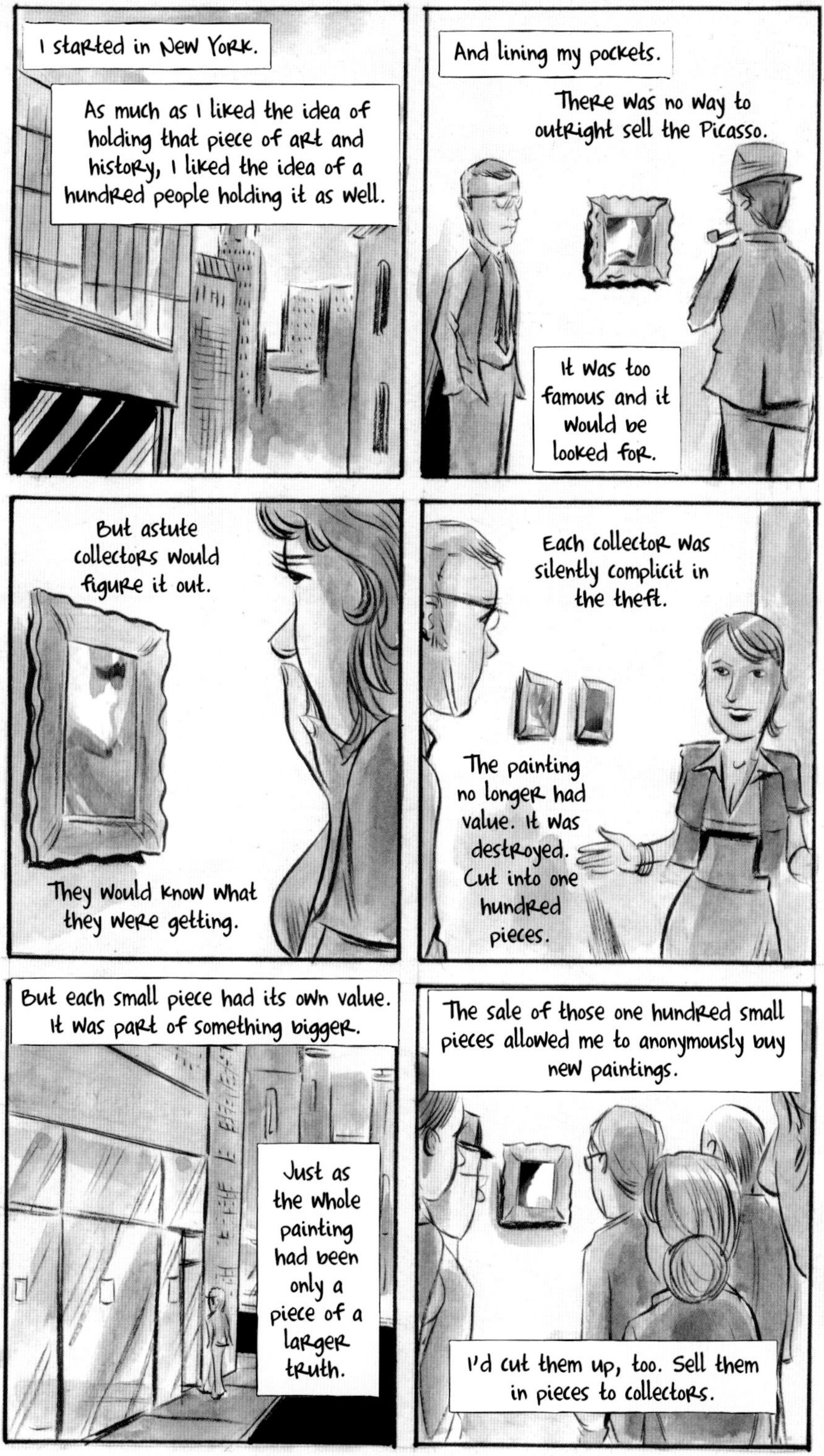
I started in New York.
As much as I liked the idea of holding that piece of art and history, I liked the idea of a hundred people holding it as well.
And lining my pockets.
There was no way to outright sell the Picasso.
It was too famous and it would be looked for.
But astute collectors would figure it out.
They would know what they were getting.
Each collector was silently complicit in the theft.
The painting no longer had value. It was destroyed. Cut into one hundred pieces.
But each small piece had its own value. It was part of something bigger.
Just as the whole painting had been only a piece of a larger truth.
The sale of those one hundred small pieces allowed me to anonymously buy new paintings.
I'd cut them up, too. Sell them in pieces to collectors.

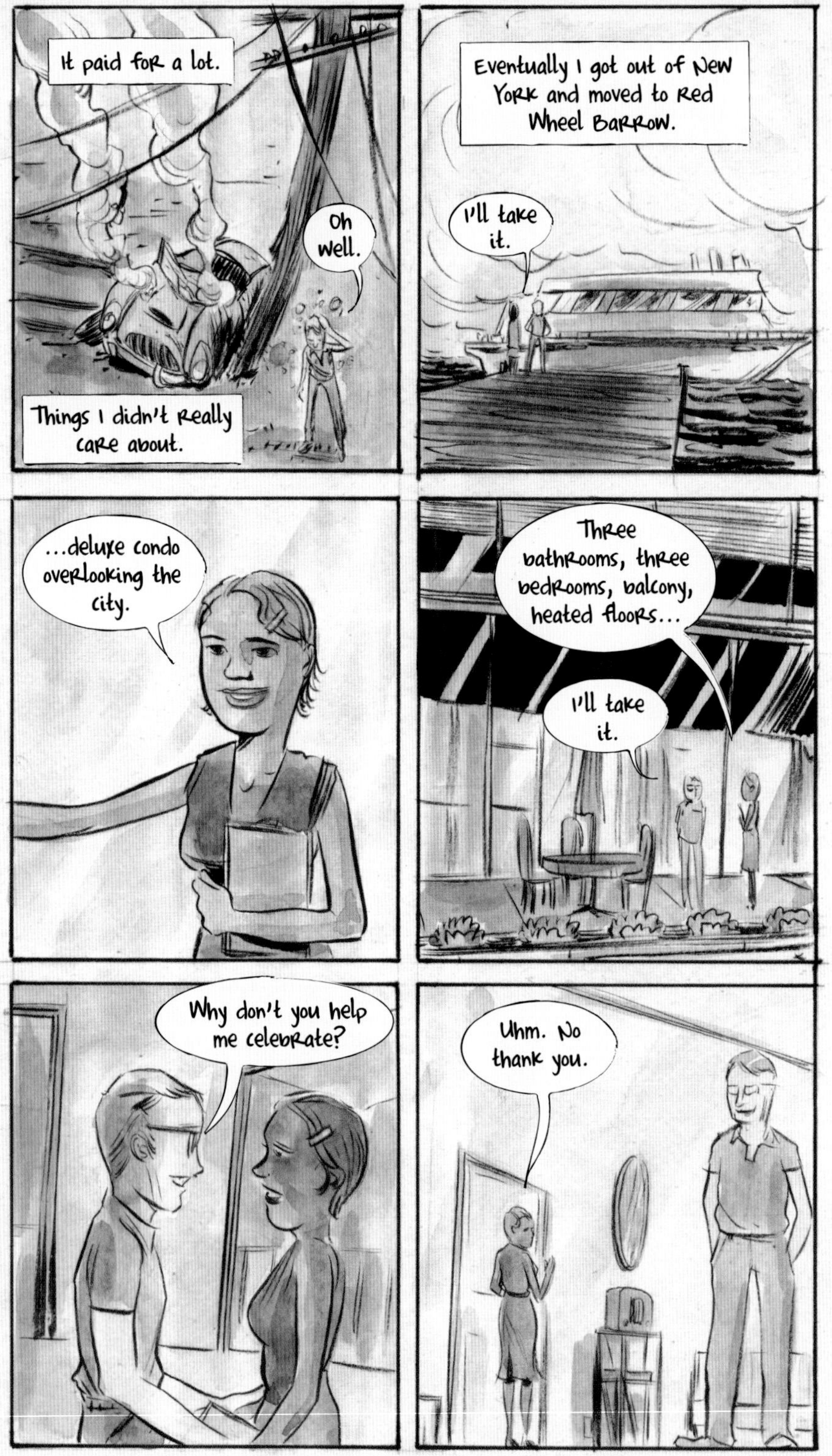
It paid for a lot.
Oh well.
Things I didn't really care about.
Eventually I got out of New York and moved to Red Wheel Barrow.
I'll take it.
...deluxe condo overlooking the city.
Three bathrooms, three bedrooms, balcony, heated floors...
I'll take it.
Why don't you help me celebrate?
Uhm. No thank you.

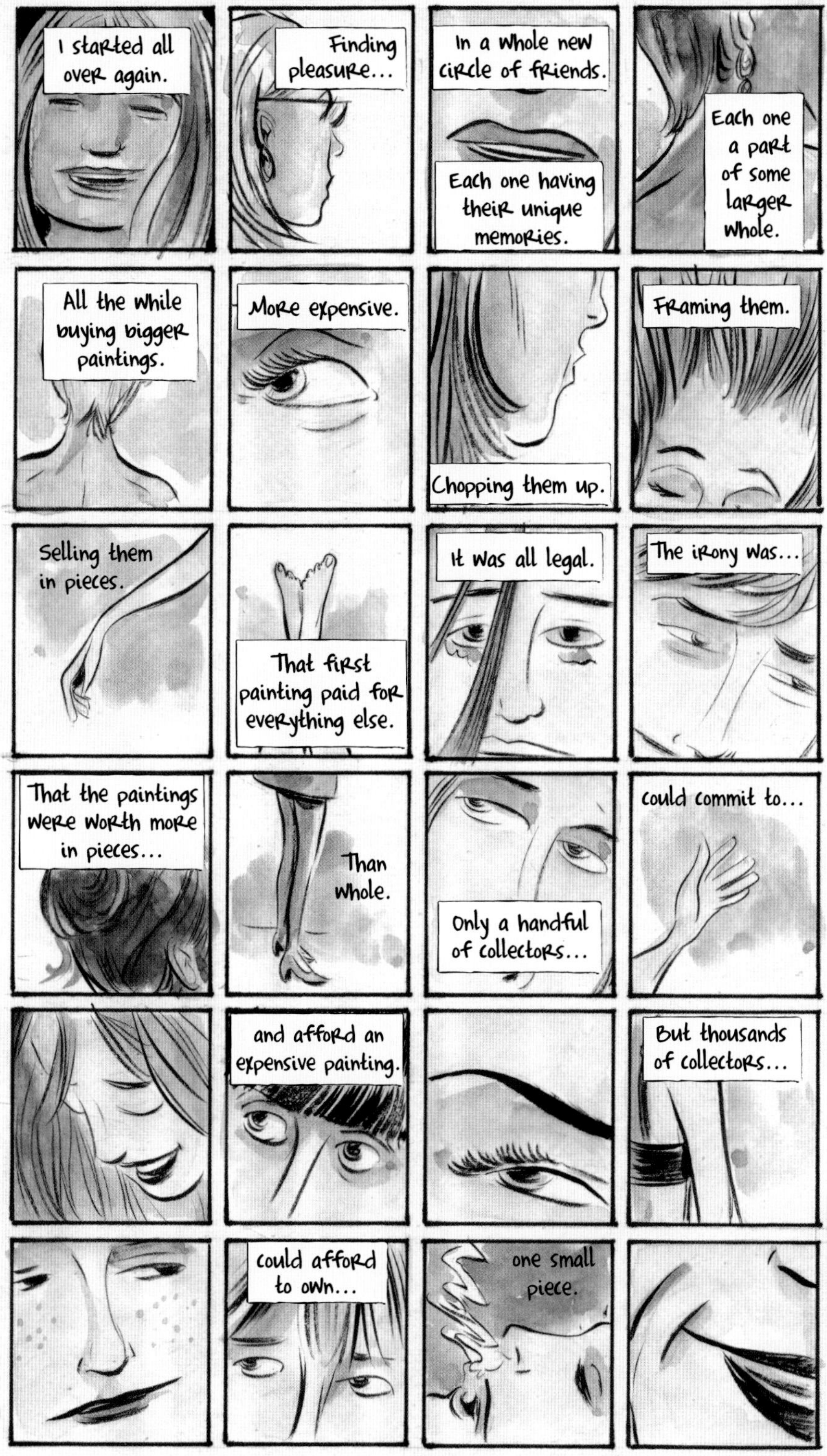

I started all over again.
Finding pleasure...
In a whole new circle of friends.
Each one having their unique memories.
Each one a part of some larger whole.
All the while buying bigger paintings.
More expensive.
Chopping them up.
Framing them.
Selling them in pieces.
That first painting paid for everything else.
It was all legal.
The irony was...
That the paintings were worth more in pieces...
Than whole.
Only a handful of collectors...
could commit to...
and afford an expensive painting.
But thousands of collectors...
could afford to own...
one small piece.

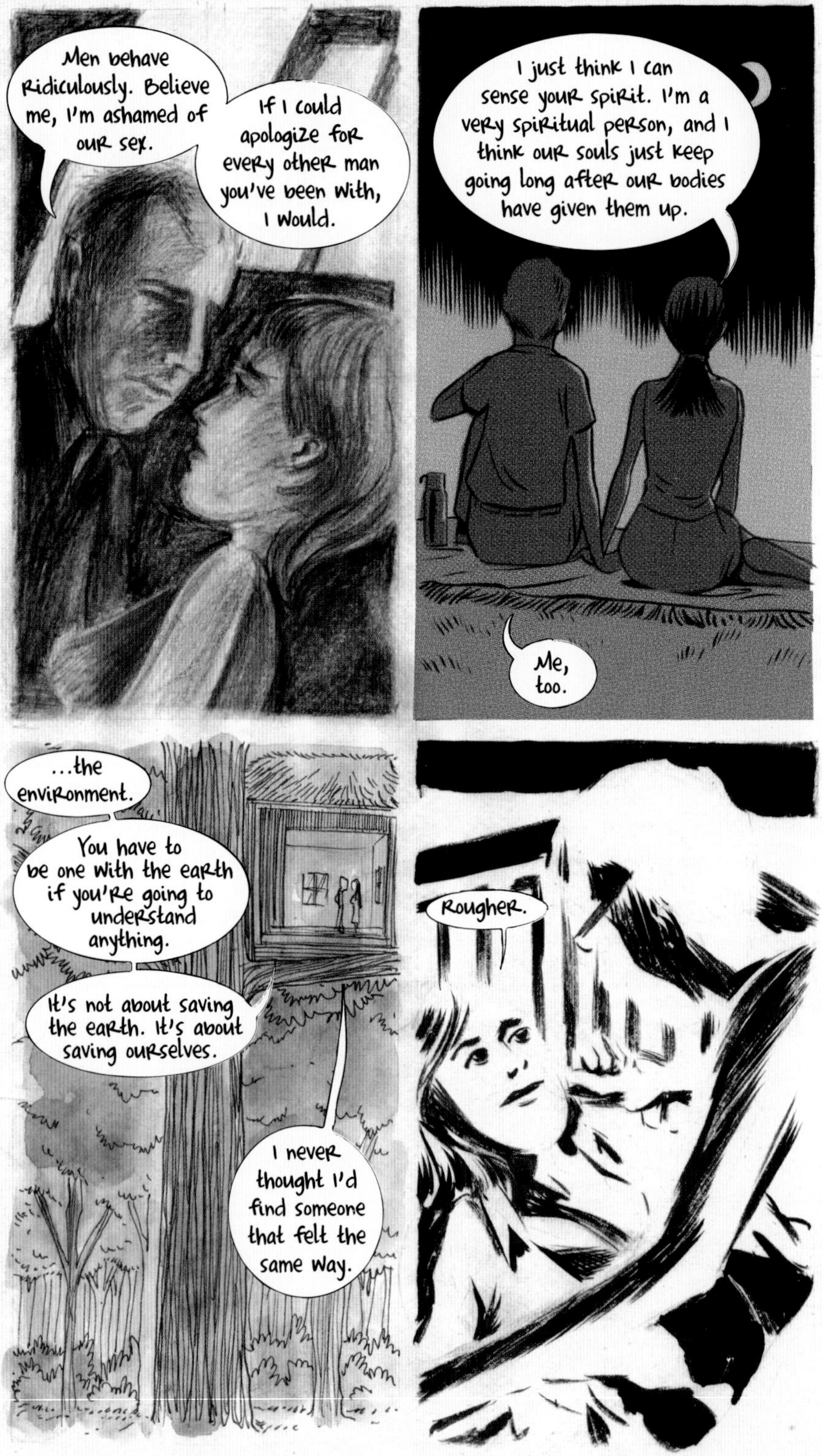
Men behave Ridiculously. Believe me, I'm ashamed of our sex.
If I could apologize for every other man you've been with, I would.
I just think I can sense your spirit. I'm a very spiritual person, and I think our souls just keep going long after our bodies have given them up.
Me, too.
...the environment.
You have to be one with the earth if you're going to understand anything.
It's not about saving the earth. It's about saving ourselves.
I never thought I'd find someone that felt the same way.
Rougher.

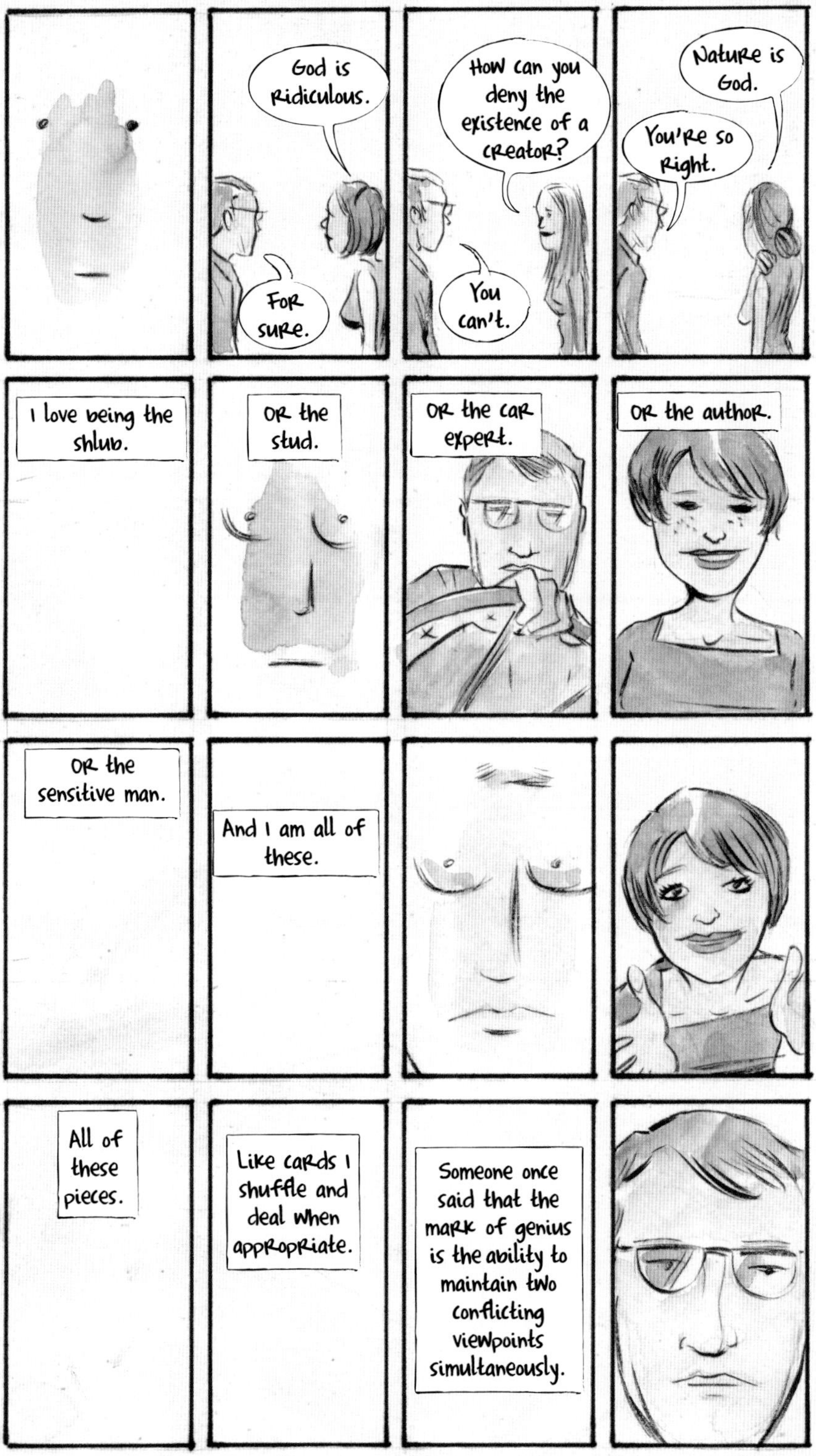
God is ridiculous.
For sure.
How can you deny the existence of a creator?
You can't.
Nature is God.
You're so right.
I love being the shlub.
Or the stud.
Or the car expert.
Or the author.
Or the sensitive man.
And I am all of these.
All of these pieces.
Like cards I shuffle and deal when appropriate.
Someone once said that the mark of genius is the ability to maintain two conflicting viewpoints simultaneously.

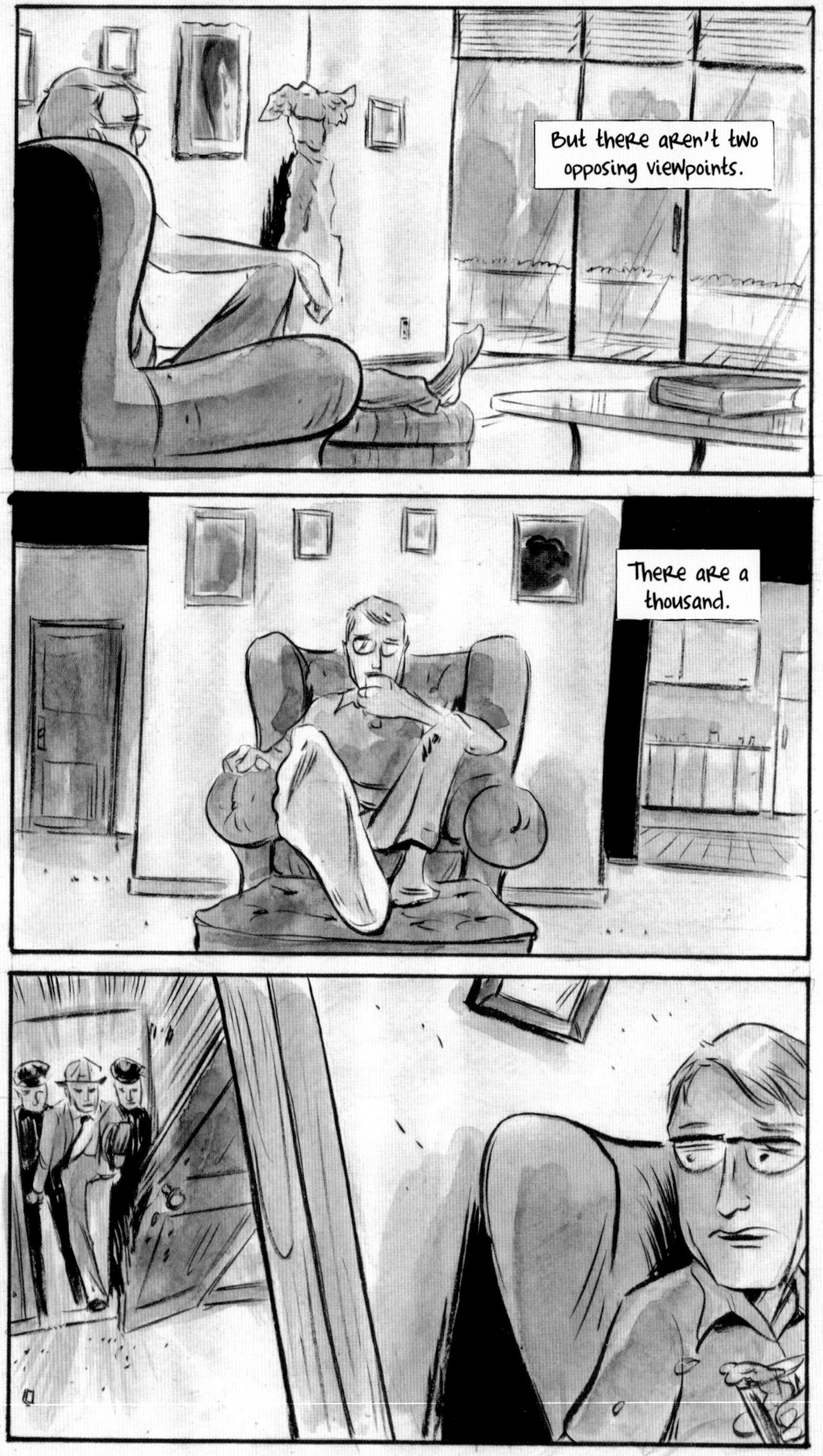
But there aren't two opposing viewpoints.
There are a thousand.

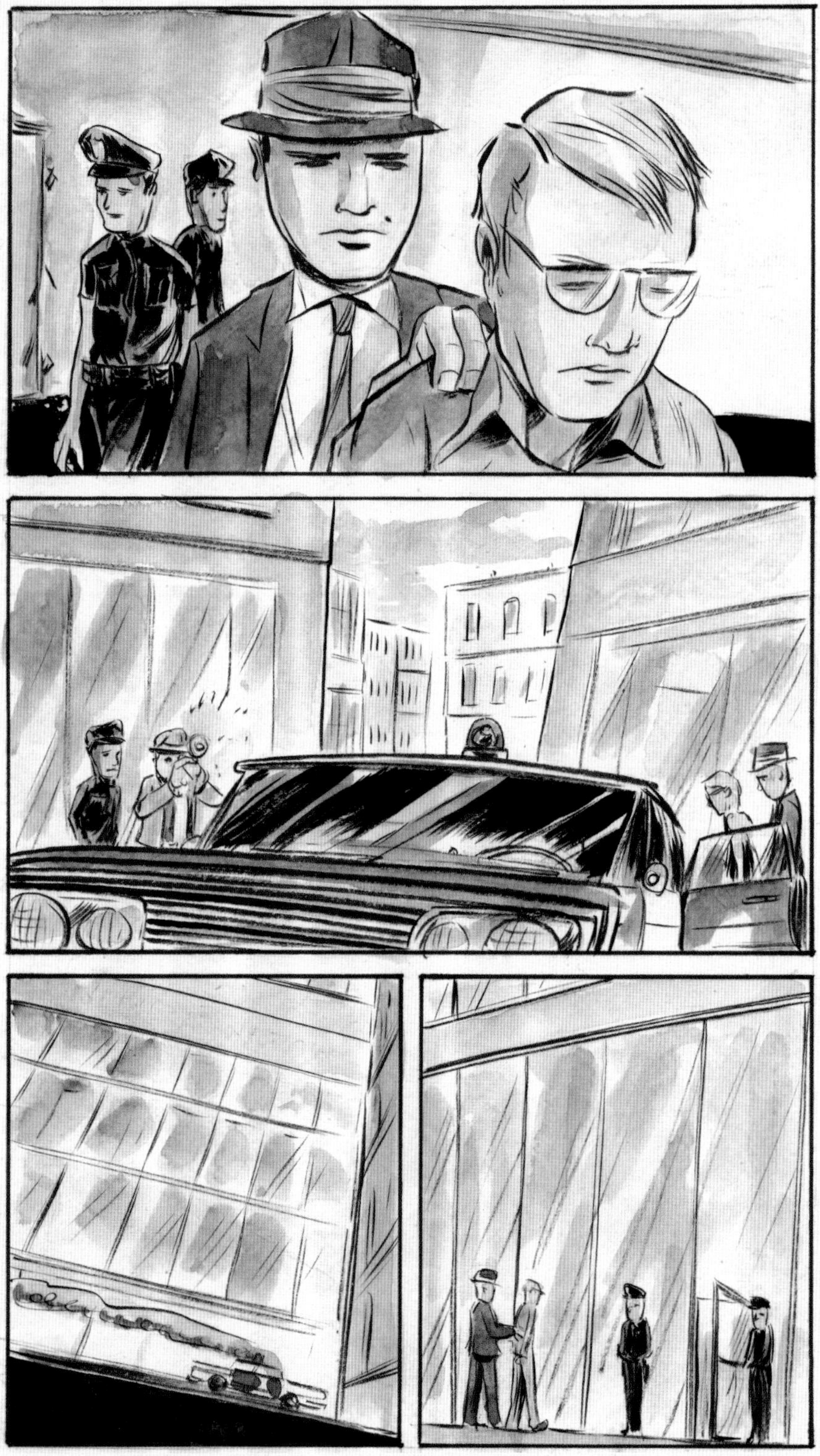

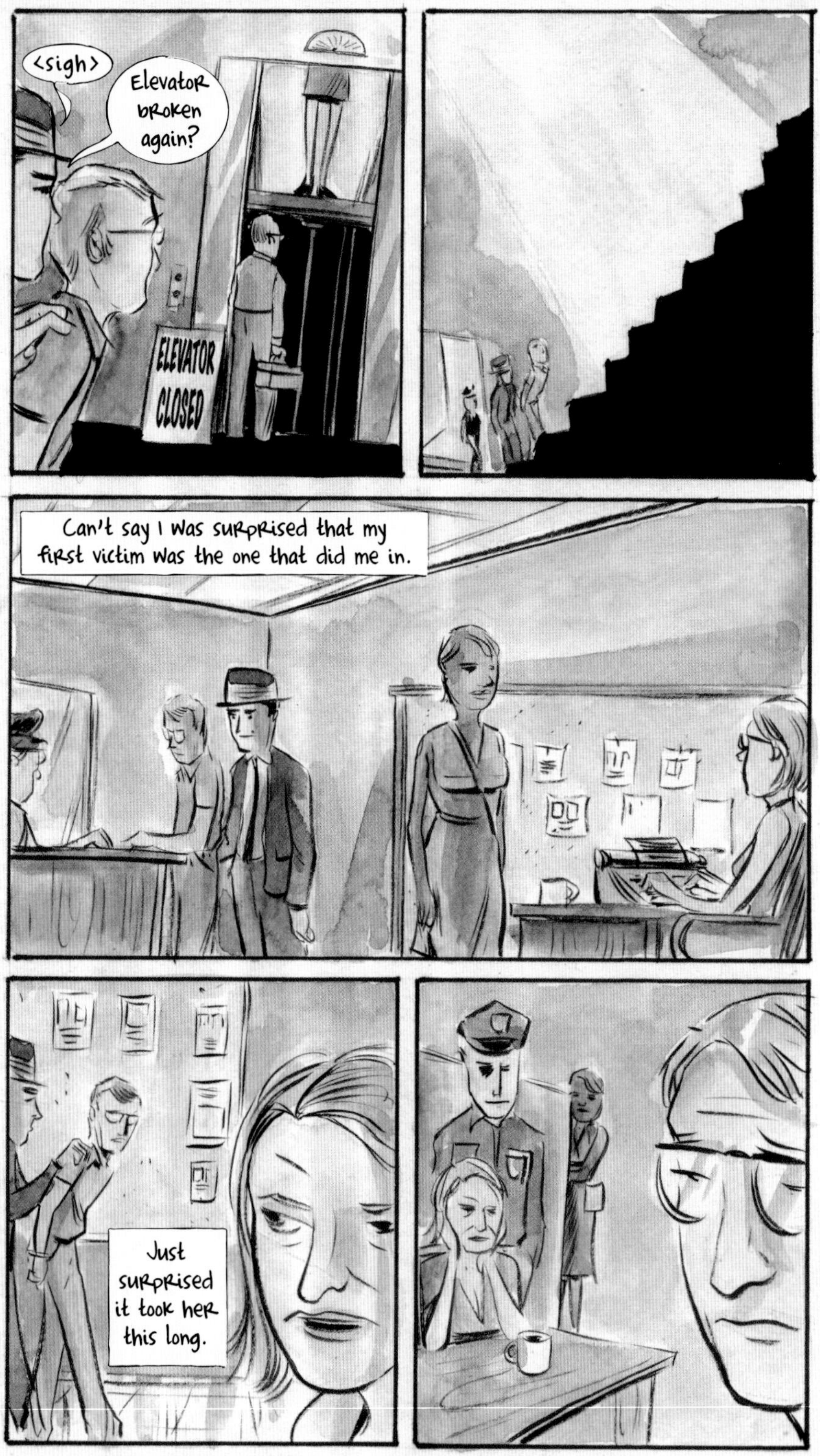
<sigh>
Elevator broken again?
ELEVATOR CLOSED
Can't say I was surprised that my first victim was the one that did me in.
Just surprised it took her this long.

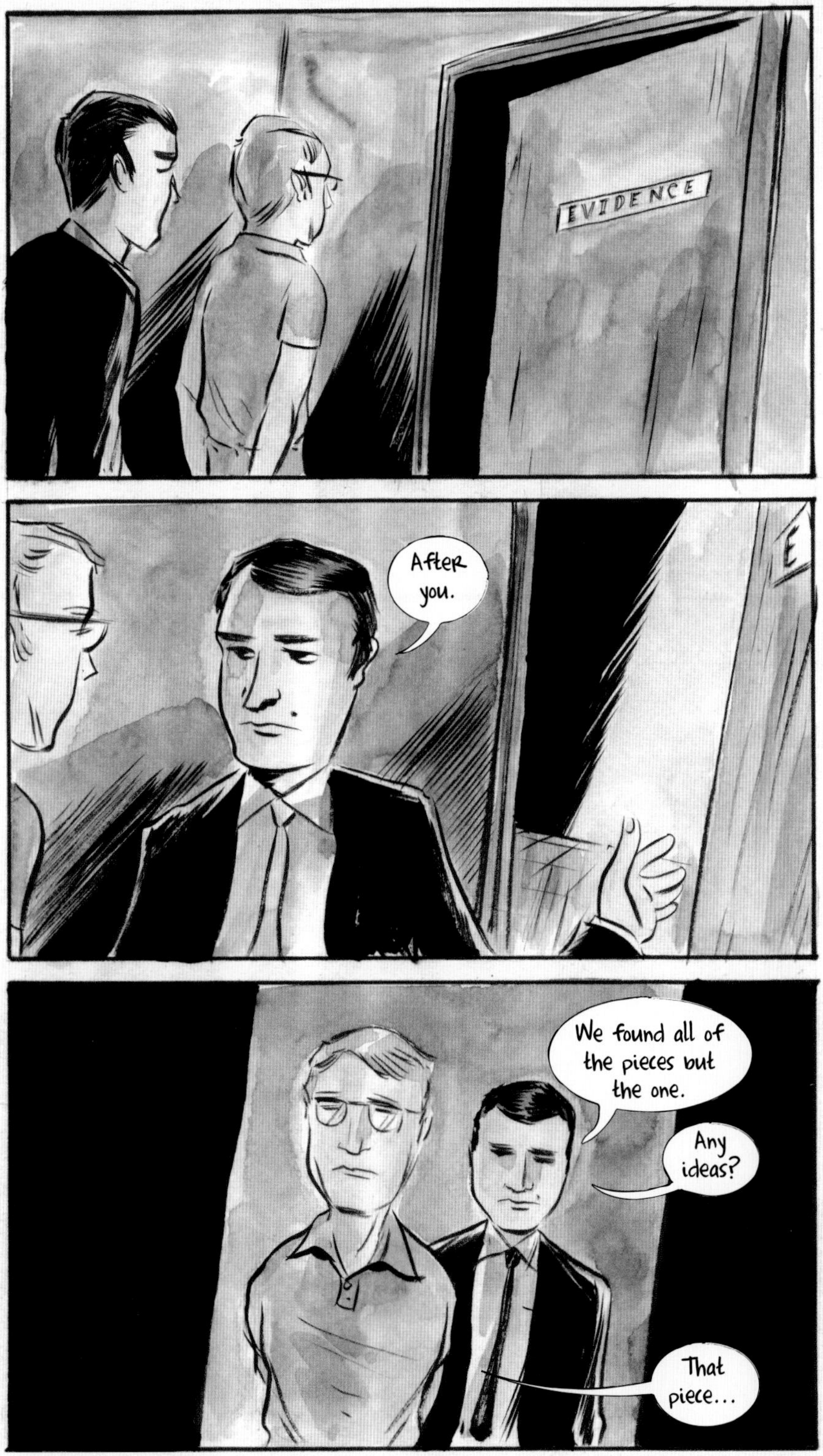
EVIDENCE
After you.
We found all of the pieces but the one.
Any ideas?
That piece...

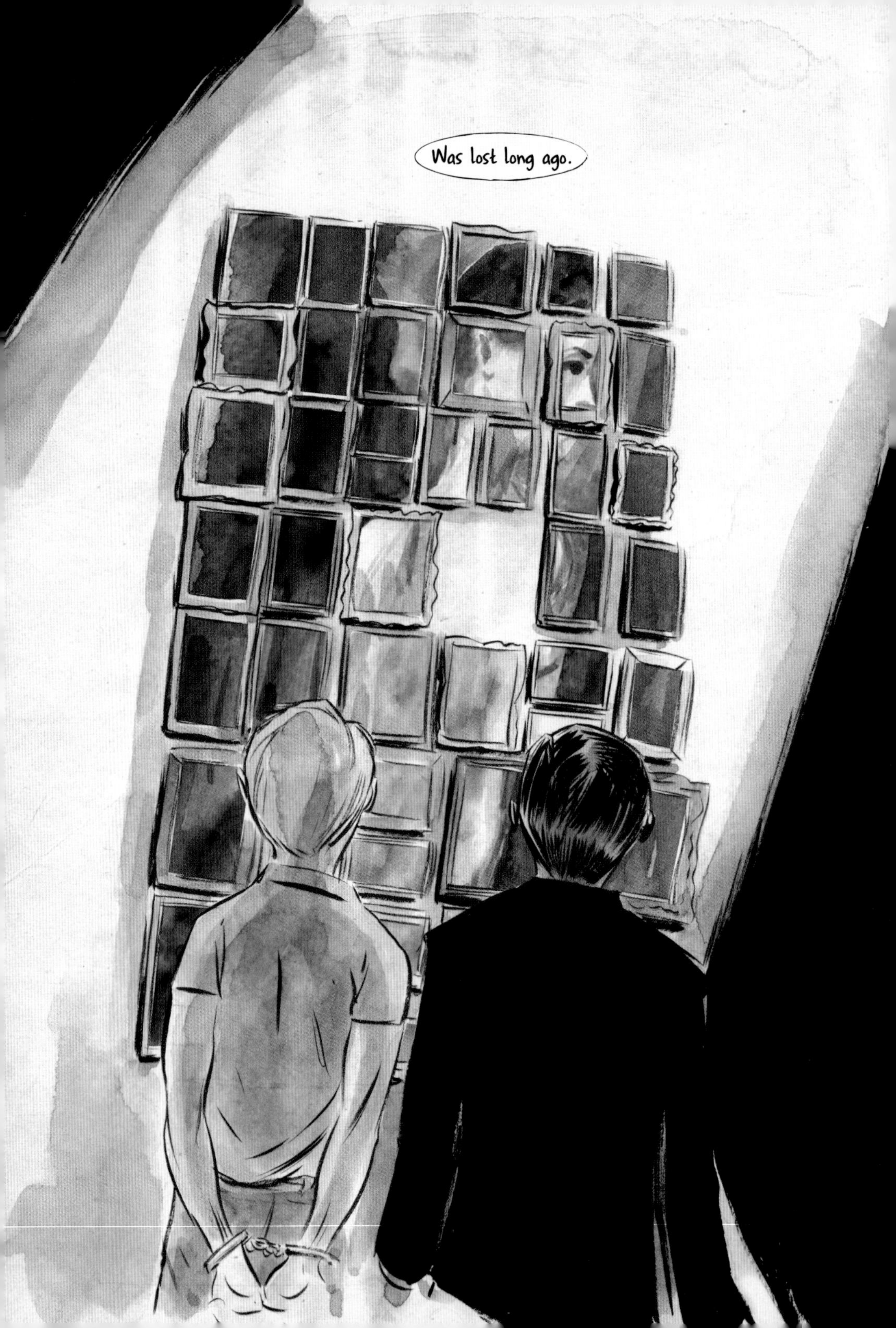
Was lost long ago.

AZ E

The famous theft of Picasso's "Woman in a Chemise" has finally been solved, thanks to Red Wheel Barrow's own ace, Detective Gould. Gould, with the help of undercover buyers and a tip from a real estate agent who wished to remain anonymous, closed in on the mysterious art thief.

All but one of the sections of "Woman in a Chemise" were recovered over the last several years, leading up to the arrest of the art thief known as "The Tiger."

Only one theft has been attributed to "The Tiger," who had established himself over the years as one of the most successful and reputable art dealers in the city. All of his property and his condominium were seized in the raid conducted yesterday afternoon.

The crucial tip came from "The Tiger's" original victim, who had lived in Monaco several years ago, and finally came forward when news of the

(continued on C8)

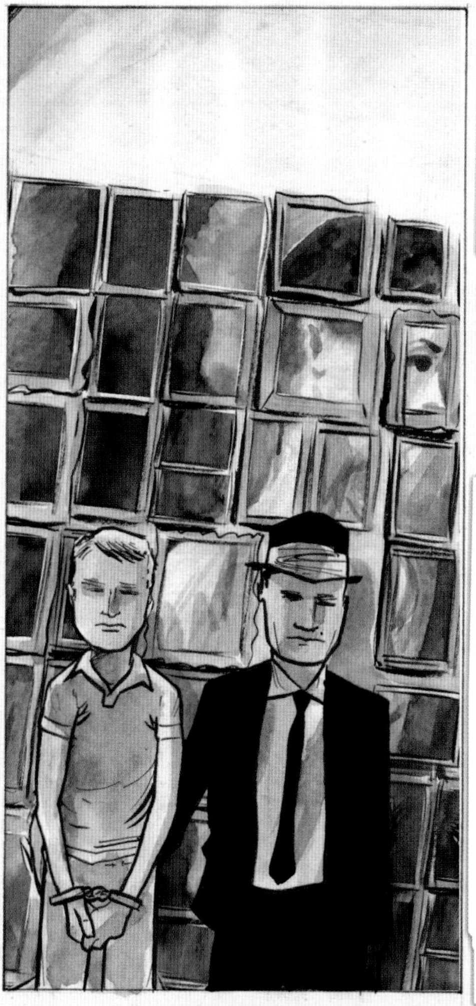

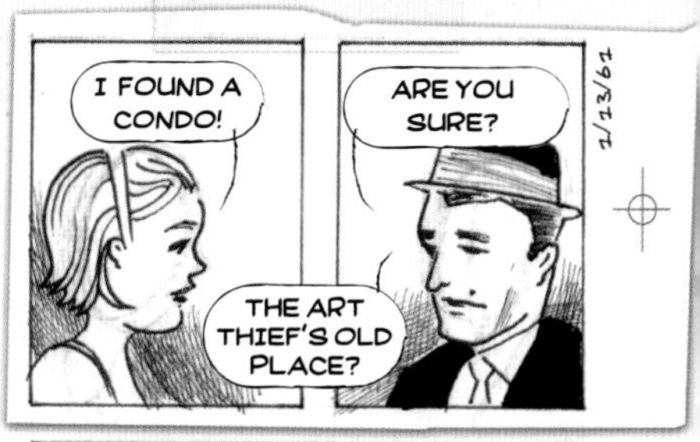
I FOUND A CONDO!
ARE YOU SURE?
THE ART THIEF'S OLD PLACE?

CONDO FOR SALE

Spacious 2-BR condo overlooking the city. Walk-out patio with gorgeous view.

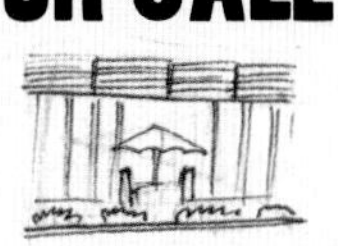

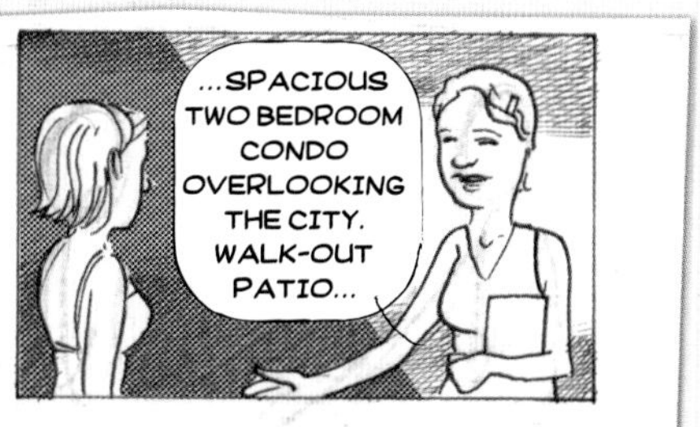
...SPACIOUS TWO BEDROOM CONDO OVERLOOKING THE CITY. WALK-OUT PATIO...

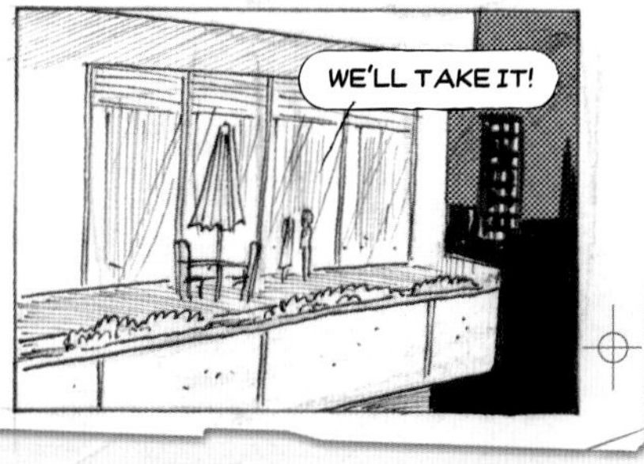
WE'LL TAKE IT!

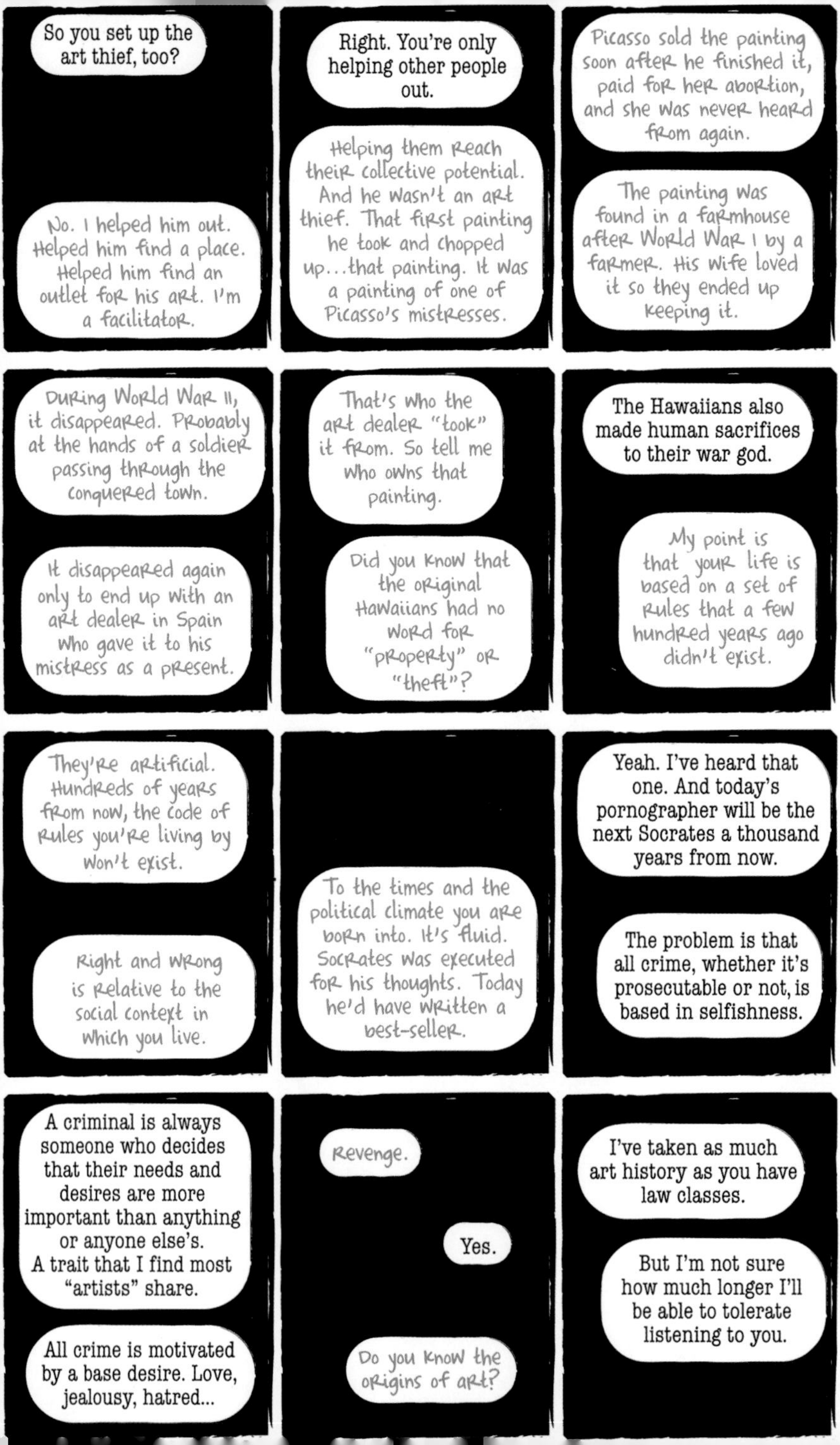
So you set up the art thief, too?
No. I helped him out. Helped him find a place. Helped him find an outlet for his art. I'm a facilitator.
Right. You're only helping other people out.
Helping them reach their collective potential. And he wasn't an art thief. That first painting he took and chopped up...that painting. It was a painting of one of Picasso's mistresses.
Picasso sold the painting soon after he finished it, paid for her abortion, and she was never heard from again.
The painting was found in a farmhouse after World War I by a farmer. His wife loved it so they ended up keeping it.
During World War II, it disappeared. Probably at the hands of a soldier passing through the conquered town.
It disappeared again only to end up with an art dealer in Spain who gave it to his mistress as a present.
That's who the art dealer "took" it from. So tell me who owns that painting.
Did you know that the original Hawaiians had no word for "property" or "theft"?
The Hawaiians also made human sacrifices to their war god.
My point is that your life is based on a set of rules that a few hundred years ago didn't exist.
They're artificial. Hundreds of years from now, the code of rules you're living by won't exist.
Right and wrong is relative to the social context in which you live.
To the times and the political climate you are born into. It's fluid. Socrates was executed for his thoughts. Today he'd have written a best-seller.
Yeah. I've heard that one. And today's pornographer will be the next Socrates a thousand years from now.
The problem is that all crime, whether it's prosecutable or not, is based in selfishness.
A criminal is always someone who decides that their needs and desires are more important than anything or anyone else's. A trait that I find most "artists" share.
All crime is motivated by a base desire. Love, jealousy, hatred...
Revenge.
Yes.
Do you know the origins of art?
I've taken as much art history as you have law classes.
But I'm not sure how much longer I'll be able to tolerate listening to you.

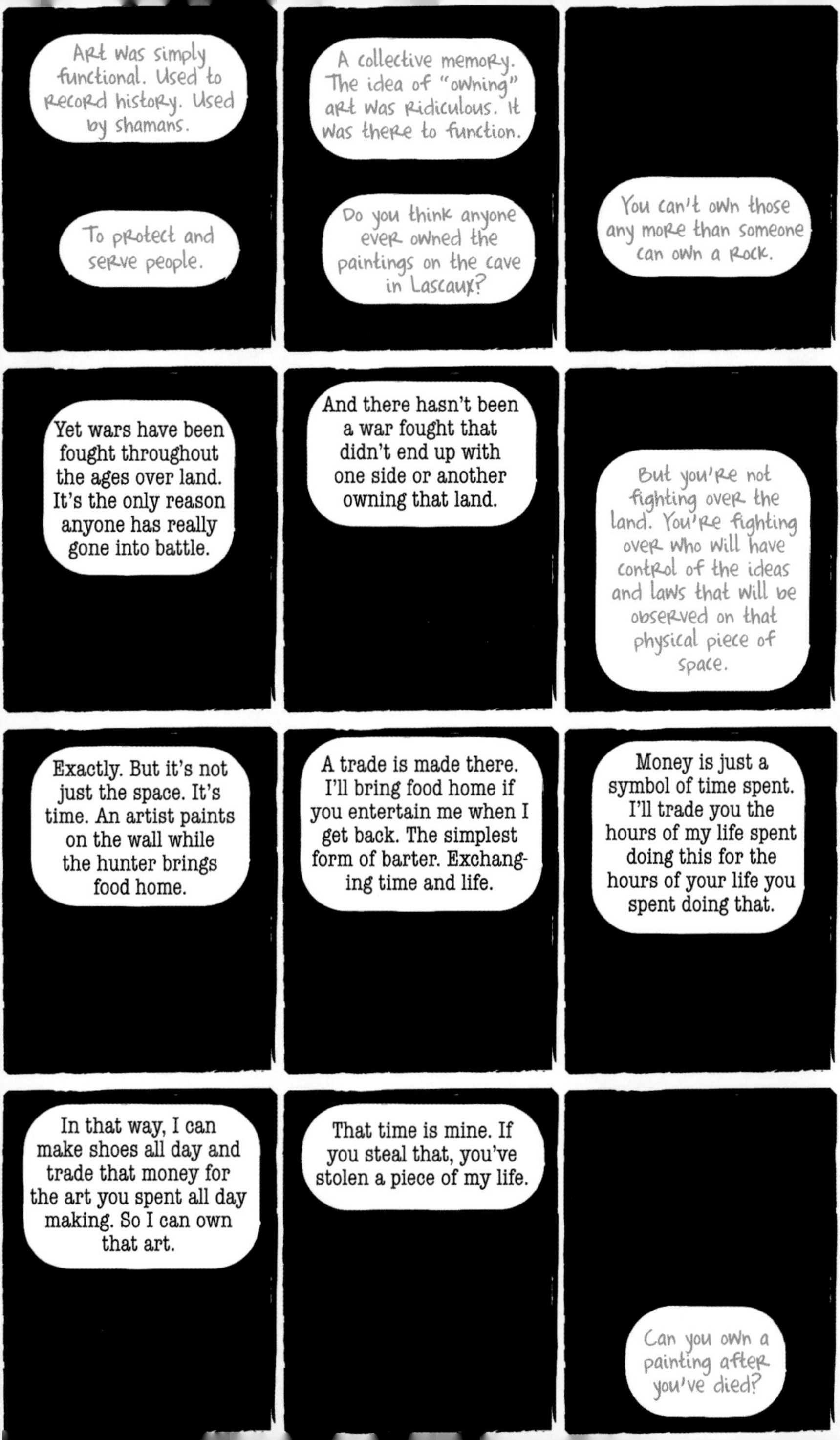
Art was simply functional. Used to record history. Used by shamans.
To protect and serve people.
A collective memory. The idea of "owning" art was ridiculous. It was there to function.
Do you think anyone ever owned the paintings on the cave in Lascaux?
You can't own those any more than someone can own a rock.
Yet wars have been fought throughout the ages over land. It's the only reason anyone has really gone into battle.
And there hasn't been a war fought that didn't end up with one side or another owning that land.
But you're not fighting over the land. You're fighting over who will have control of the ideas and laws that will be observed on that physical piece of space.
Exactly. But it's not just the space. It's time. An artist paints on the wall while the hunter brings food home.
A trade is made there. I'll bring food home if you entertain me when I get back. The simplest form of barter. Exchanging time and life.
Money is just a symbol of time spent. I'll trade you the hours of my life spent doing this for the hours of your life you spent doing that.
In that way, I can make shoes all day and trade that money for the art you spent all day making. So I can own that art.
That time is mine. If you steal that, you've stolen a piece of my life.
Can you own a painting after you've died?

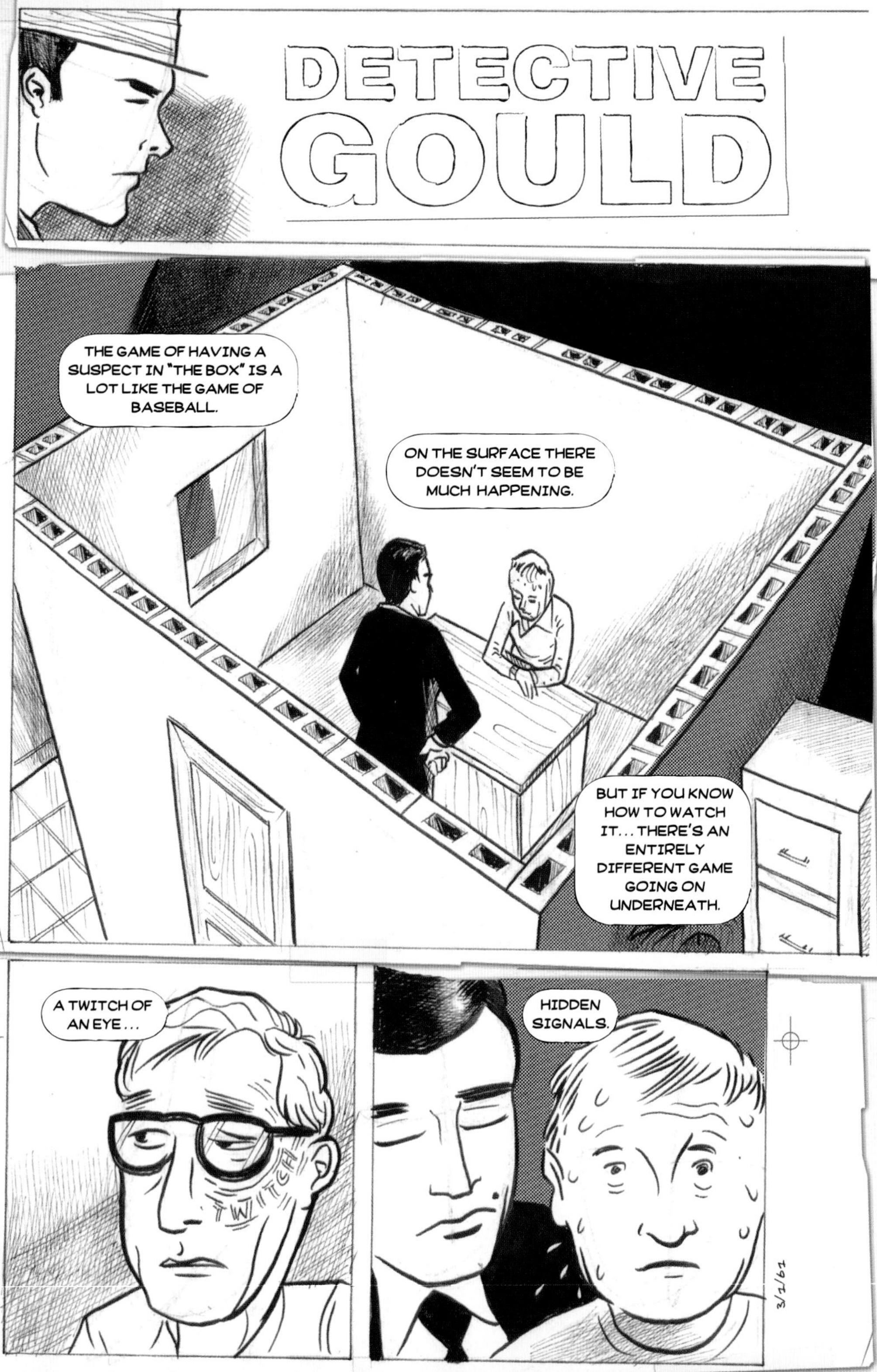
DETECTIVE GOULD
THE GAME OF HAVING A SUSPECT IN "THE BOX" IS A LOT LIKE THE GAME OF BASEBALL.
ON THE SURFACE THERE DOESN'T SEEM TO BE MUCH HAPPENING.
BUT IF YOU KNOW HOW TO WATCH IT... THERE'S AN ENTIRELY DIFFERENT GAME GOING ON UNDERNEATH.
A TWITCH OF AN EYE...
TWITCH
TWITCH
HIDDEN SIGNALS.

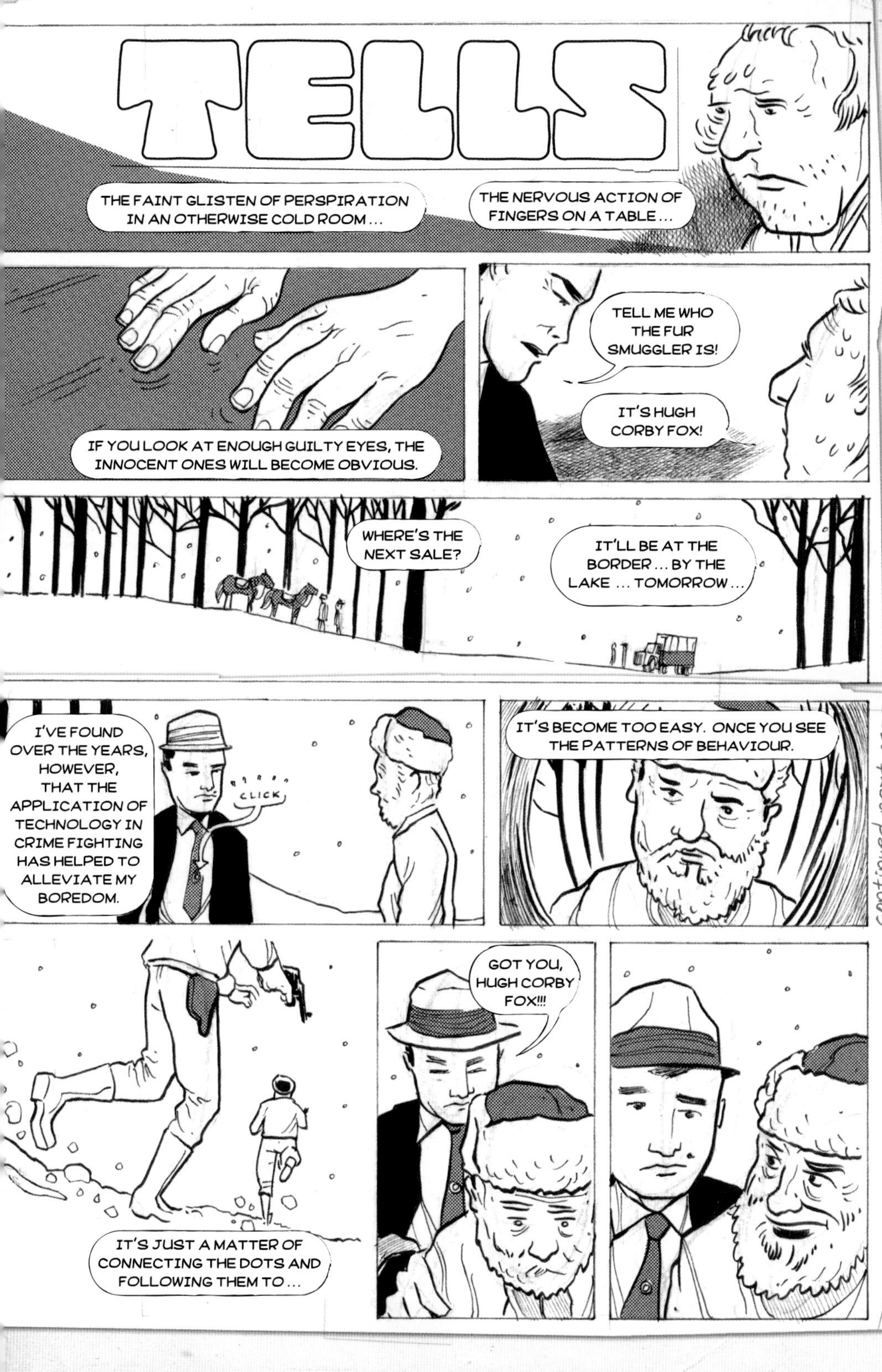
TELLS
THE FAINT GLISTEN OF PERSPIRATION IN AN OTHERWISE COLD ROOM ...
THE NERVOUS ACTION OF FINGERS ON A TABLE ...
IF YOU LOOK AT ENOUGH GUILTY EYES, THE INNOCENT ONES WILL BECOME OBVIOUS.
TELL ME WHO THE FUR SMUGGLER IS!
IT'S HUGH CORBY FOX!
WHERE'S THE NEXT SALE?
IT'LL BE AT THE BORDER ... BY THE LAKE ... TOMORROW ...
I'VE FOUND OVER THE YEARS, HOWEVER, THAT THE APPLICATION OF TECHNOLOGY IN CRIME FIGHTING HAS HELPED TO ALLEVIATE MY BOREDOM.
CLICK
IT'S BECOME TOO EASY. ONCE YOU SEE THE PATTERNS OF BEHAVIOUR.
IT'S JUST A MATTER OF CONNECTING THE DOTS AND FOLLOWING THEM TO ...
GOT YOU, HUGH CORBY FOX!!!
continued next page

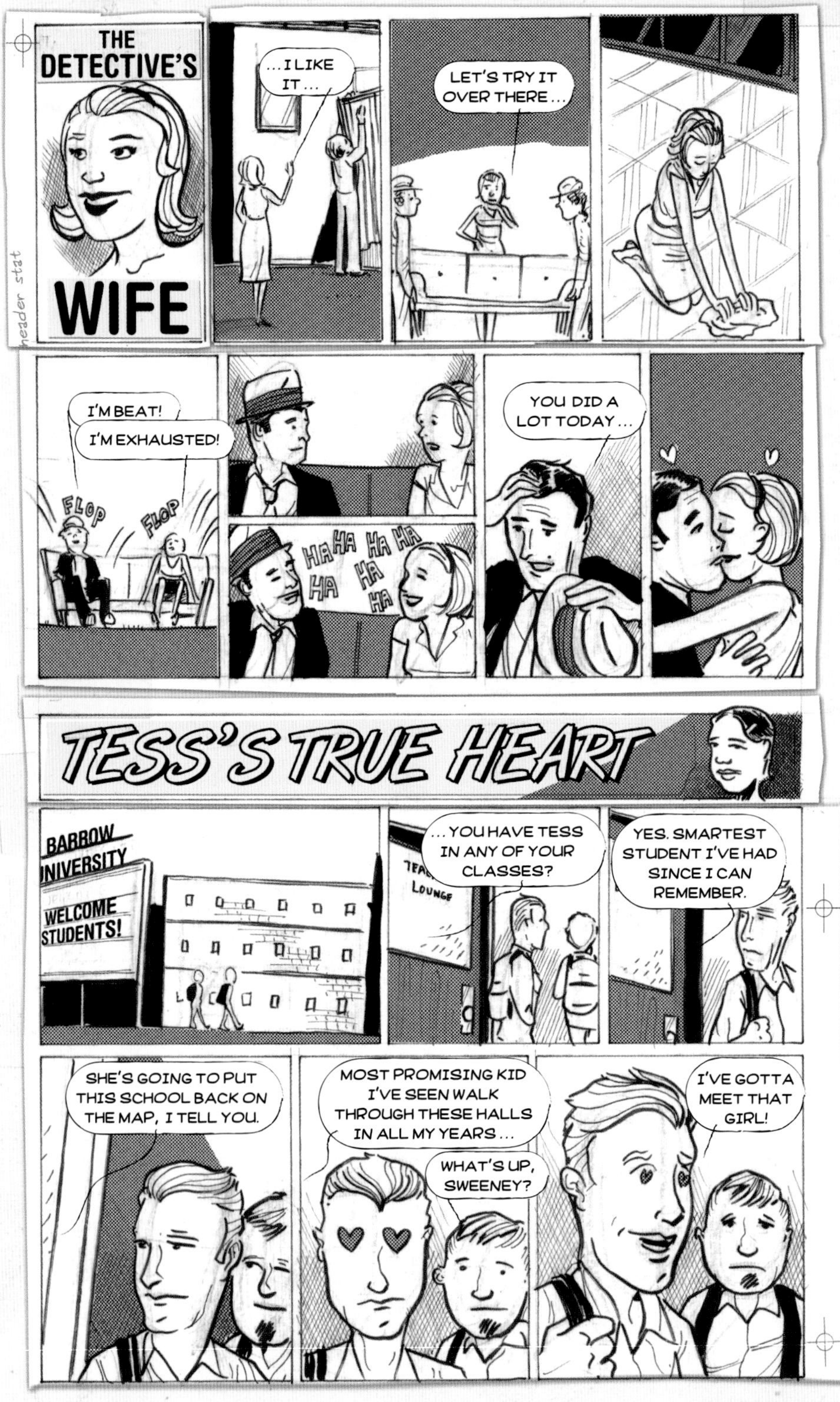
THE DETECTIVE'S
WIFE
header stat
...I LIKE IT...
LET'S TRY IT OVER THERE...
I'M BEAT!
I'M EXHAUSTED!
FLOP
FLOP
HA HA HA HA HA HA HA HA
YOU DID A LOT TODAY...
TESS'S TRUE HEART
BARROW UNIVERSITY
WELCOME STUDENTS!
TEACHERS' LOUNGE
...YOU HAVE TESS IN ANY OF YOUR CLASSES?
YES. SMARTEST STUDENT I'VE HAD SINCE I CAN REMEMBER.
SHE'S GOING TO PUT THIS SCHOOL BACK ON THE MAP, I TELL YOU.
MOST PROMISING KID I'VE SEEN WALK THROUGH THESE HALLS IN ALL MY YEARS...
WHAT'S UP, SWEENEY?
I'VE GOTTA MEET THAT GIRL!

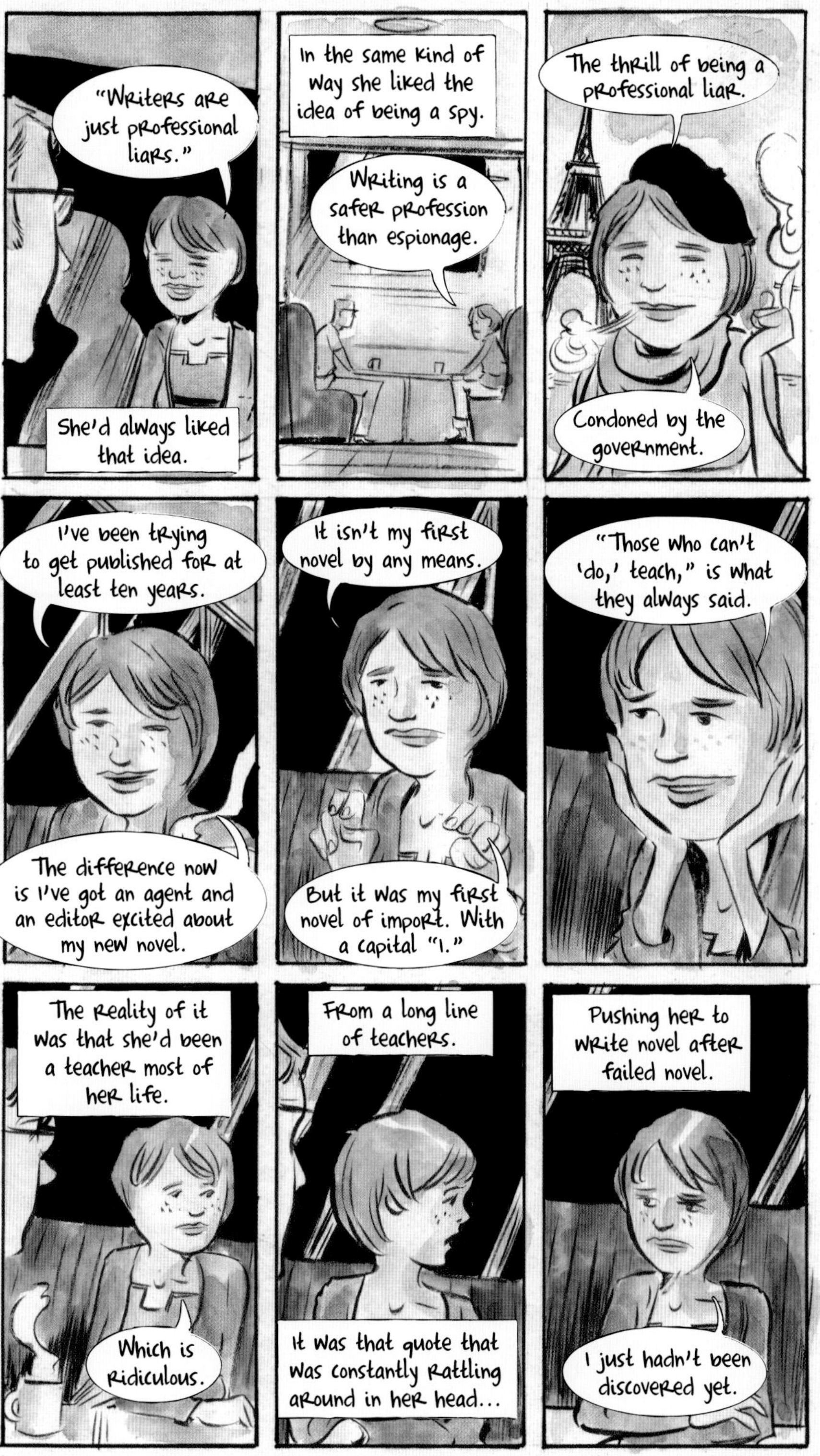
"Writers are just professional liars."
She'd always liked that idea.
In the same kind of way she liked the idea of being a spy.
Writing is a safer profession than espionage.
The thrill of being a professional liar.
Condoned by the government.
I've been trying to get published for at least ten years.
The difference now is I've got an agent and an editor excited about my new novel.
It isn't my first novel by any means.
But it was my first novel of import. With a capital "I."
"Those who can't 'do,' teach," is what they always said.
The reality of it was that she'd been a teacher most of her life.
Which is ridiculous.
From a long line of teachers.
It was that quote that was constantly rattling around in her head...
Pushing her to write novel after failed novel.
I just hadn't been discovered yet.

THE
ANT

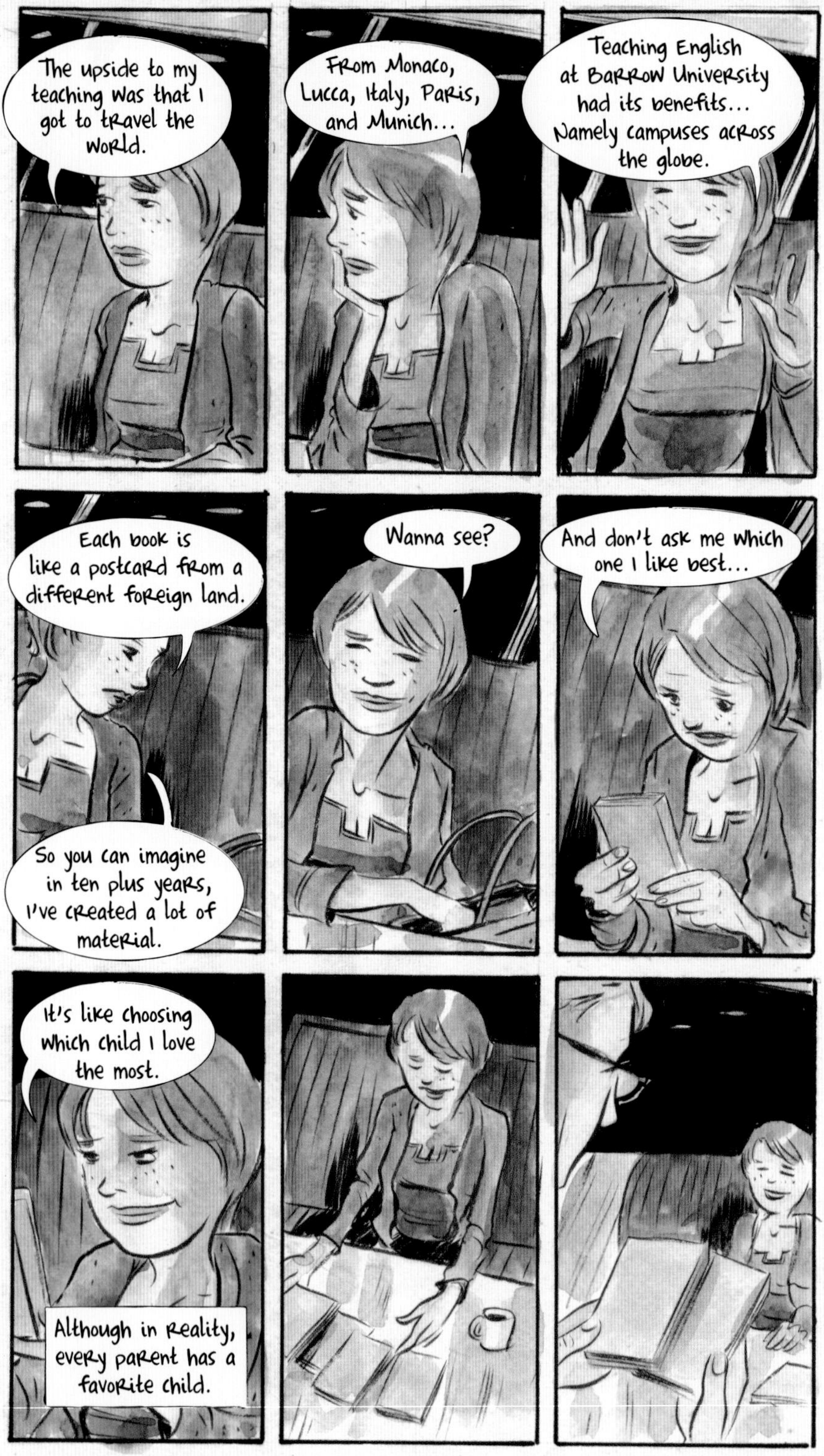
The upside to my teaching was that I got to travel the world.
From Monaco, Lucca, Italy, Paris, and Munich...
Teaching English at Barrow University had its benefits... Namely campuses across the globe.
Each book is like a postcard from a different foreign land.
So you can imagine in ten plus years, I've created a lot of material.
Wanna see?
And don't ask me which one I like best...
It's like choosing which child I love the most.
Although in reality, every parent has a favorite child.

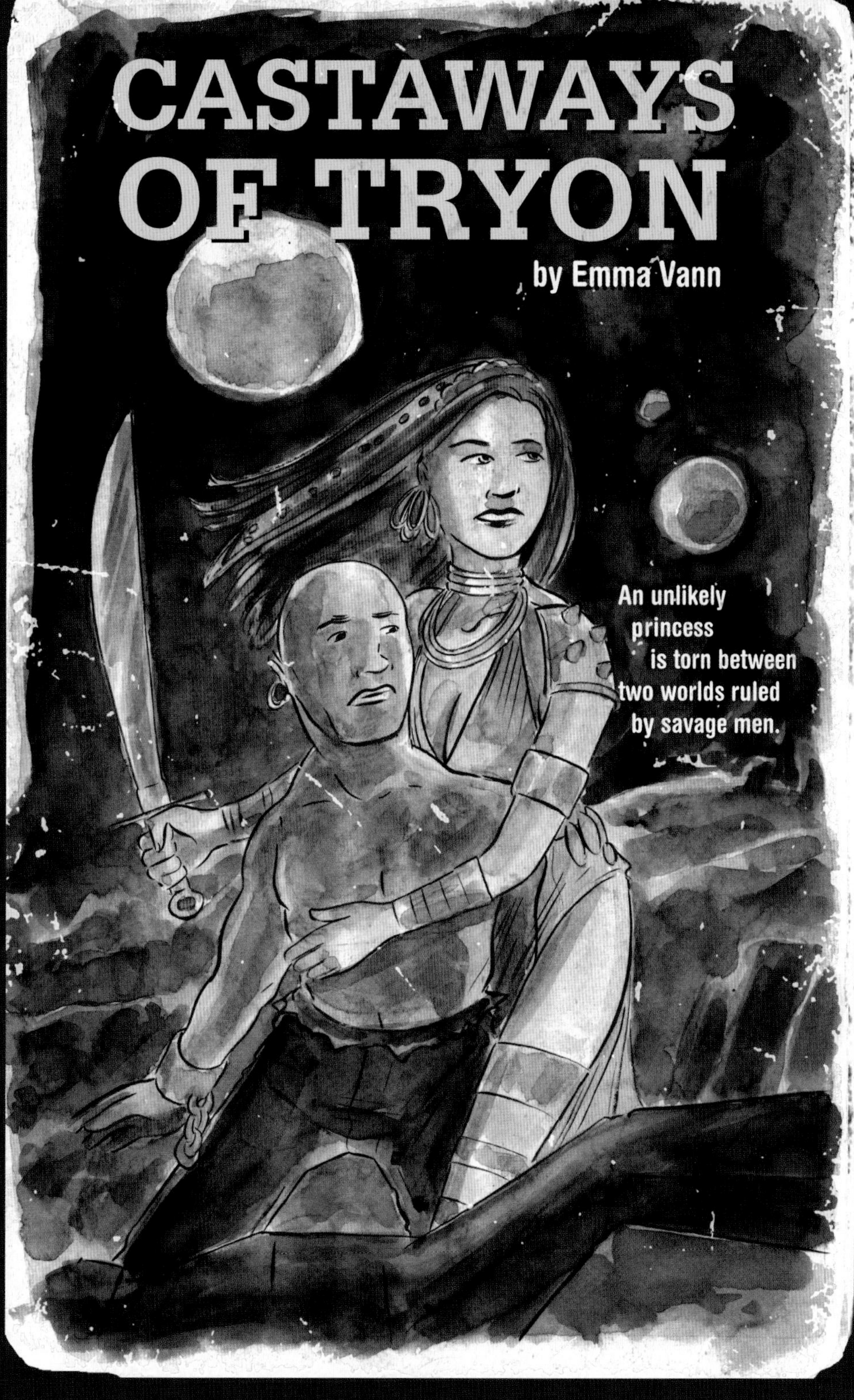
CASTAWAYS OF TRYON
by Emma Vann
An unlikely princess is torn between two worlds ruled by savage men.

a novel of dreams lost and fantasies come to life...

Eva is kidnapped from her day job as a night nurse – a
hood is thrown over her head and she is thrown into the
trunk of a car. The next thing she knows, she is waking up
in the grand palace of the ReJectasy – the despotic king of
a planet thousands of light years from earth. Her captors
tell her that she is to become the mate of Grande
Potent-Hate III and provide him with offspring.

All of Eva's fantastical daydreams seem to be realized
until she meets Potent-Hate and she realizes that her
fantasies may actually turn into a nightmare of sadistic
orgies, torturous games of sport, and a populace on the
verge of boiling over into civil war. Can Eva set things
right without dying an unimaginably horrible death? She
must tackle all of this while avoiding another
uncomfortable question – is any of this even real?

CASTAWAYS
OF TRYON

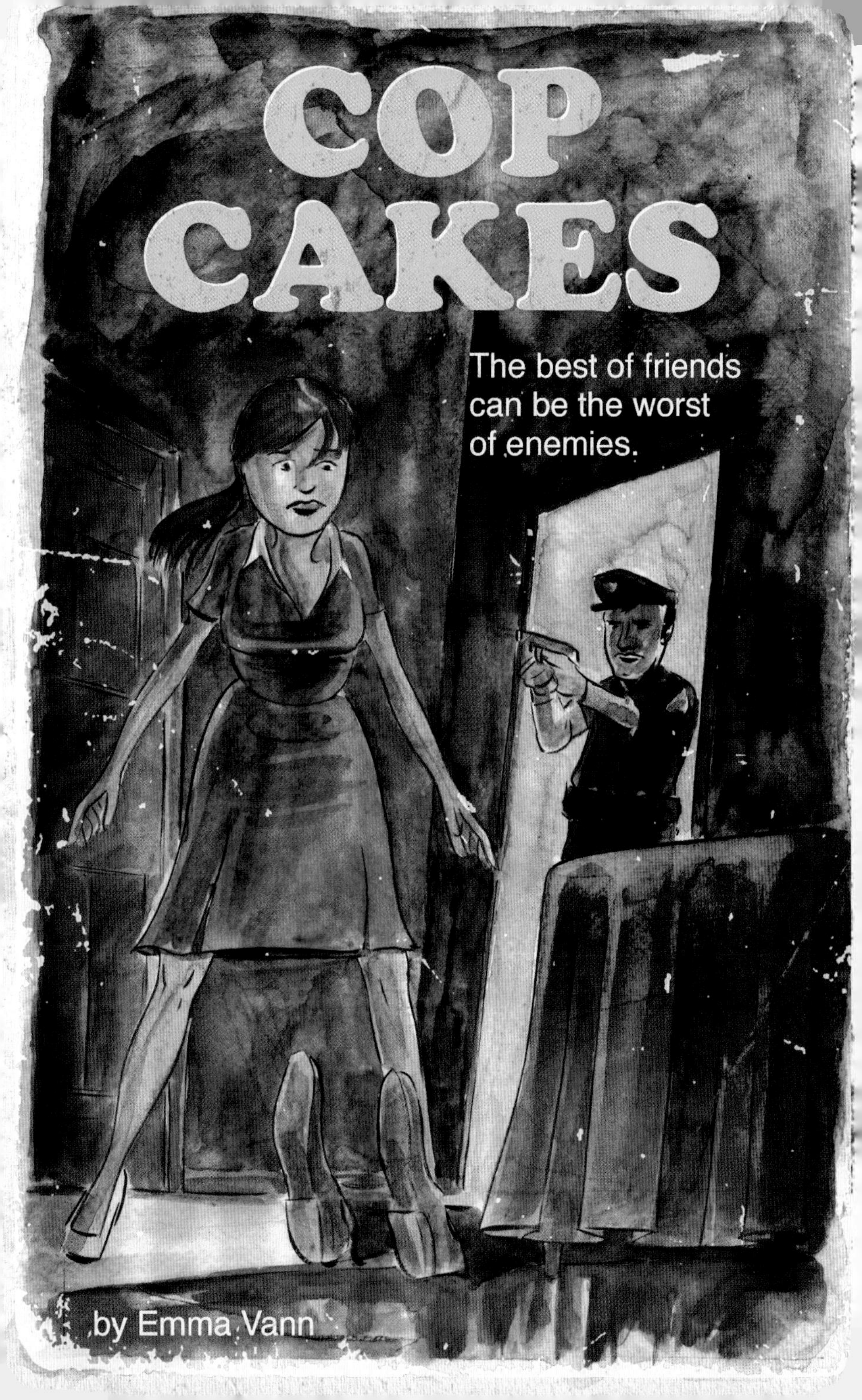
COP
CAKES
The best of friends can be the worst of enemies.
by Emma Vann

searching for her innocence even as she loses it...

by Emma Vann

Ila had run her donut shop "Copcakes" for years
and was a favorite of the local police force who made
up nearly all of her business. She knew them all by
name and was even invited to their birthday parties
and summer picnics. That is how it used to be before
she woke up in her shop one morning with a dead
body behind the counter, blood on her hands, and a
shop full of policemen waiting to order donuts, but
finding her seemingly guilty of murder instead.

Ila runs, convinced that she has been set up. How
could you murder someone and not know it? She
knows she's been set up but by who and why? Her
cross-country search will take her through the deepest
bowels of society in search of her innocence – made
all the harder by her instant celebrity status as the
nation follows her exploits – the most famous "killer"
of the century – the "Copcake Killer."

Can she find out who set the pieces of her life
toppling into chaos before her celebrity status
becomes more real than reality?

COP
CAKES

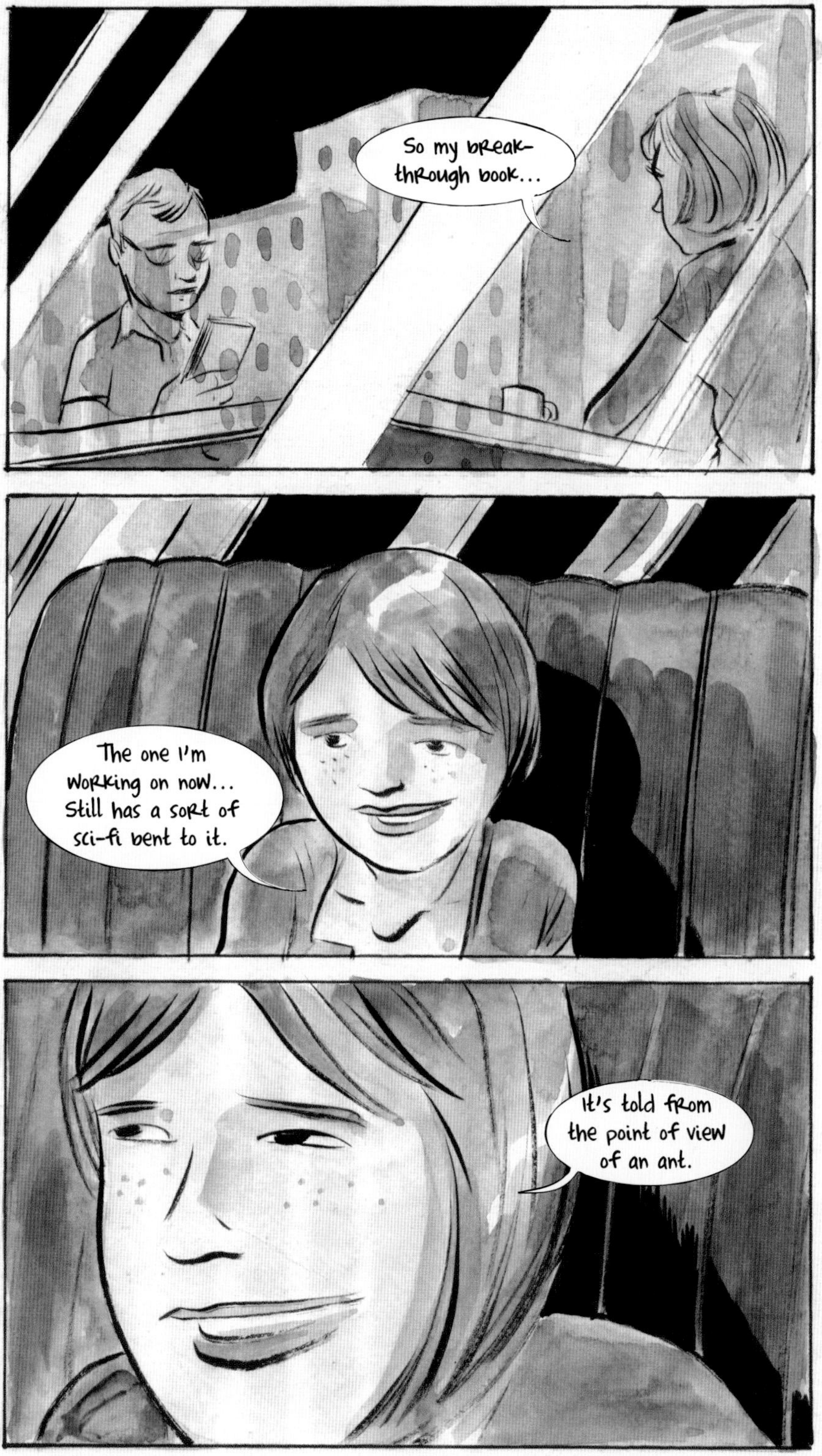
So my break-through book...
The one I'm working on now... Still has a sort of sci-fi bent to it.
It's told from the point of view of an ant.

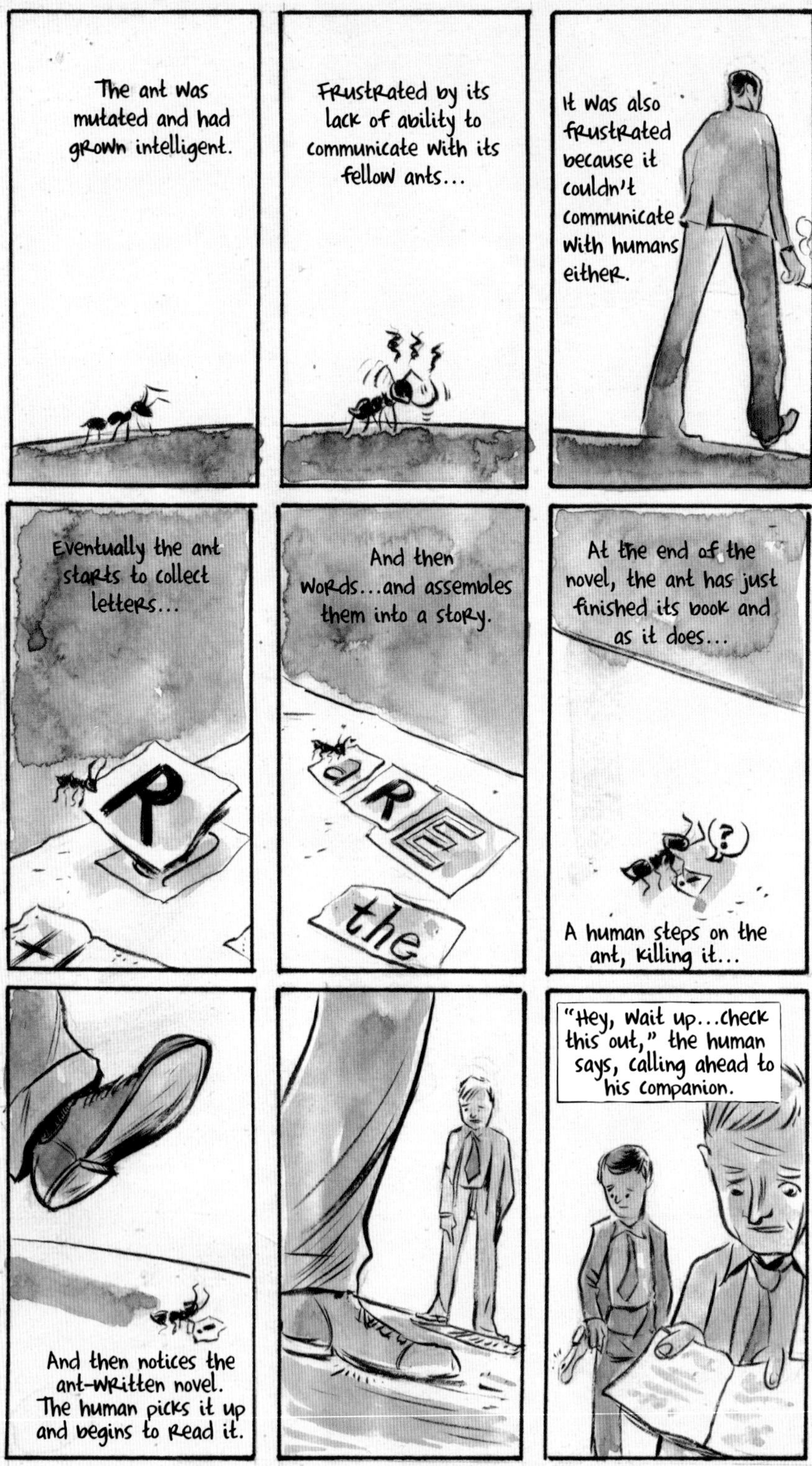
The ant was mutated and had grown intelligent.
Frustrated by its lack of ability to communicate with its fellow ants...
It was also frustrated because it couldn't communicate with humans either.
Eventually the ant starts to collect letters...
R
And then words...and assembles them into a story.
a
R
E
the
At the end of the novel, the ant has just finished its book and as it does...
?
A human steps on the ant, killing it...
And then notices the ant-written novel. The human picks it up and begins to read it.
"Hey, wait up...check this out," the human says, calling ahead to his companion.

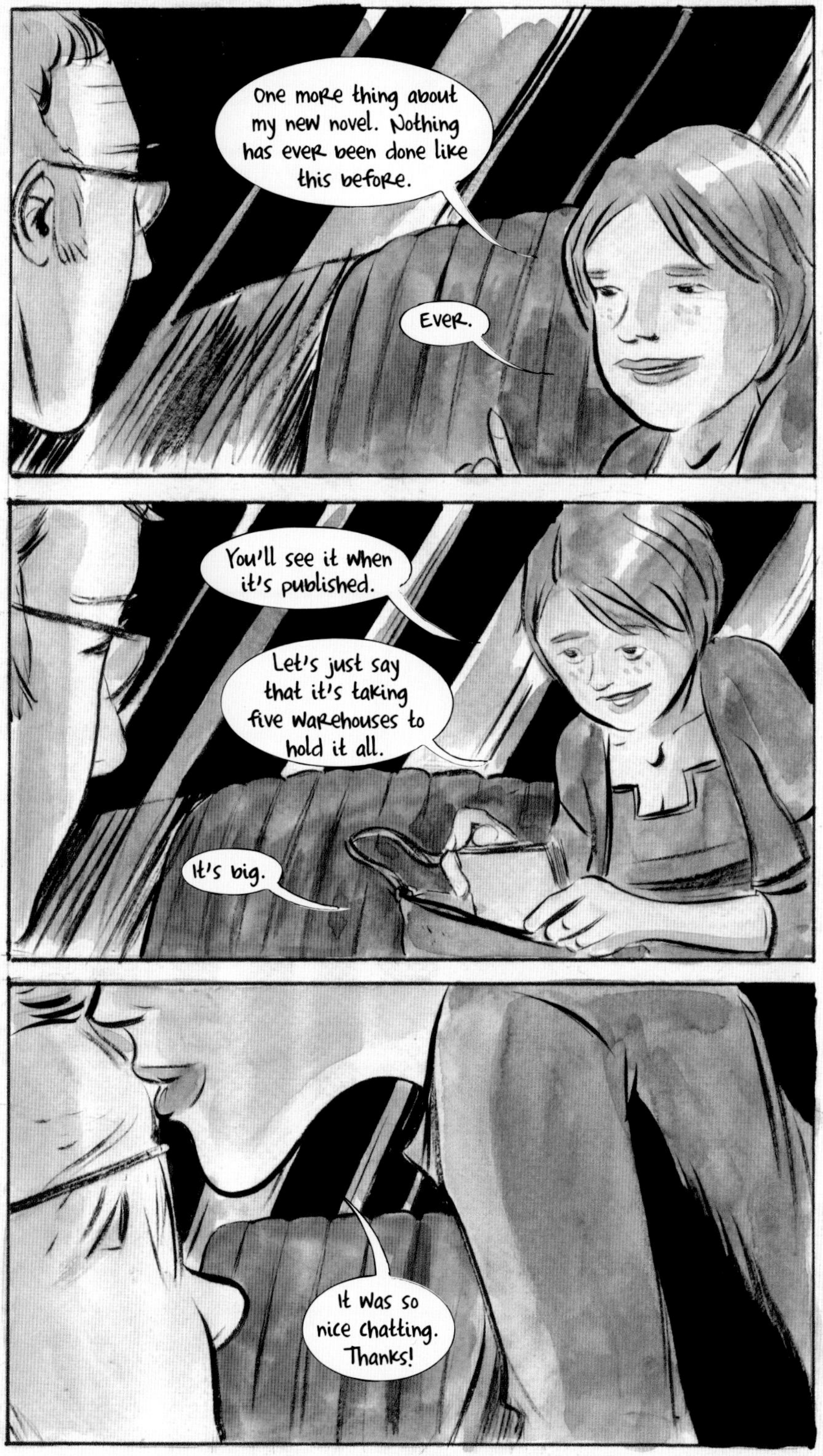
One more thing about my new novel. Nothing has ever been done like this before.
Ever.
You'll see it when it's published.
Let's just say that it's taking five warehouses to hold it all.
It's big.
It was so nice chatting. Thanks!

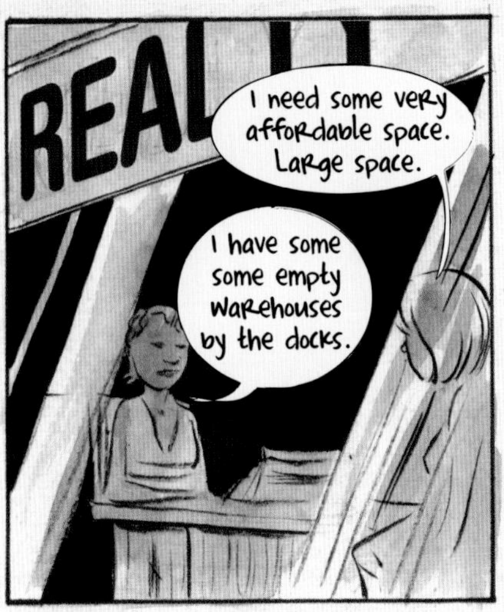
REAL
I need some very affordable space. Large space.
I have some some empty warehouses by the docks.

perseverance over all the odds

I have about ten warehouses available right now.

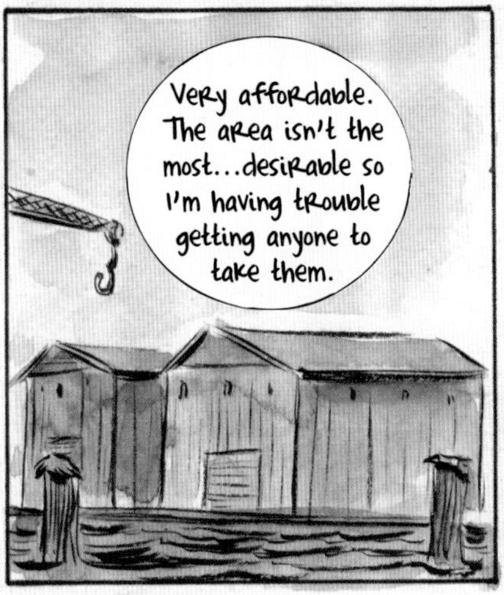
Very affordable. The area isn't the most...desirable so I'm having trouble getting anyone to take them.

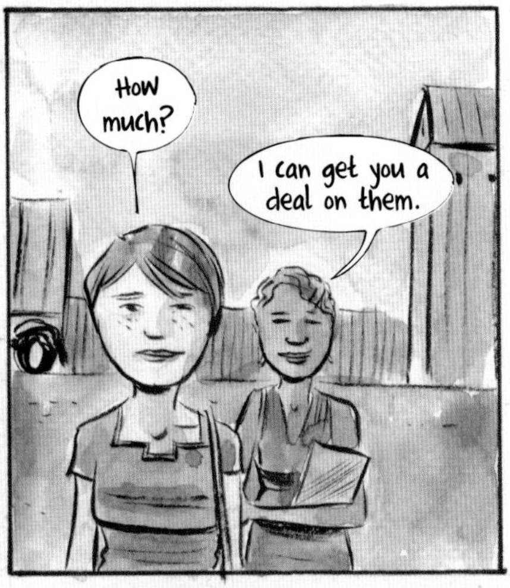
How much?
I can get you a deal on them.

as Ant placed the last letter on the page

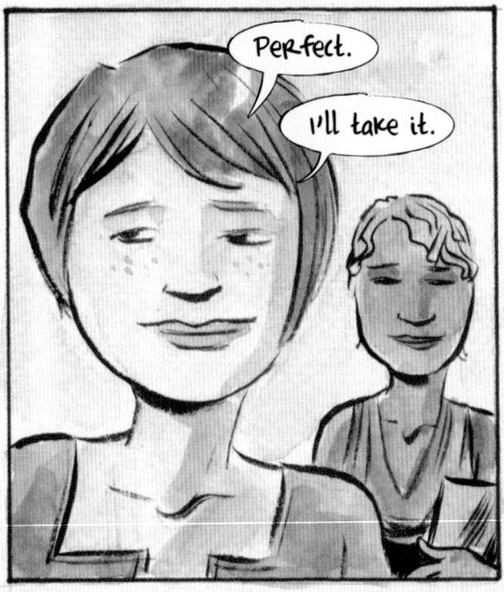
Perfect.
I'll take it.

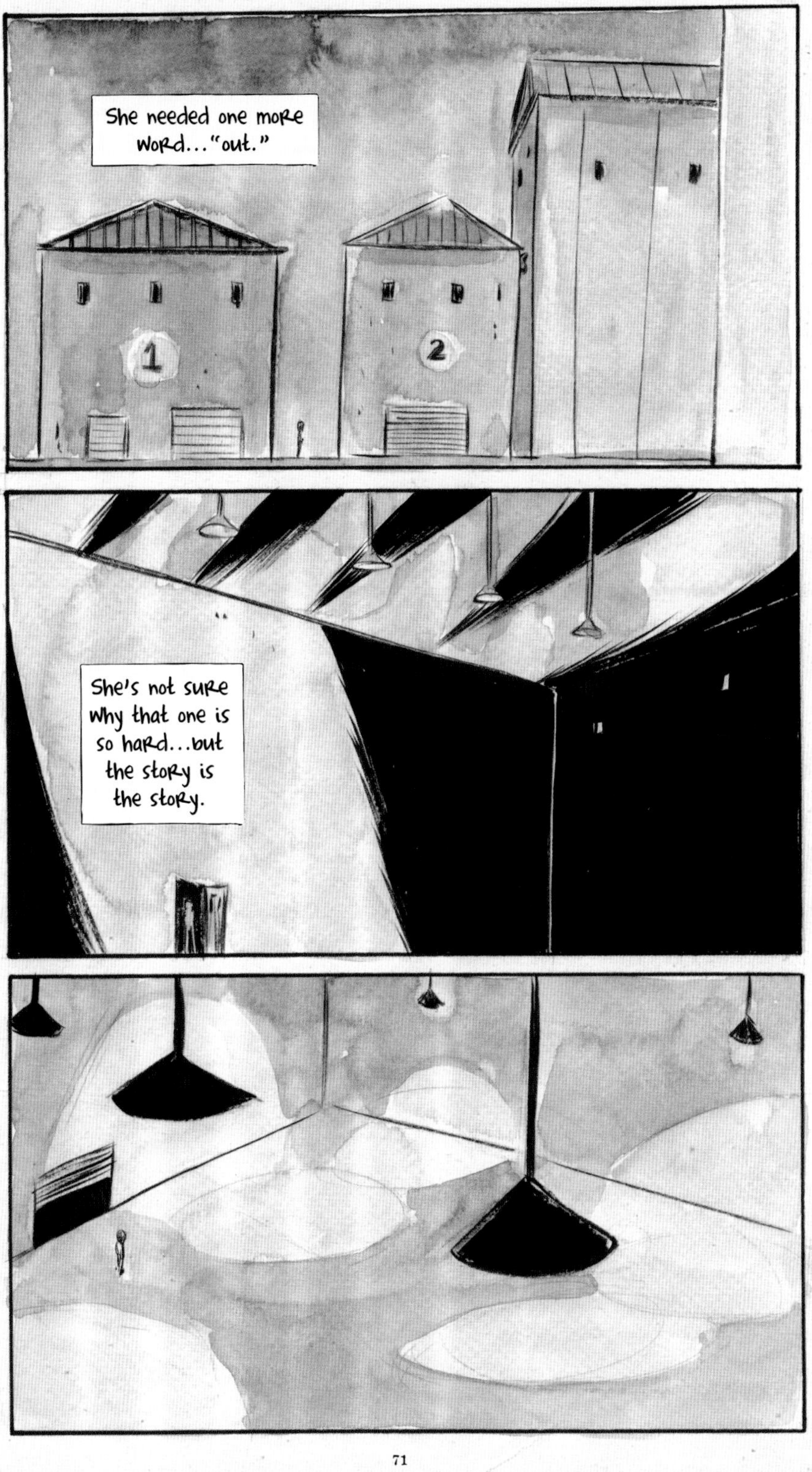
She needed one more word... "out."
1
2
She's not sure why that one is so hard...but the story is the story.

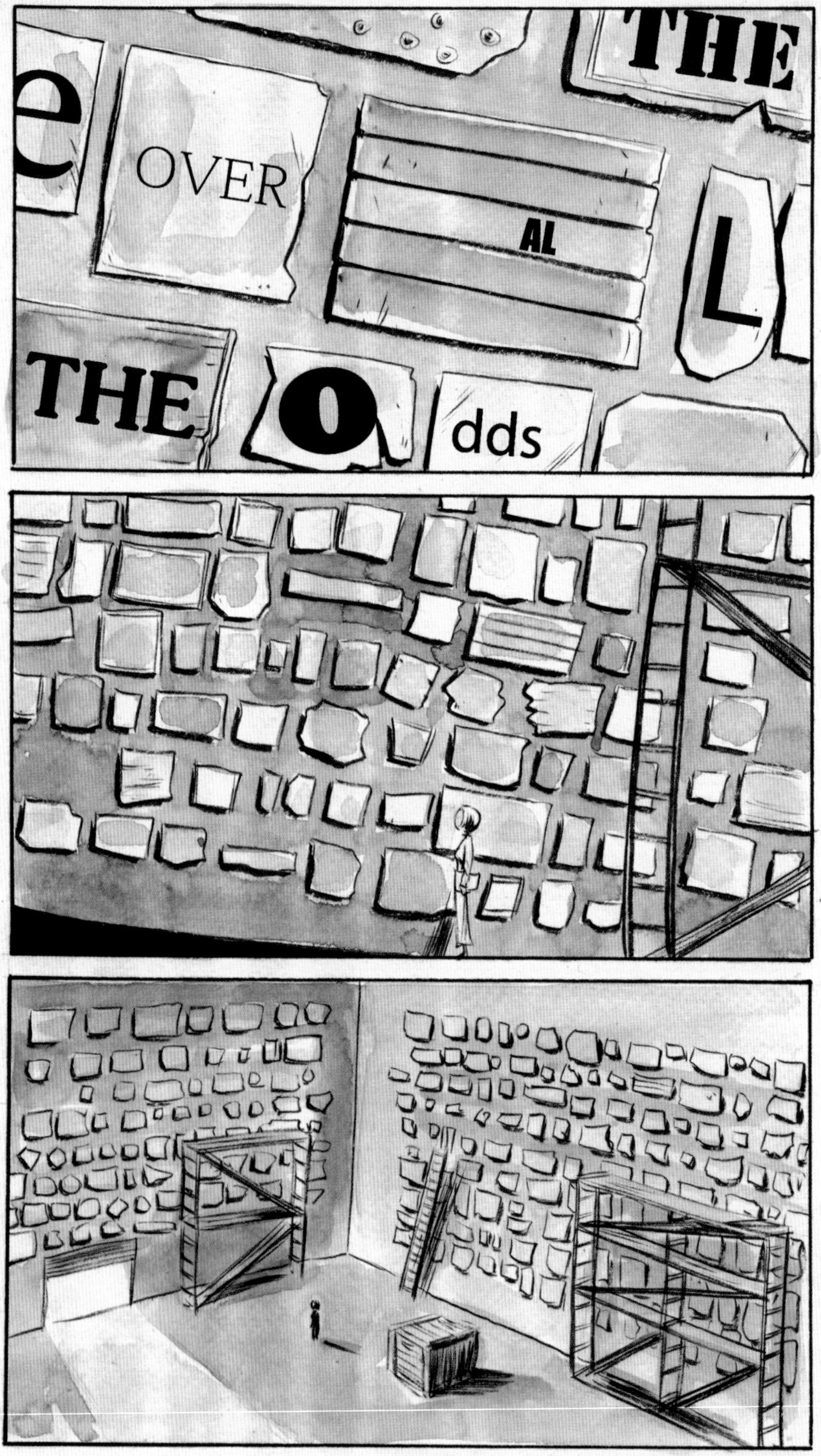
THE
e
OVER
AL
L
THE
O
dds

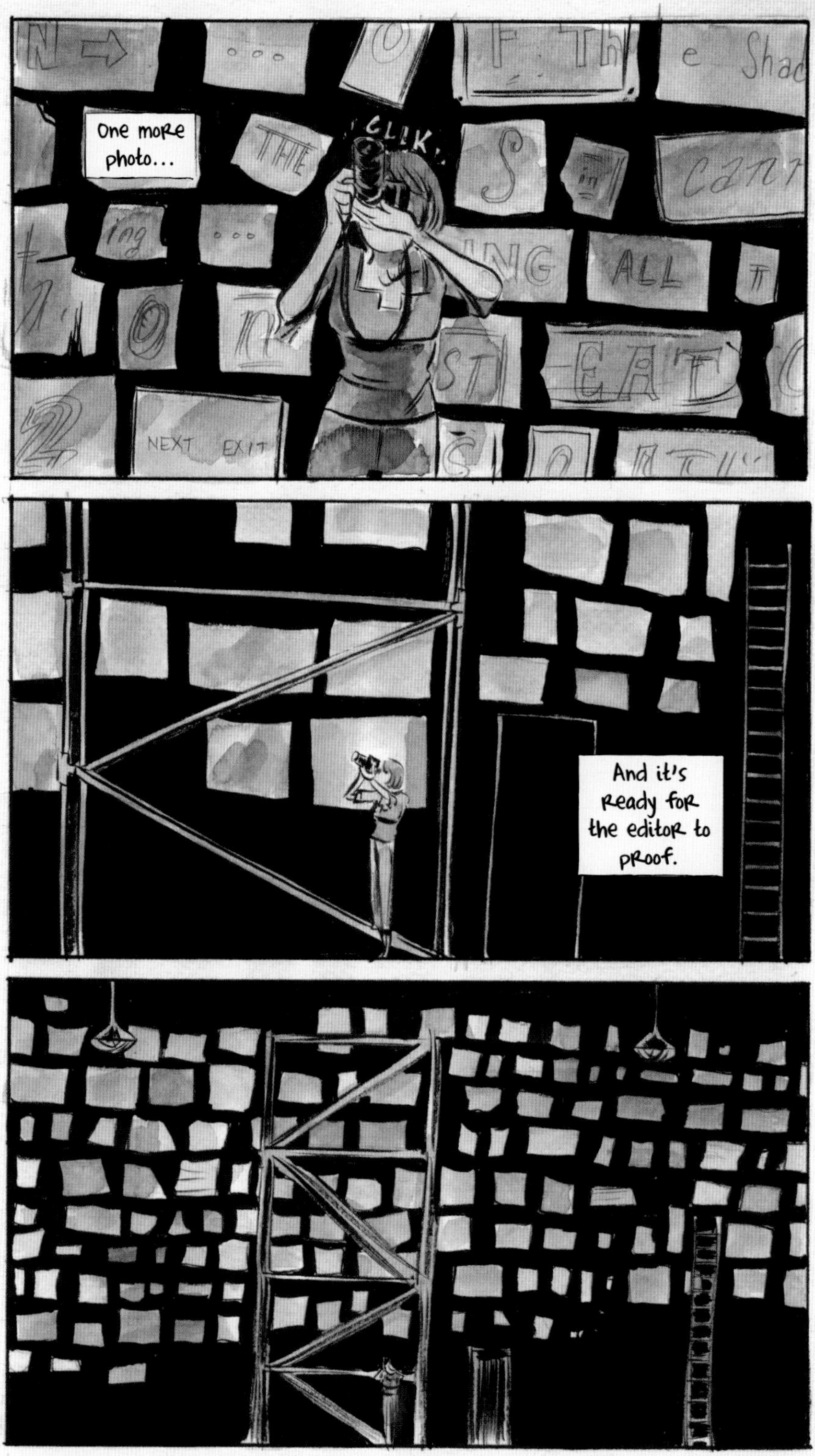
One more photo...
NEXT EXIT
And it's ready for the editor to proof.

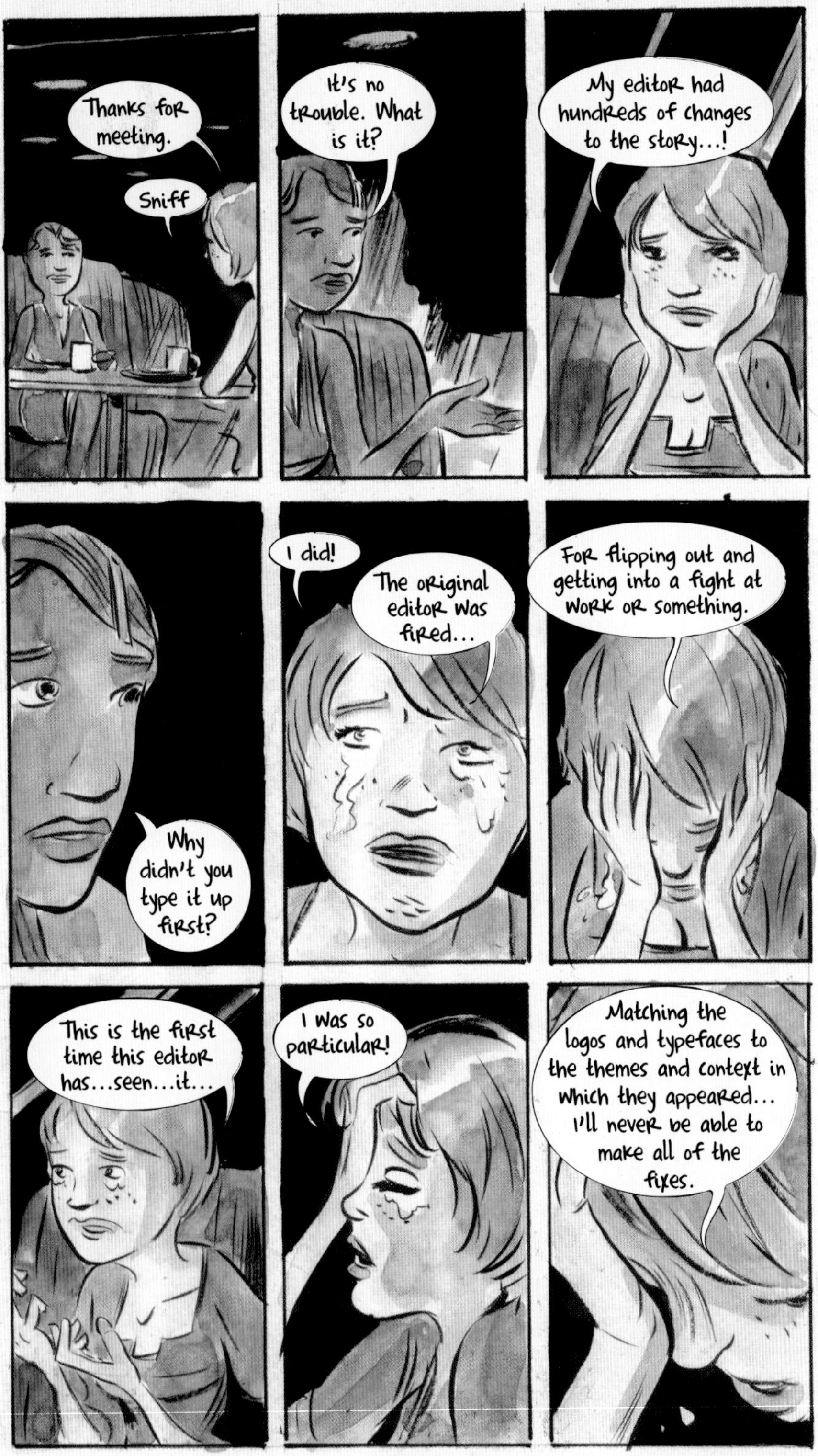
Thanks for meeting.
Sniff
It's no trouble. What is it?
My editor had hundreds of changes to the story...!
Why didn't you type it up first?
I did!
The original editor was fired...
For flipping out and getting into a fight at work or something.
This is the first time this editor has...seen...it...
I was so particular!
Matching the logos and typefaces to the themes and context in which they appeared... I'll never be able to make all of the fixes.

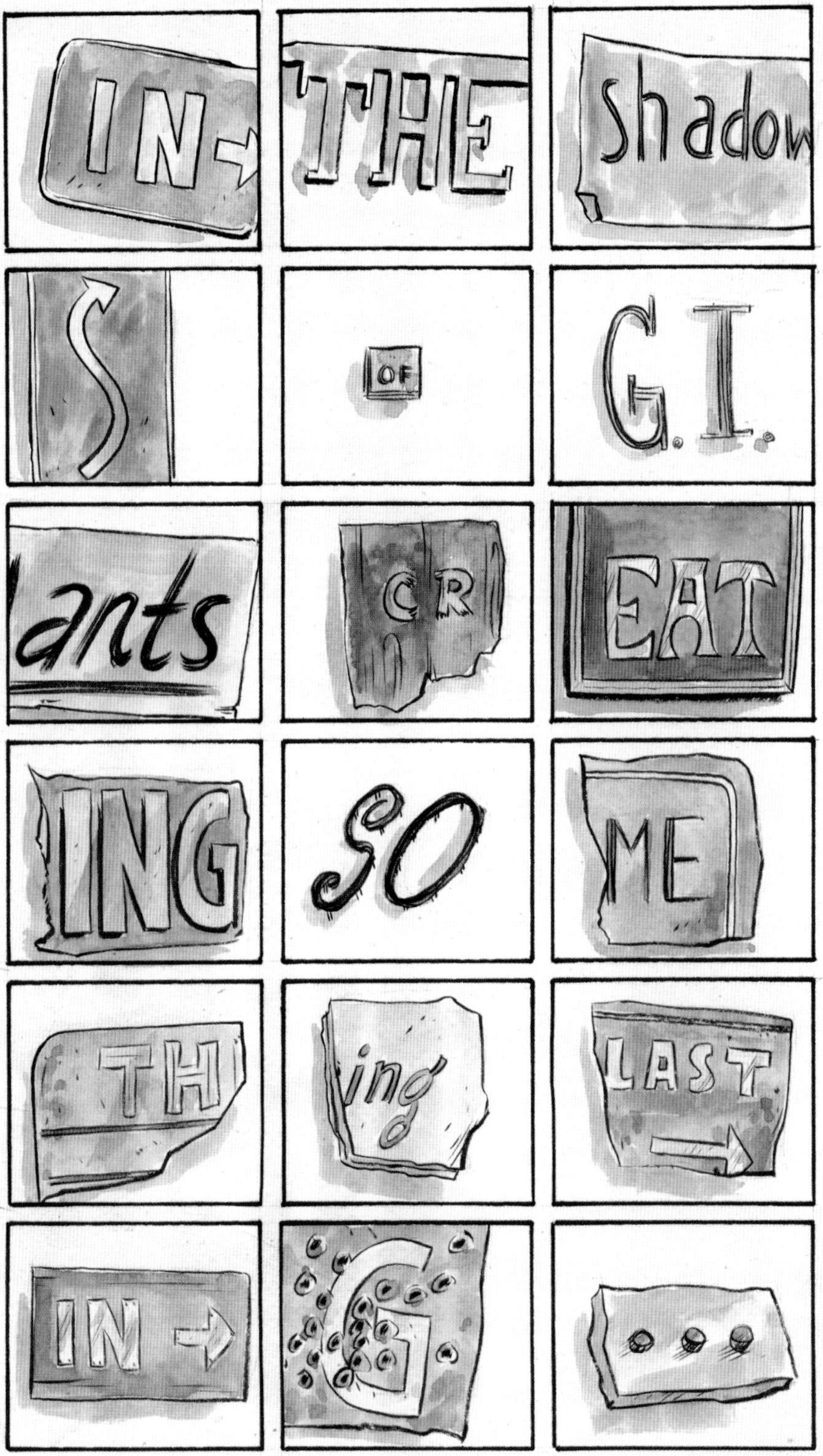
IN
THE
Shadow
S
OF
G.I.
ants
CR
EAT
ING
SO
ME
TH
ing
LAST
IN
G
...

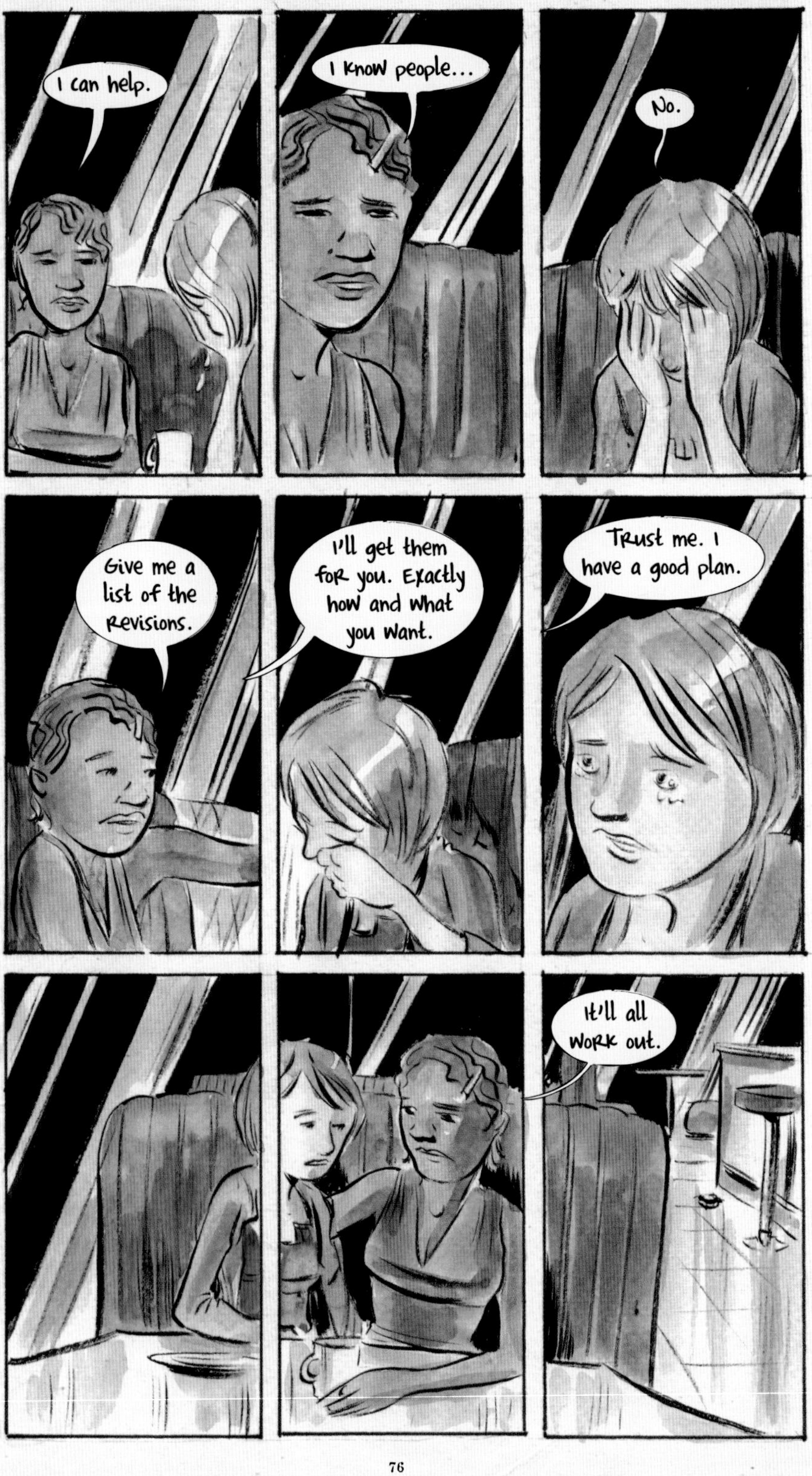
I can help.
I know people...
No.
Give me a list of the revisions.
I'll get them for you. Exactly how and what you want.
Trust me. I have a good plan.
It'll all work out.

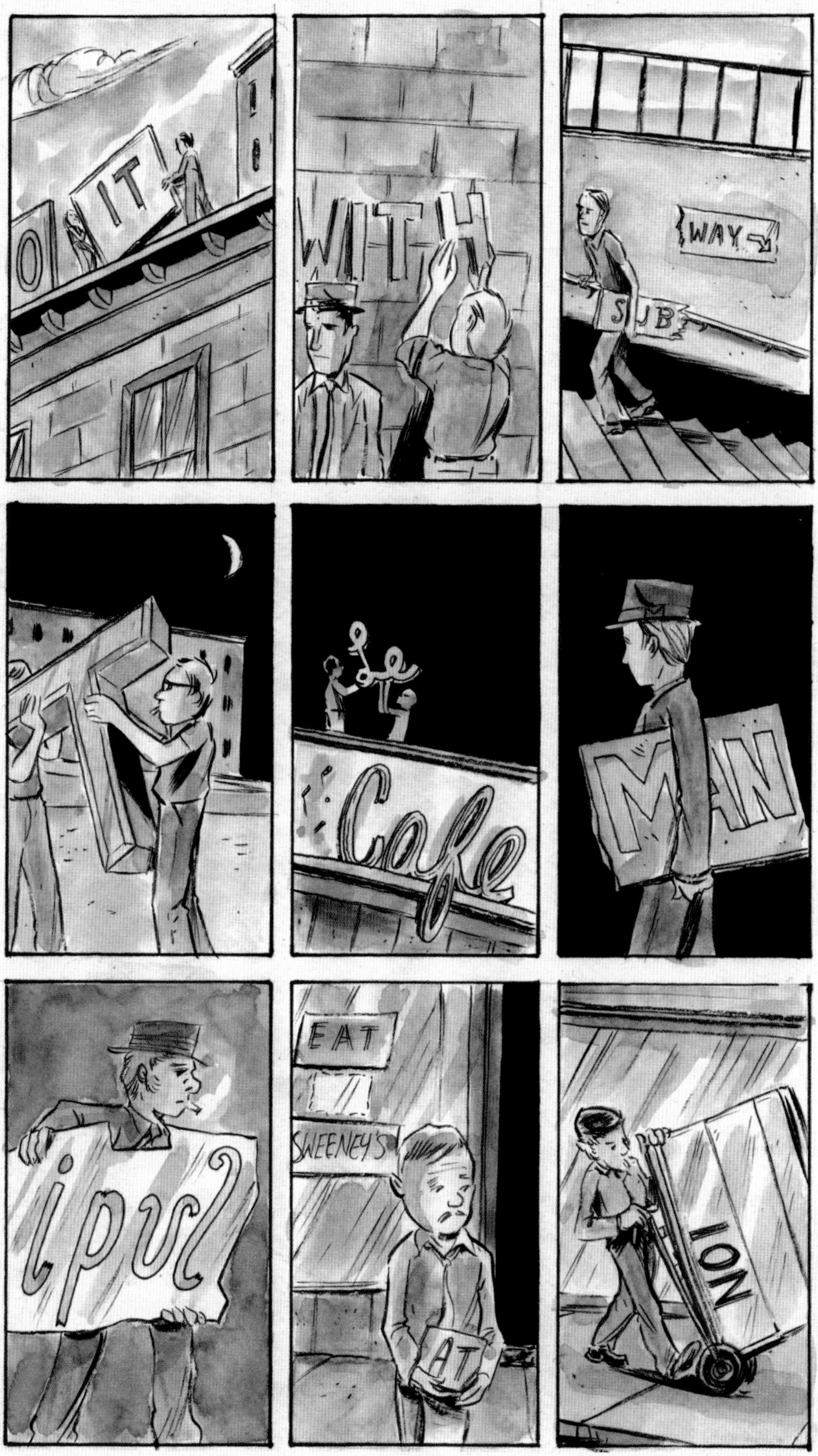
O
IT
WITH
WAY
SUB
Cafe
MAN
ipul
EAT
SWEENEY'S
AT
ION

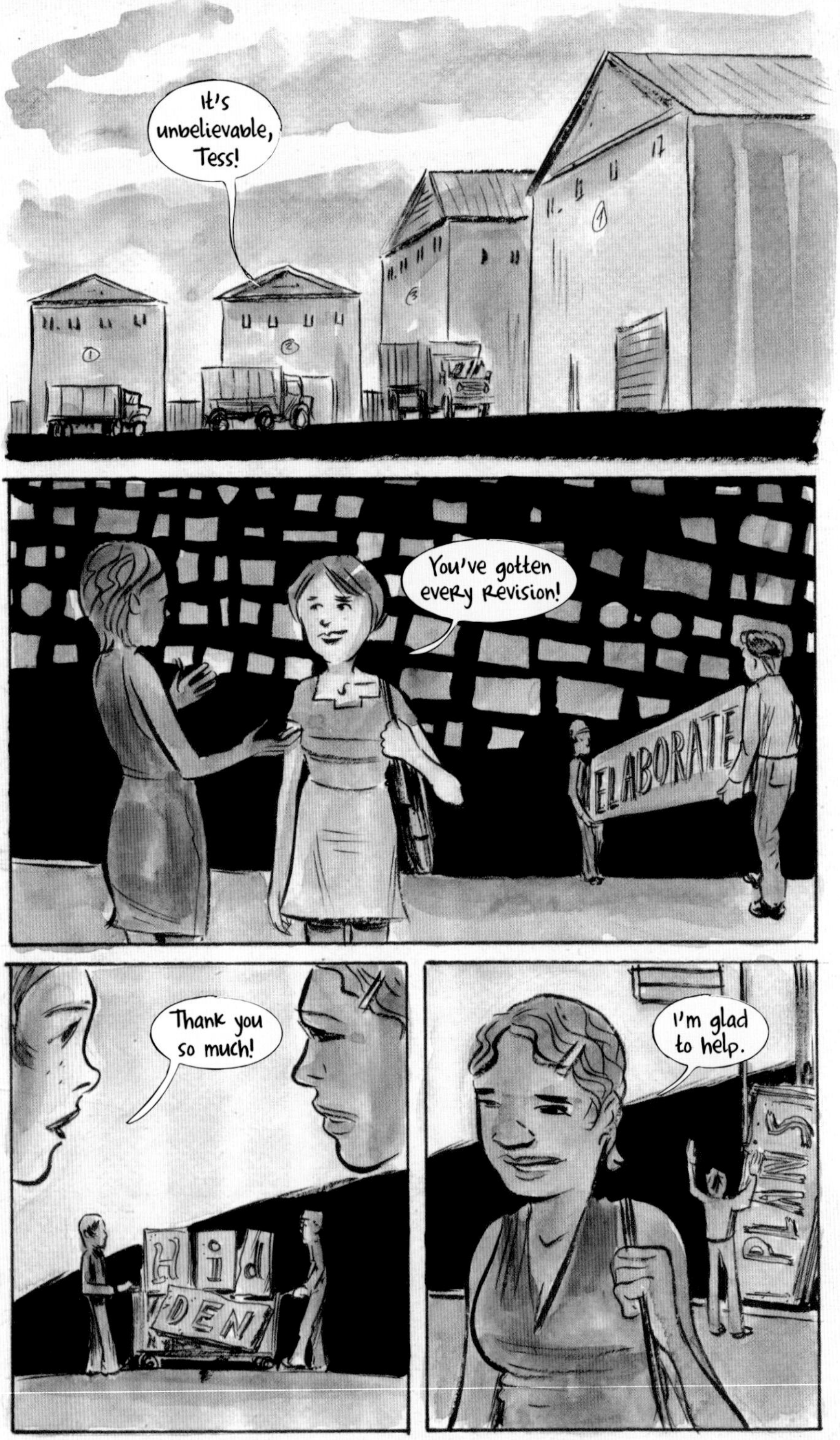
It's unbelievable, Tess!
You've gotten every revision!
ELABORATE
Thank you so much!
Hid
DEN
I'm glad to help.
PLANS

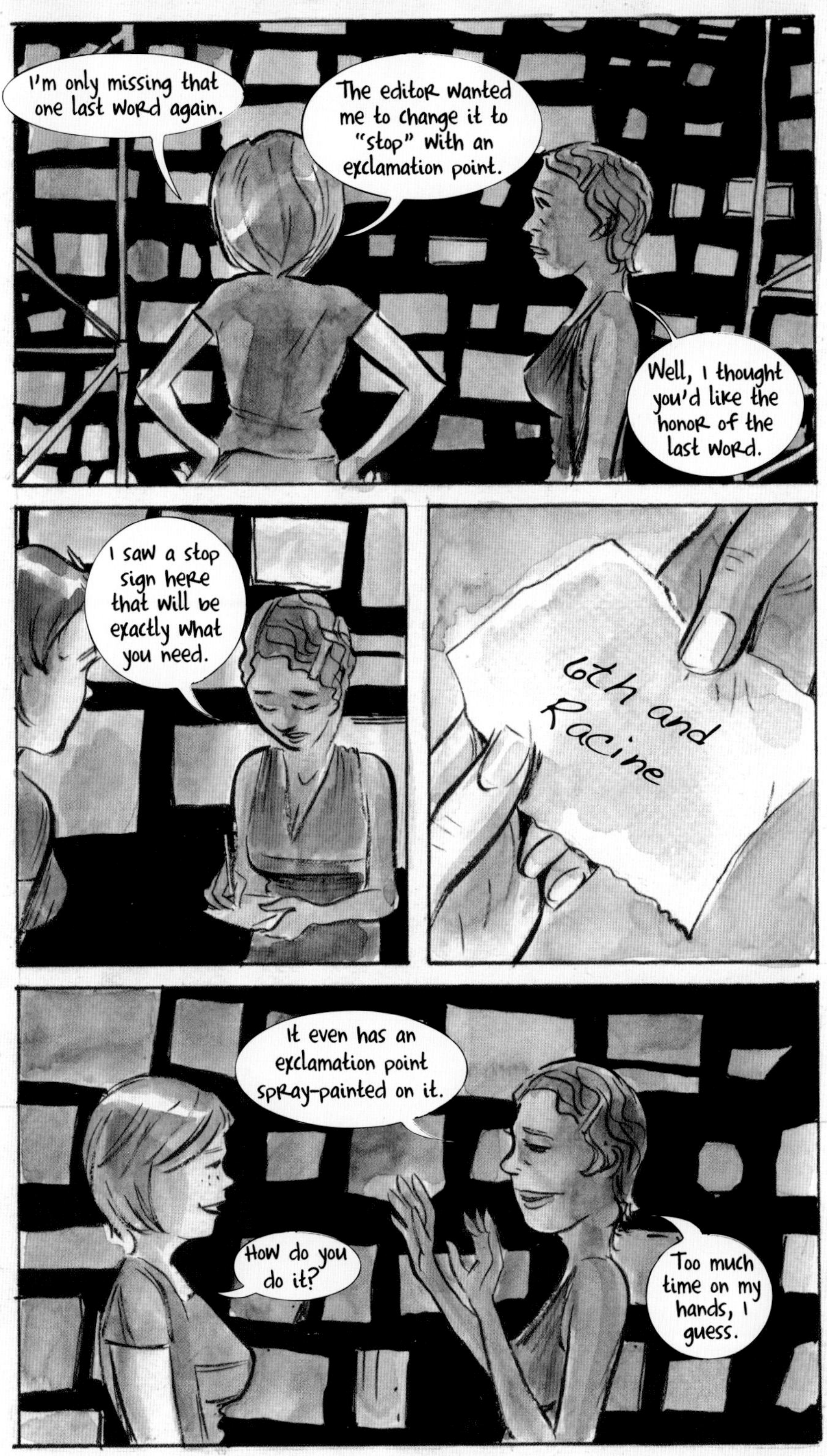
I'm only missing that one last word again.
The editor wanted me to change it to "stop" with an exclamation point.
Well, I thought you'd like the honor of the last word.
I saw a stop sign here that will be exactly what you need.
6th and Racine
It even has an exclamation point spray-painted on it.
How do you do it?
Too much time on my hands, I guess.

Detective Gould, in one of the most fascinating and confounding cases of his illustrious career, finally found the culprit responsible for the mystery disappearance of street signs, store signage, and letters that has been plaguing the city for years.

Gould, using a new system of modern video surveillance and computer analysis of the specific letters and words stolen, deducted the motive for the thefts. Gould then explained how he cross-referenced the list of words with all novels submitted for publication over the last five years. This eventually led him to one suspect: Emma Vann. Vann had reportedly submitted a record number of novel submissions and received a record number of rejections. All of this happening during the same time that the signs started disappearing.

(continued B3)

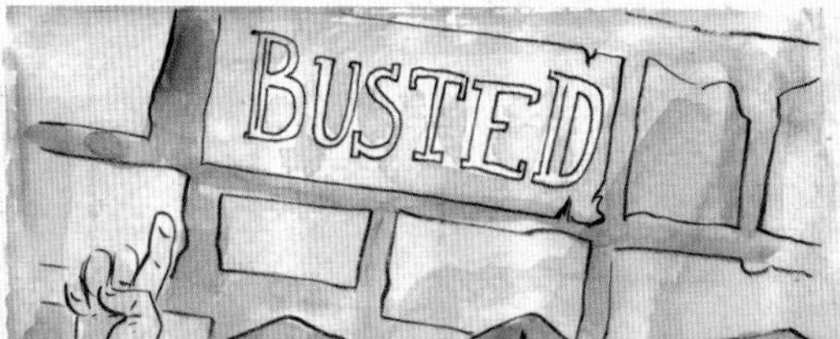
BUSTED

Gould and fellow officers break the case.

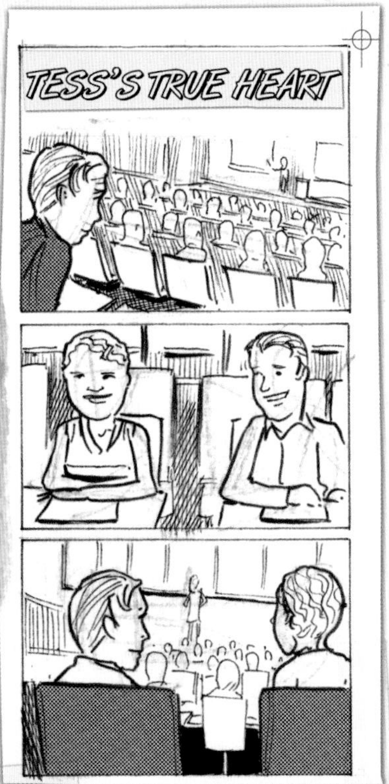
TESS'S TRUE HEART

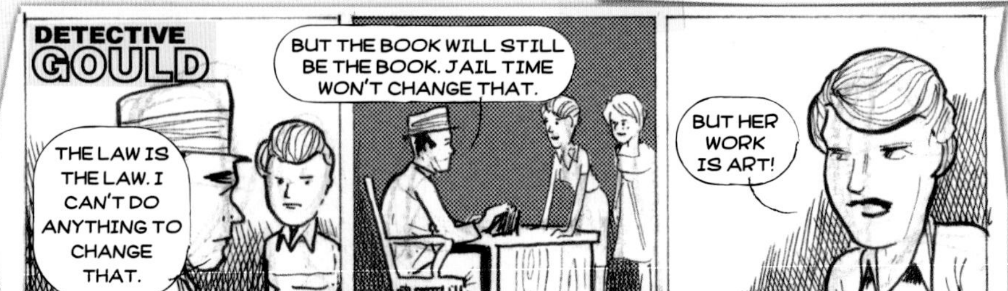
DETECTIVE GOULD
THE LAW IS THE LAW. I CAN'T DO ANYTHING TO CHANGE THAT.
BUT THE BOOK WILL STILL BE THE BOOK. JAIL TIME WON'T CHANGE THAT.
BUT HER WORK IS ART!

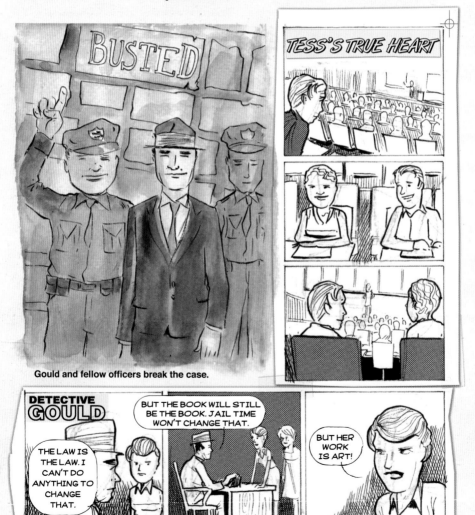

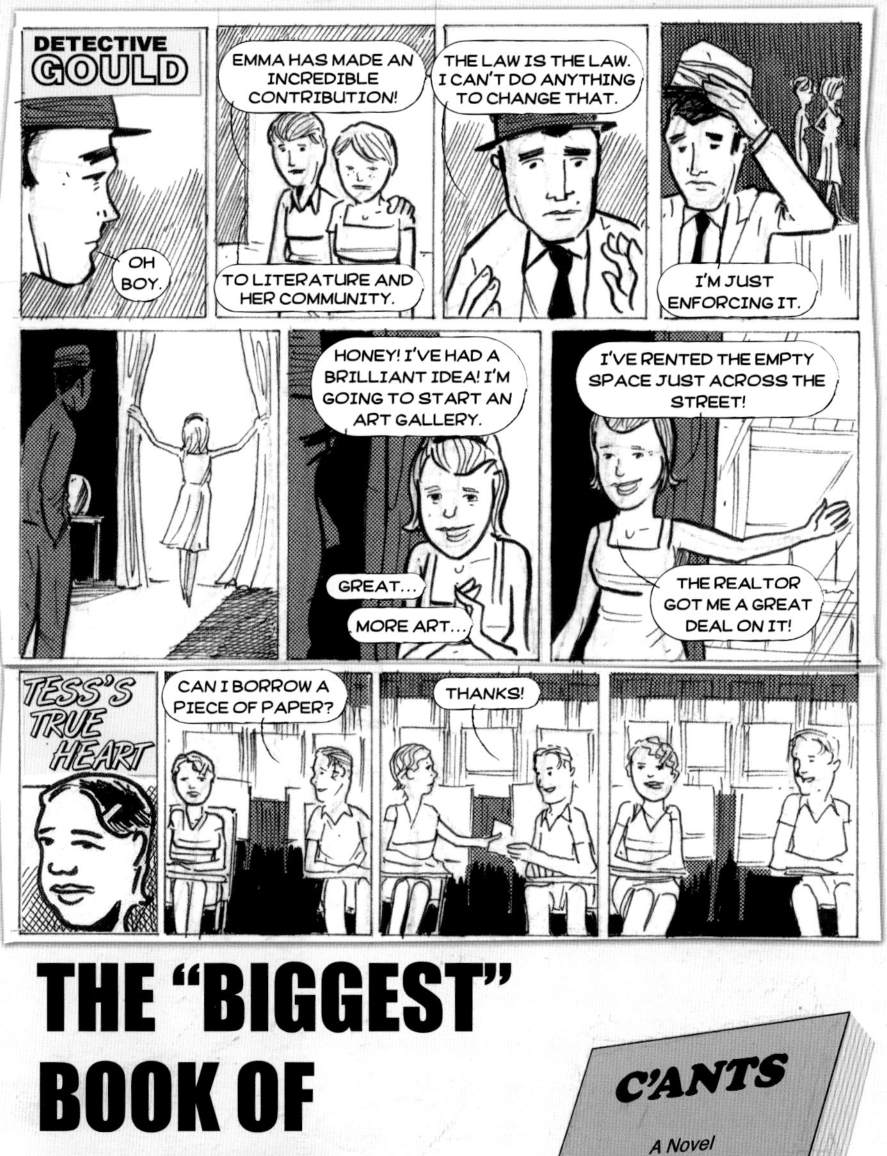
DETECTIVE GOULD
OH BOY.
EMMA HAS MADE AN INCREDIBLE CONTRIBUTION!
TO LITERATURE AND HER COMMUNITY.
THE LAW IS THE LAW. I CAN'T DO ANYTHING TO CHANGE THAT.
I'M JUST ENFORCING IT.
HONEY! I'VE HAD A BRILLIANT IDEA! I'M GOING TO START AN ART GALLERY.
GREAT...
MORE ART...
I'VE RENTED THE EMPTY SPACE JUST ACROSS THE STREET!
THE REALTOR GOT ME A GREAT DEAL ON IT!
TESS'S TRUE HEART
CAN I BORROW A PIECE OF PAPER?
THANKS!

THE "BIGGEST" BOOK OF ALL TIME!

FROM THE AUTHOR FAMOUSLY ARRESTED FOR THE CRIME OF WRITING HER NOVEL — YEARS IN THE MAKING COMES… *C'ANTS*, A NOVEL ABOUT STRIVING FOR SIGNIFICANCE AND THE STRUGGLE TO BE HEARD IN MODERN SOCIETY WHERE THE SMALLEST OF VOICES ARE EASILY DROWNED OUT.

"A TINY ACHIEVEMENT OF MONUMENTAL PROPORTIONS."—*THE BARROW BOOK REVIEW*

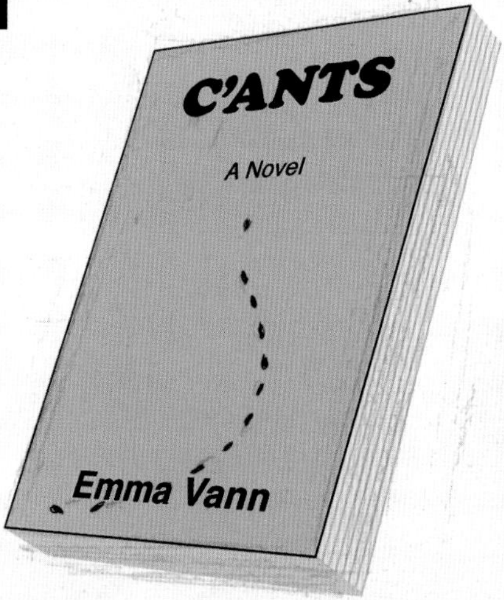
C'ANTS
A Novel
Emma Vann

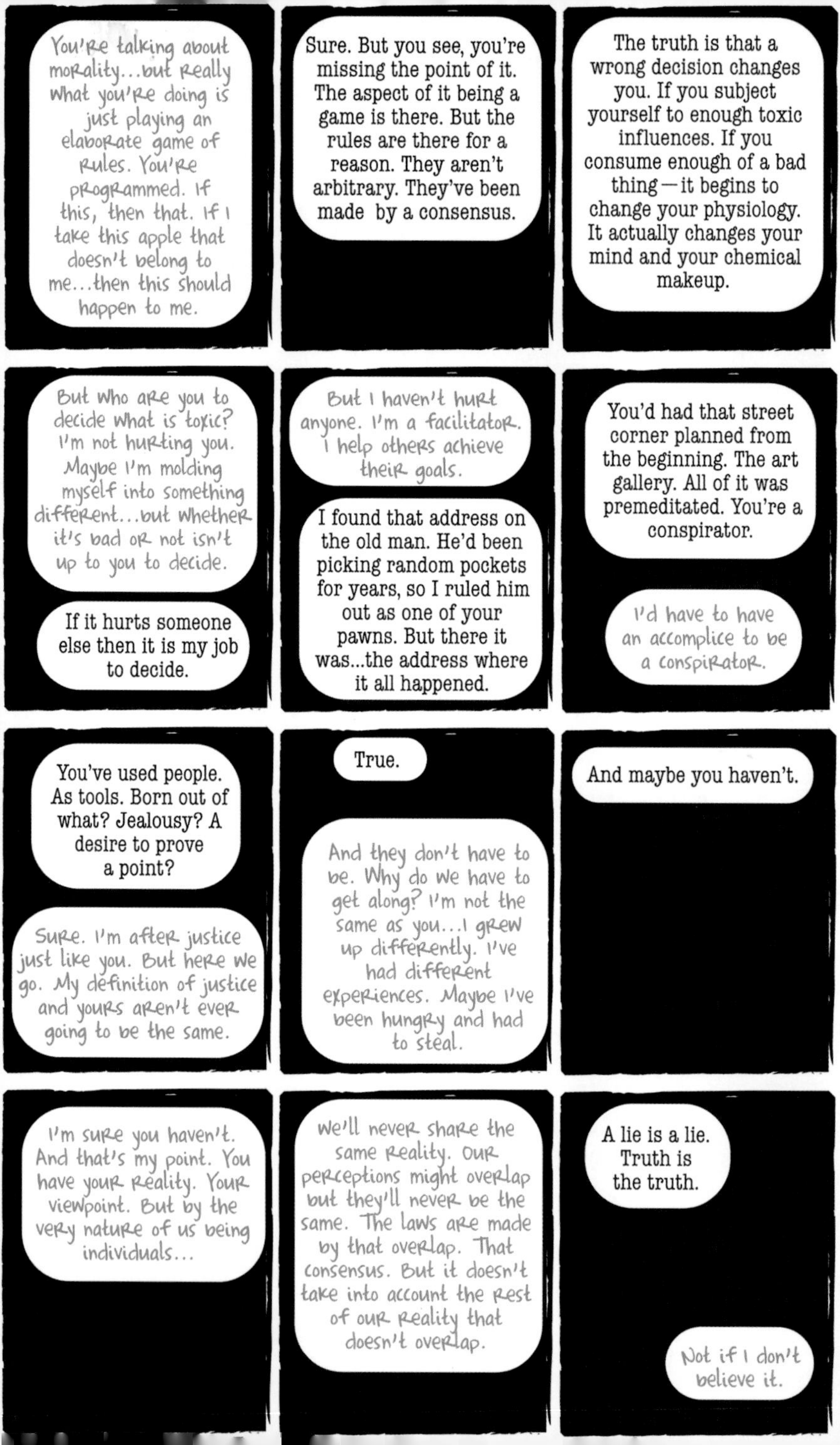
You're talking about morality...but really what you're doing is just playing an elaborate game of rules. You're programmed. If this, then that. If I take this apple that doesn't belong to me...then this should happen to me.
Sure. But you see, you're missing the point of it. The aspect of it being a game is there. But the rules are there for a reason. They aren't arbitrary. They've been made by a consensus.
The truth is that a wrong decision changes you. If you subject yourself to enough toxic influences. If you consume enough of a bad thing—it begins to change your physiology. It actually changes your mind and your chemical makeup.
But who are you to decide what is toxic? I'm not hurting you. Maybe I'm molding myself into something different...but whether it's bad or not isn't up to you to decide.
If it hurts someone else then it is my job to decide.
But I haven't hurt anyone. I'm a facilitator. I help others achieve their goals.
I found that address on the old man. He'd been picking random pockets for years, so I ruled him out as one of your pawns. But there it was...the address where it all happened.
You'd had that street corner planned from the beginning. The art gallery. All of it was premeditated. You're a conspirator.
I'd have to have an accomplice to be a conspirator.
You've used people. As tools. Born out of what? Jealousy? A desire to prove a point?
Sure. I'm after justice just like you. But here we go. My definition of justice and yours aren't ever going to be the same.
True.
And they don't have to be. Why do we have to get along? I'm not the same as you...I grew up differently. I've had different experiences. Maybe I've been hungry and had to steal.
And maybe you haven't.
I'm sure you haven't. And that's my point. You have your reality. Your viewpoint. But by the very nature of us being individuals...
We'll never share the same reality. Our perceptions might overlap but they'll never be the same. The laws are made by that overlap. That consensus. But it doesn't take into account the rest of our reality that doesn't overlap.
A lie is a lie. Truth is the truth.
Not if I don't believe it.

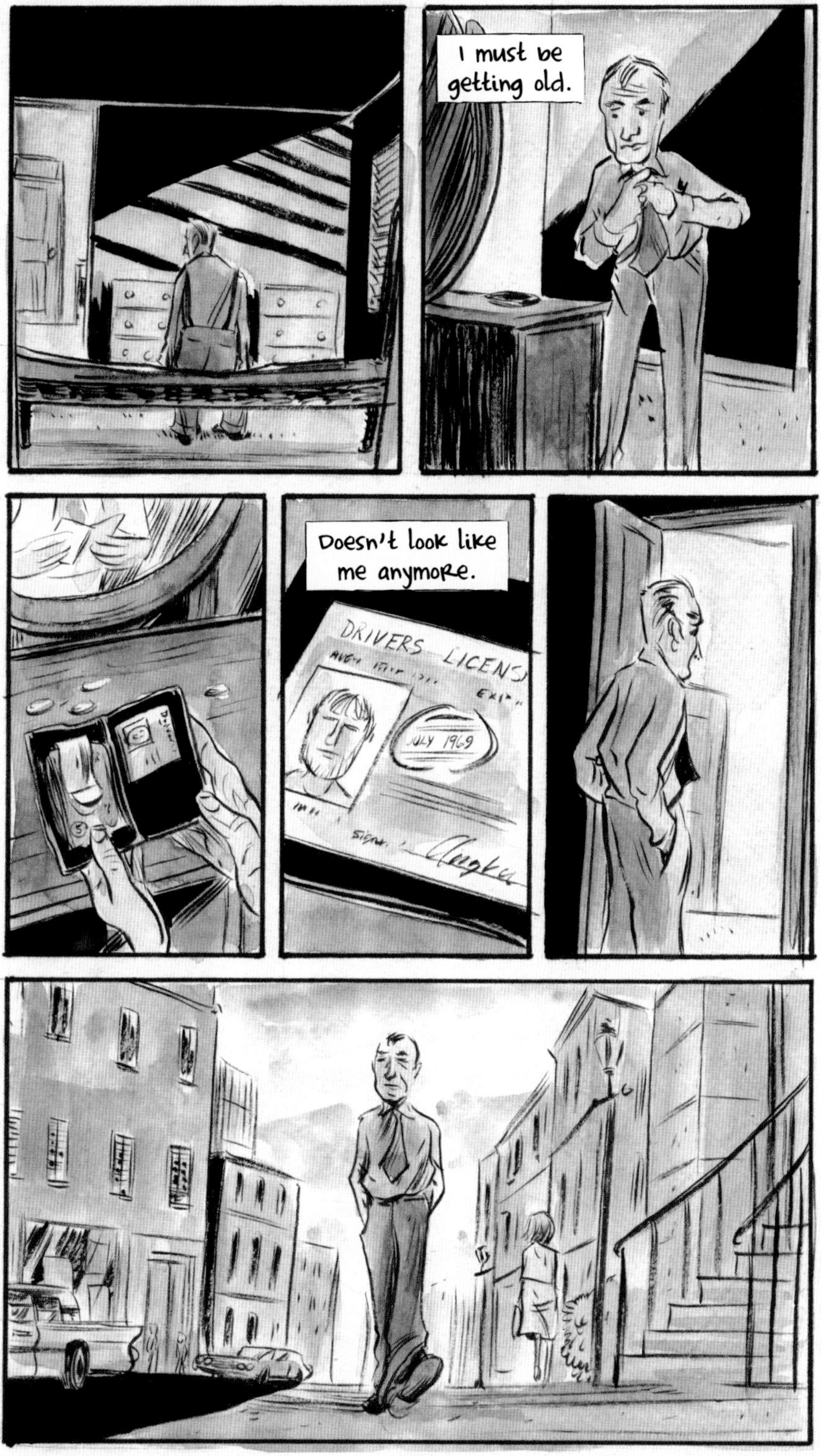
I must be getting old.
Doesn't look like me anymore.
DRIVERS LICENS
JULY 1969

THE
FORGOTTEN

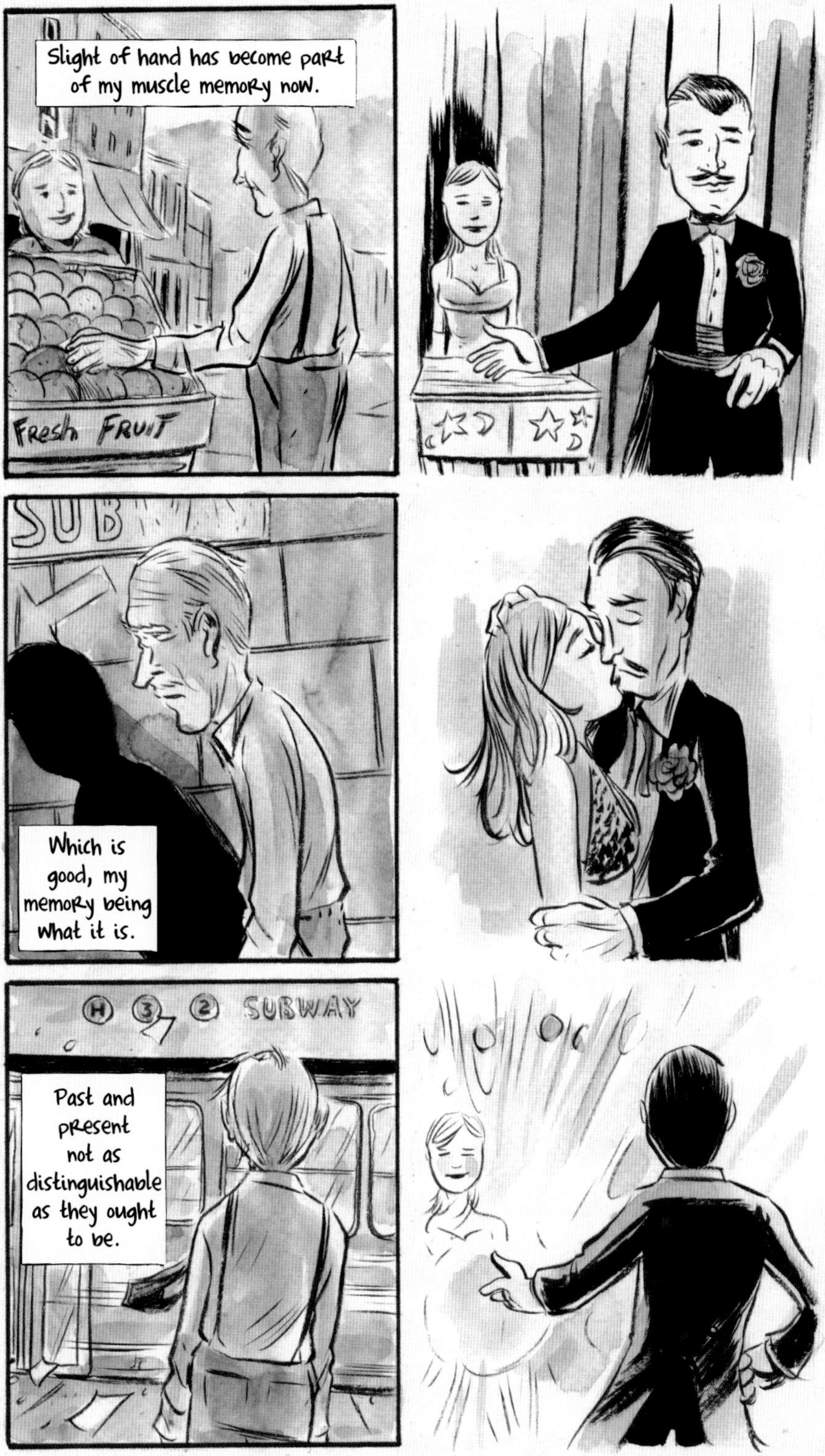
Slight of hand has become part of my muscle memory now.
FRESH FRUIT
SUB
Which is good, my memory being what it is.
H 3 2 SUBWAY
Past and present not as distinguishable as they ought to be.

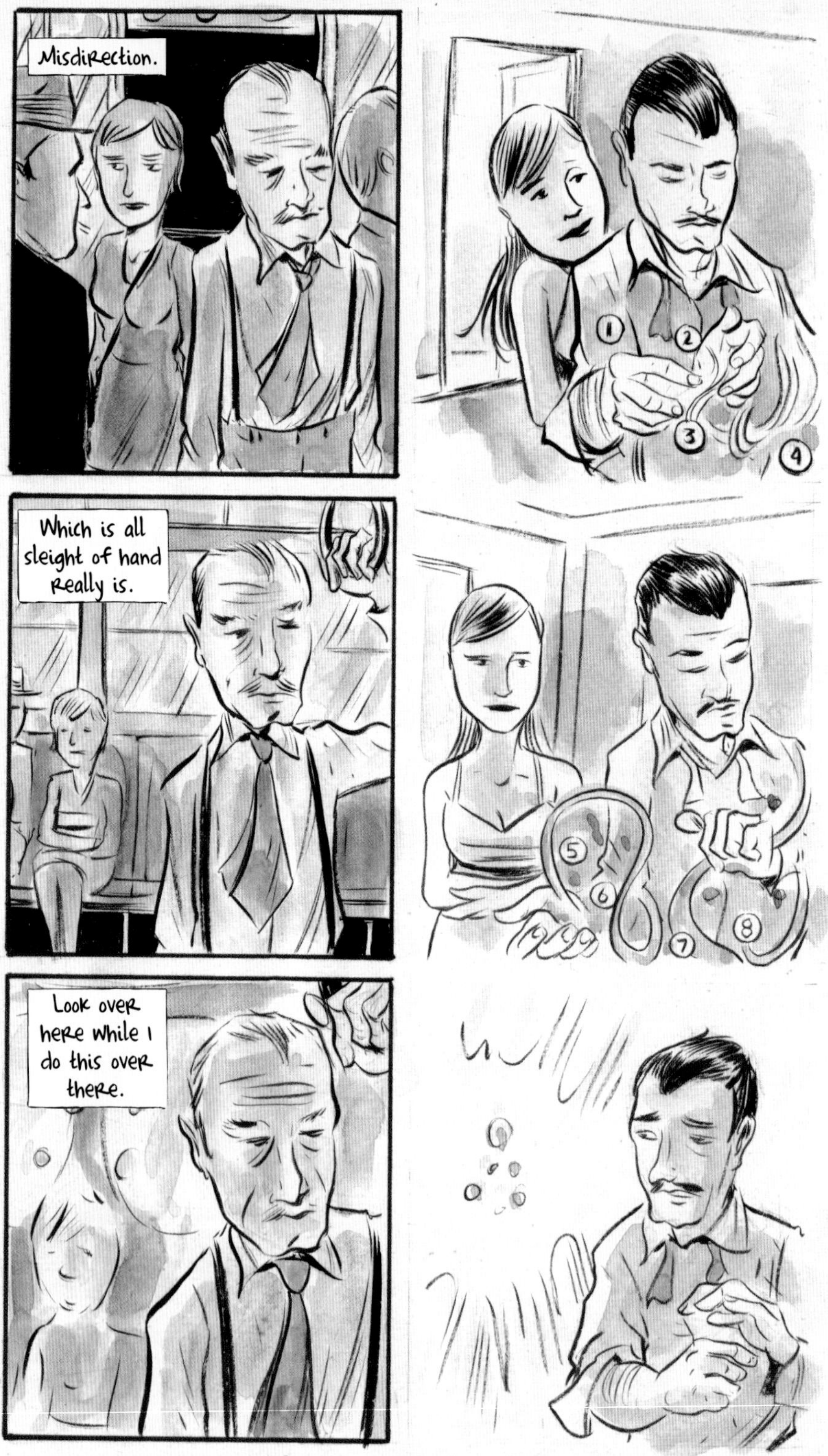
Misdirection.
Which is all sleight of hand really is.
Look over here while I do this over there.
1
2
3
4
5
6
7
8

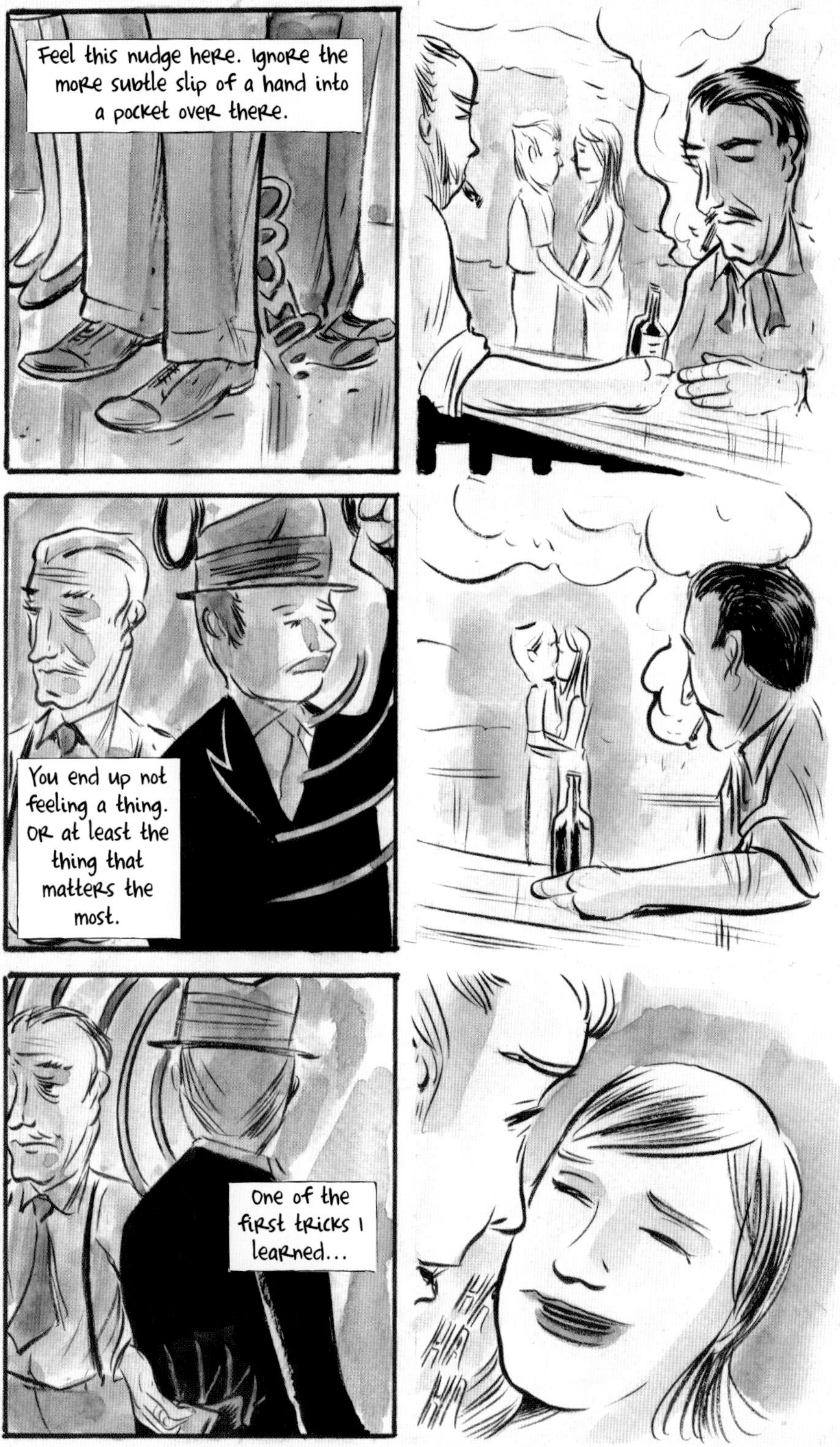
Feel this nudge here. Ignore the more subtle slip of a hand into a pocket over there.
You end up not feeling a thing. Or at least the thing that matters the most.
One of the first tricks I learned...

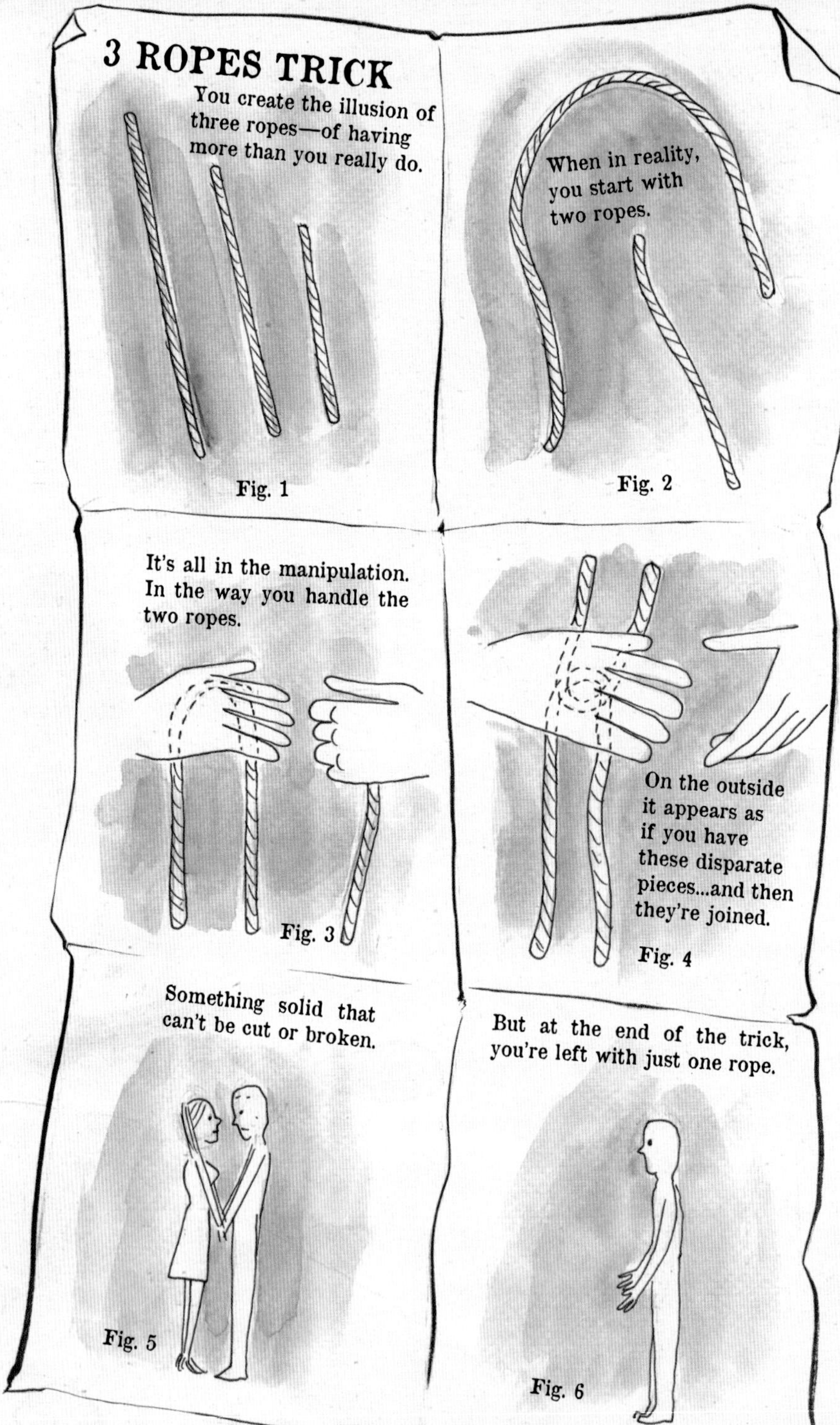
3 ROPES TRICK
You create the illusion of three ropes—of having more than you really do.
Fig. 1
When in reality, you start with two ropes.
Fig. 2
It's all in the manipulation. In the way you handle the two ropes.
Fig. 3
On the outside it appears as if you have these disparate pieces...and then they're joined.
Fig. 4
Something solid that can't be cut or broken.
Fig. 5
But at the end of the trick, you're left with just one rope.
Fig. 6

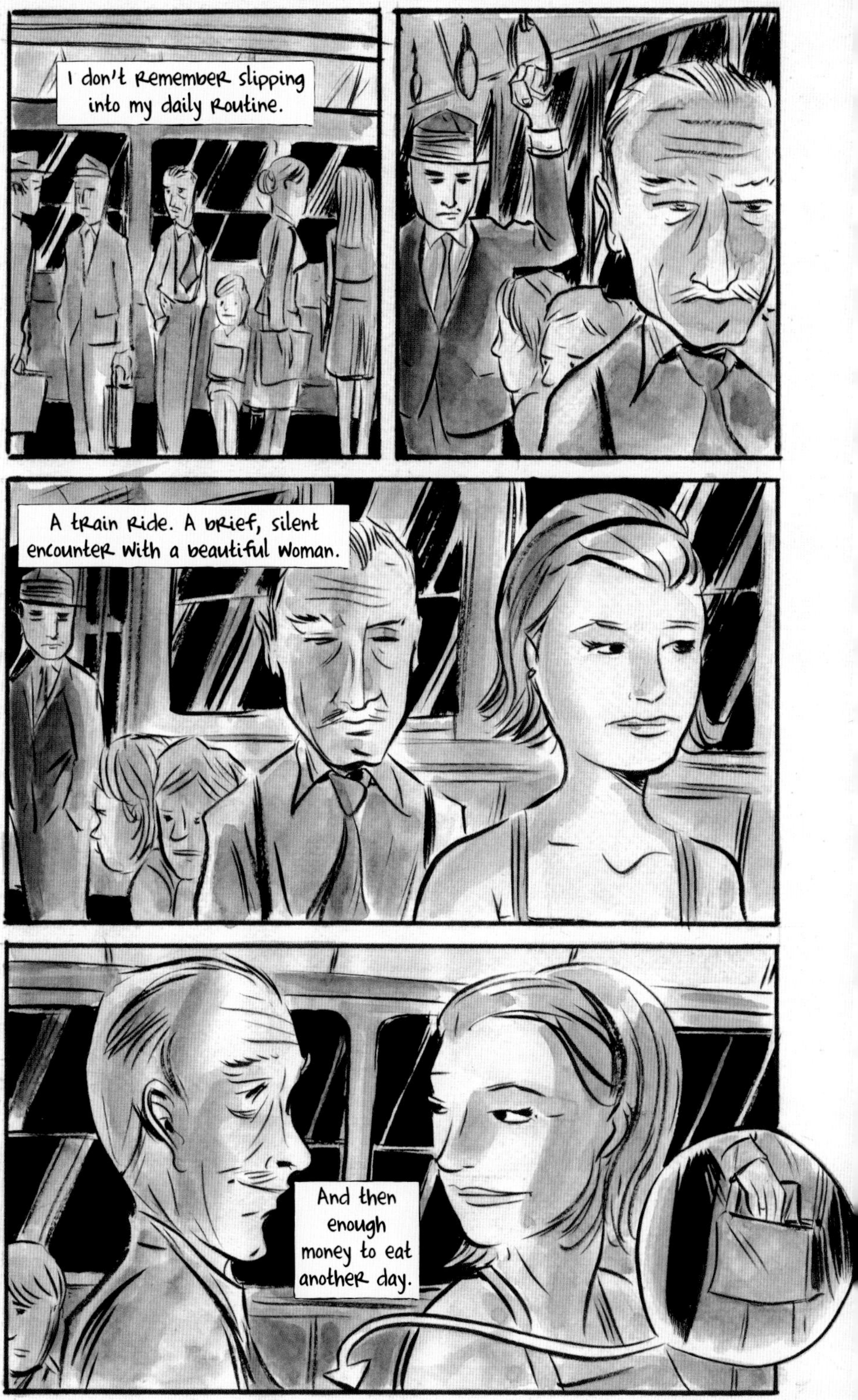
I don't remember slipping into my daily routine.
A train ride. A brief, silent encounter with a beautiful woman.
And then enough money to eat another day.

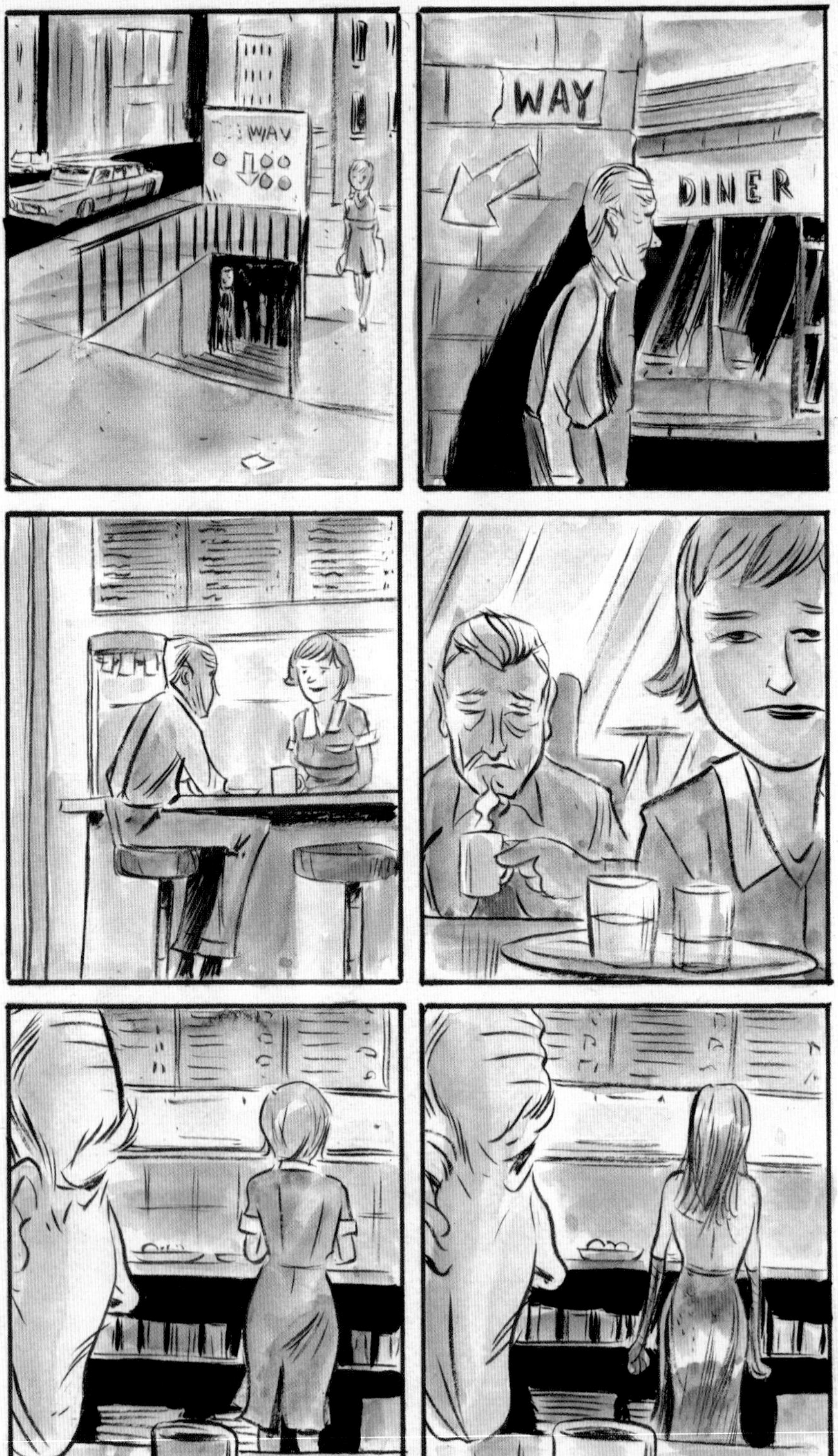

WAY
WAY
DINER

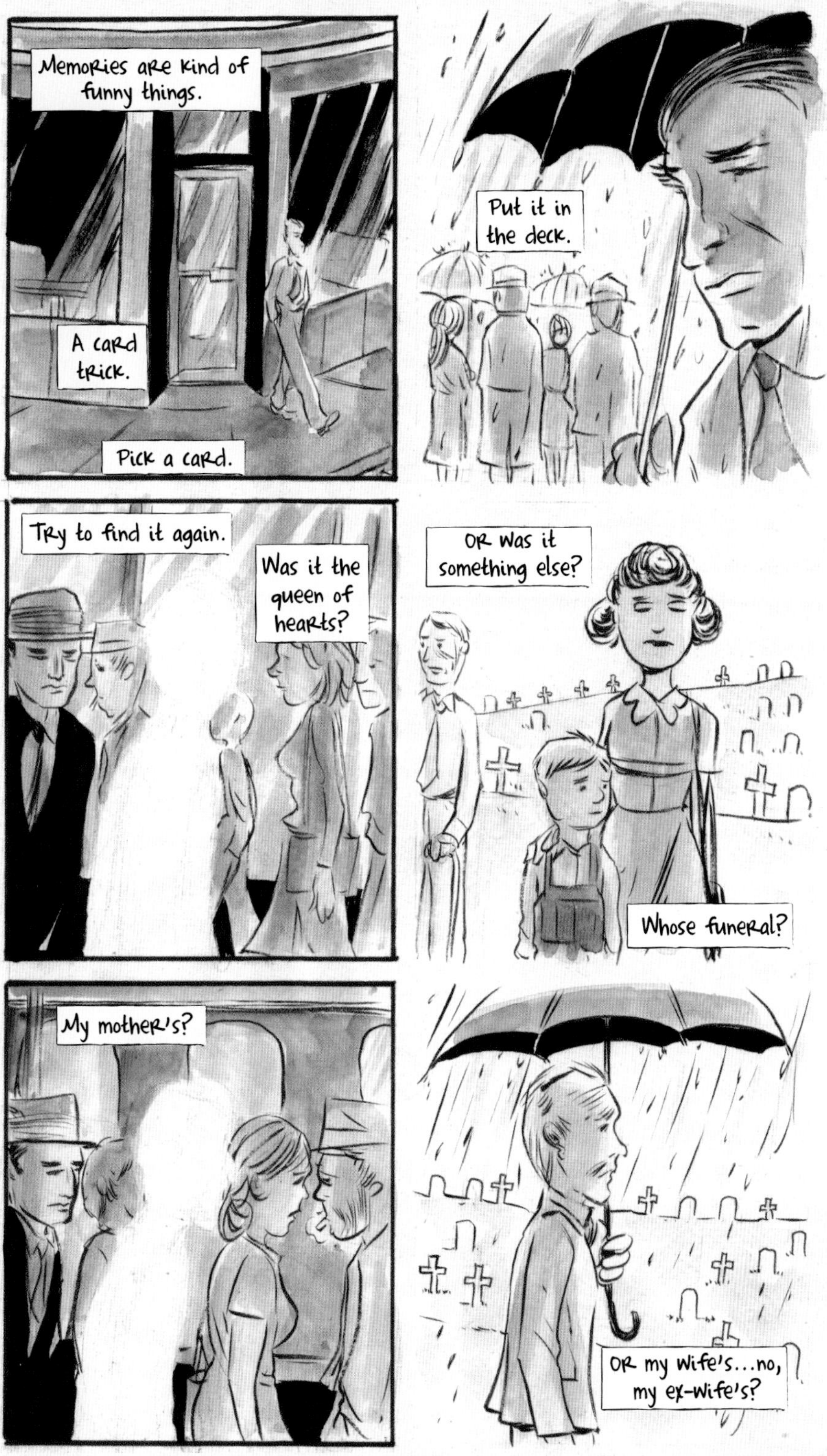
Memories are kind of funny things.
A card trick.
Pick a card.
Put it in the deck.
Try to find it again.
Was it the queen of hearts?
Or was it something else?
Whose funeral?
My mother's?
Or my wife's...no, my ex-wife's?

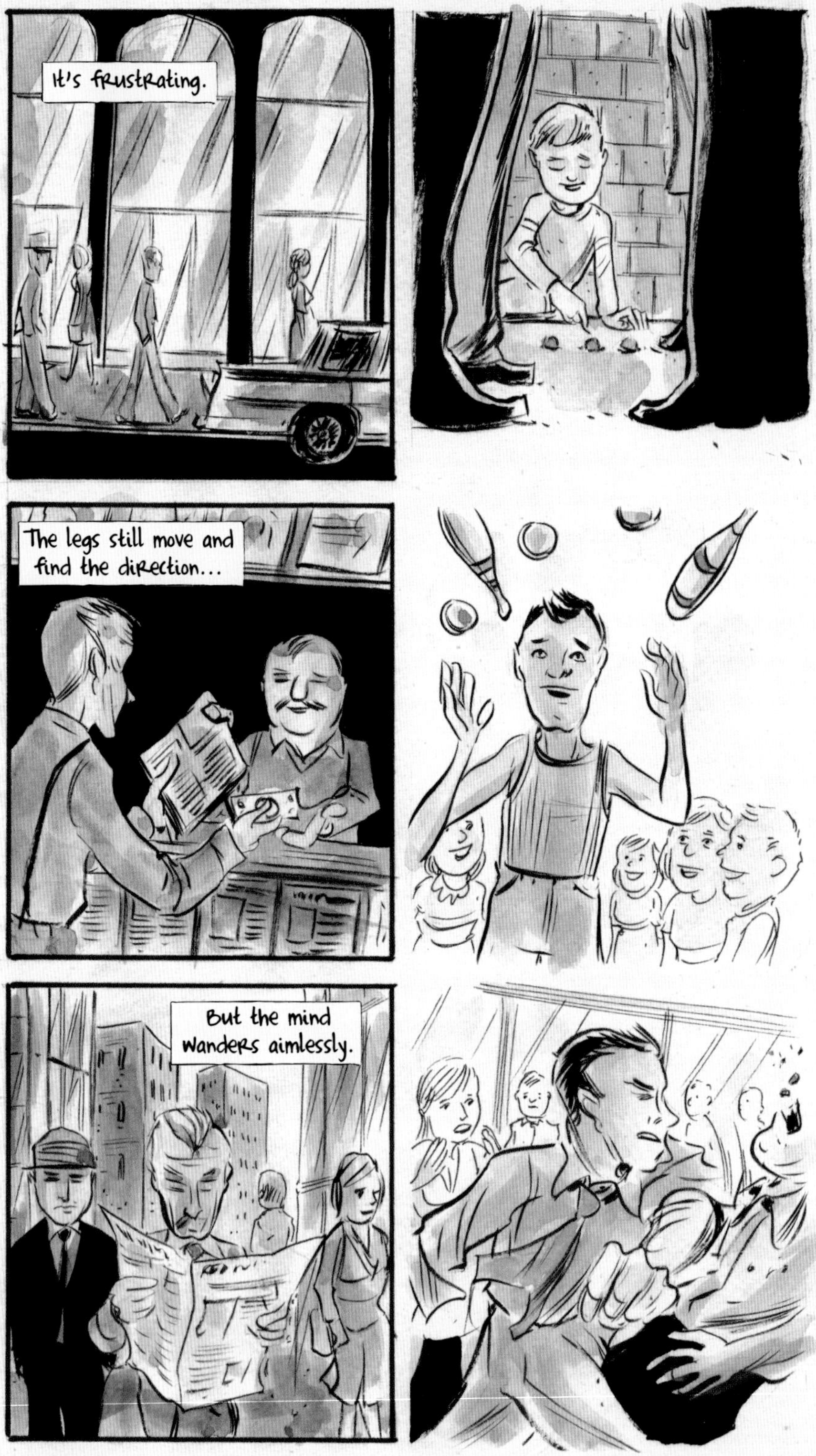
It's frustrating.
The legs still move and find the direction...
But the mind wanders aimlessly.

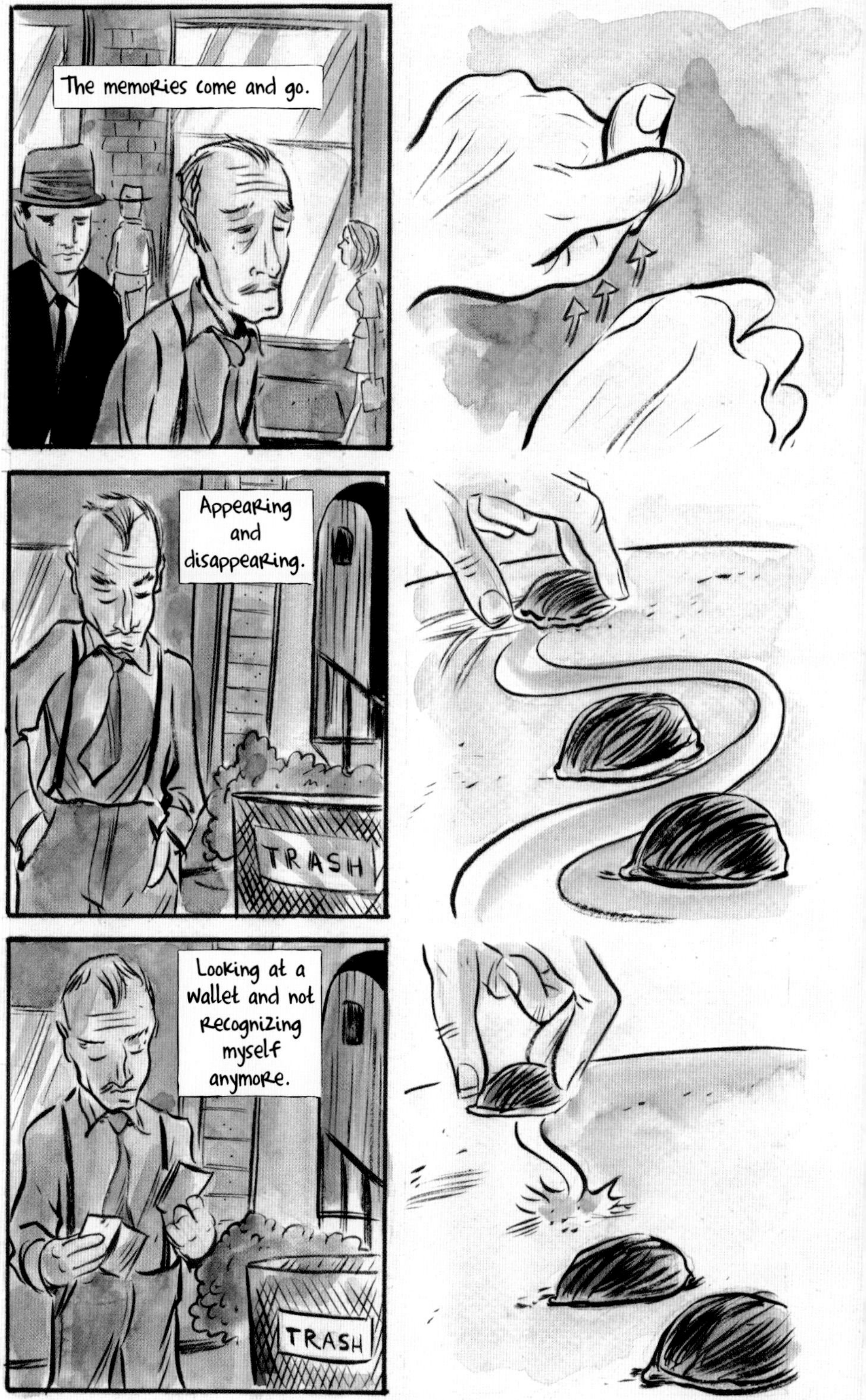
The memories come and go.
Appearing and disappearing.
TRASH
Looking at a wallet and not recognizing myself anymore.
TRASH

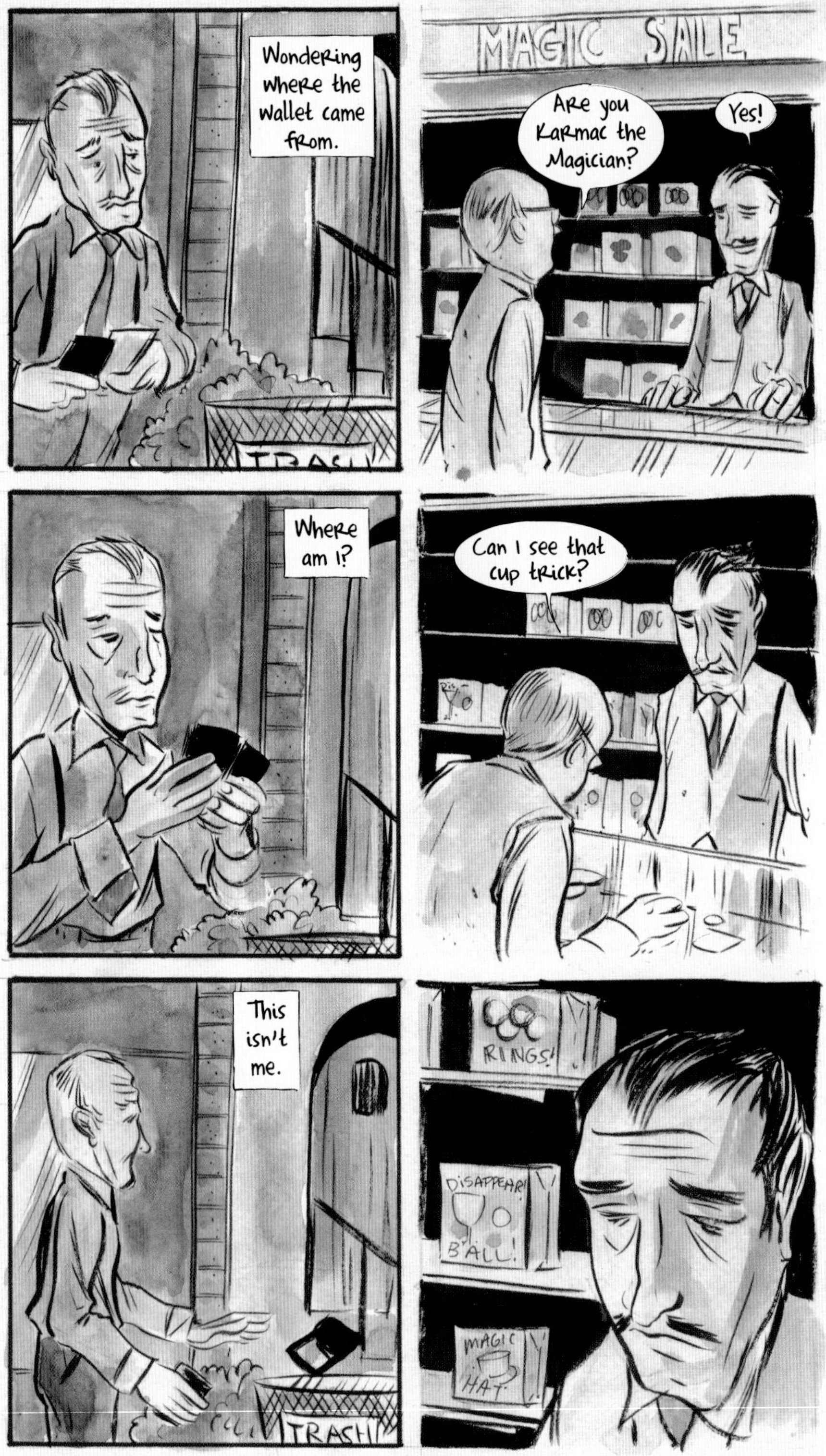
Wondering where the wallet came from.
MAGIC SALE
Are you Karmac the Magician?
Yes!
Where am I?
Can I see that cup trick?
This isn't me.
TRASH
RINGS!
DISAPPEAR! BALL!
MAGIC HAT

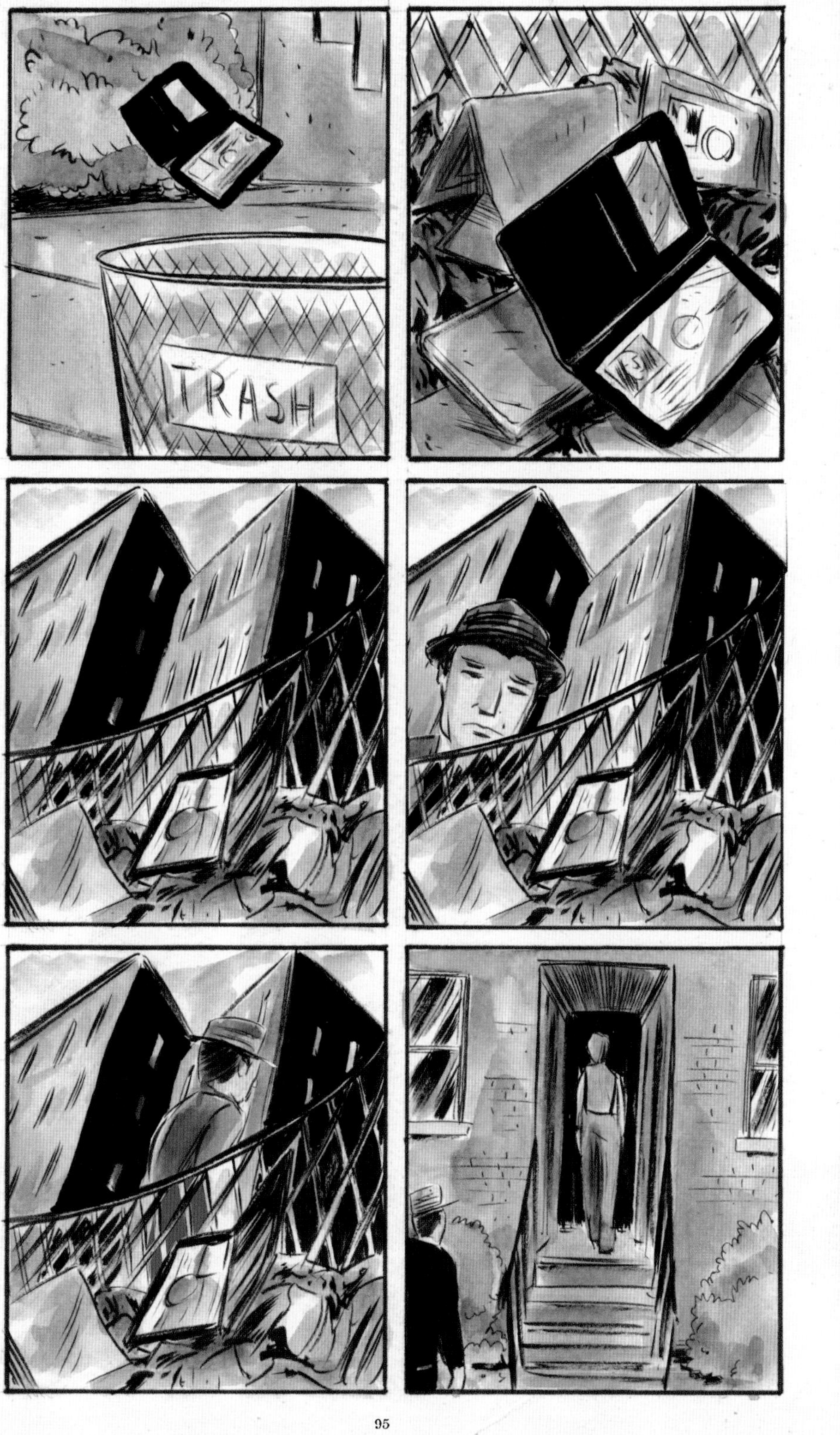
TRASH

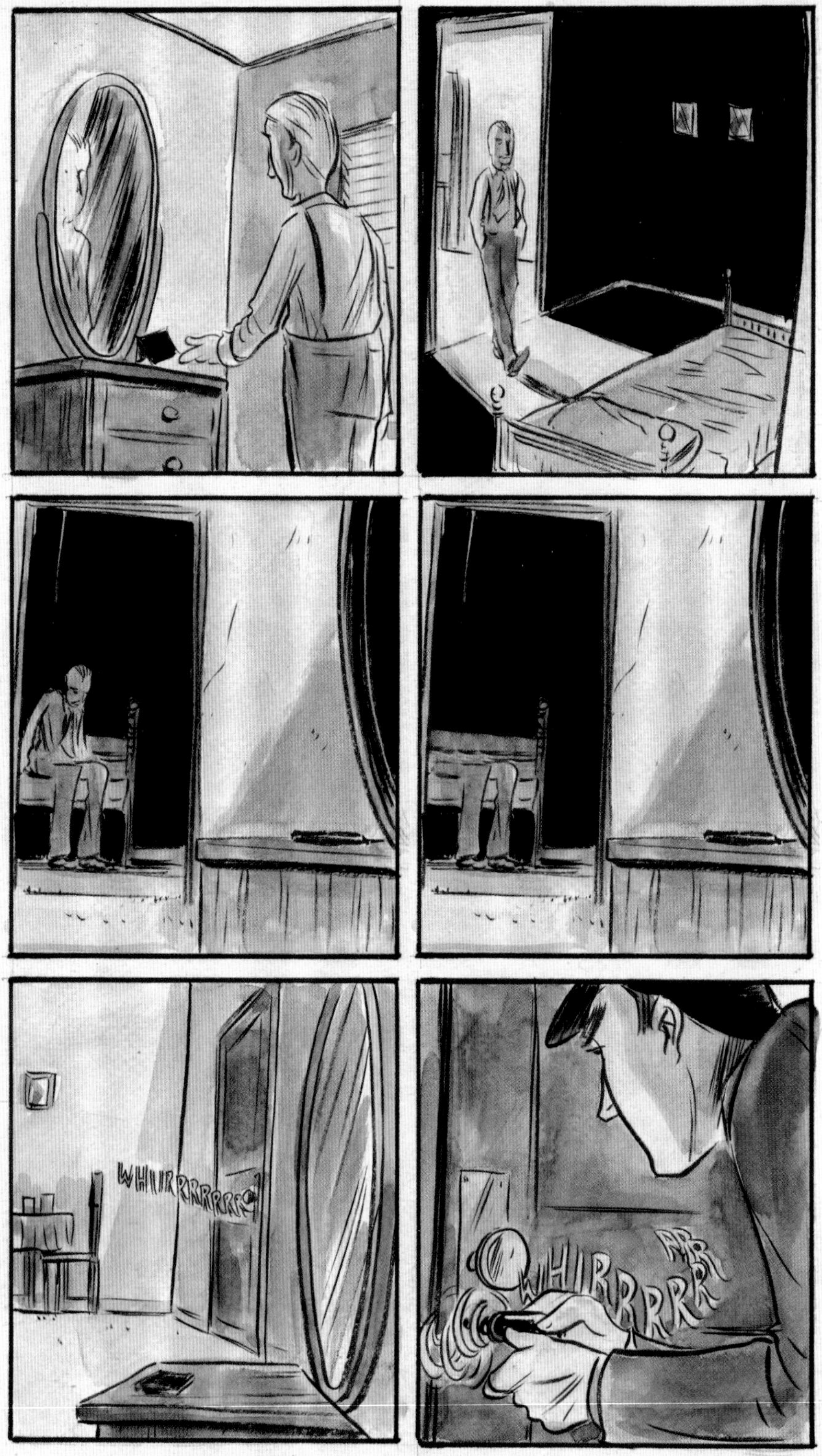
WHIRRRRRRR
WHIRRRRRRRR

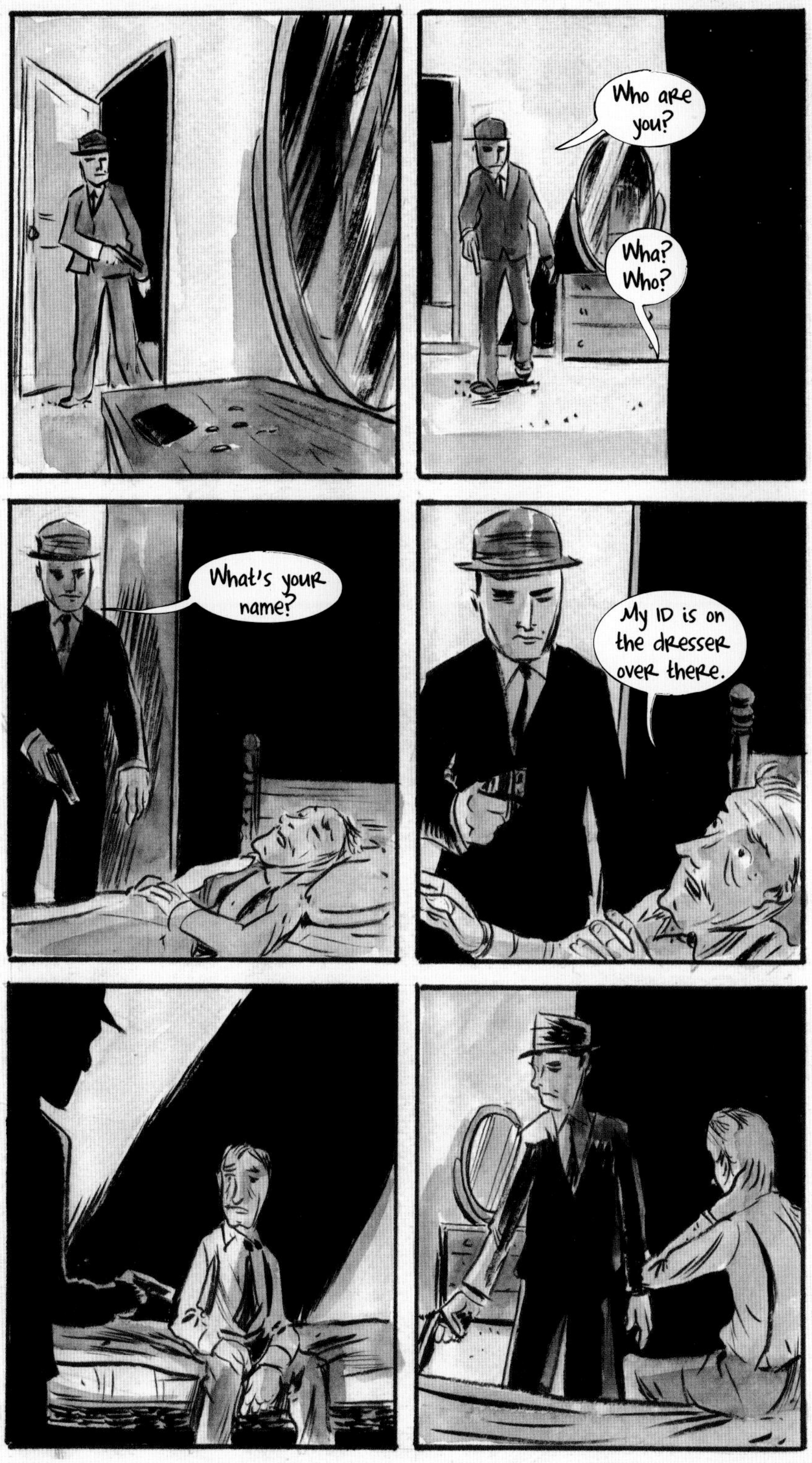
Who are you?
Wha? Who?
What's your name?
My ID is on the dresser over there.

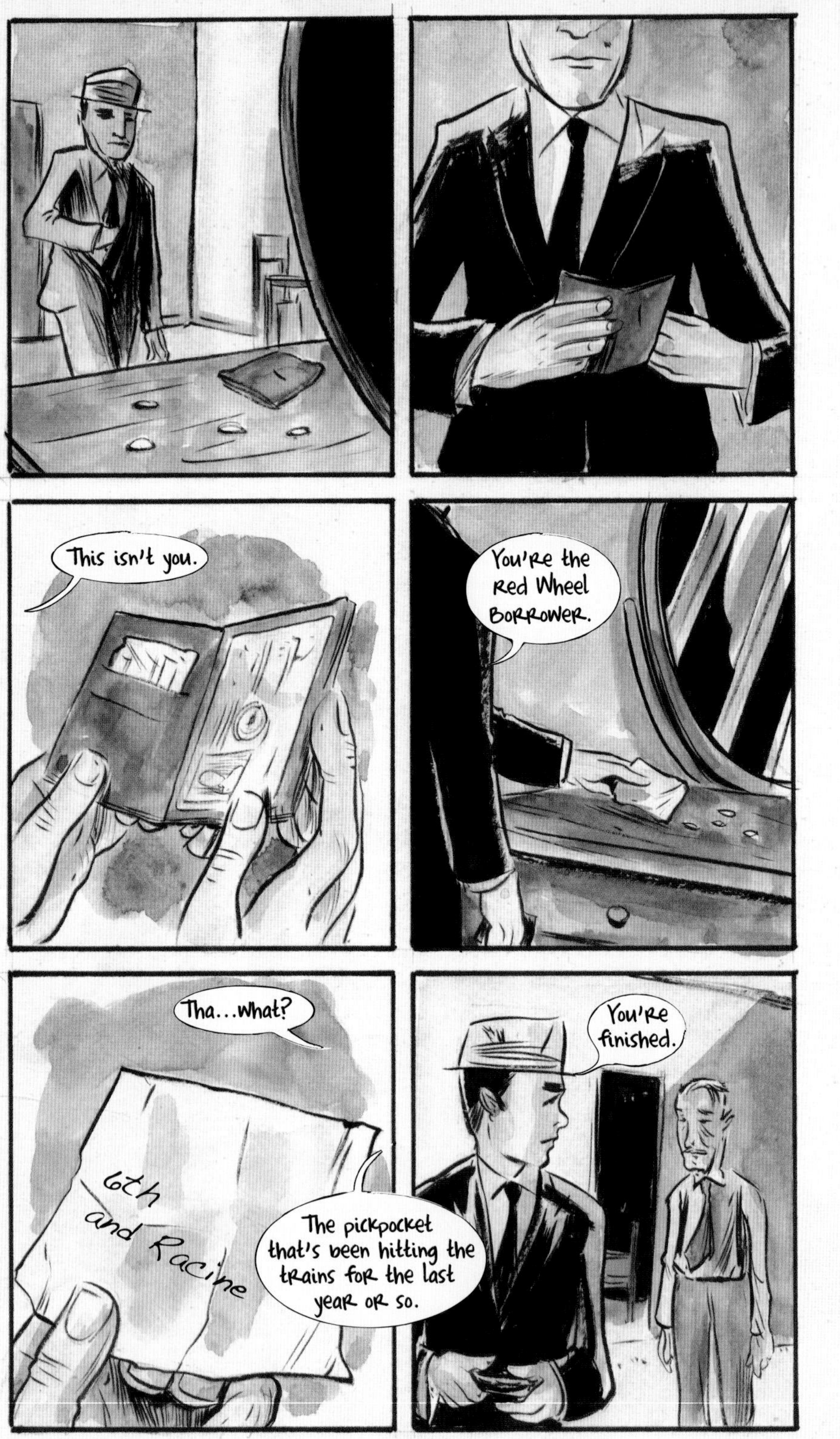
This isn't you.
You're the Red Wheel Borrower.
Tha...what?
6th and Racine
The pickpocket that's been hitting the trains for the last year or so.
You're finished.

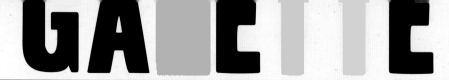

GA E E

Karmac the Magician was arrested yesterday afternoon and has admitted to the rash of pick-pockets that have been plaguing the afternoon trains for weeks.

Karmac reached the height of his popularity in the 1940s. He soon fell onto hard times as his wife left him and he left the spotlight for good. He'd since been rarely seen—arrested once in the 1950s as part of an alleged fur-smuggling ring at the northern border. Since then, he has lived a quiet life—no one suspecting that he was the Red Wheel Borrower—responsible for an estimated 1,000 pickpocket thefts.

(continued on C14)

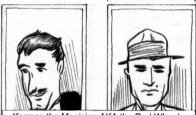

Karmac the Magician AKA the Red Wheel Borrower (left) nabbed by Gould (right).

DETECTIVE GOULD
Don't use that one.
Why?
This is our most compelling shot.
It makes me look like a jerk.
continued

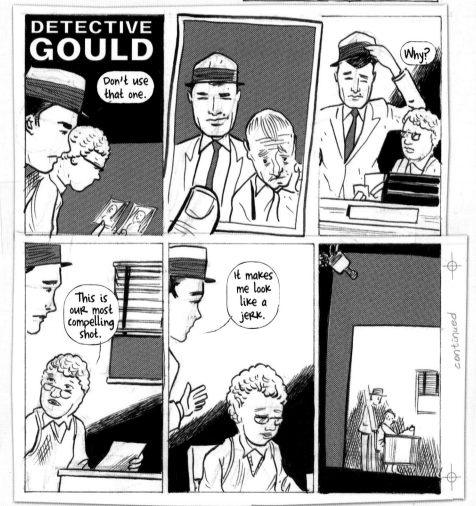

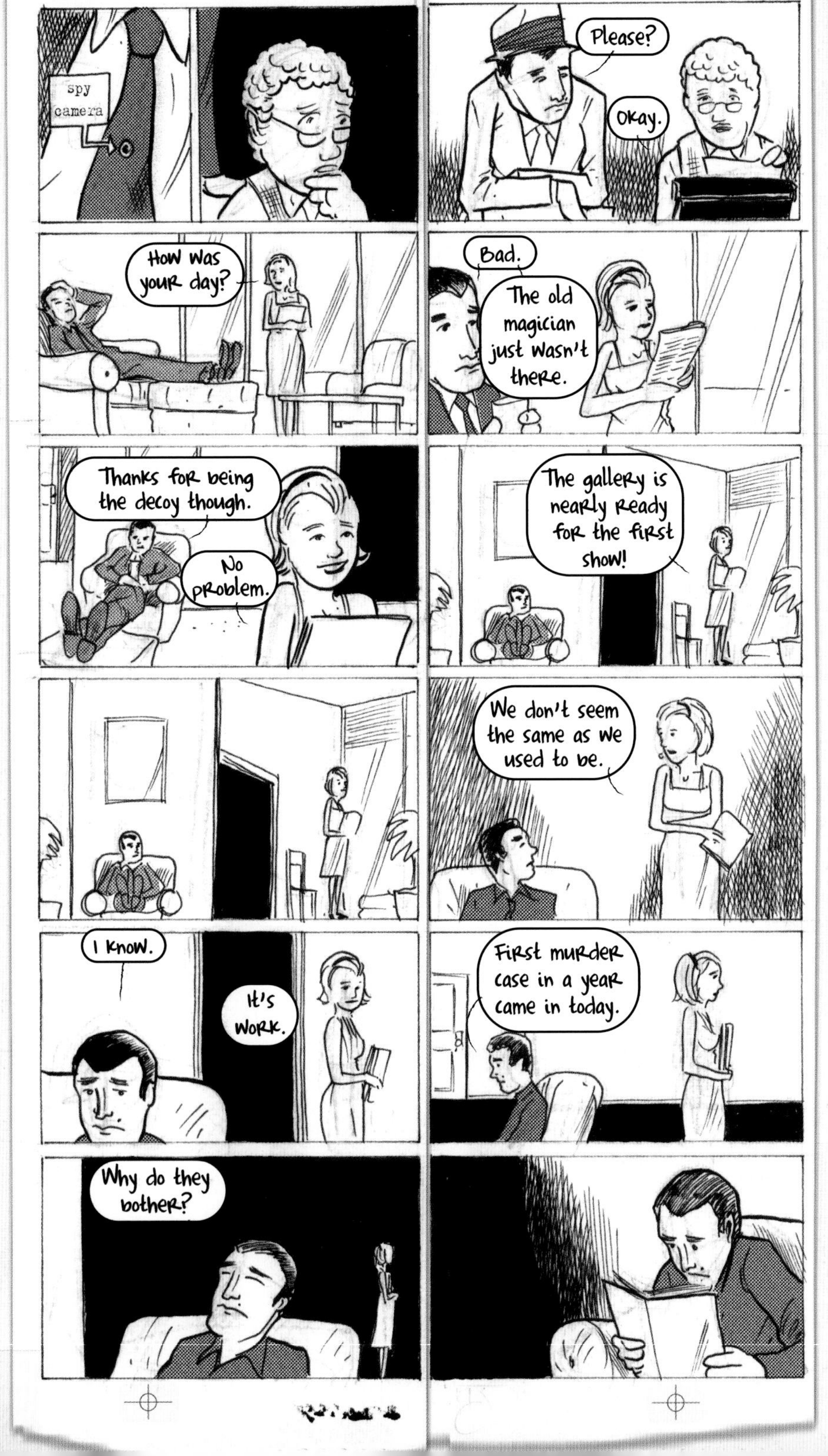
spy
camera
Please?
Okay.
How was your day?
Bad.
The old magician just wasn't there.
Thanks for being the decoy though.
No problem.
The gallery is nearly ready for the first show!
We don't seem the same as we used to be.
I know.
It's work.
First murder case in a year came in today.
Why do they bother?

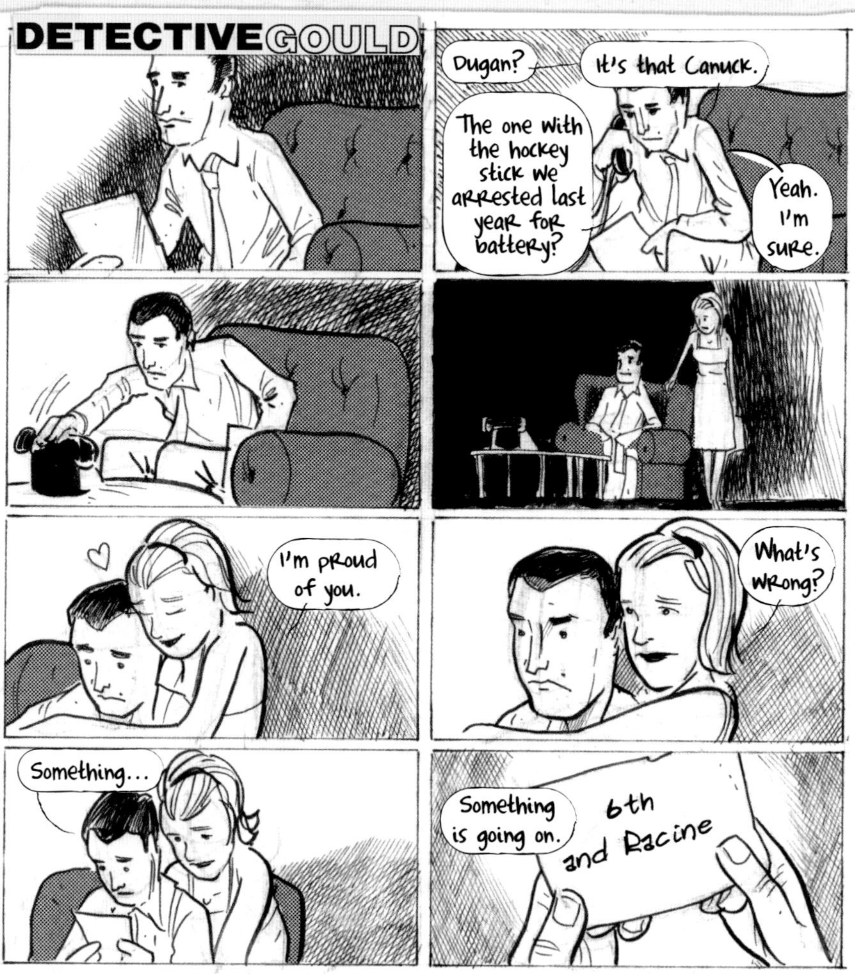
DETECTIVE GOULD
Dugan?
It's that Canuck.
The one with the hockey stick we arrested last year for battery?
Yeah. I'm sure.
I'm proud of you.
What's wrong?
Something...
Something is going on.
6th and Racine

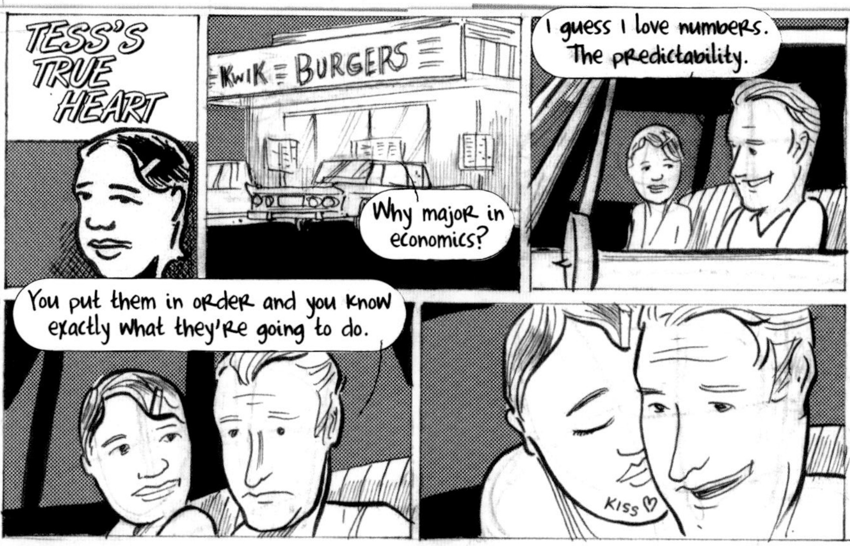
TESS'S TRUE HEART
KWIK BURGERS
Why major in economics?
I guess I love numbers. The predictability.
You put them in order and you know exactly what they're going to do.
KISS

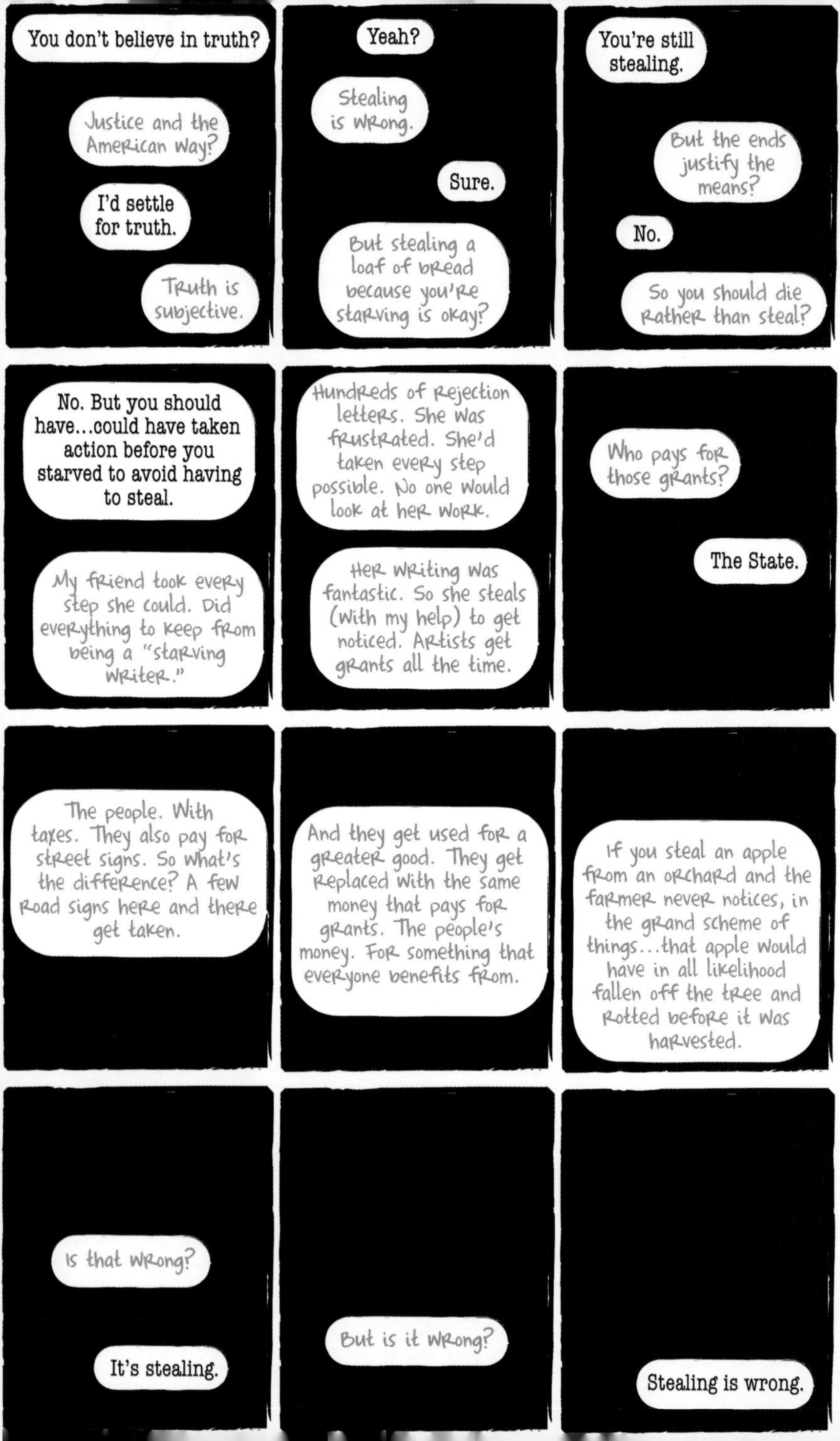
You don't believe in truth?
Justice and the American way?
I'd settle for truth.
Truth is subjective.
Yeah?
Stealing is wrong.
Sure.
But stealing a loaf of bread because you're starving is okay?
You're still stealing.
But the ends justify the means?
No.
So you should die rather than steal?
No. But you should have...could have taken action before you starved to avoid having to steal.
My friend took every step she could. Did everything to keep from being a "starving writer."
Hundreds of rejection letters. She was frustrated. She'd taken every step possible. No one would look at her work.
Her writing was fantastic. So she steals (with my help) to get noticed. Artists get grants all the time.
Who pays for those grants?
The State.
The people. With taxes. They also pay for street signs. So what's the difference? A few road signs here and there get taken.
And they get used for a greater good. They get replaced with the same money that pays for grants. The people's money. For something that everyone benefits from.
If you steal an apple from an orchard and the farmer never notices, in the grand scheme of things...that apple would have in all likelihood fallen off the tree and rotted before it was harvested.
Is that wrong?
It's stealing.
But is it wrong?
Stealing is wrong.

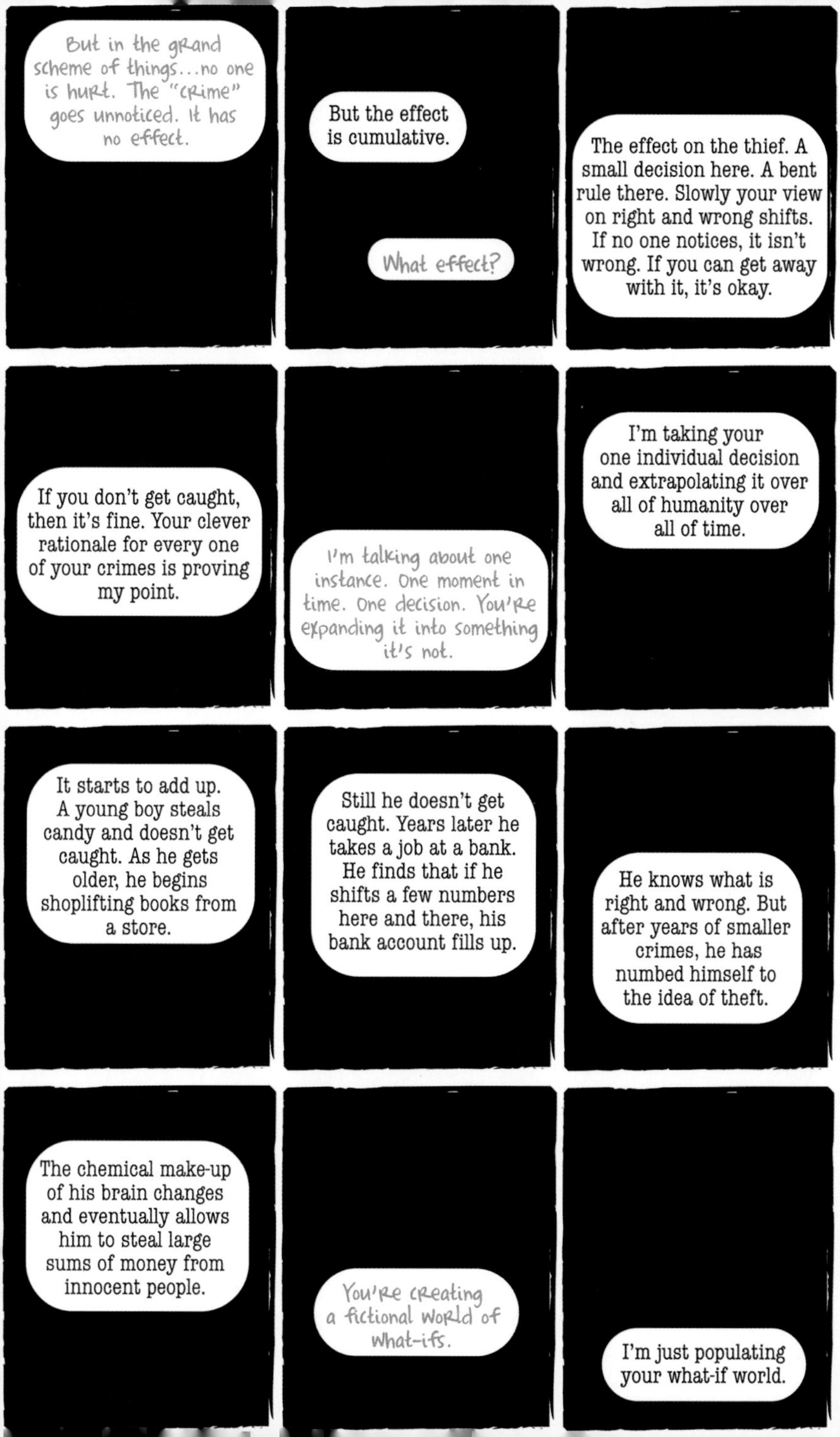
But in the grand scheme of things...no one is hurt. The "crime" goes unnoticed. It has no effect.
But the effect is cumulative.
What effect?
The effect on the thief. A small decision here. A bent rule there. Slowly your view on right and wrong shifts. If no one notices, it isn't wrong. If you can get away with it, it's okay.
If you don't get caught, then it's fine. Your clever rationale for every one of your crimes is proving my point.
I'm talking about one instance. One moment in time. One decision. You're expanding it into something it's not.
I'm taking your one individual decision and extrapolating it over all of humanity over all of time.
It starts to add up. A young boy steals candy and doesn't get caught. As he gets older, he begins shoplifting books from a store.
Still he doesn't get caught. Years later he takes a job at a bank. He finds that if he shifts a few numbers here and there, his bank account fills up.
He knows what is right and wrong. But after years of smaller crimes, he has numbed himself to the idea of theft.
The chemical make-up of his brain changes and eventually allows him to steal large sums of money from innocent people.
You're creating a fictional world of what-ifs.
I'm just populating your what-if world.

HOTEL DEL LA
DING
17
ALARM
1 2 3 4 5 6 7 8 9 10

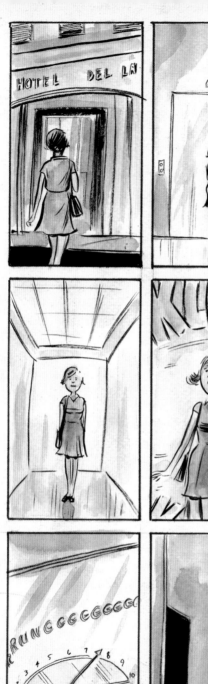

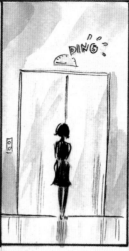

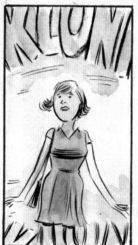

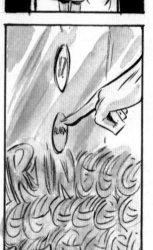

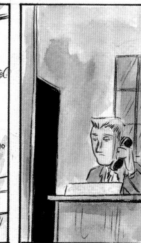

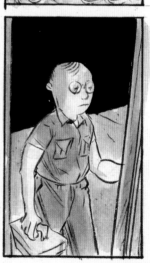

THE
REPAIR MAN

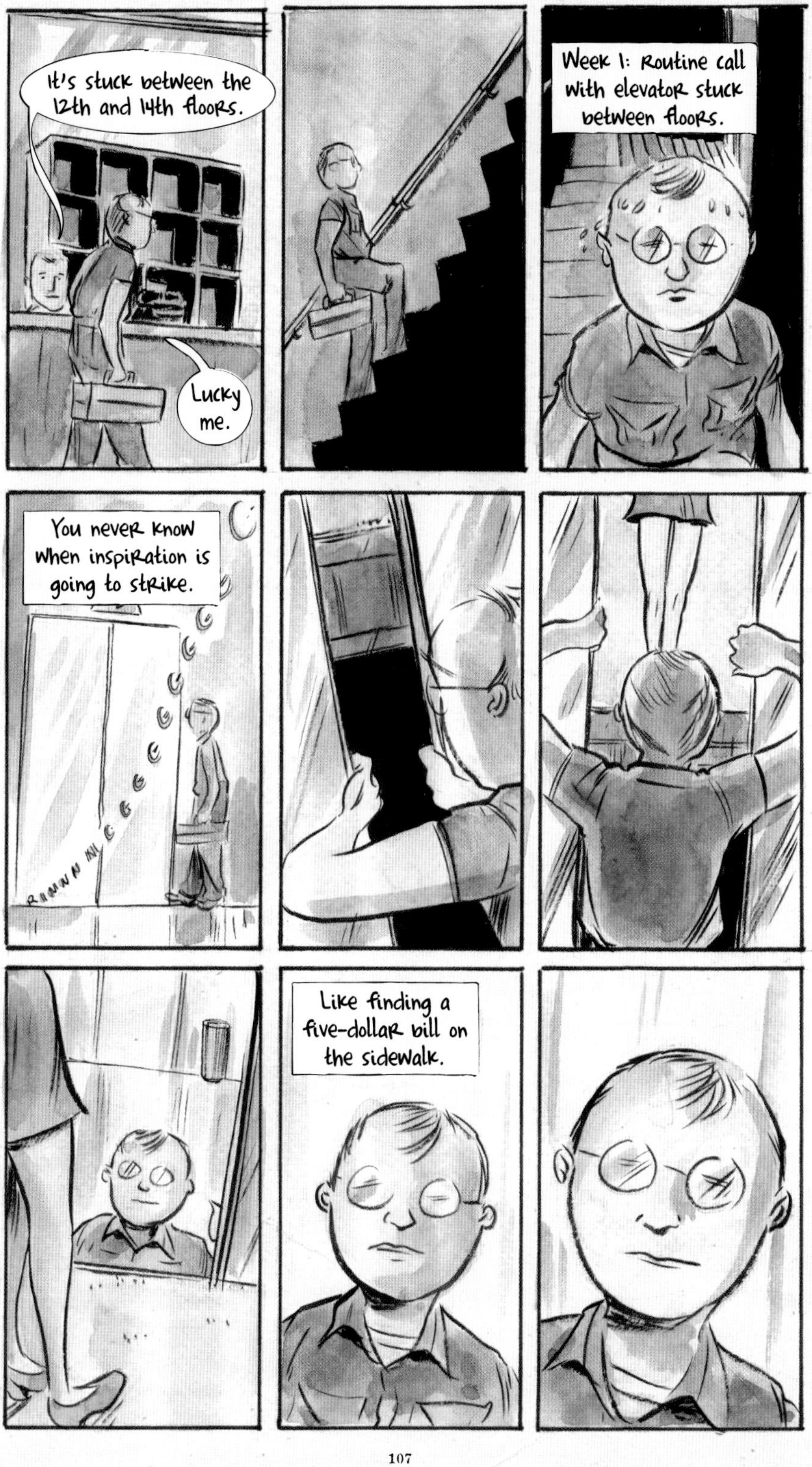
It's stuck between the 12th and 14th floors.
Lucky me.
Week 1: Routine call with elevator stuck between floors.
You never know when inspiration is going to strike.
Like finding a five-dollar bill on the sidewalk.

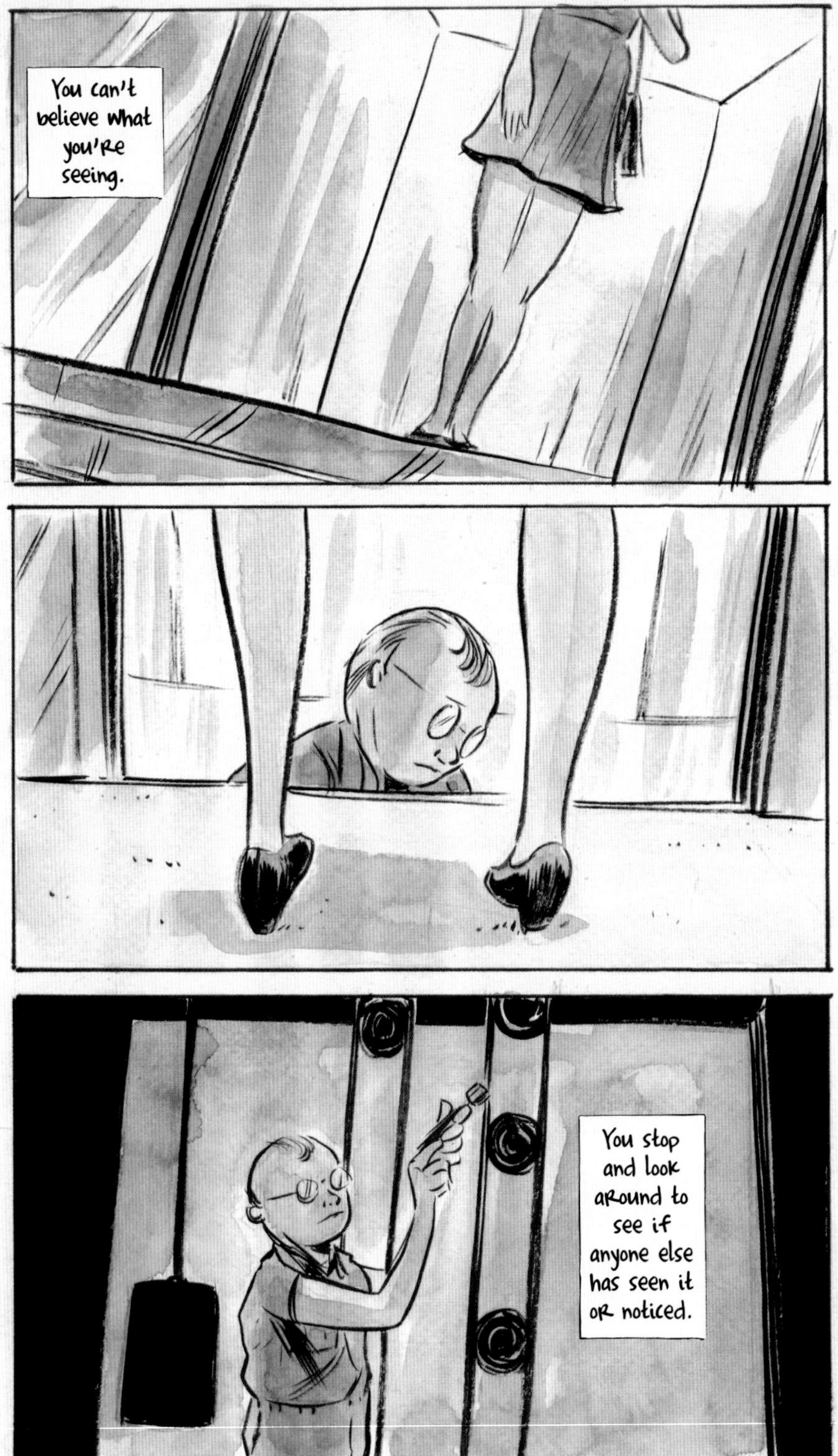
You can't believe what you're seeing.
You stop and look around to see if anyone else has seen it or noticed.

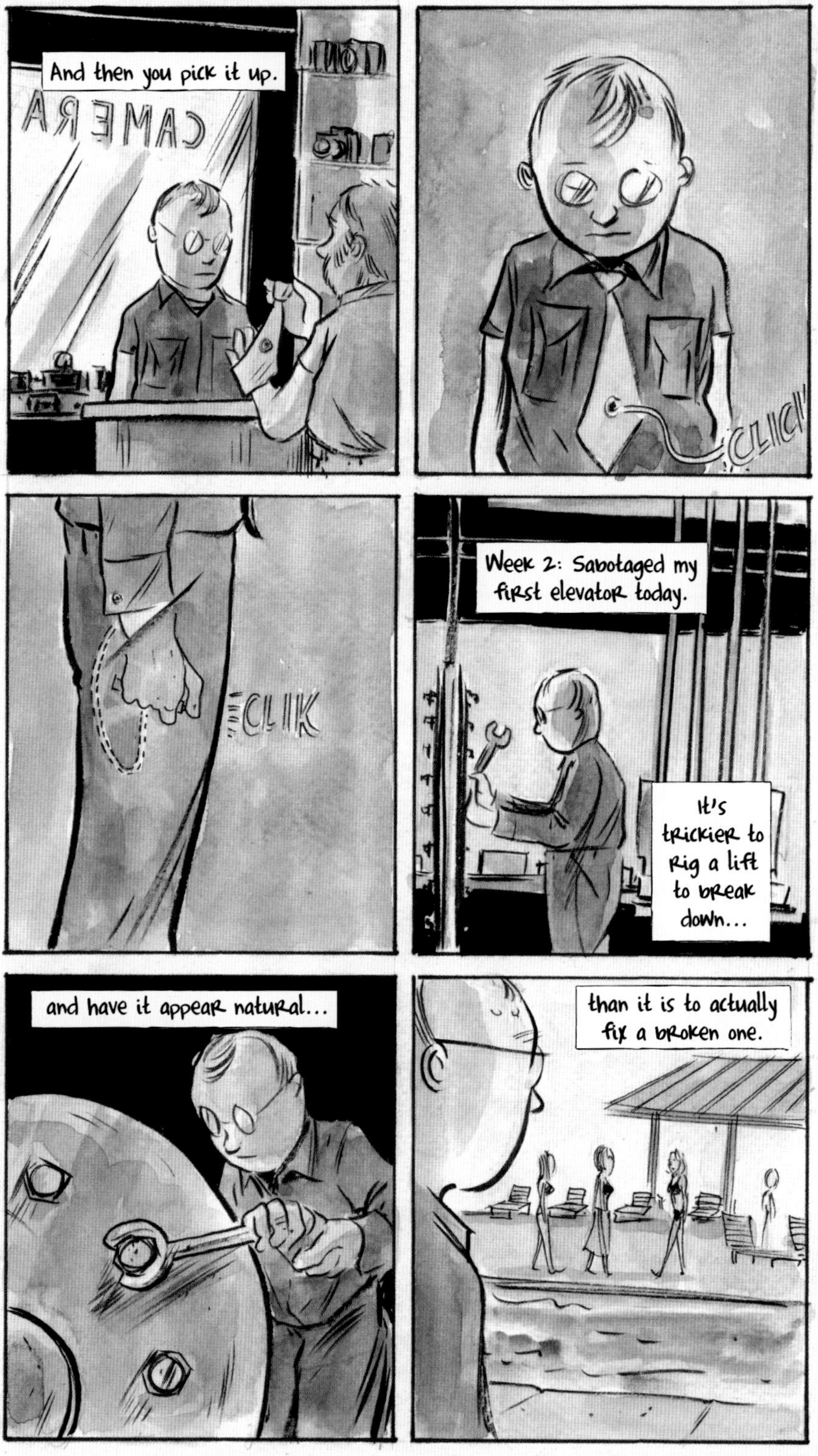

CAMERA
And then you pick it up.
CLICK
CLIK
Week 2: Sabotaged my first elevator today.
It's trickier to rig a lift to break down...
and have it appear natural...
than it is to actually fix a broken one.

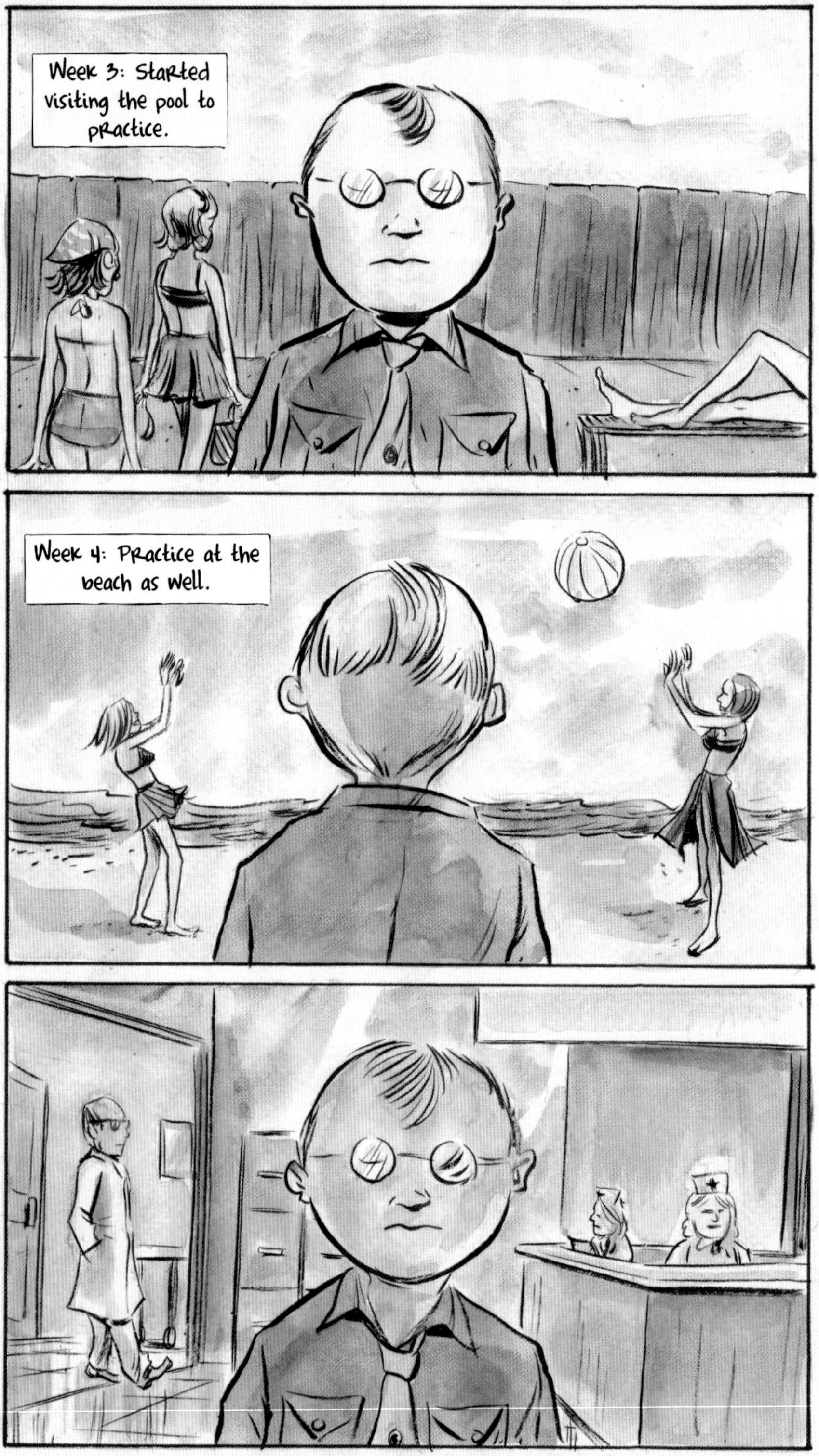
Week 3: Started visiting the pool to practice.
Week 4: Practice at the beach as well.

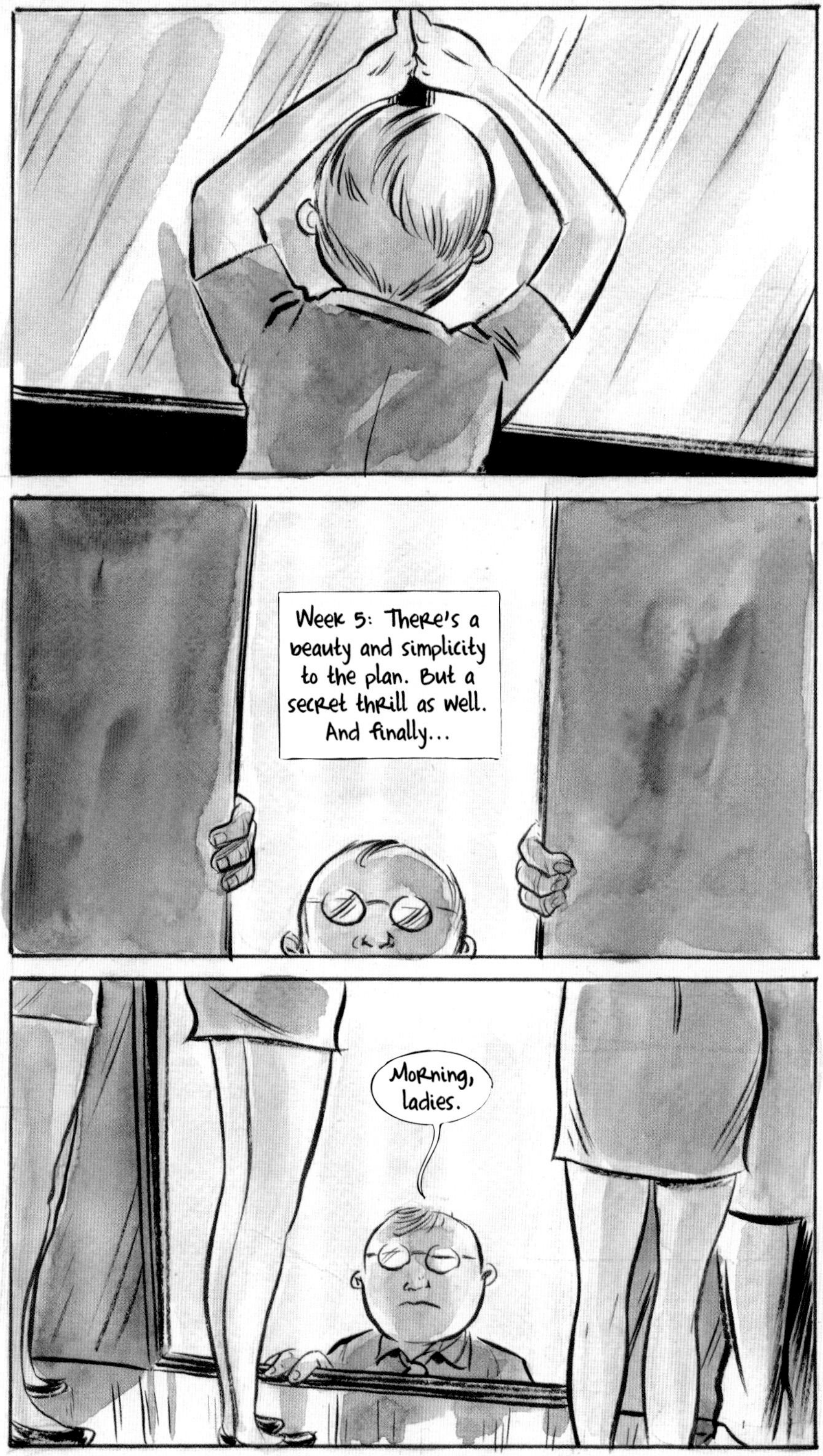
Week 5: There's a beauty and simplicity to the plan. But a secret thrill as well. And finally...
Morning, ladies.

A burst of
adrenalin when the
shutter is pushed.
The first of many.

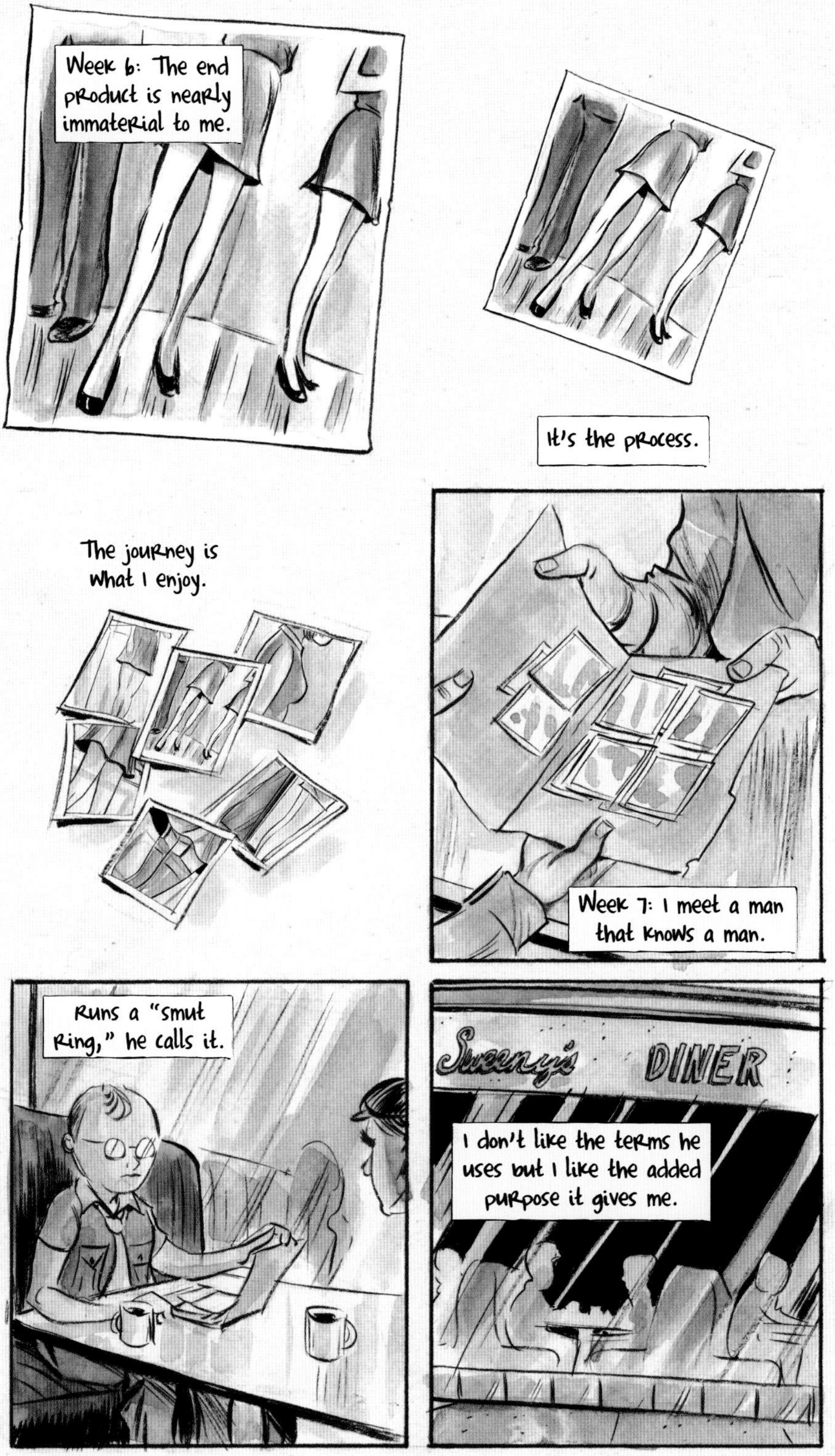
Week 6: The end product is nearly immaterial to me.
It's the process.
The journey is what I enjoy.
Week 7: I meet a man that knows a man.
Runs a "smut ring," he calls it.
Sweeny's DINER
I don't like the terms he uses but I like the added purpose it gives me.

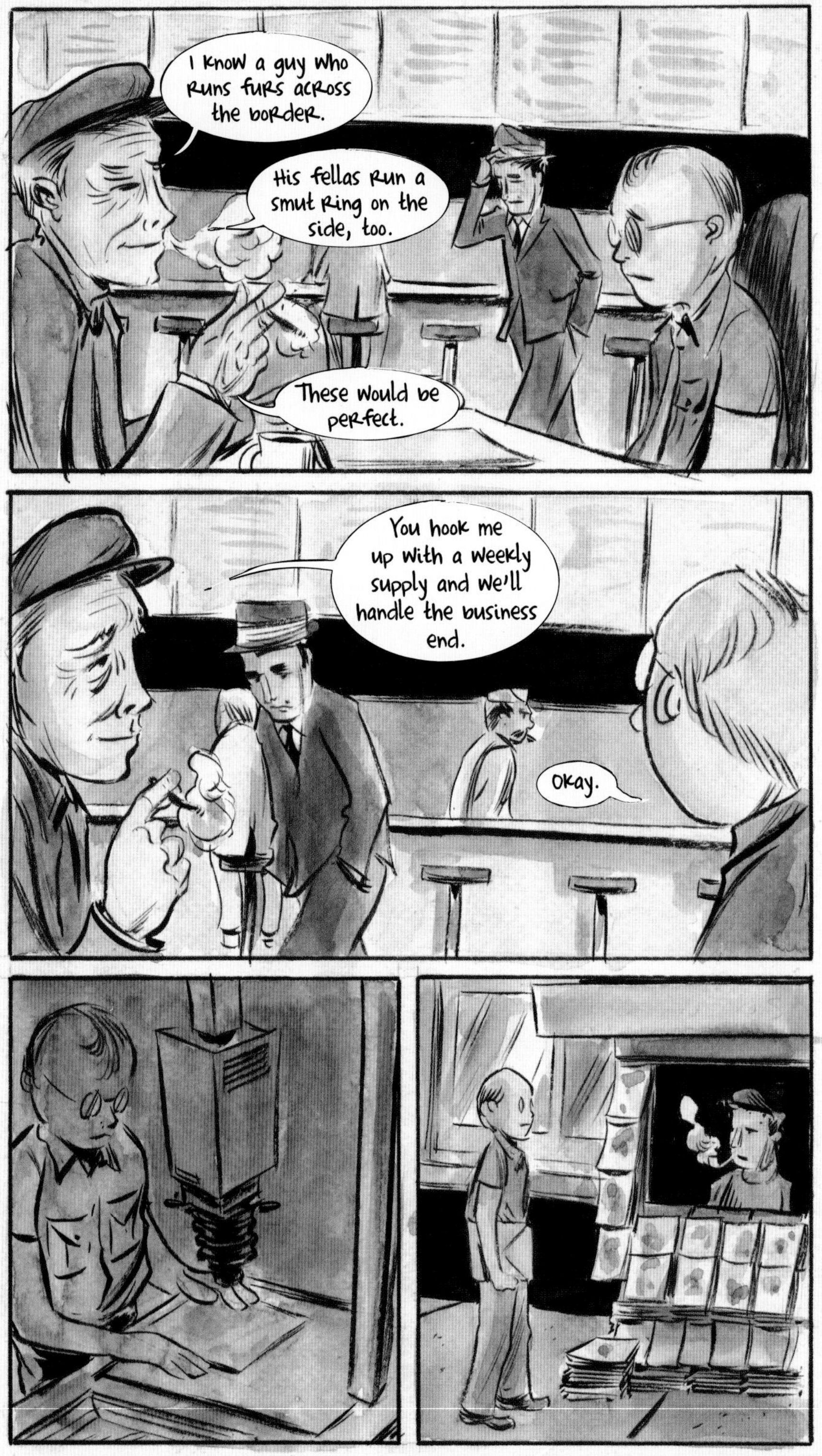
I know a guy who runs furs across the border.
His fellas run a smut ring on the side, too.
These would be perfect.
You hook me up with a weekly supply and we'll handle the business end.
Okay.

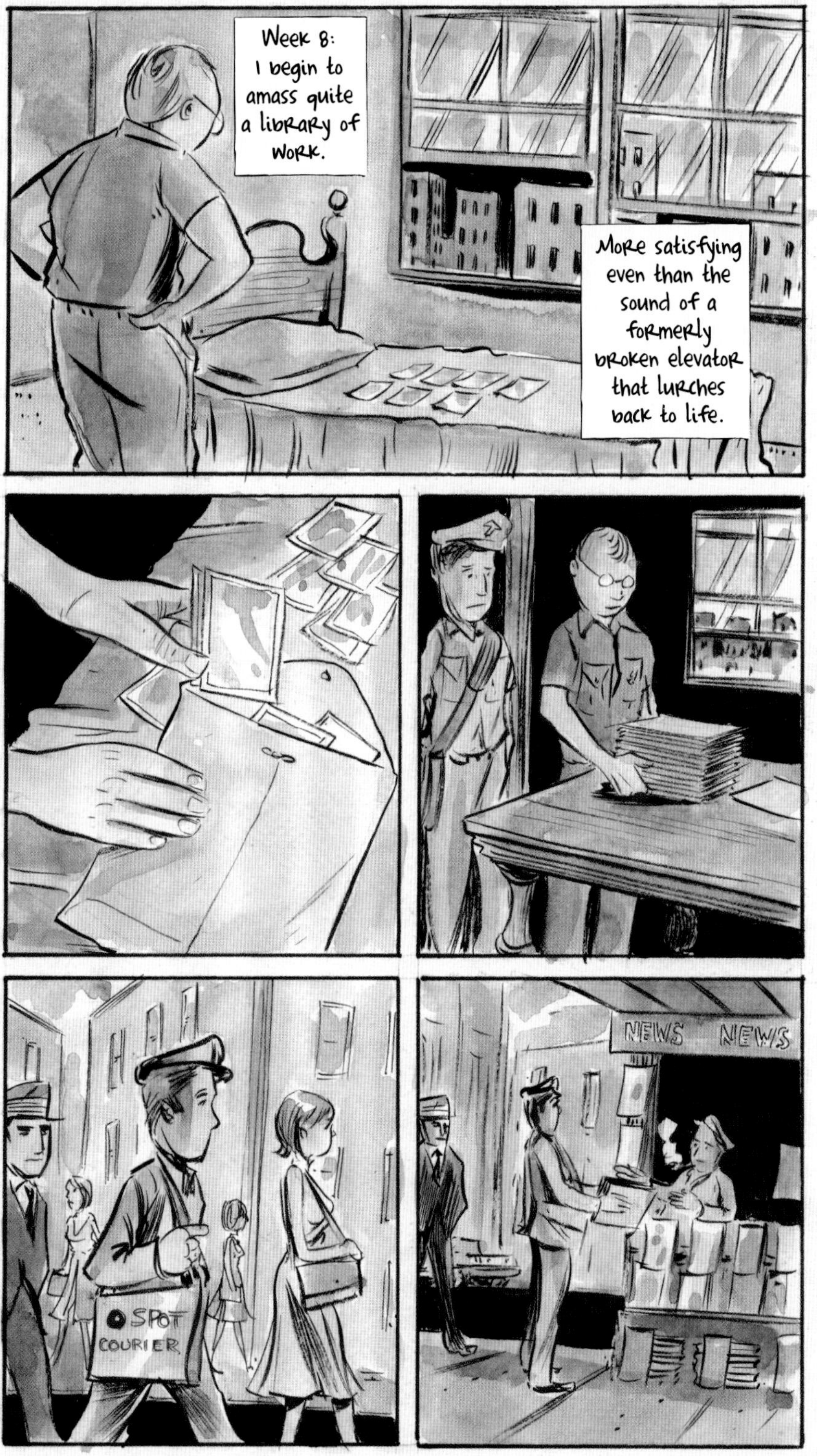
Week 8:
I begin to amass quite a library of work.
More satisfying even than the sound of a formerly broken elevator that lurches back to life.
SPOT
COURIER
NEWS
NEWS

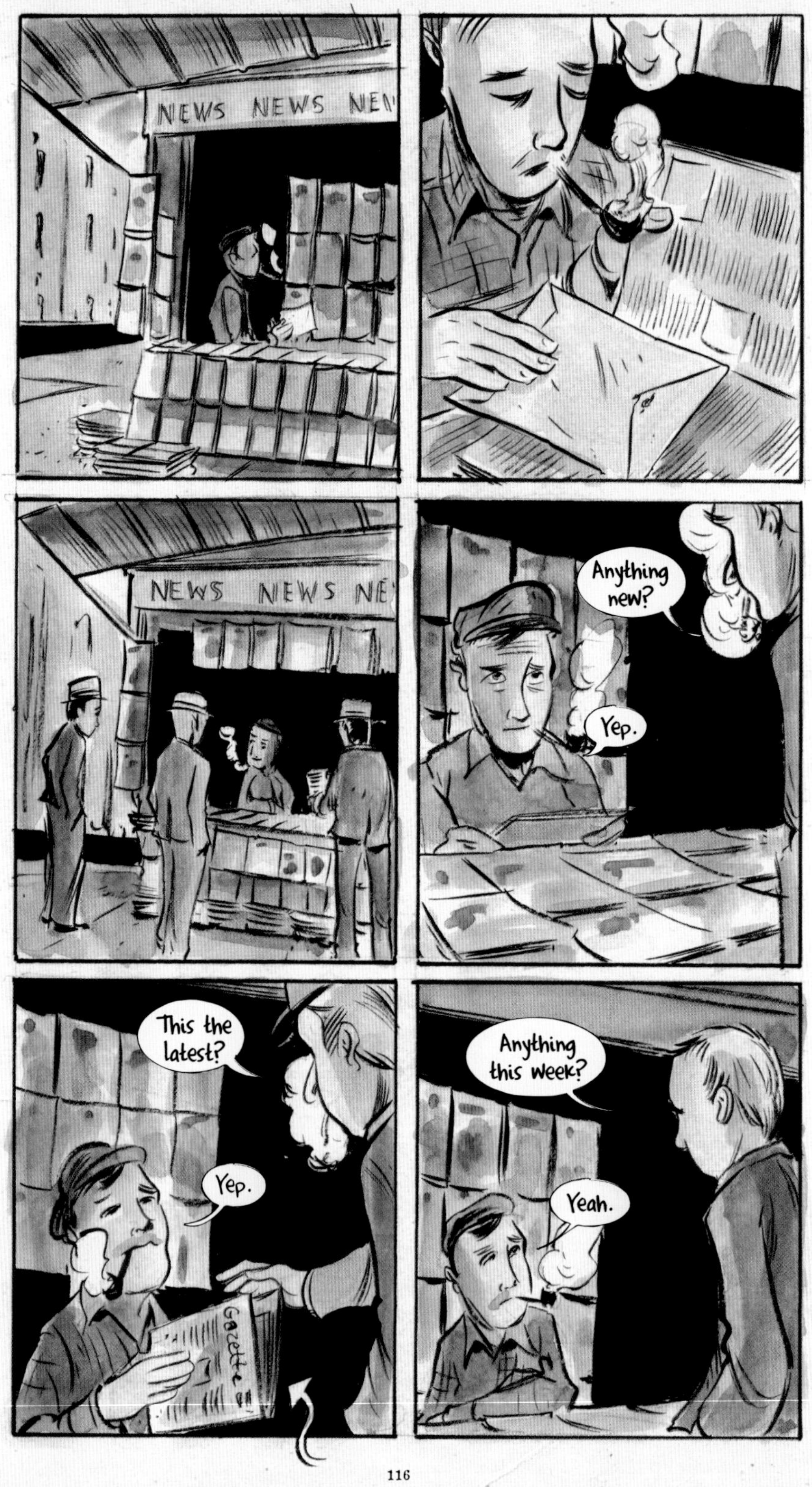
NEWS NEWS NE
NEWS NEWS NE
Anything new?
Yep.
This the latest?
Yep.
Gazette
Anything this week?
Yeah.

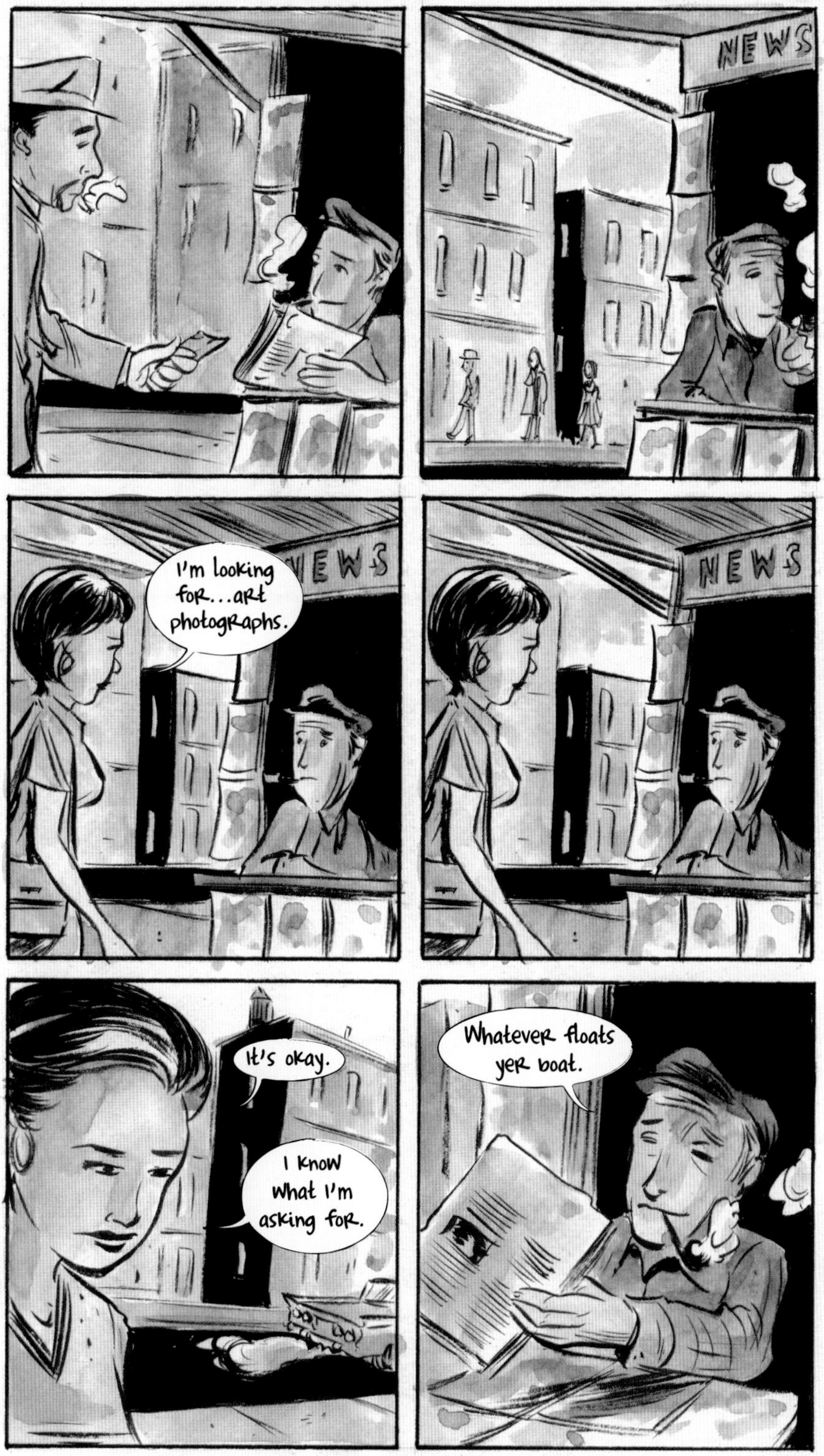
NEWS
I'm looking for...art photographs.
NEWS
NEWS
It's okay.
I know what I'm asking for.
Whatever floats yer boat.

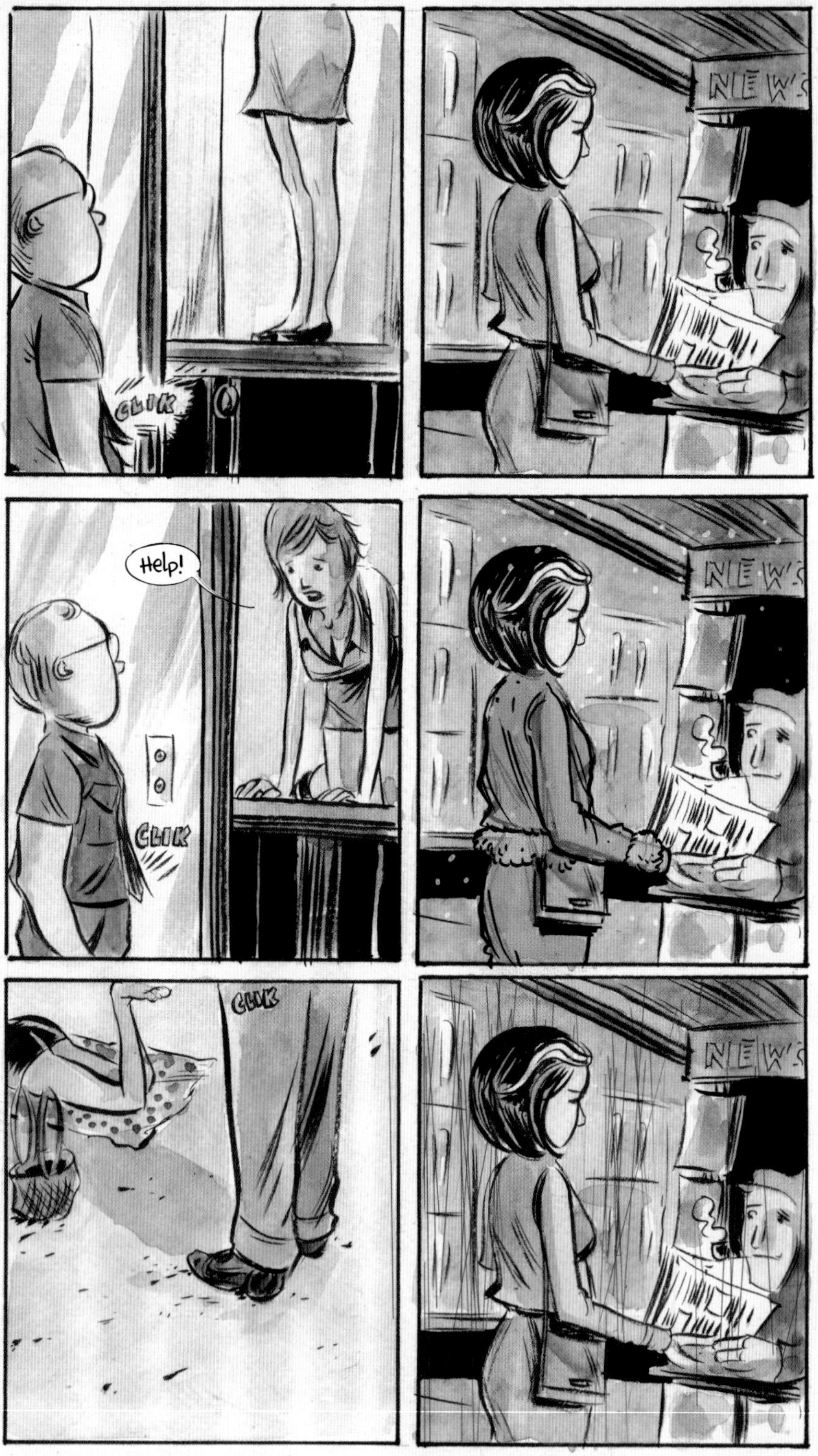
NEW'S
CLIK
Help!
CLIK
NEW'S
CLIK
NEW'S

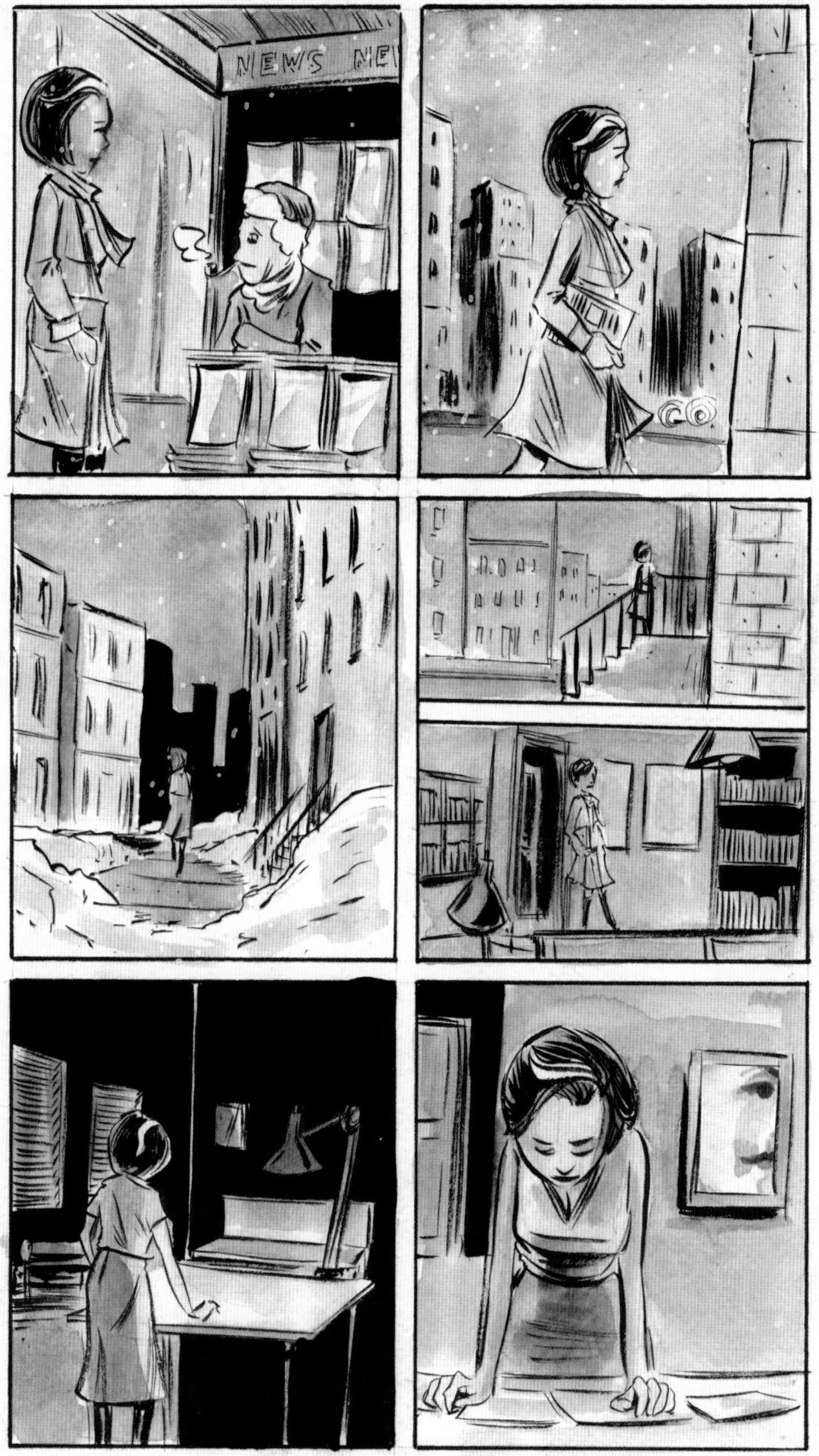
NEWS NE

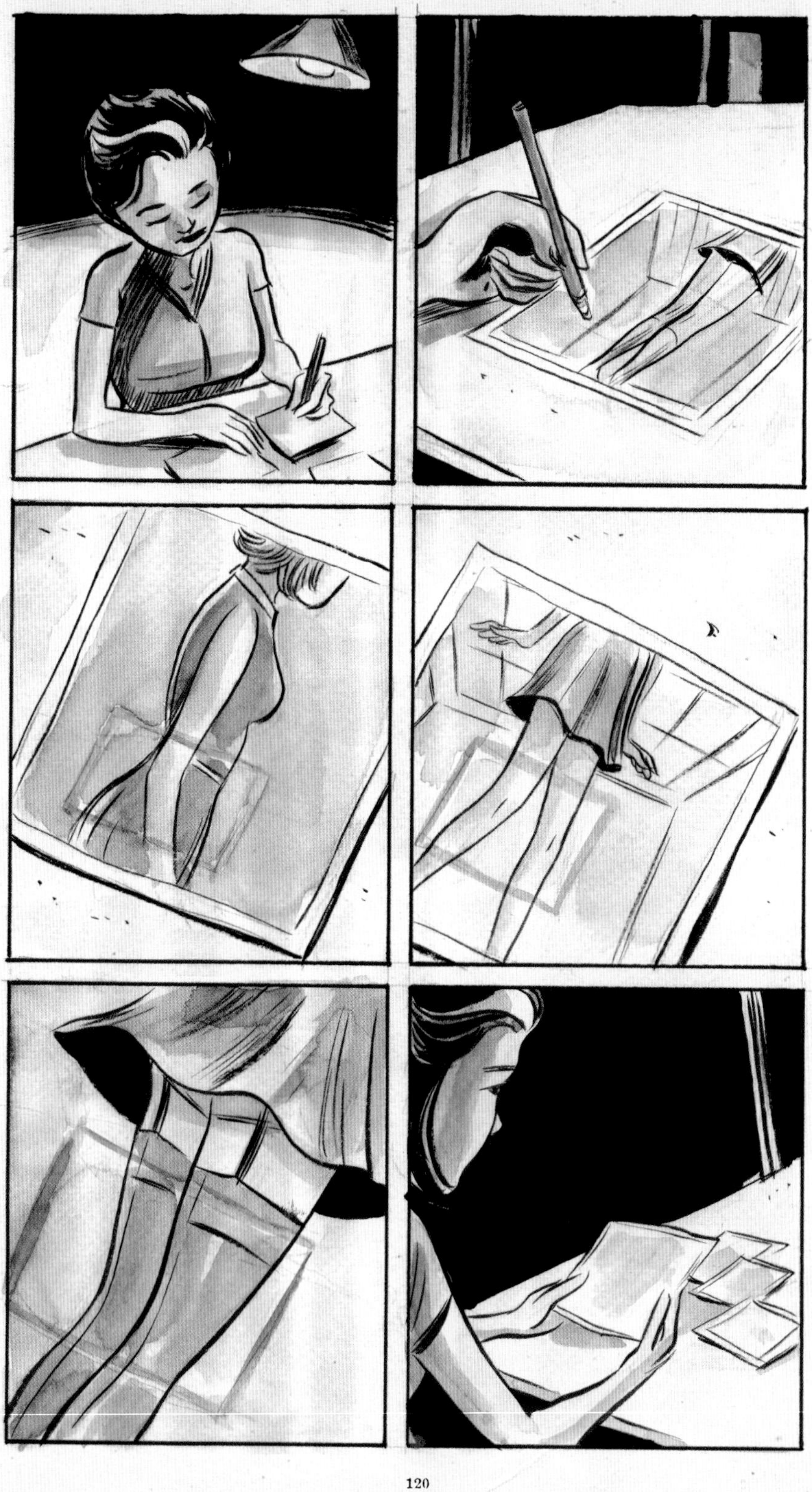

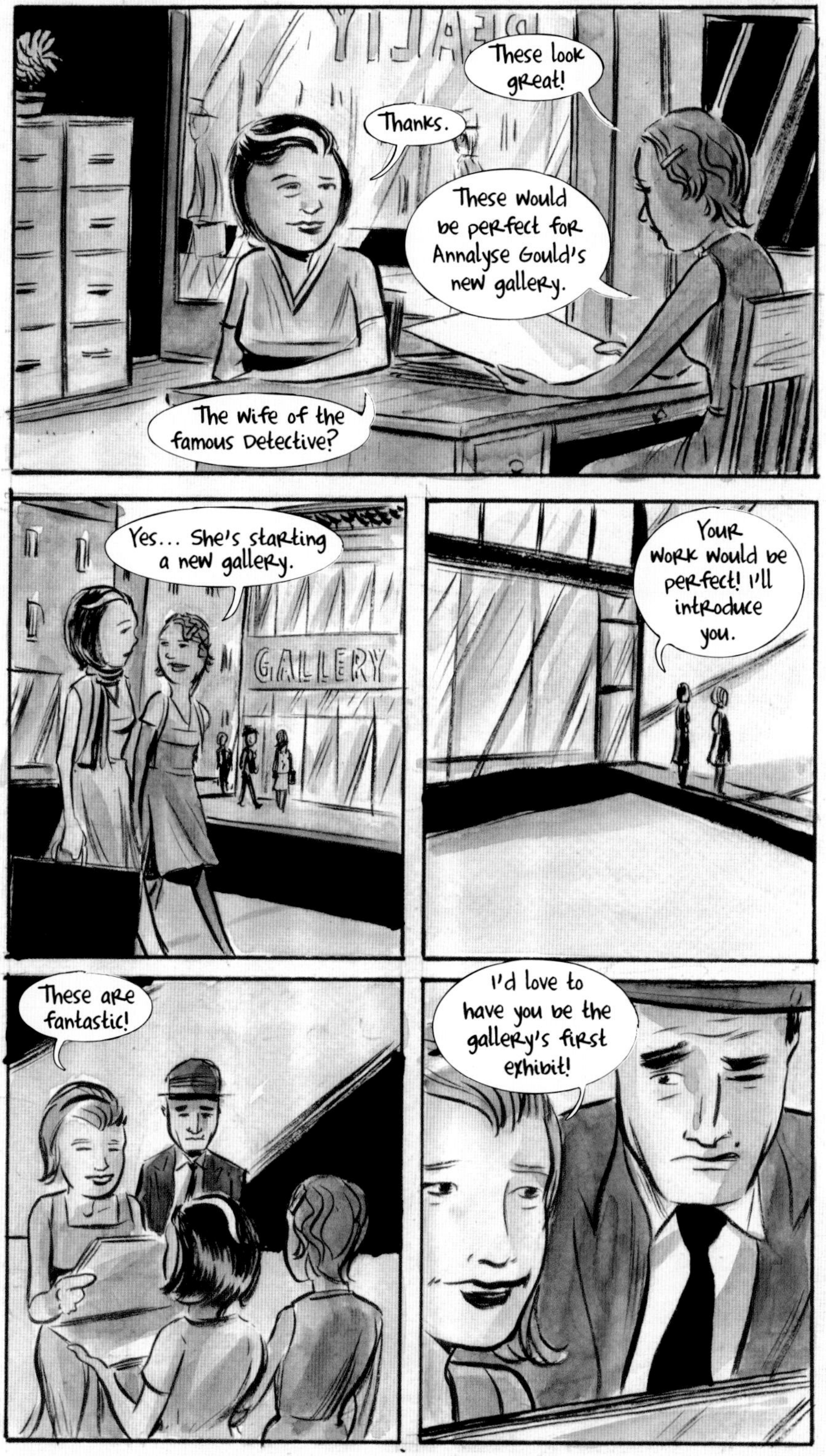
These look great!
Thanks.
These would be perfect for Annalyse Gould's new gallery.
The wife of the famous Detective?
Yes... She's starting a new gallery.
GALLERY
Your work would be perfect! I'll introduce you.
These are fantastic!
I'd love to have you be the gallery's first exhibit!

The leading suspect in a recently uncovered smut ring has been apprehended by Detective Gould this week. Gould's wife, Annalyse, was actually partially responsible in helping to crack the case as some of the photographs (which will be on exhibit at her gallery opening next month) were linked to the smut ring photographer. Gould also credits his expert use of a battery of hidden cameras and recording equipment with helping to nab the suspect—Brighton Diggs.

Also key in the arrest was the testimony of artist Carol Hixson, whose photos helped lead Gould in the right direction. When asked about her thoughts on the case, Hixson was pragmatic: "The only thing worse than being talked about is not being talked about. I hope this will bring even more patrons of the arts out to the opening exhibit."

When questioned about a possible link between the smut ring and the fur smuggling trade at the border, Gould was elusive but did say that the smut ring investigation and the fur smuggler may be linked.

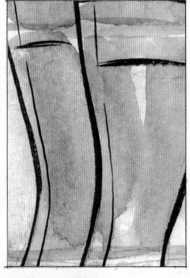

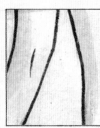

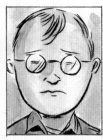

Art from the upcoming exhibit and Brighton Diggs's original photo.

DETECTIVE GOULD
HIS BODY IS AN ECONOMY OF MOVEMENT, BELYING THE RACING OF HIS MIND.
HE STRUGGLES TO BALANCE EVERYTHING IN HIS HEAD.

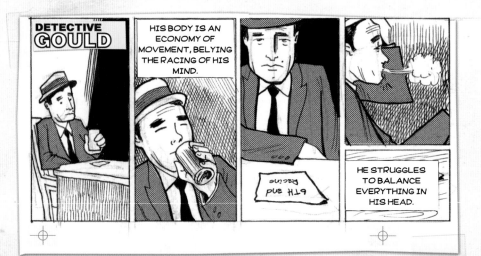

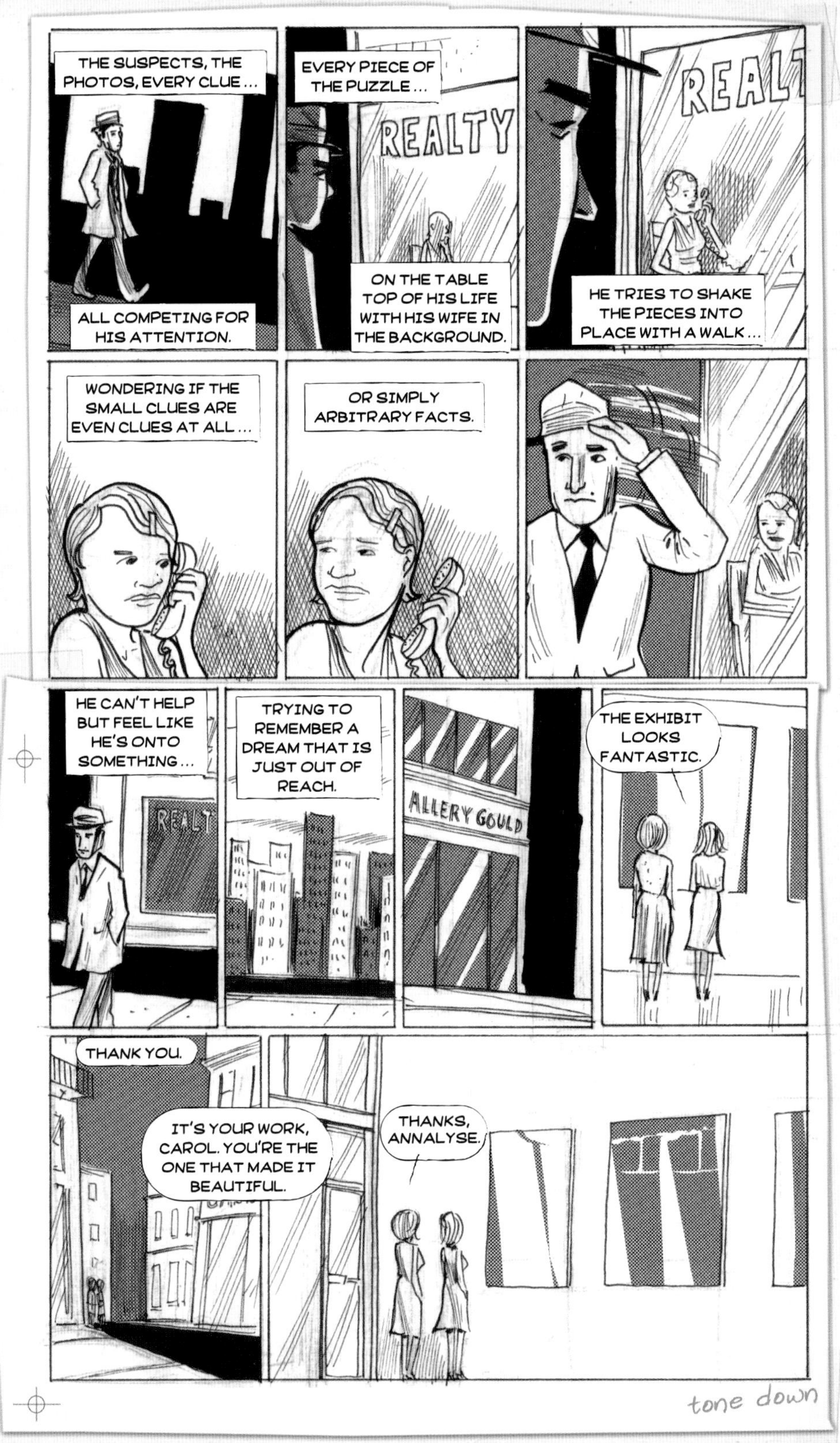
THE SUSPECTS, THE PHOTOS, EVERY CLUE...
ALL COMPETING FOR HIS ATTENTION.
EVERY PIECE OF THE PUZZLE...
REALTY
ON THE TABLE TOP OF HIS LIFE WITH HIS WIFE IN THE BACKGROUND.
REALT
HE TRIES TO SHAKE THE PIECES INTO PLACE WITH A WALK...
WONDERING IF THE SMALL CLUES ARE EVEN CLUES AT ALL...
OR SIMPLY ARBITRARY FACTS.
HE CAN'T HELP BUT FEEL LIKE HE'S ONTO SOMETHING...
REALT
TRYING TO REMEMBER A DREAM THAT IS JUST OUT OF REACH.
ALLERY GOULD
THE EXHIBIT LOOKS FANTASTIC.
THANK YOU.
IT'S YOUR WORK, CAROL. YOU'RE THE ONE THAT MADE IT BEAUTIFUL.
THANKS, ANNALYSE.
tone down

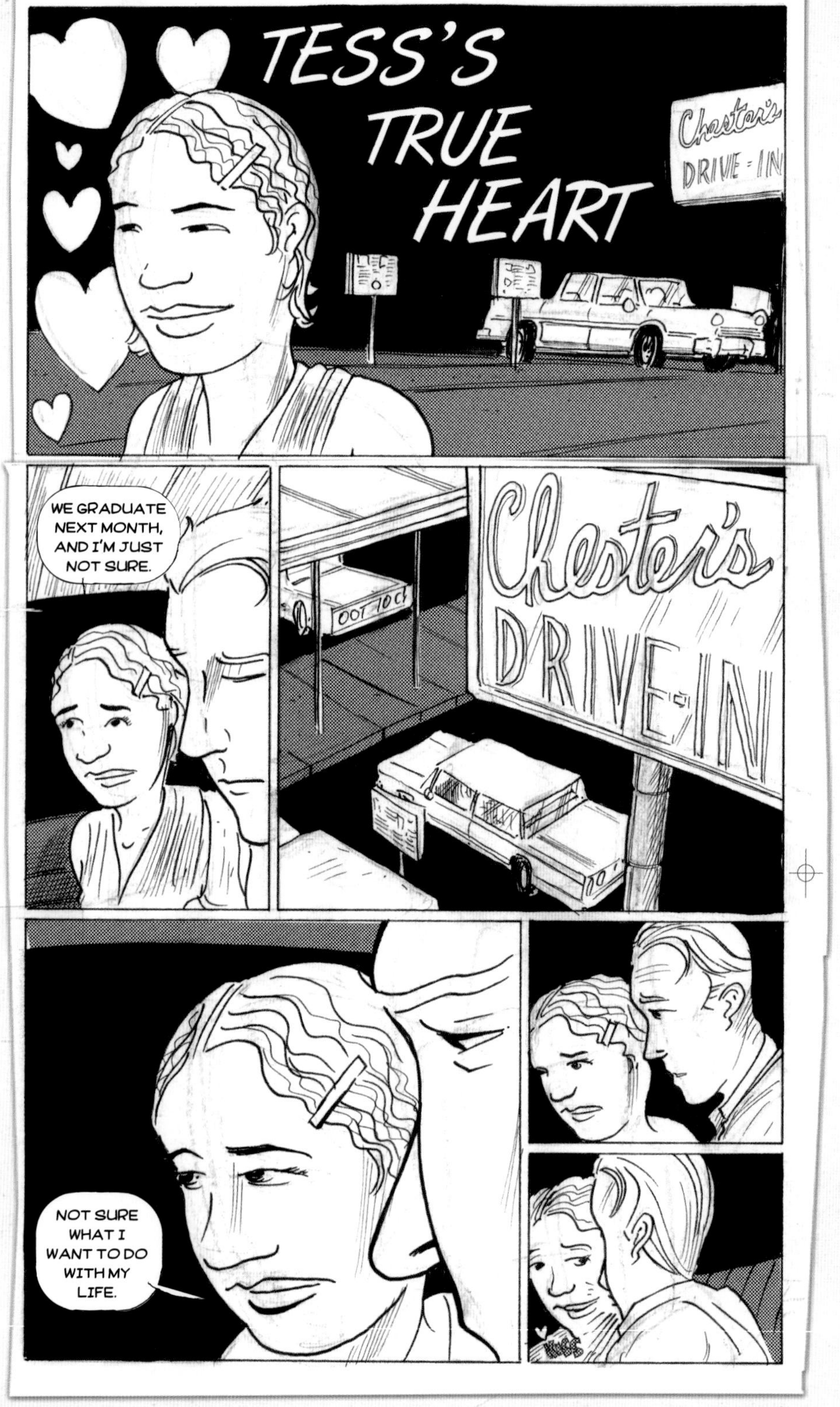
TESS'S TRUE HEART
Chester's DRIVE-IN
WE GRADUATE NEXT MONTH, AND I'M JUST NOT SURE.
Chester's DRIVE-IN
NOT SURE WHAT I WANT TO DO WITH MY LIFE.

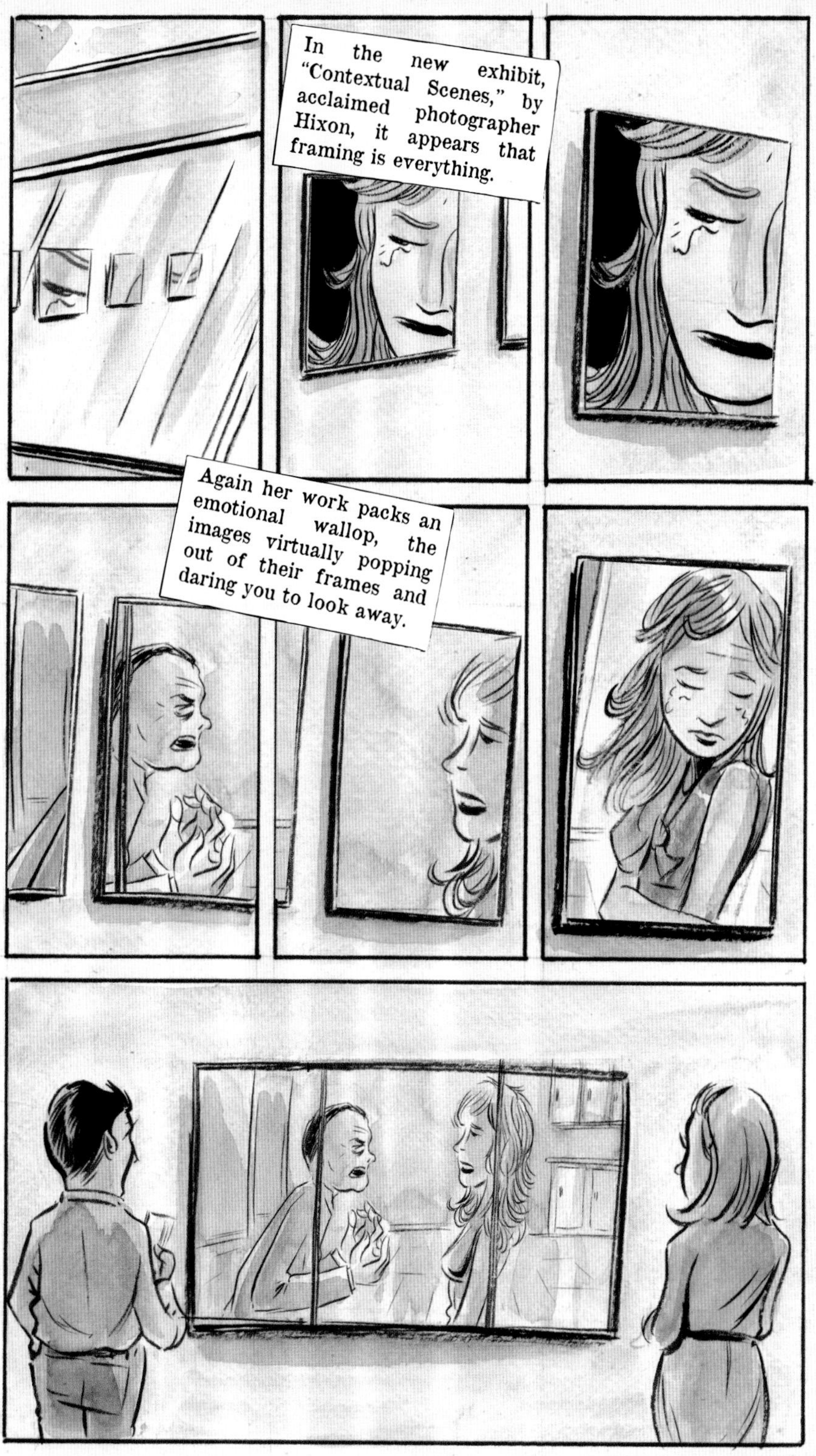
In the new exhibit, "Contextual Scenes," by acclaimed photographer Hixon, it appears that framing is everything.
Again her work packs an emotional wallop, the images virtually popping out of their frames and daring you to look away.

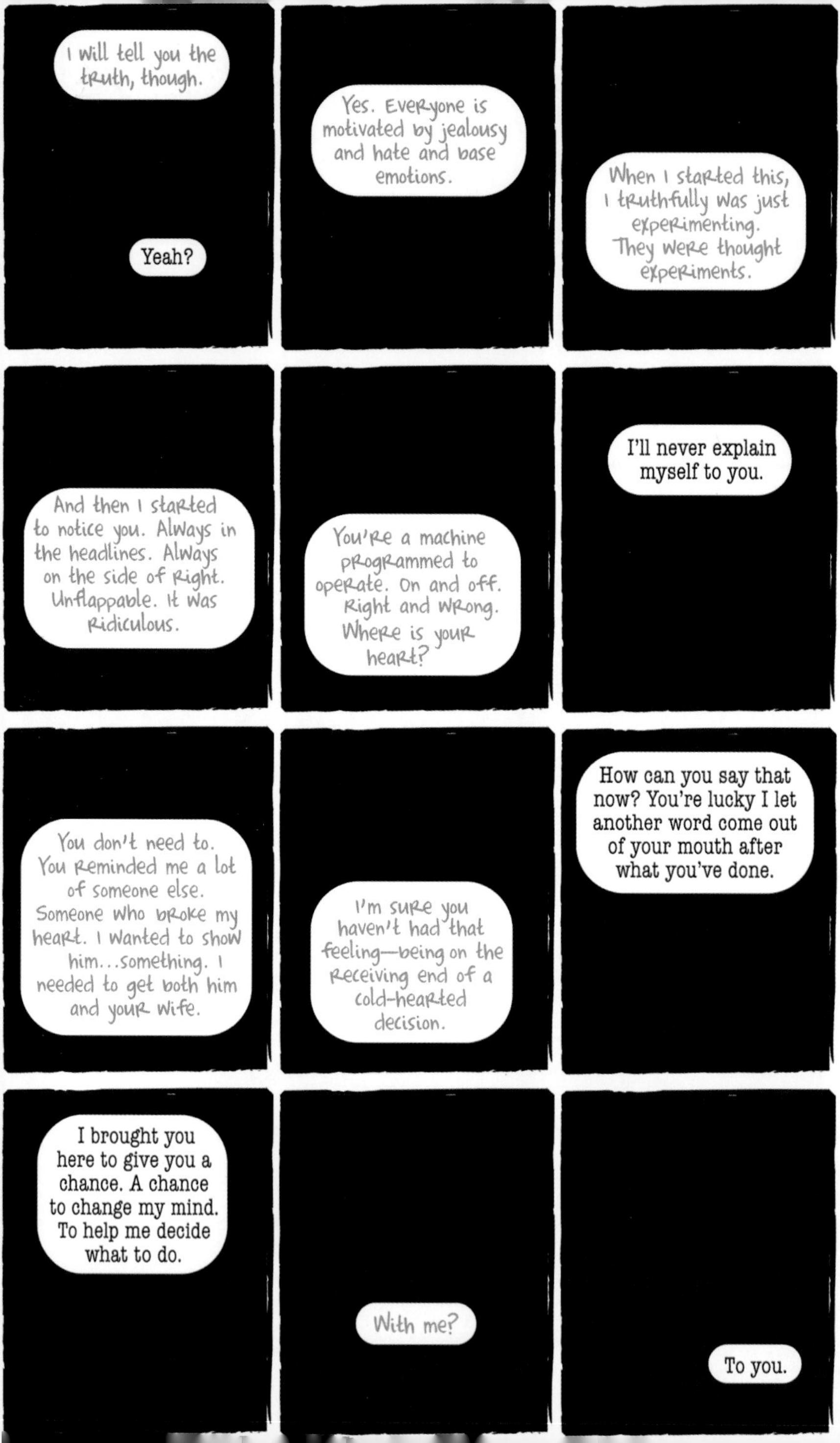
I will tell you the truth, though.
Yeah?
Yes. Everyone is motivated by jealousy and hate and base emotions.
When I started this, I truthfully was just experimenting. They were thought experiments.
And then I started to notice you. Always in the headlines. Always on the side of right. Unflappable. It was ridiculous.
You're a machine programmed to operate. On and off. Right and wrong. Where is your heart?
I'll never explain myself to you.
You don't need to. You reminded me a lot of someone else. Someone who broke my heart. I wanted to show him…something. I needed to get both him and your wife.
I'm sure you haven't had that feeling—being on the receiving end of a cold-hearted decision.
How can you say that now? You're lucky I let another word come out of your mouth after what you've done.
I brought you here to give you a chance. A chance to change my mind. To help me decide what to do.
With me?
To you.

THE
PERFORMANCE
ARTIST

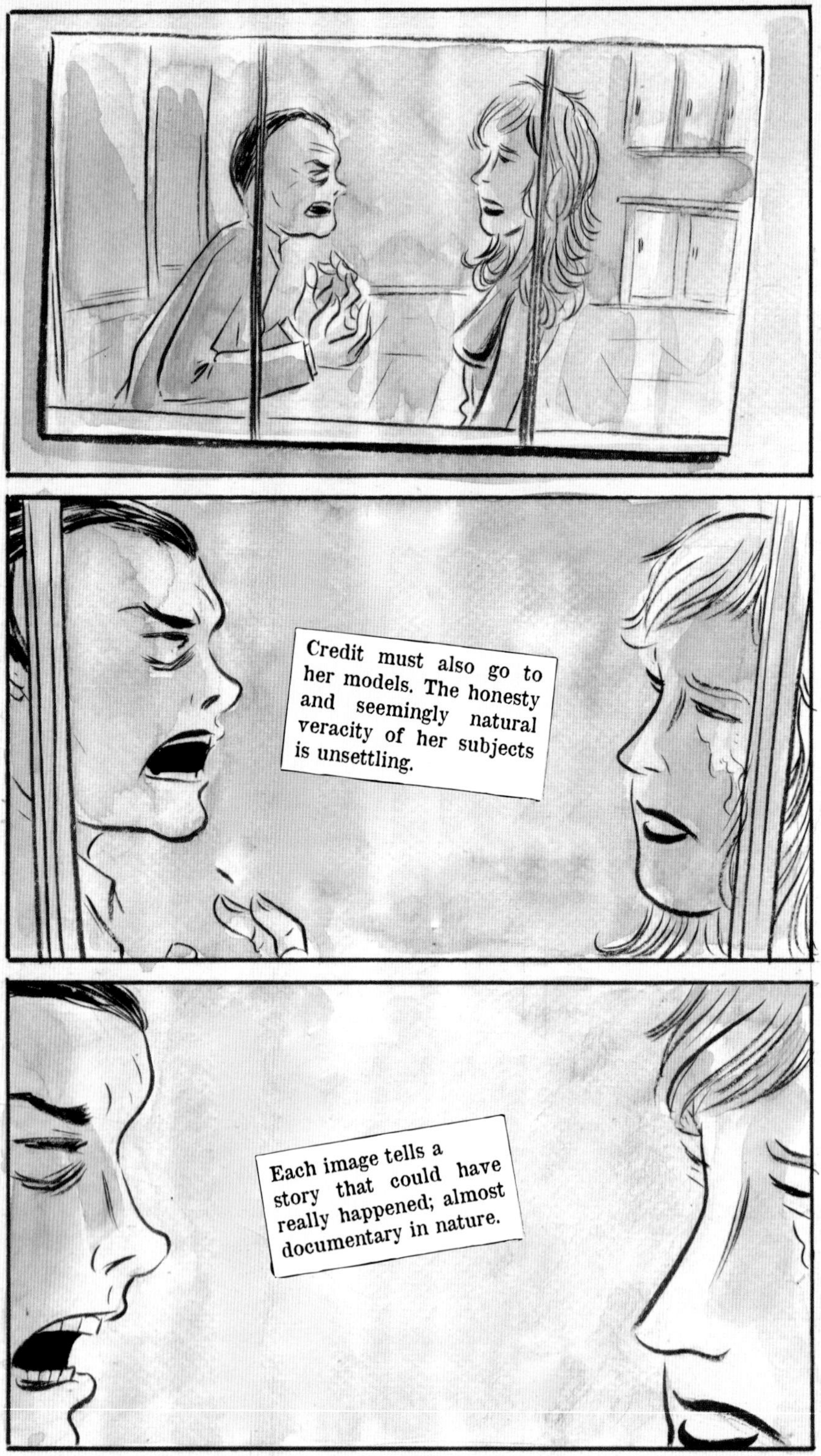
Credit must also go to her models. The honesty and seemingly natural veracity of her subjects is unsettling.
Each image tells a story that could have really happened; almost documentary in nature.

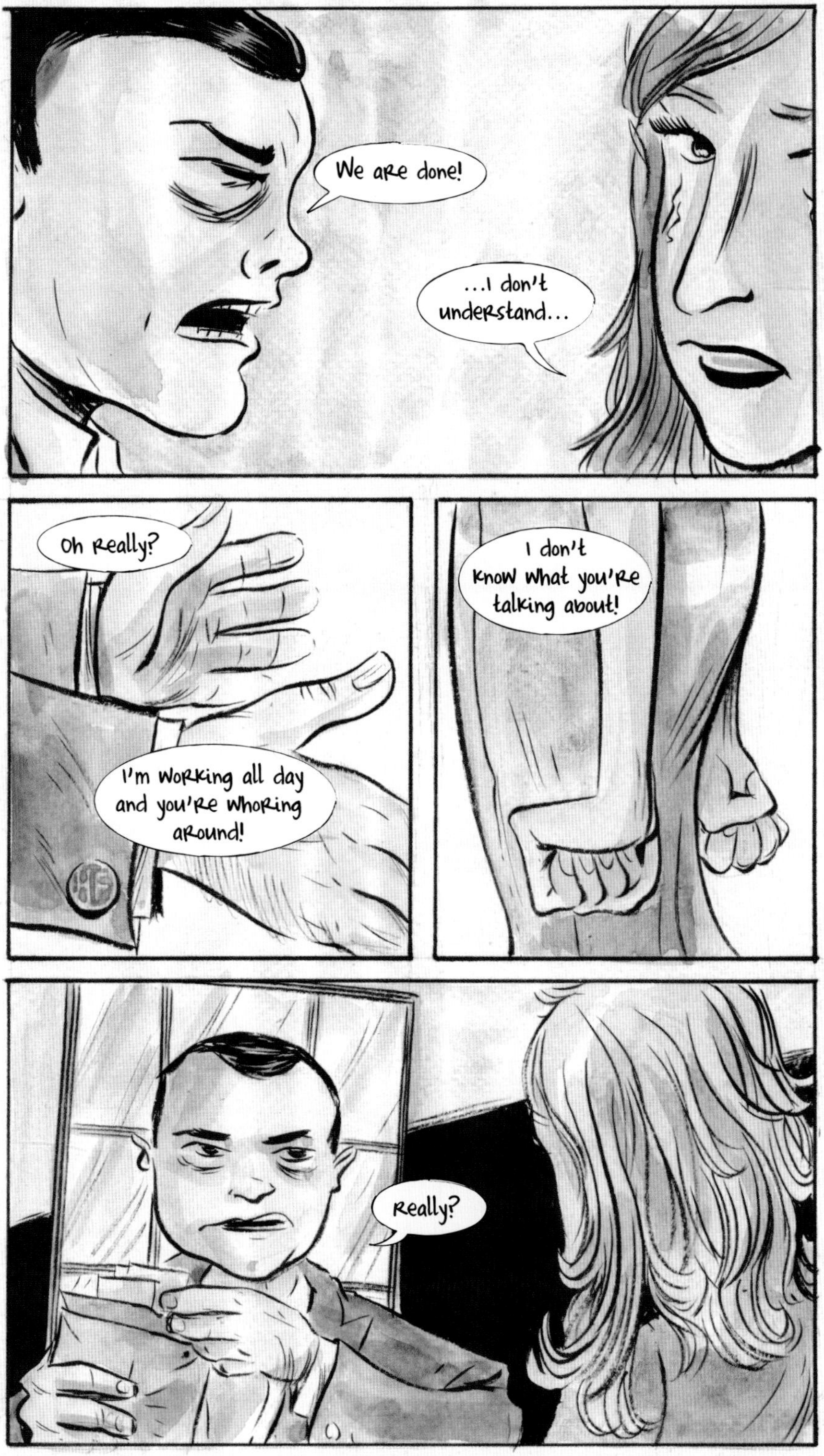

We are done!
...I don't understand...
Oh really?
I don't know what you're talking about!
I'm working all day and you're whoring around!
Really?

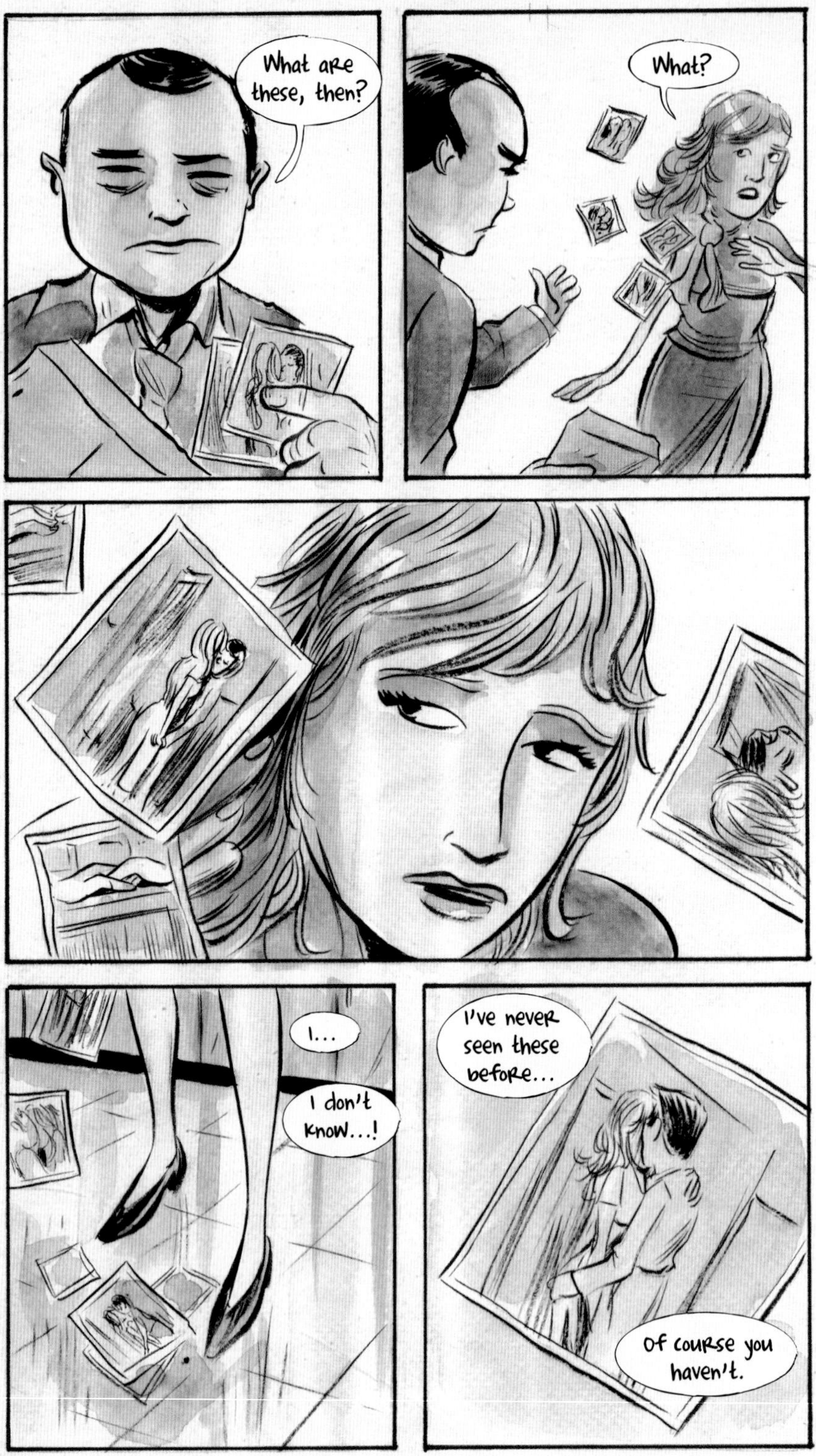
What are these, then?
What?
I...
I don't know...!
I've never seen these before...
Of course you haven't.

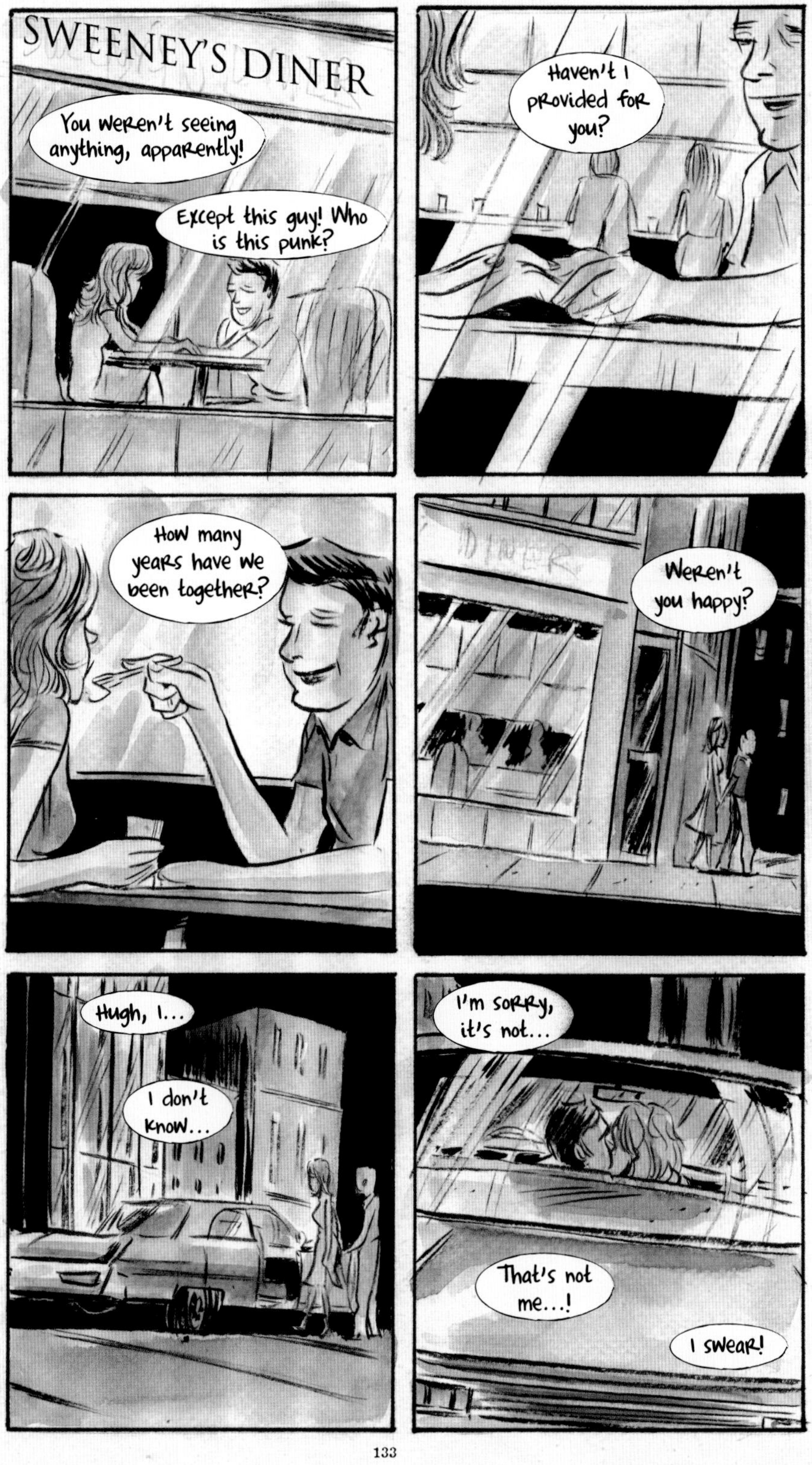
SWEENEY'S DINER
You weren't seeing anything, apparently!
Except this guy! Who is this punk?
Haven't I provided for you?
How many years have we been together?
DINER
Weren't you happy?
Hugh, I...
I don't know...
I'm sorry, it's not...
That's not me...!
I swear!

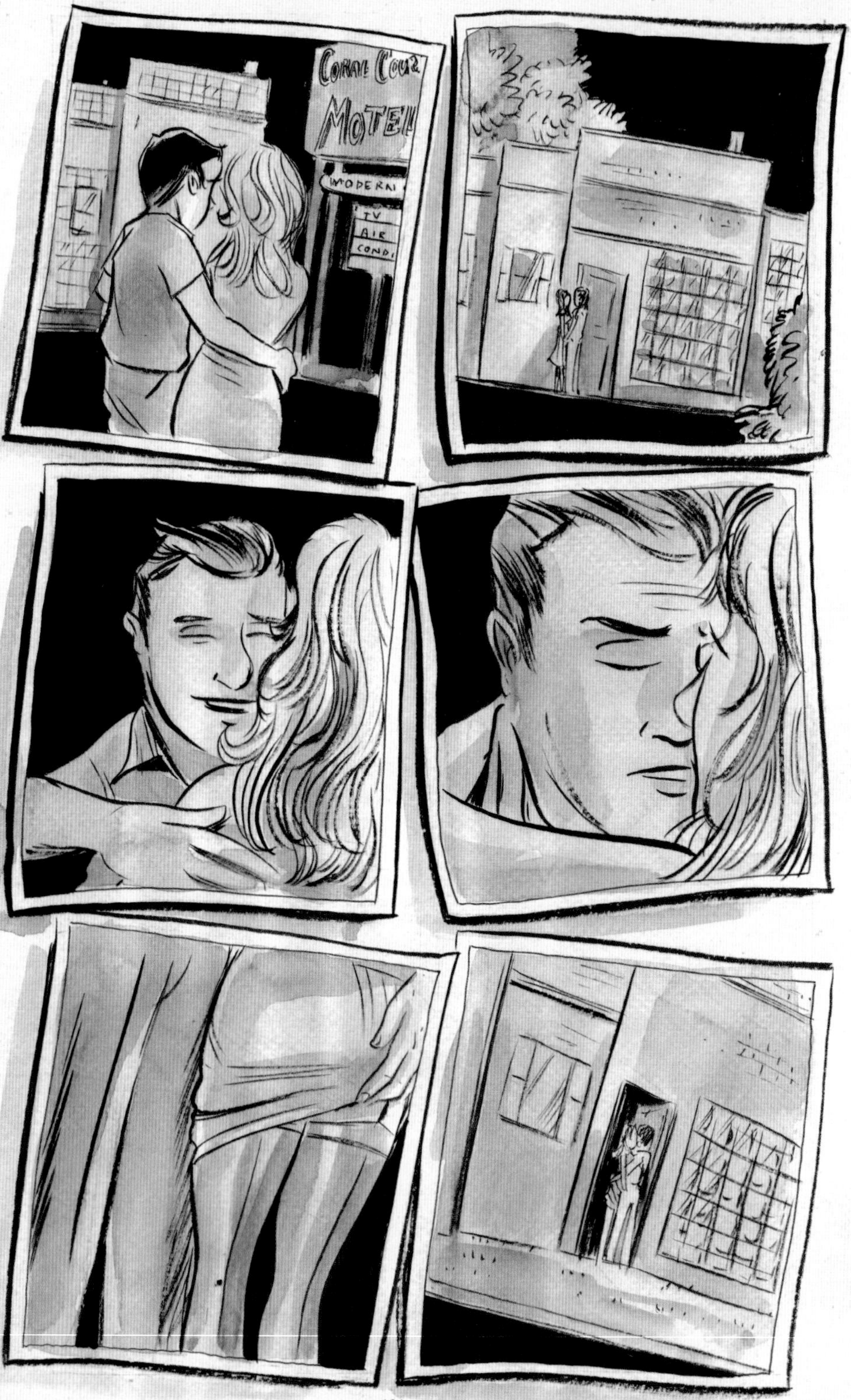
CORAL COUR
MOTEL
MODERN
TV
AIR
COND.

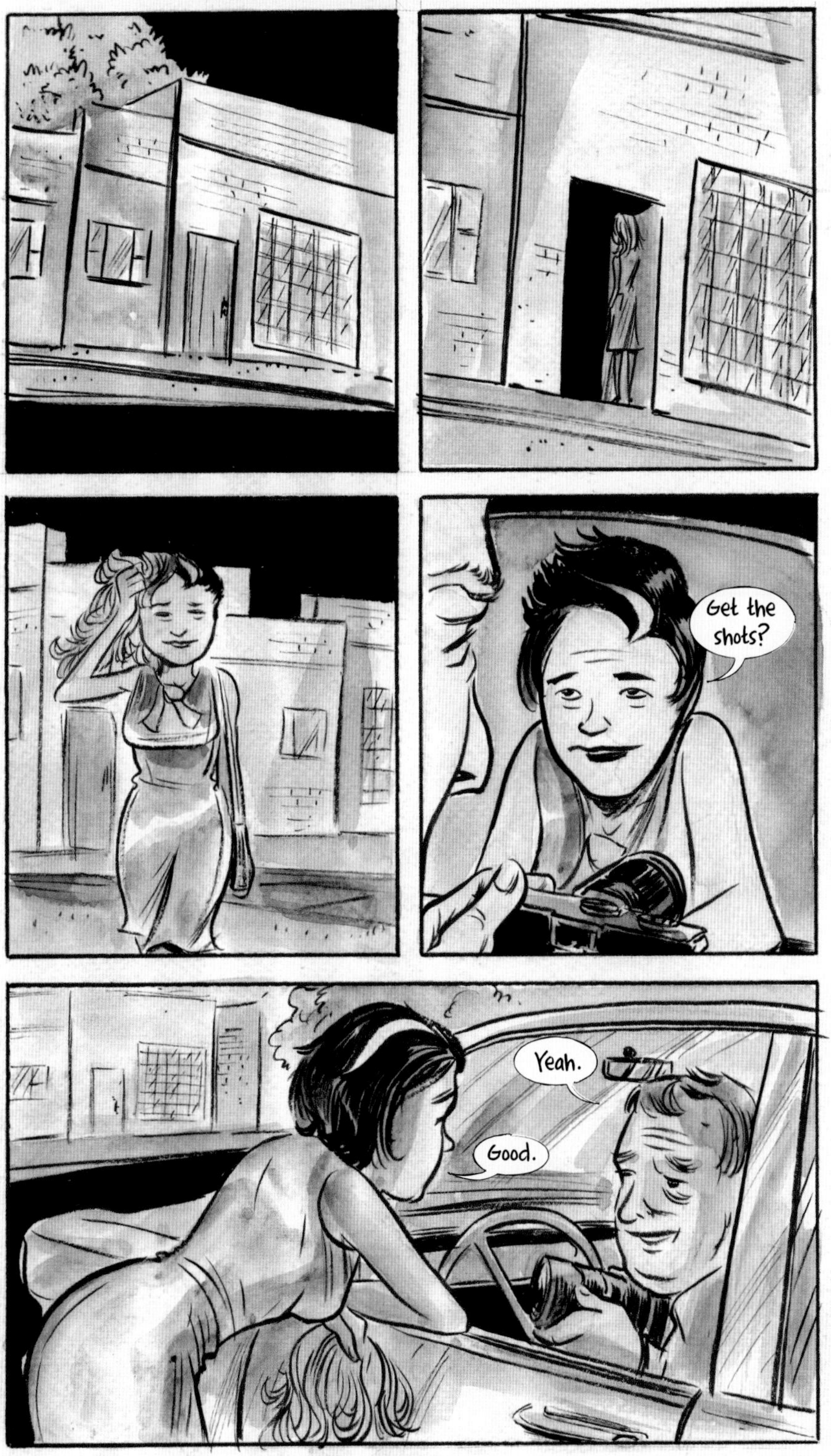
Get the shots?
Yeah.
Good.

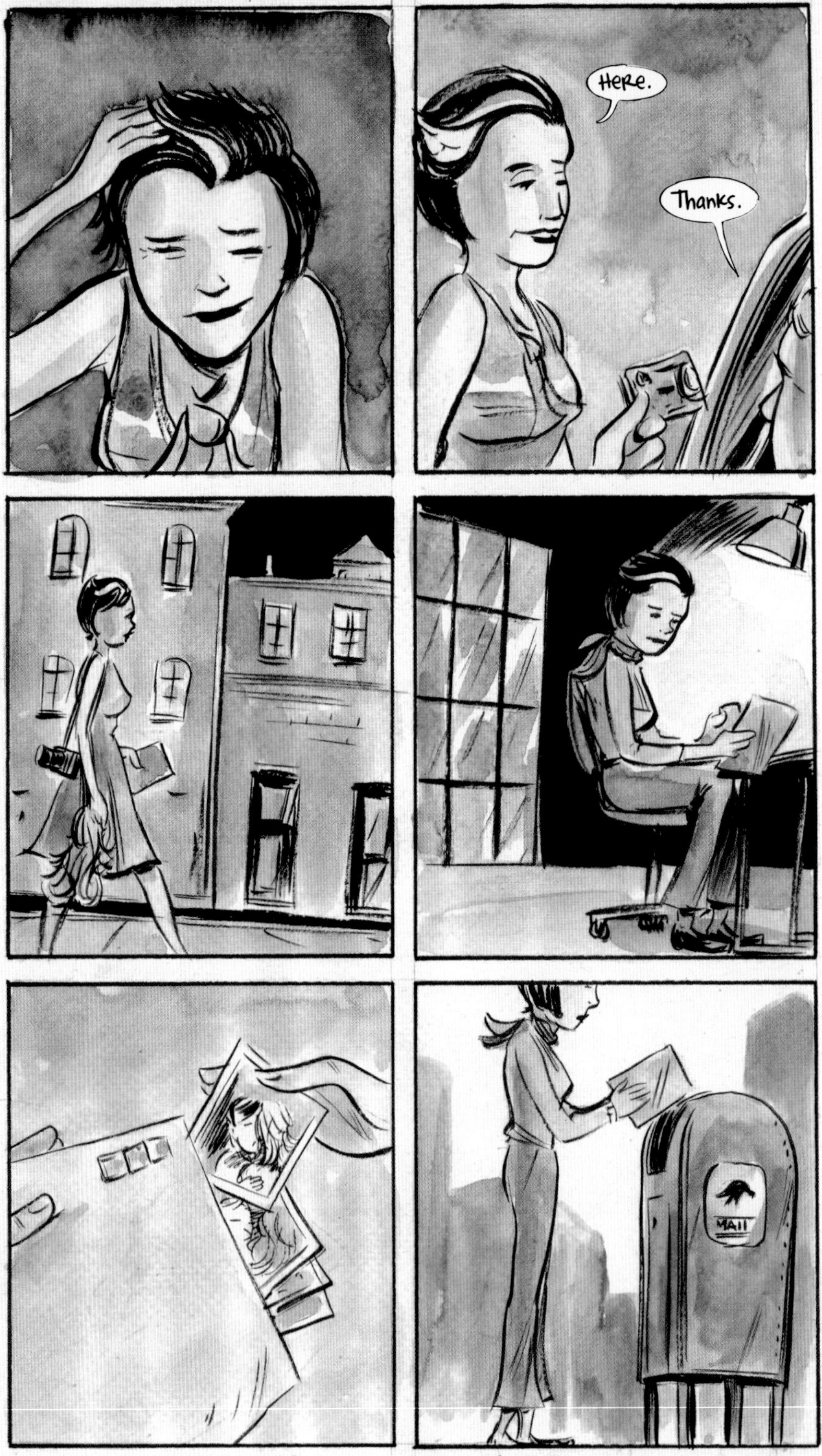
Here.
Thanks.
MAIL

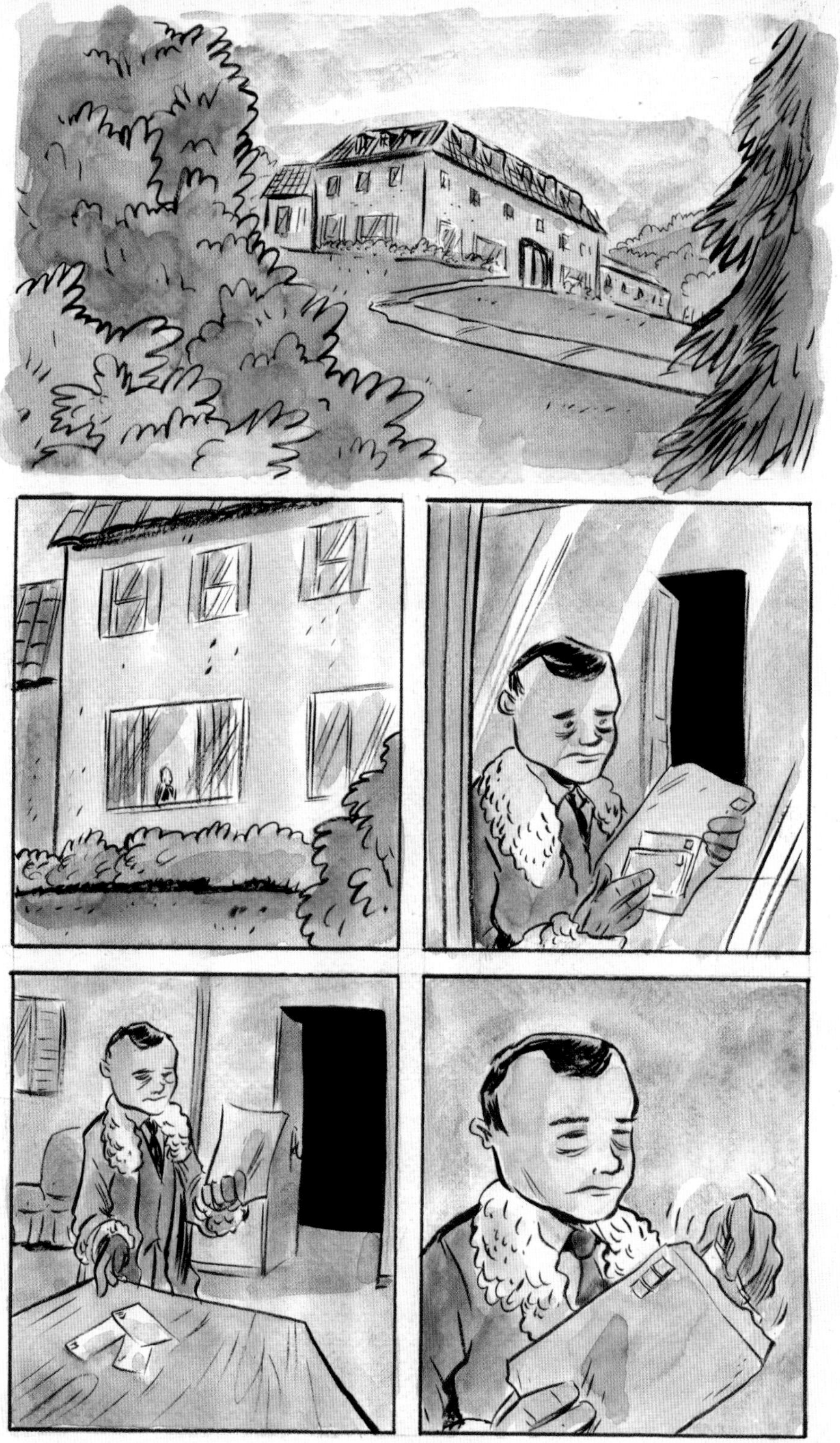

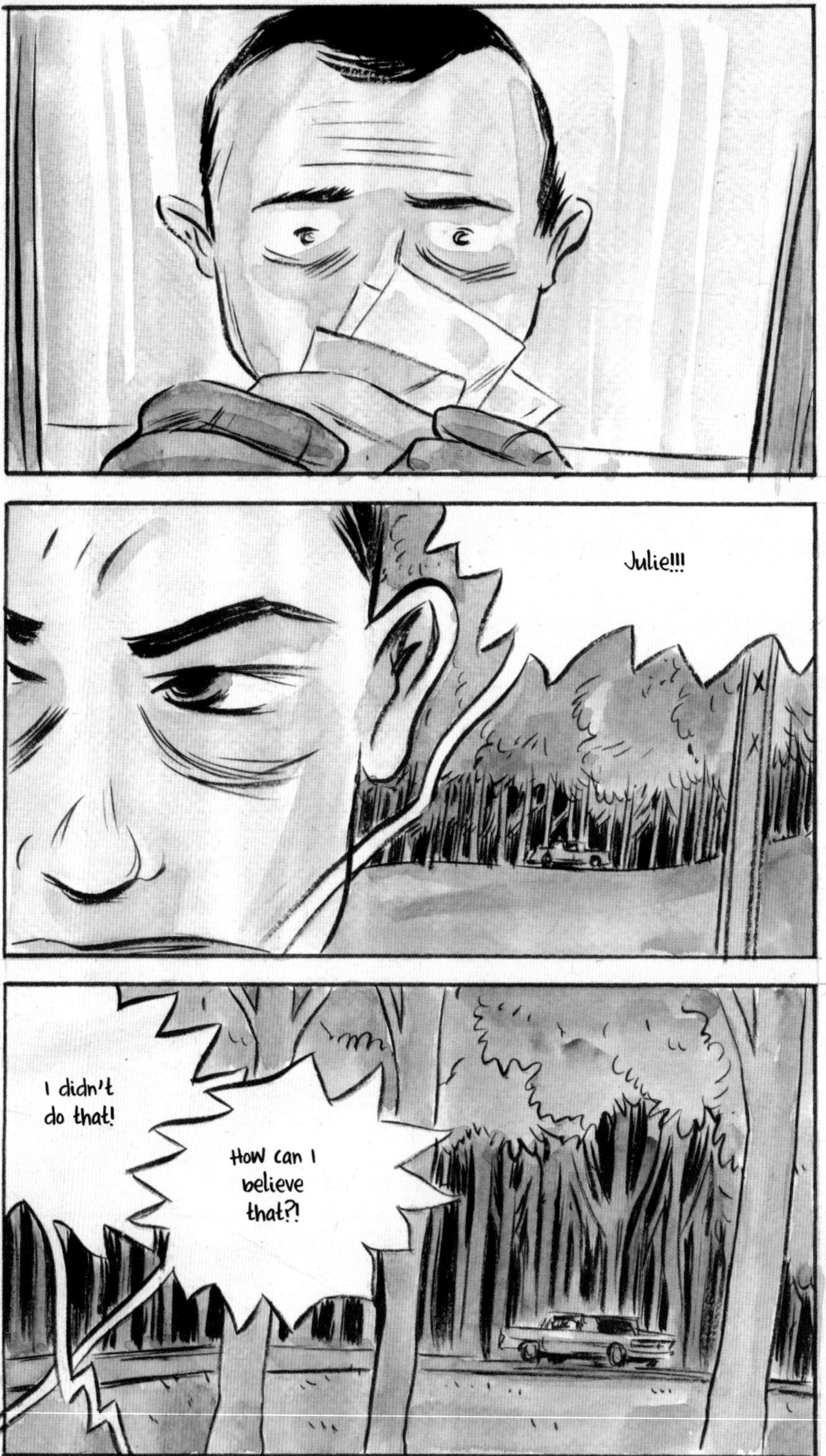
Julie!!!
I didn't do that!
How can I believe that?!

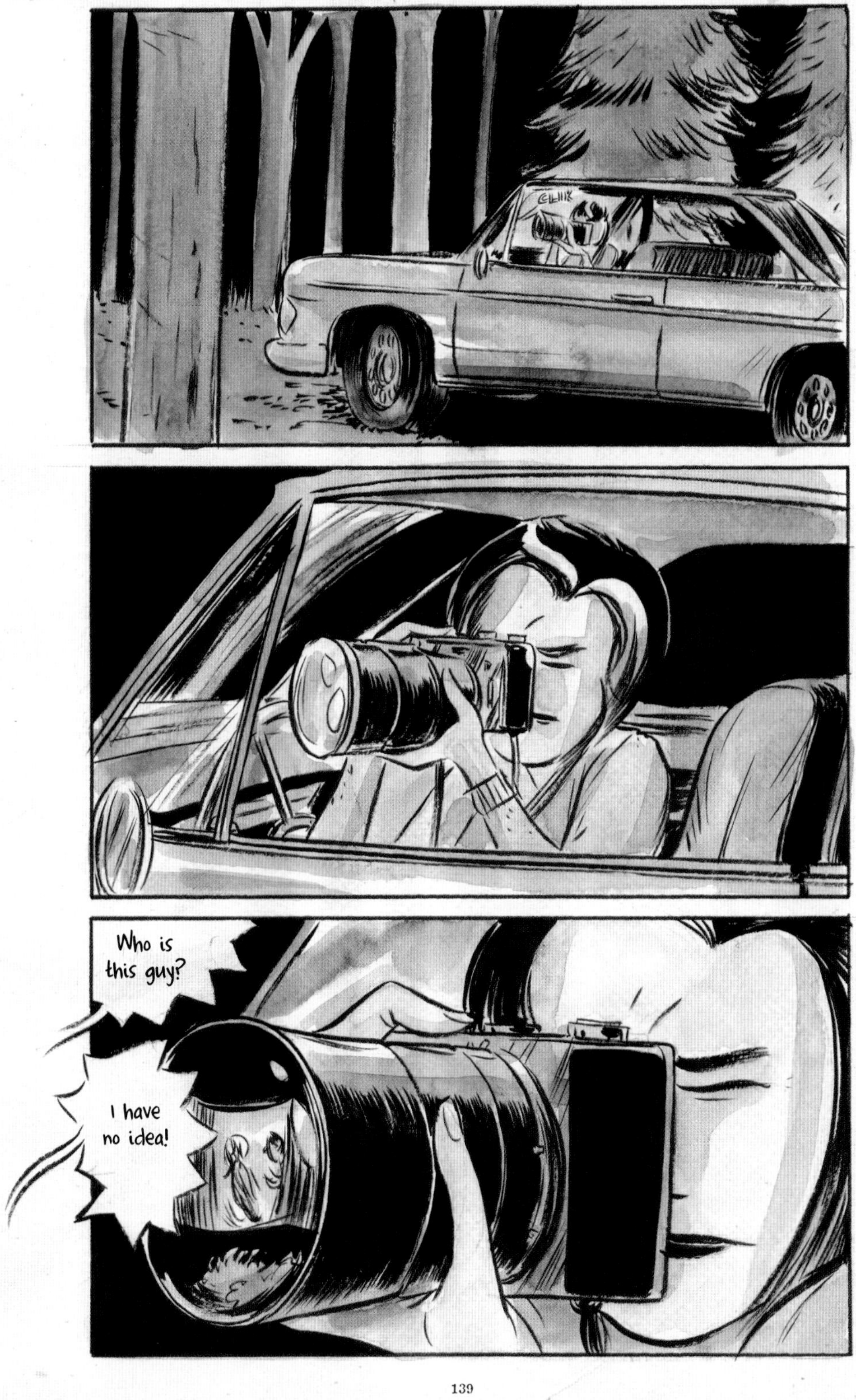
CLIK
Who is this guy?
I have no idea!

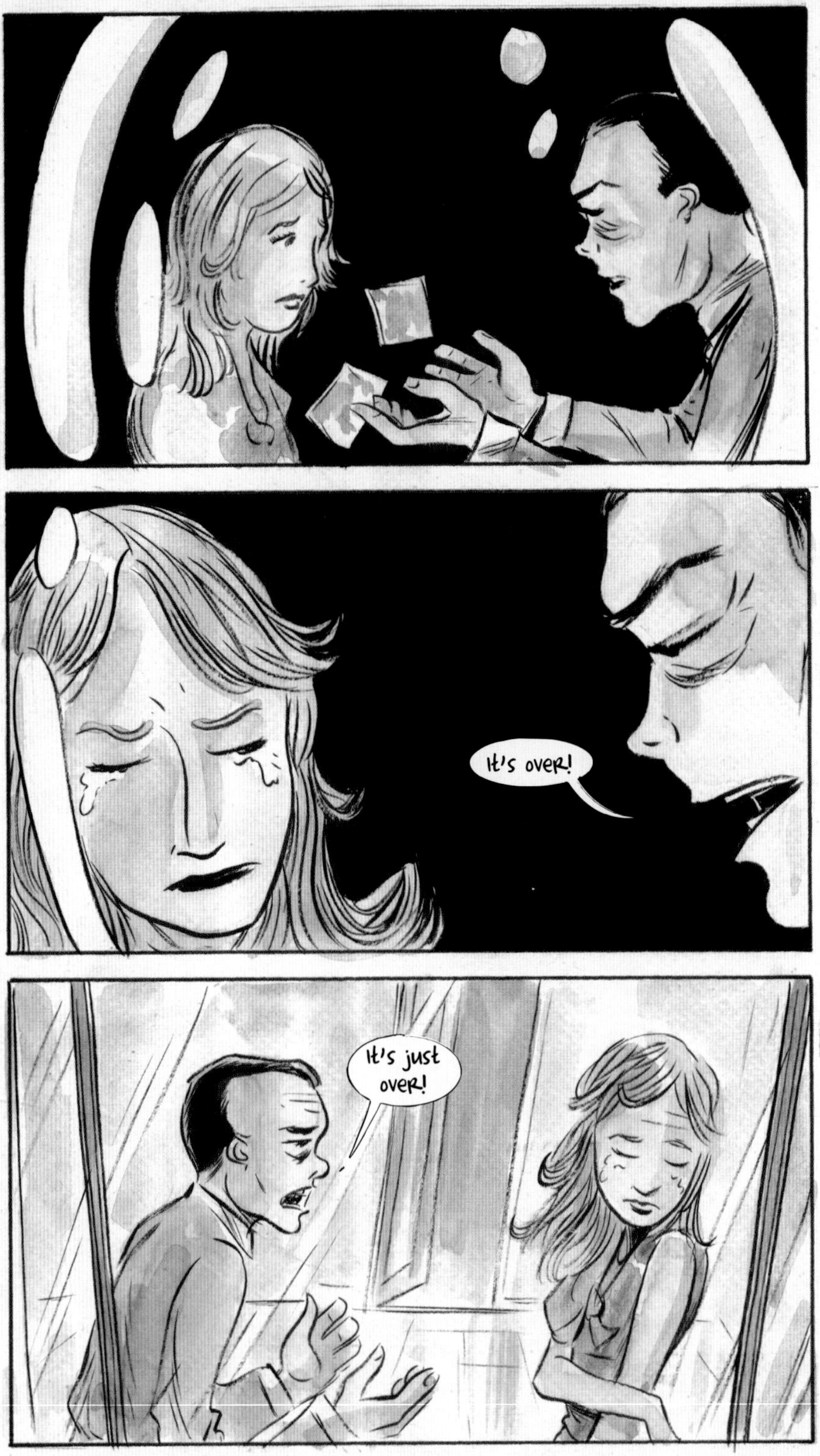
It's over!
It's just over!

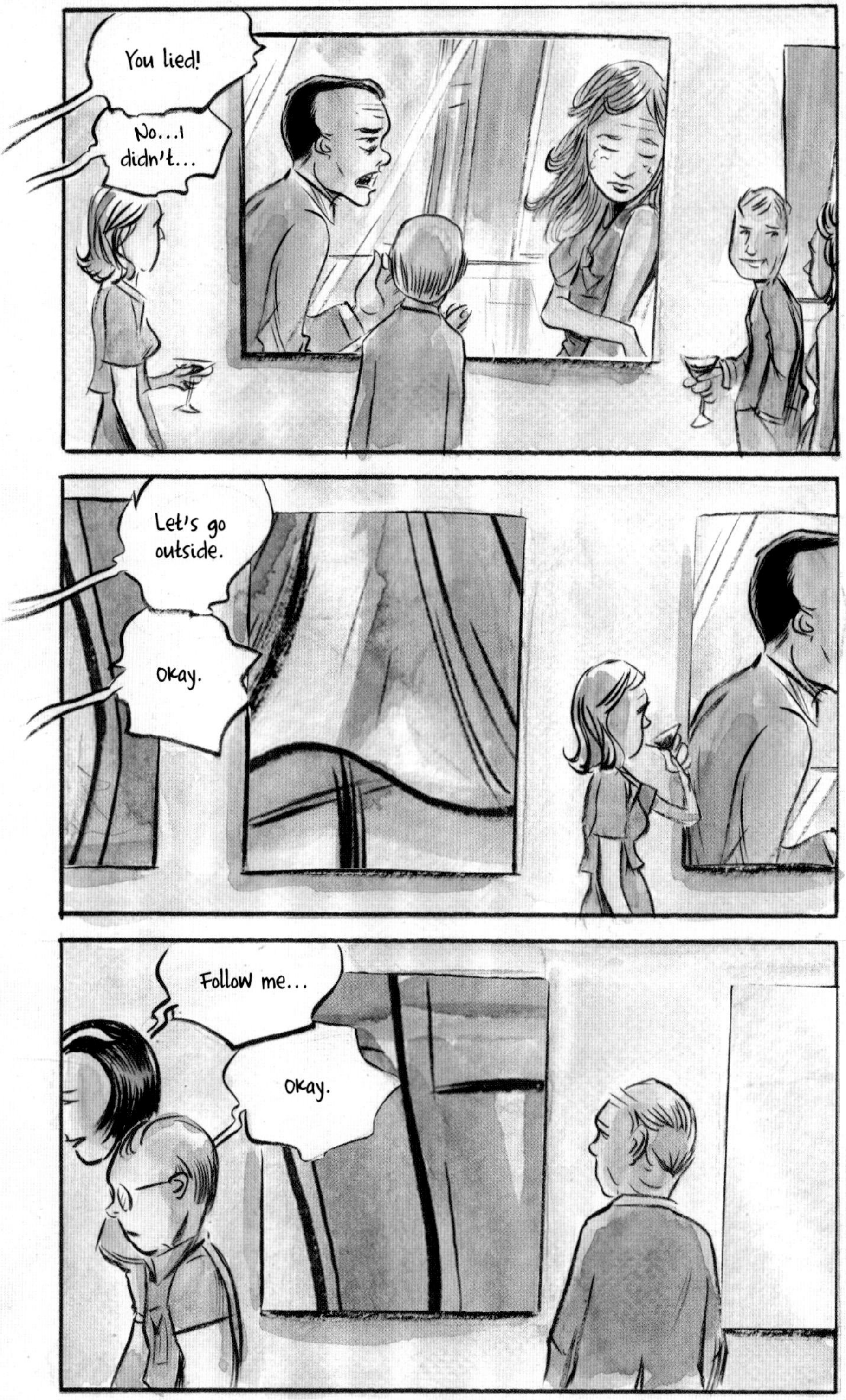
You lied!
No...I didn't...
Let's go outside.
Okay.
Follow me...
Okay.

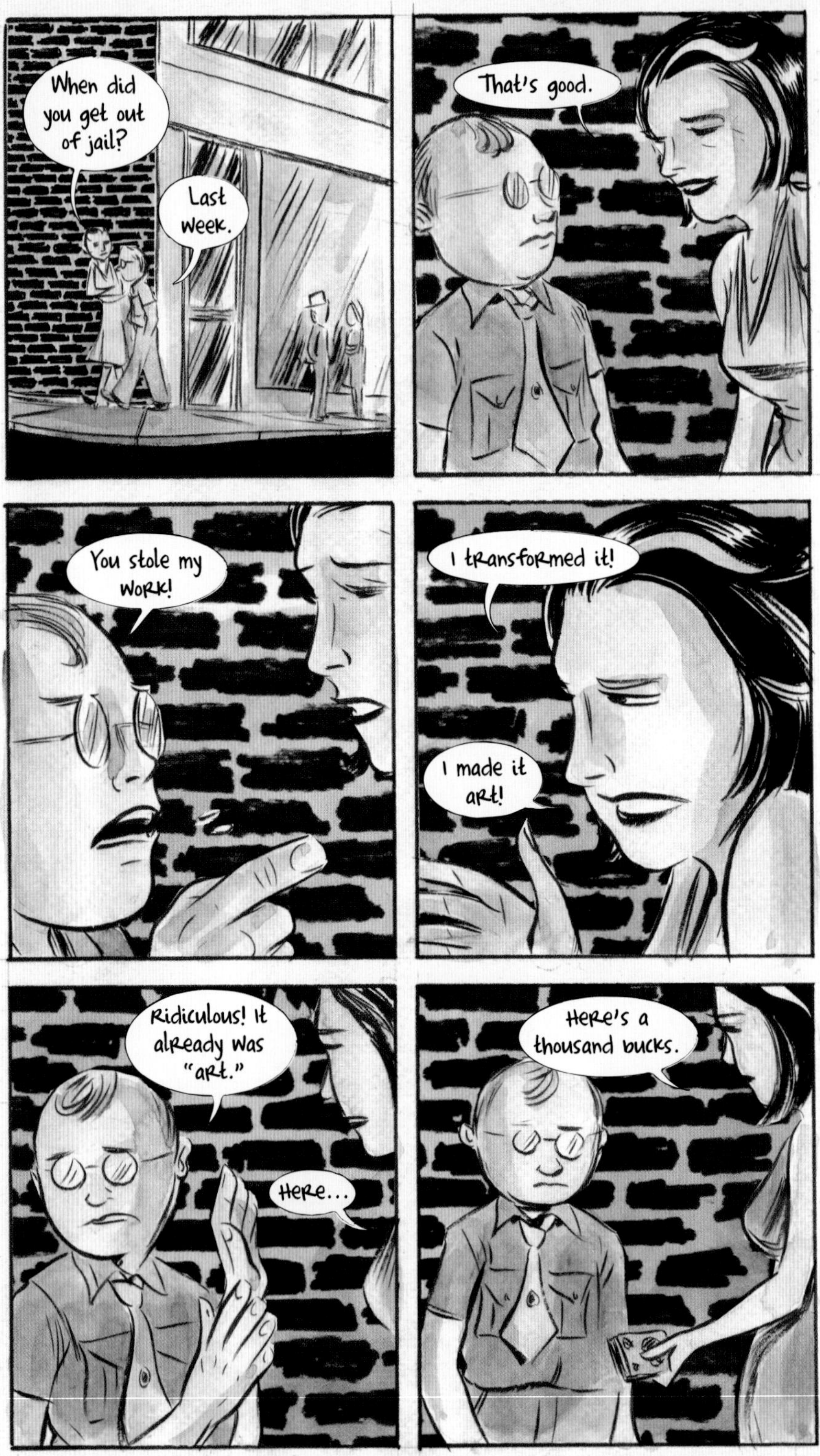
When did you get out of jail?
Last week.
That's good.
You stole my work!
I transformed it!
I made it art!
Ridiculous! It already was "art."
Here...
Here's a thousand bucks.

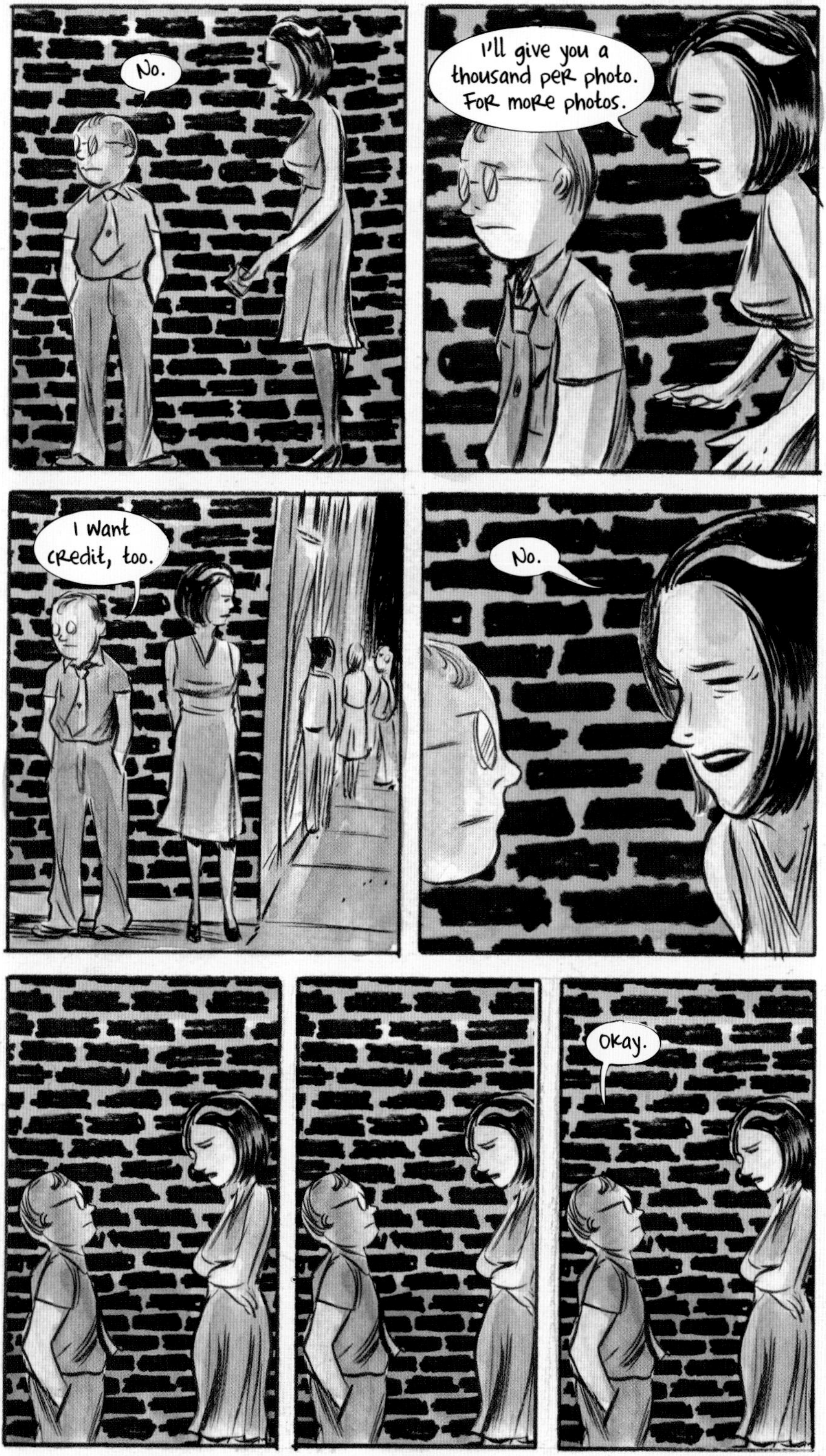
No.
I'll give you a thousand per photo. For more photos.
I want credit, too.
No.
Okay.

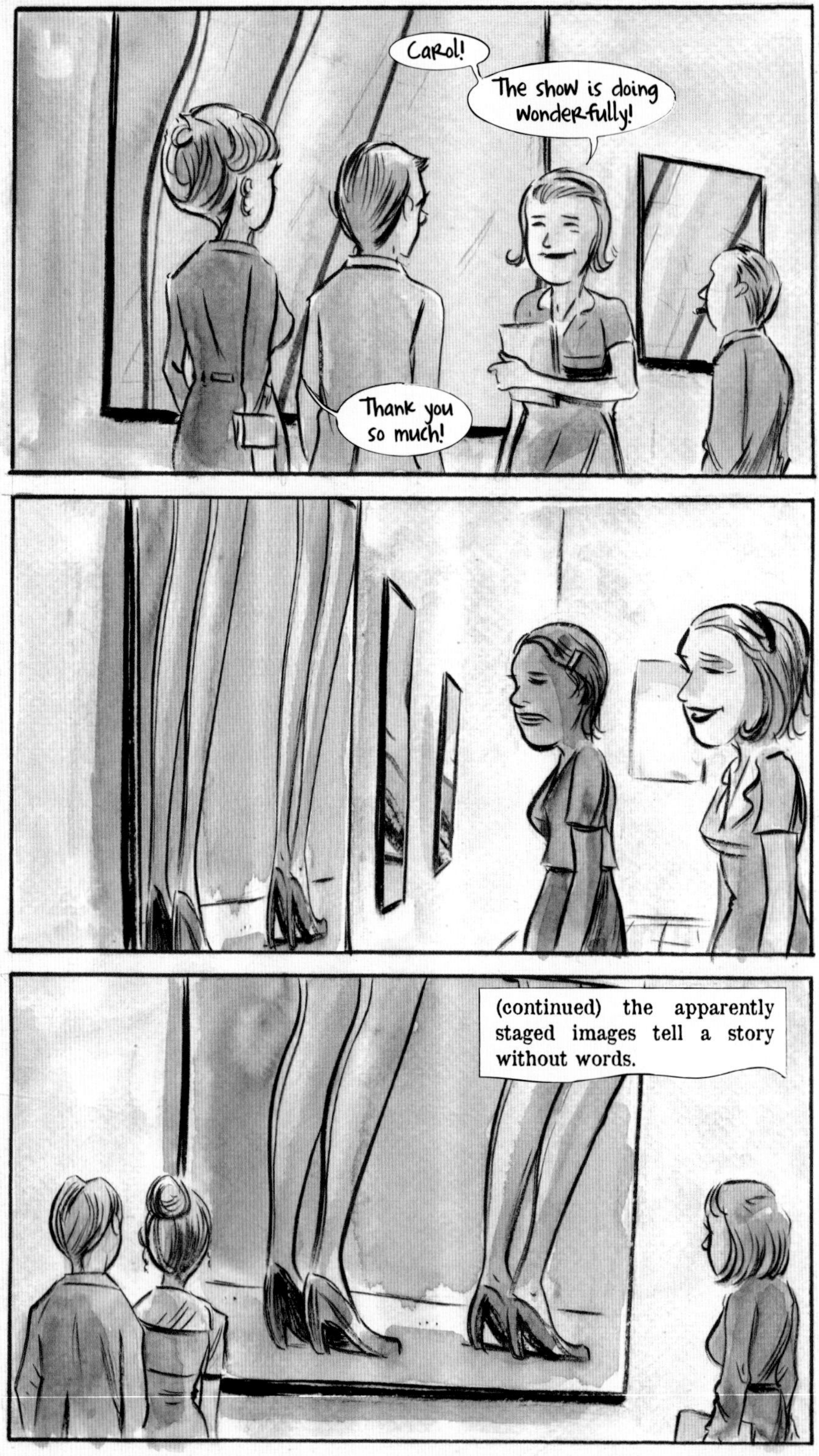
Carol!
The show is doing wonderfully!
Thank you so much!
(continued) the apparently staged images tell a story without words.

GA

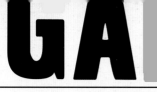

(continued from page C1)
were lucky to get a sneak preview of Annalyse Gould's photo exhibit opening next month.

The photos on exhibit have an uncanny honesty to them. The staging and models ring true. Each snapshot becomes its own devastating masterpiece. We can only hope that Gallery Gould brings work of this high caliber to the city in the months and years to come.

Gould Interview (continued)

We caught up to Gould the night before the capture of the elusive Fur Smuggler. He attributes the capture to a nearly obsessive attention to detail and the vigilant help of the good citizens of Red Wheel Barrow. Crime reports would indicate that the city owes Gould more than a heartfelt thanks. Crime rates may be on the rise, but the conviction rate of suspects is nearly perfect in all of Gould's cases.

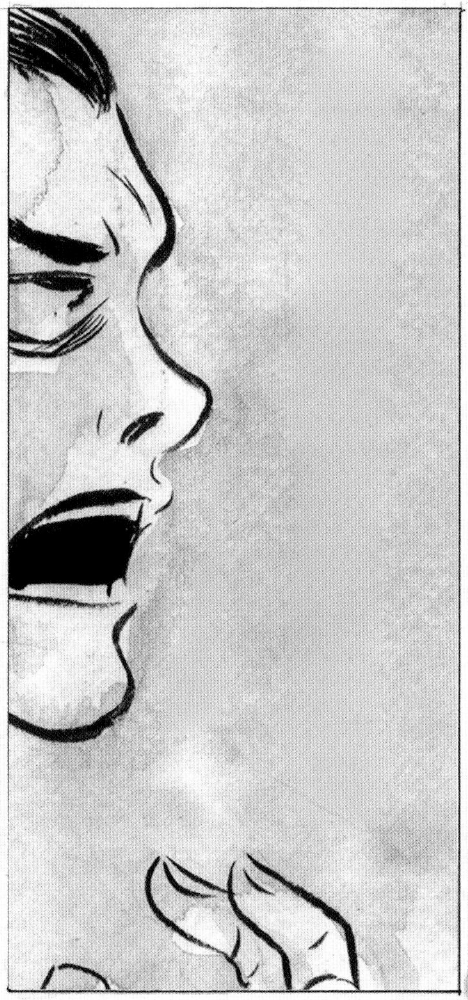

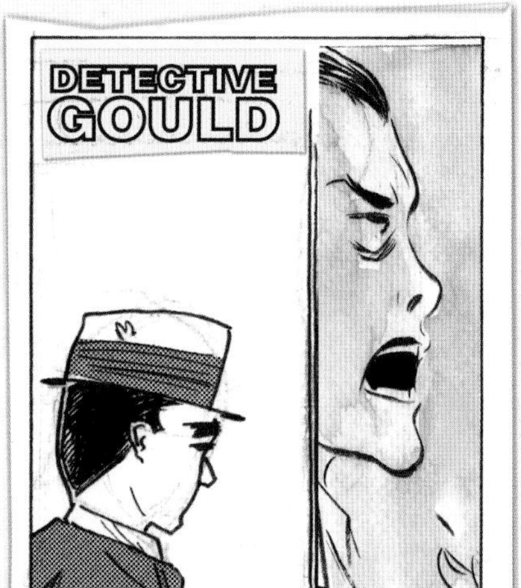
DETECTIVE
GOULD
repro from following page
15

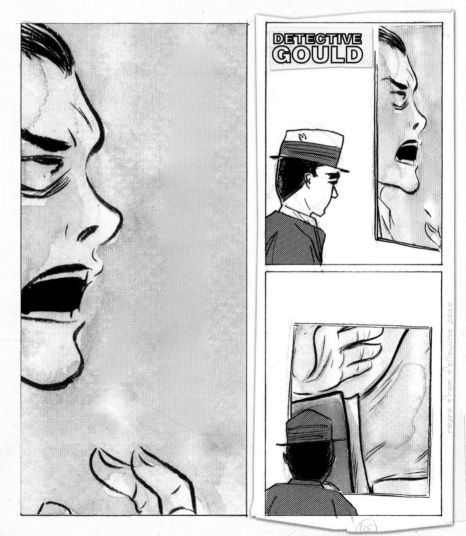

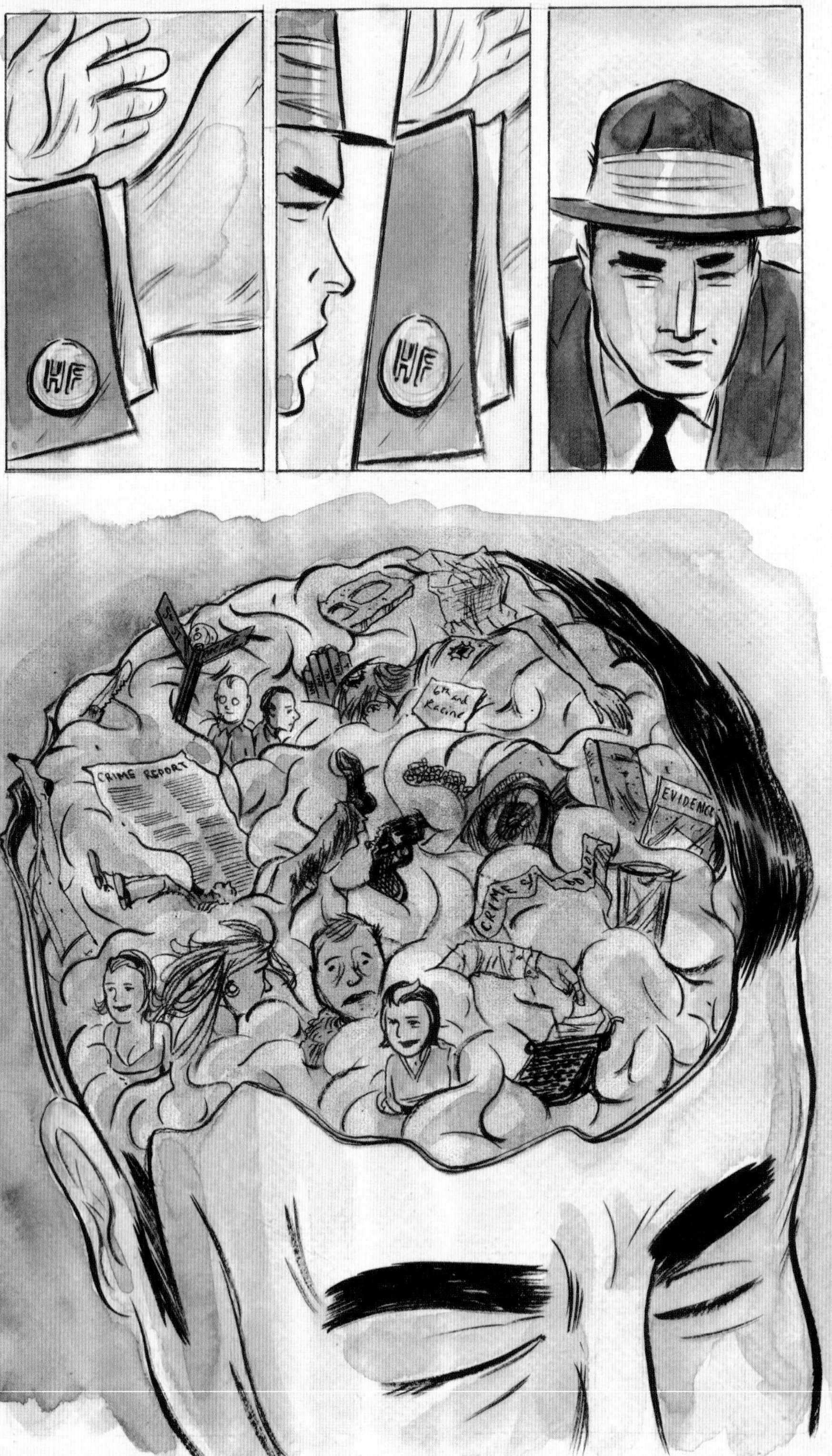
HF
HF
CRIME REPORT
6th and Racine
EVIDENCE

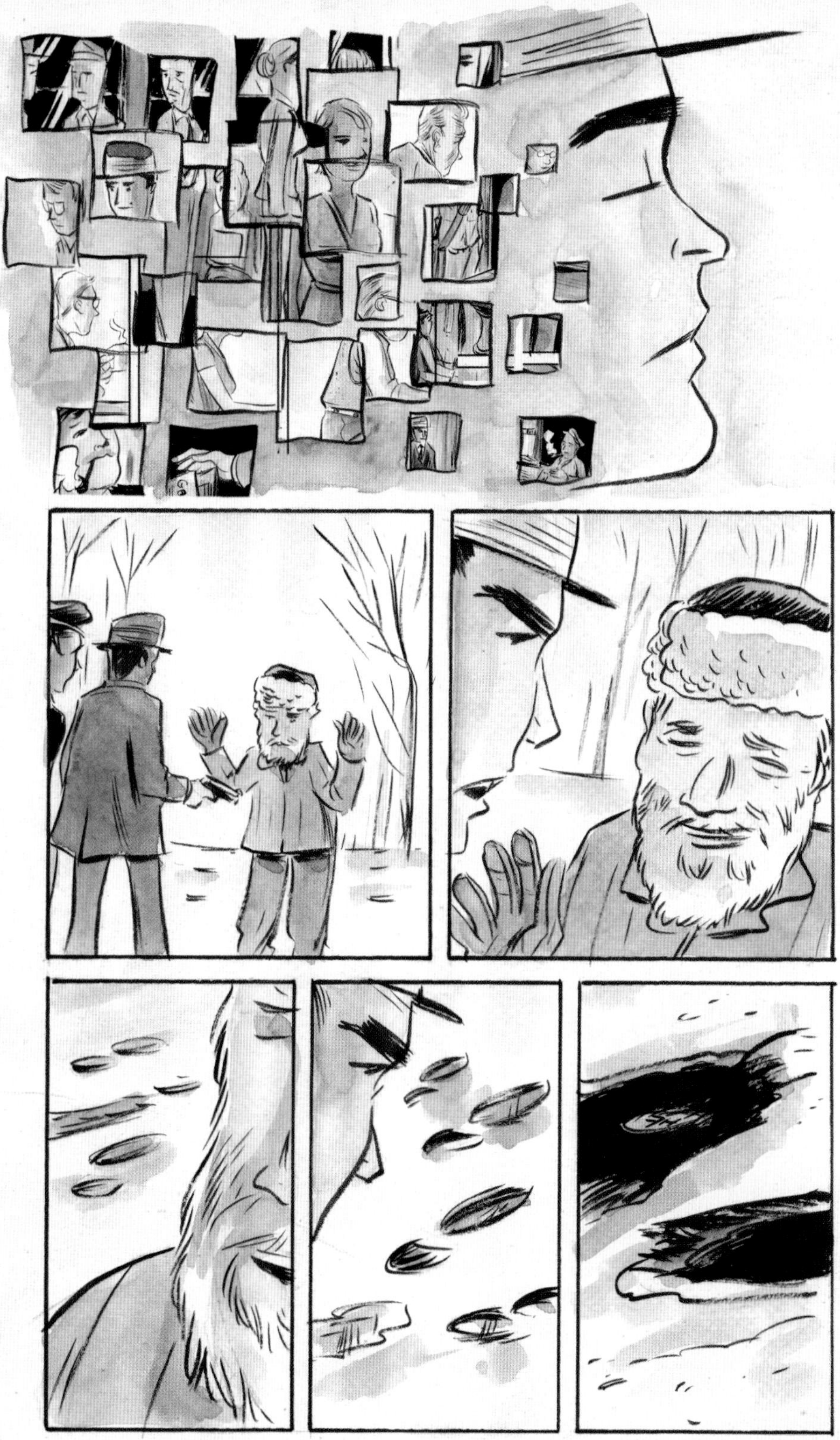

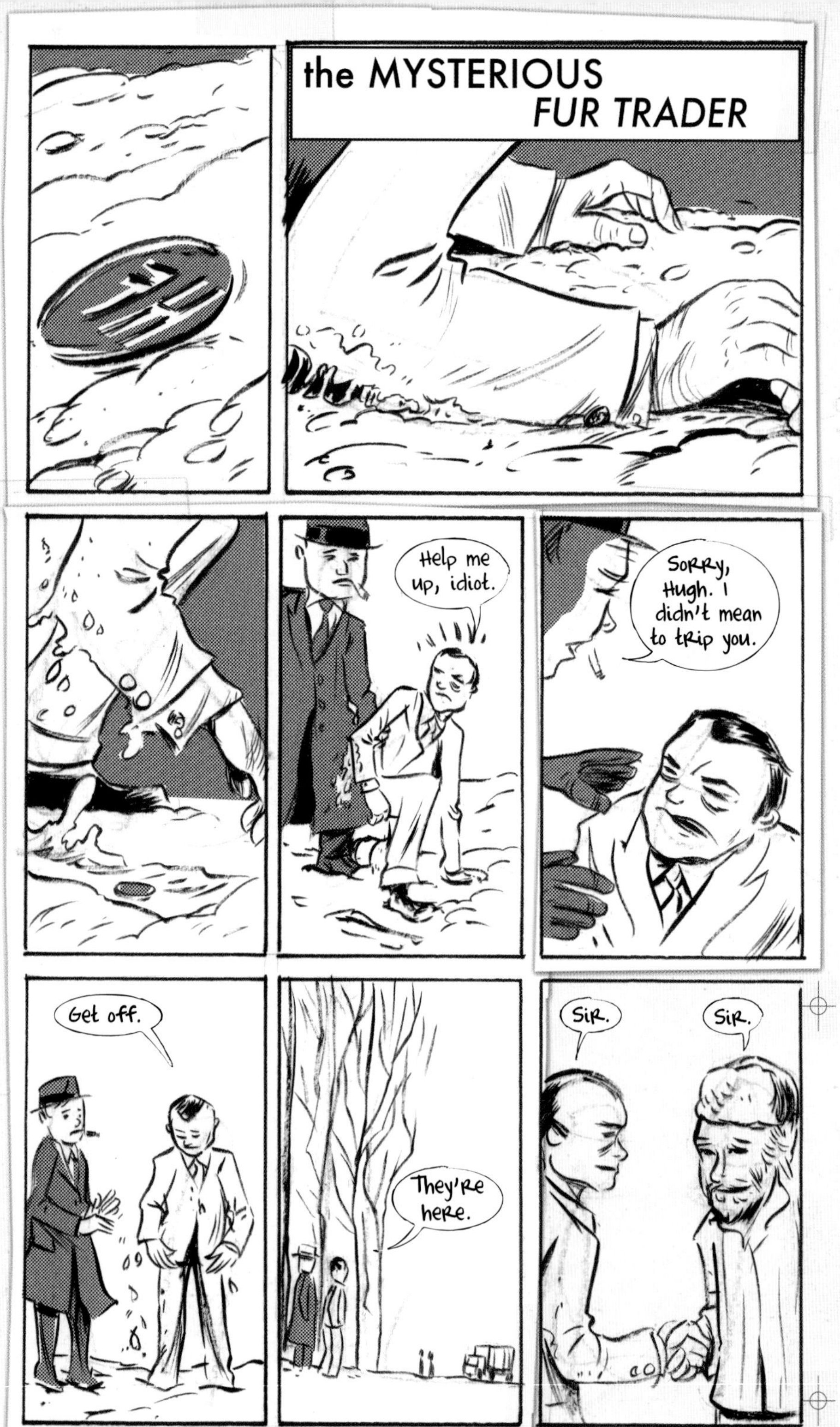

the MYSTERIOUS FUR TRADER
Help me up, idiot.
Sorry, Hugh. I didn't mean to trip you.
Get off.
They're here.
Sir.
Sir.

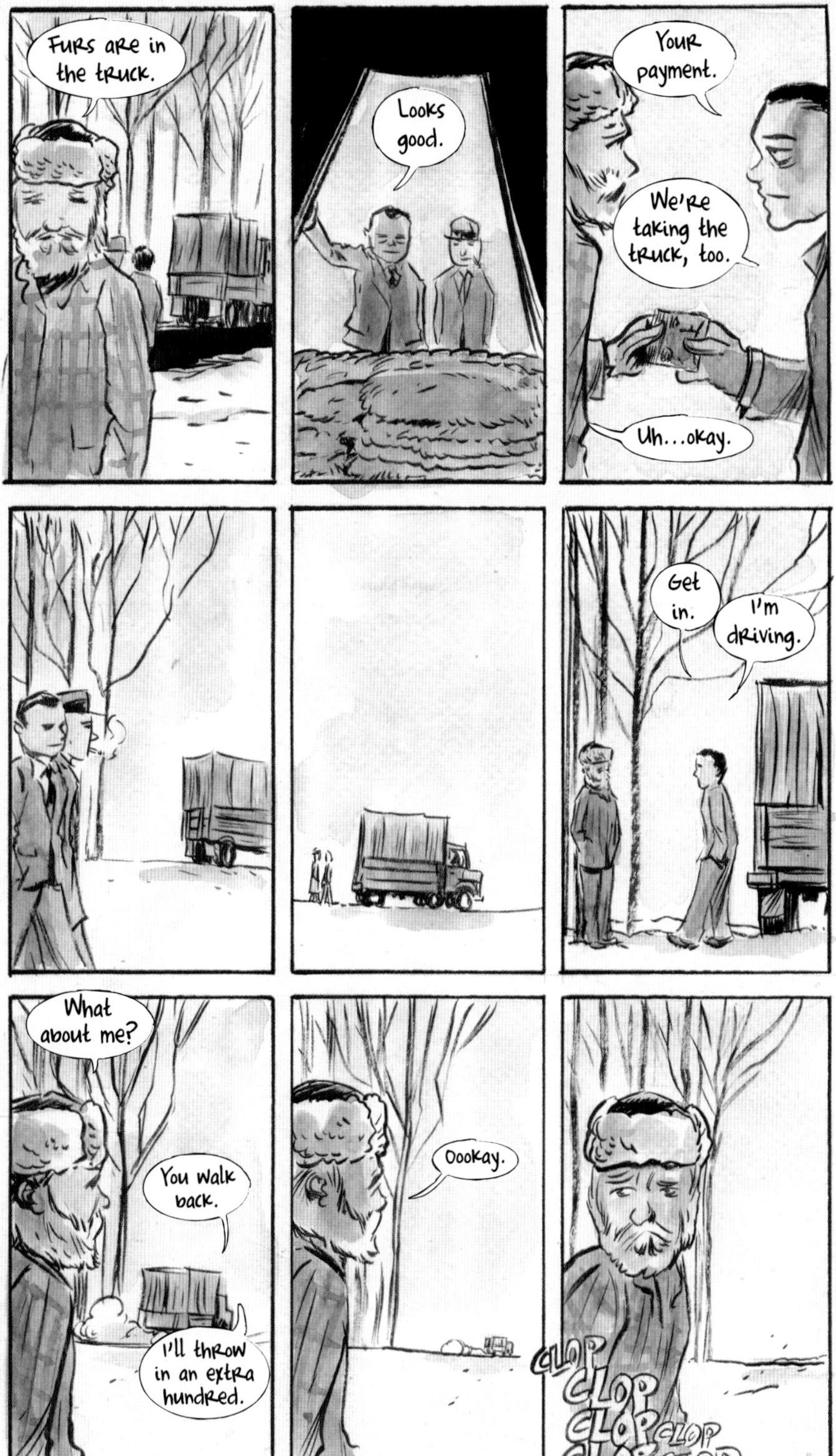

Furs are in the truck.
Looks good.
Your payment.
We're taking the truck, too.
Uh...okay.
Get in.
I'm driving.
What about me?
You walk back.
I'll throw in an extra hundred.
Oookay.
CLOP
CLOP
CLOP CLOP
CLOP CLOP
CLOP

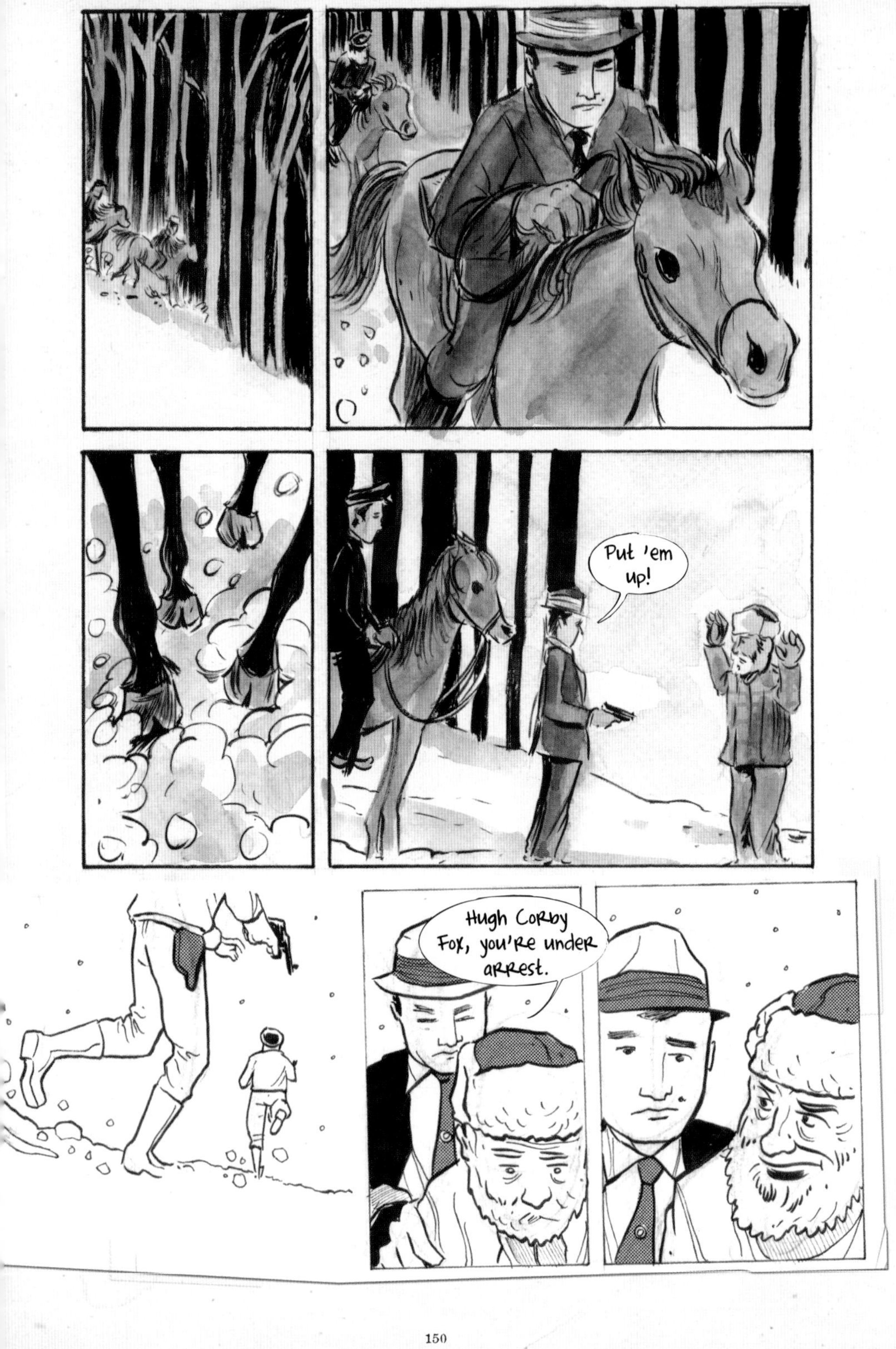
Put 'em up!
Hugh Corby Fox, you're under arrest.

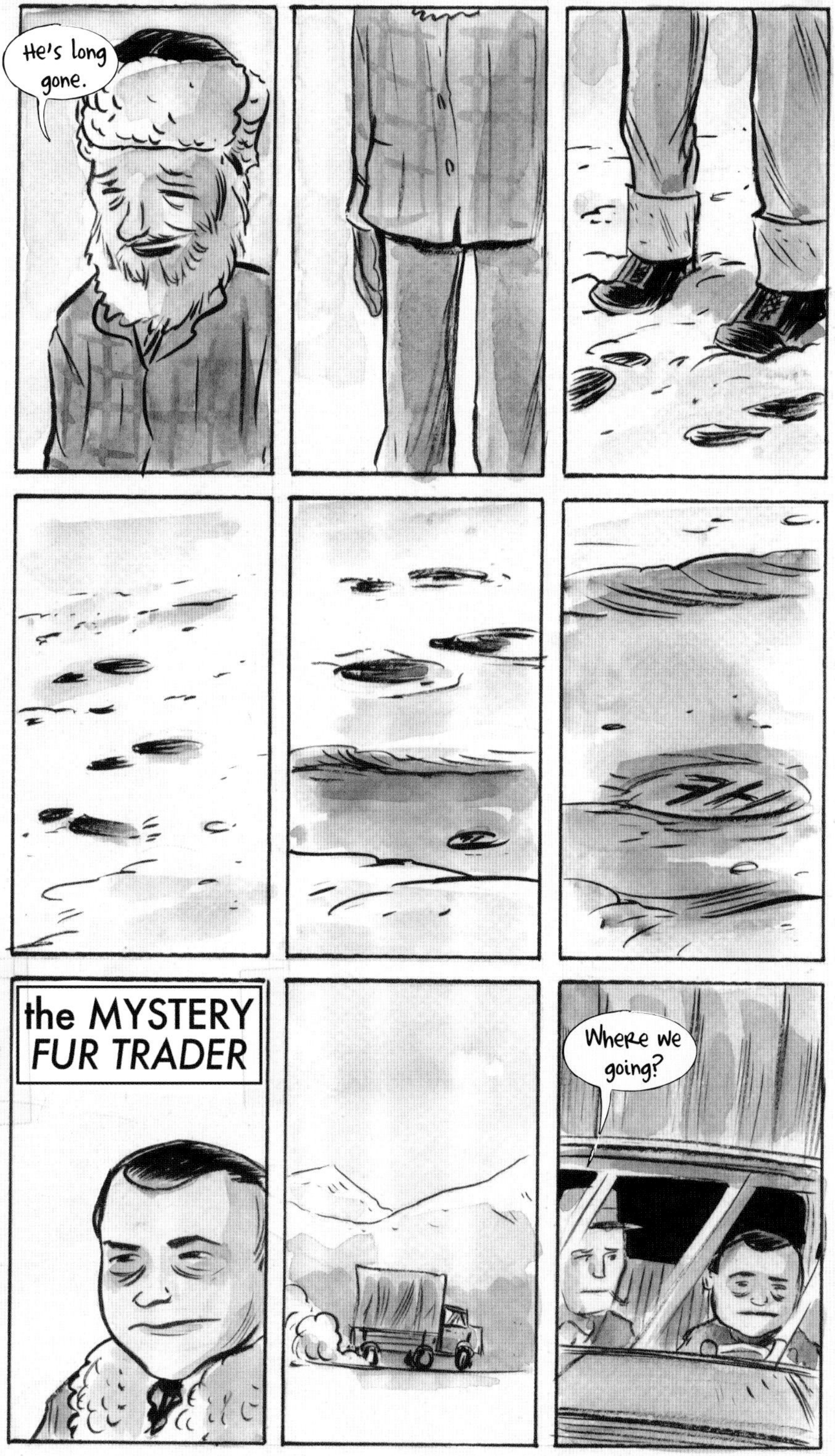
He's long gone.
the MYSTERY FUR TRADER
Where we going?

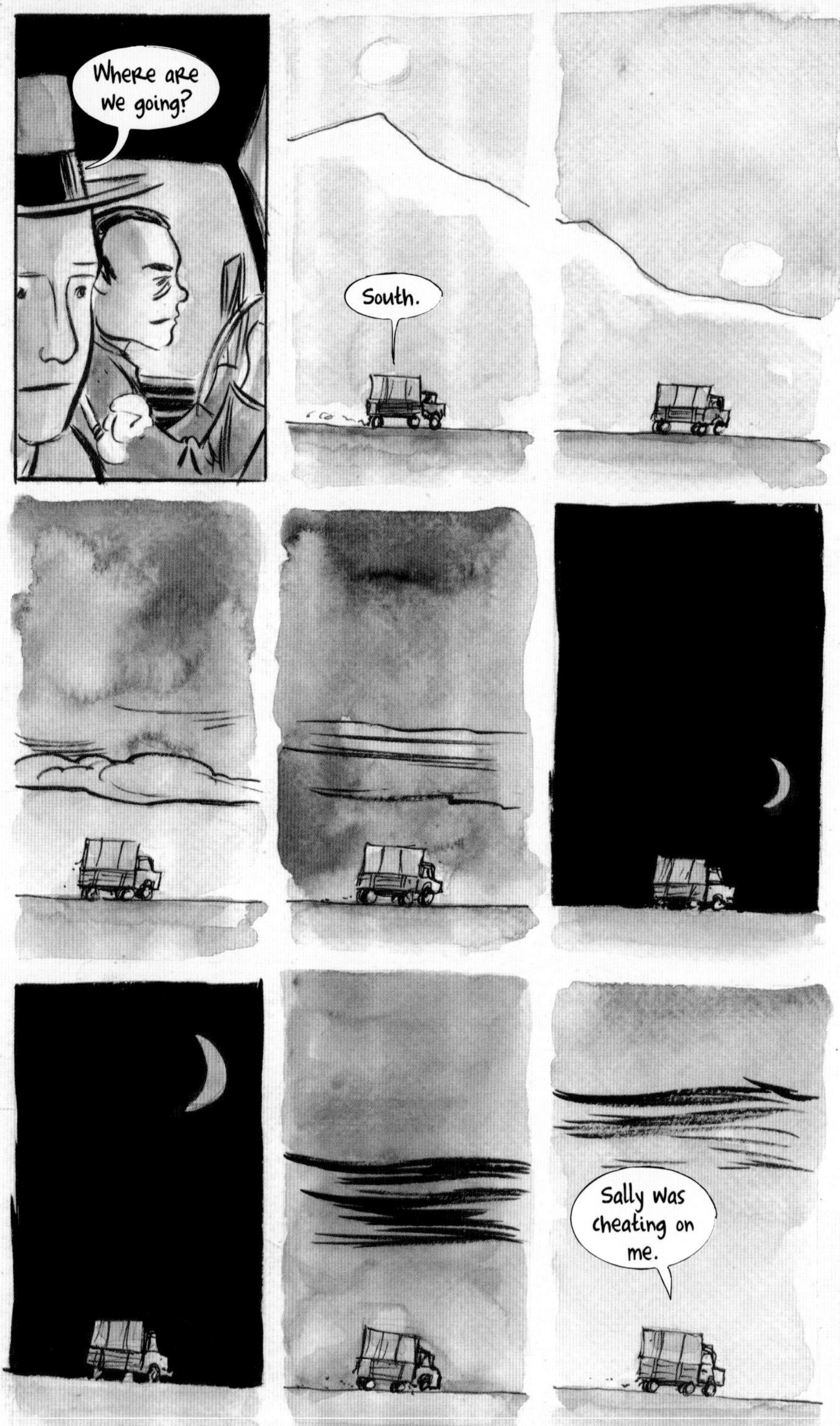
Where are we going?
South.
Sally was cheating on me.

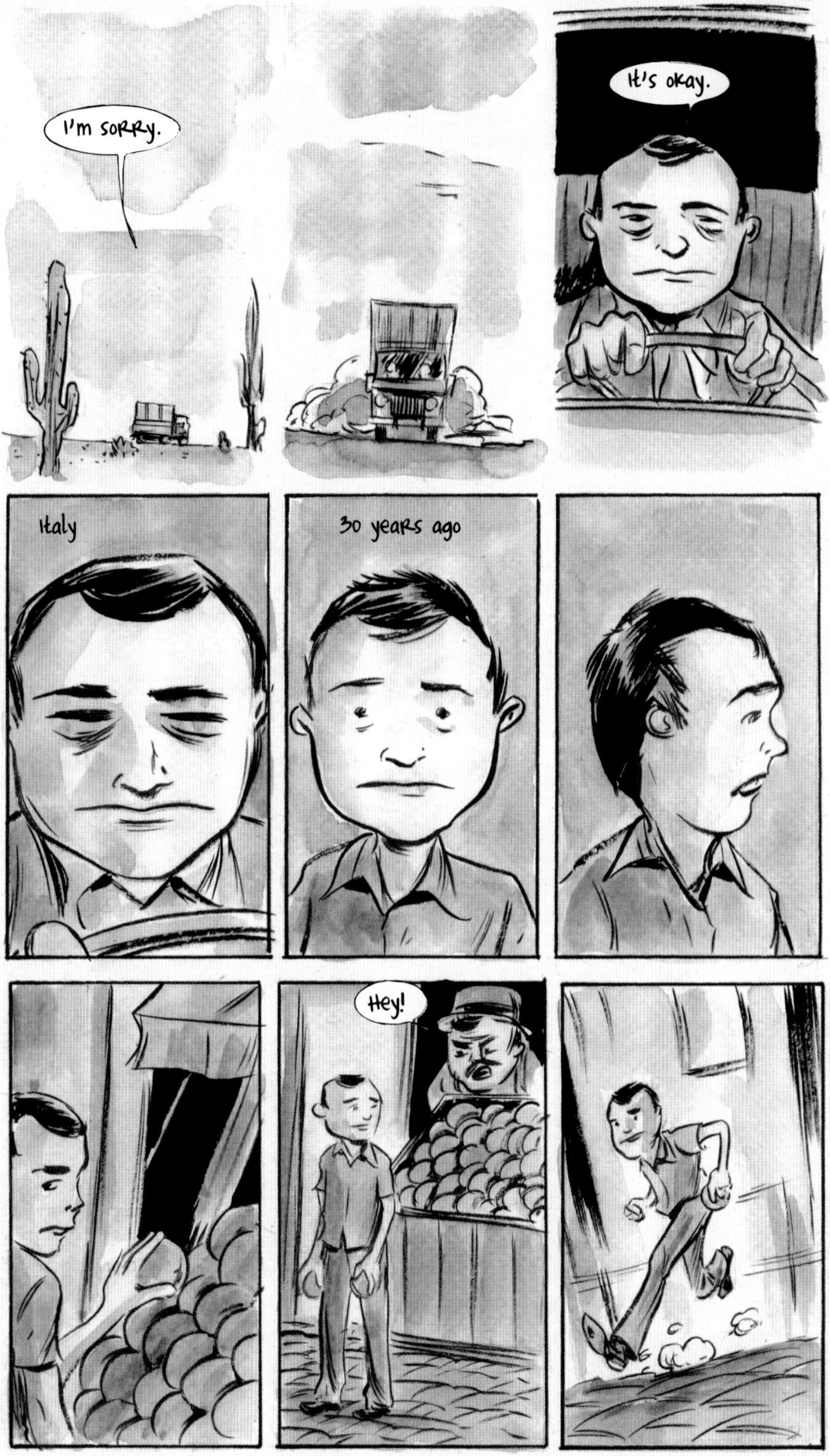
I'm sorry.
It's okay.
Italy
30 years ago
Hey!

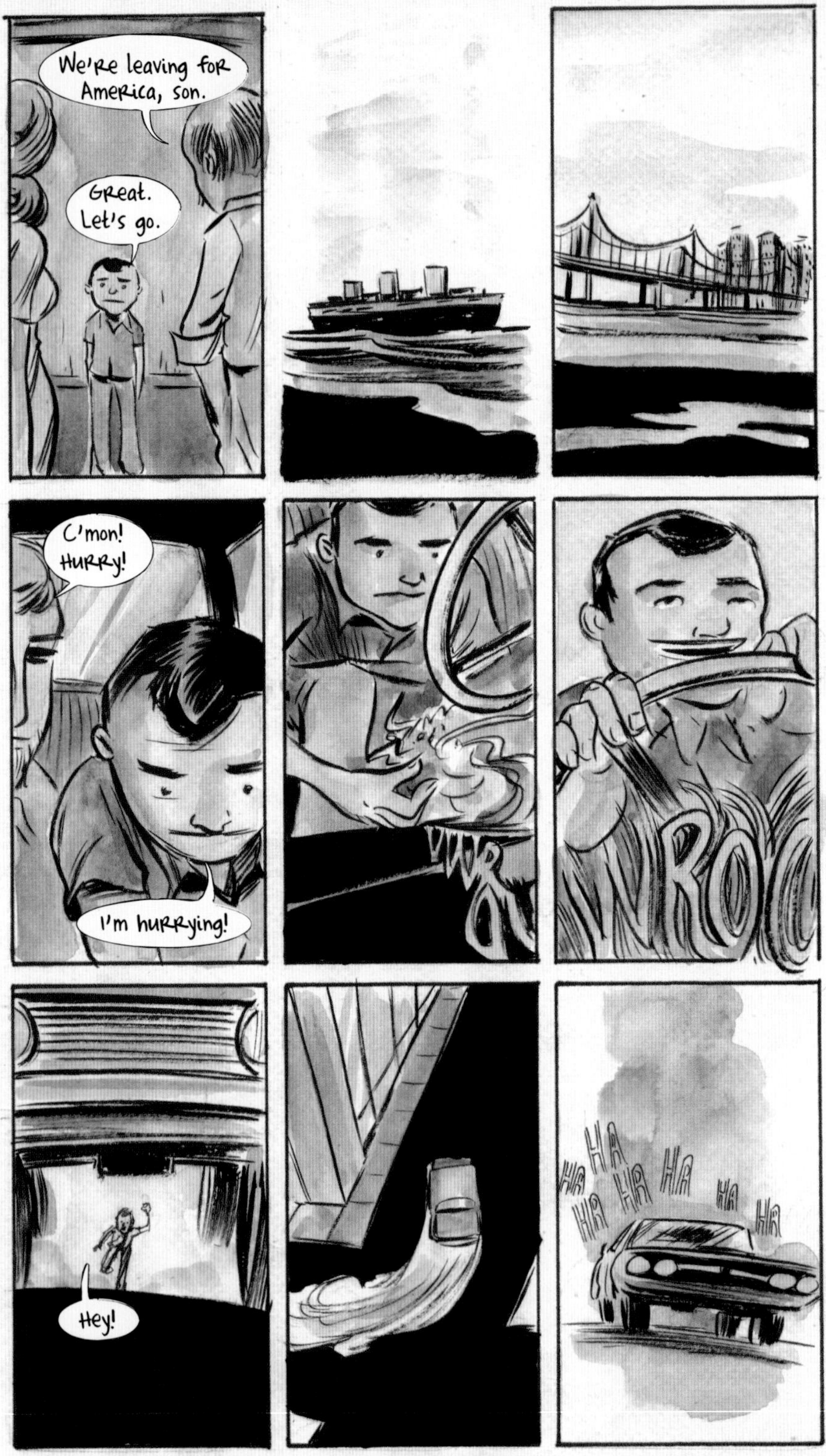
We're leaving for America, son.
Great. Let's go.
C'mon! Hurry!
I'm hurrying!
Hey!
HA HA HA HA HA HA HA HA

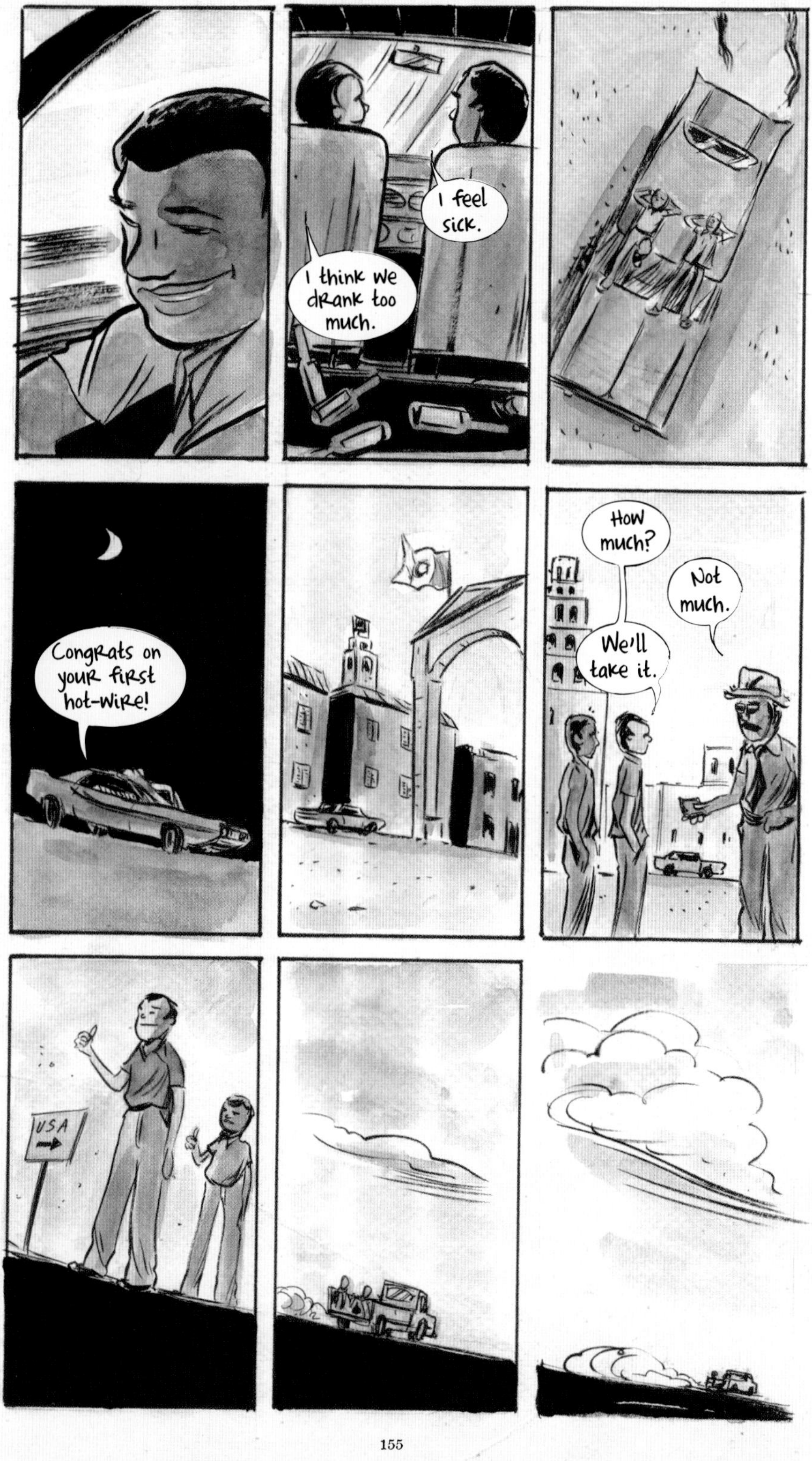
I feel sick.
I think we drank too much.
Congrats on your first hot-wire!
How much?
Not much.
We'll take it.
USA

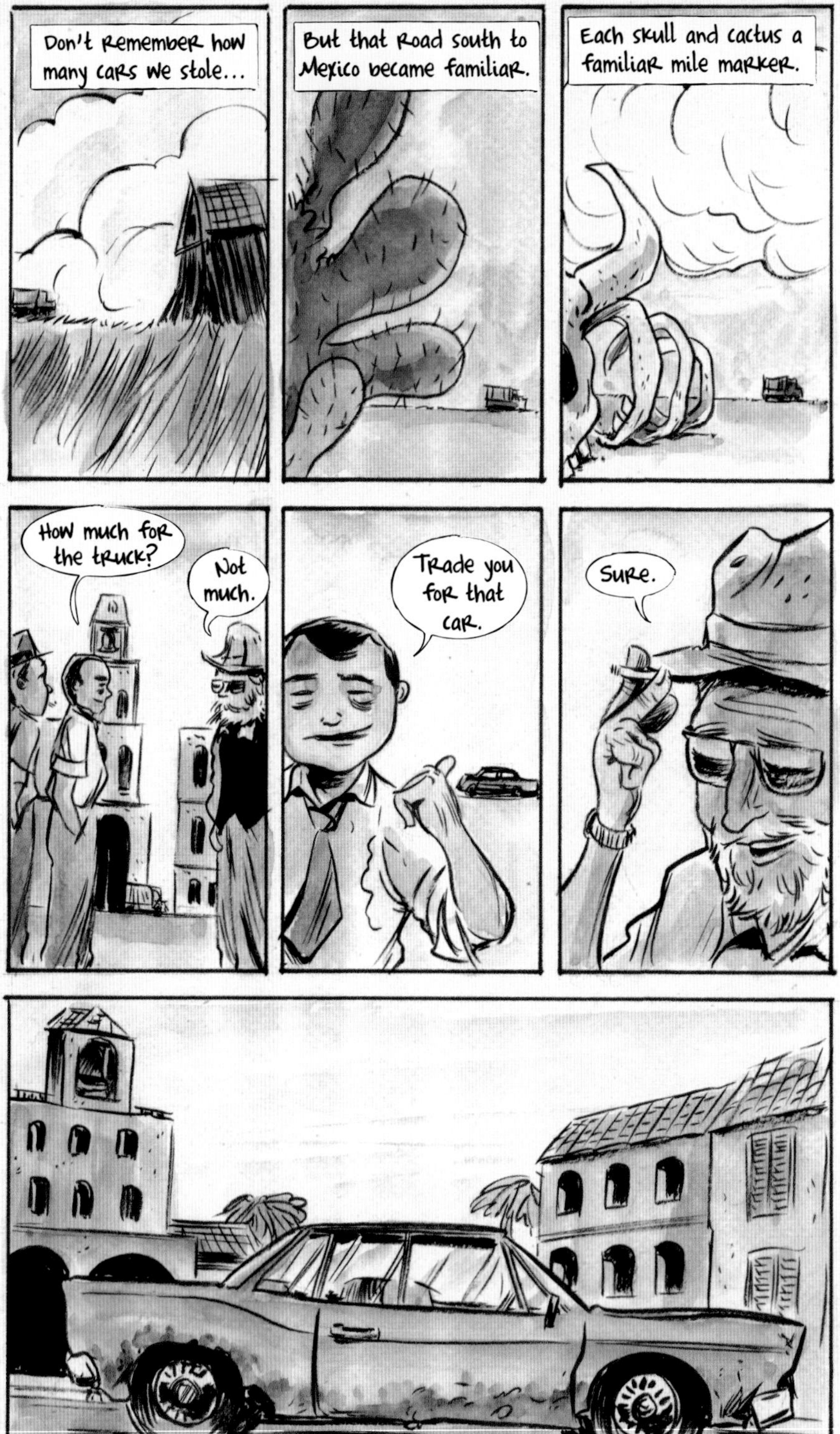

Don't remember how many cars we stole...
But that road south to Mexico became familiar.
Each skull and cactus a familiar mile marker.
How much for the truck?
Not much.
Trade you for that car.
Sure.

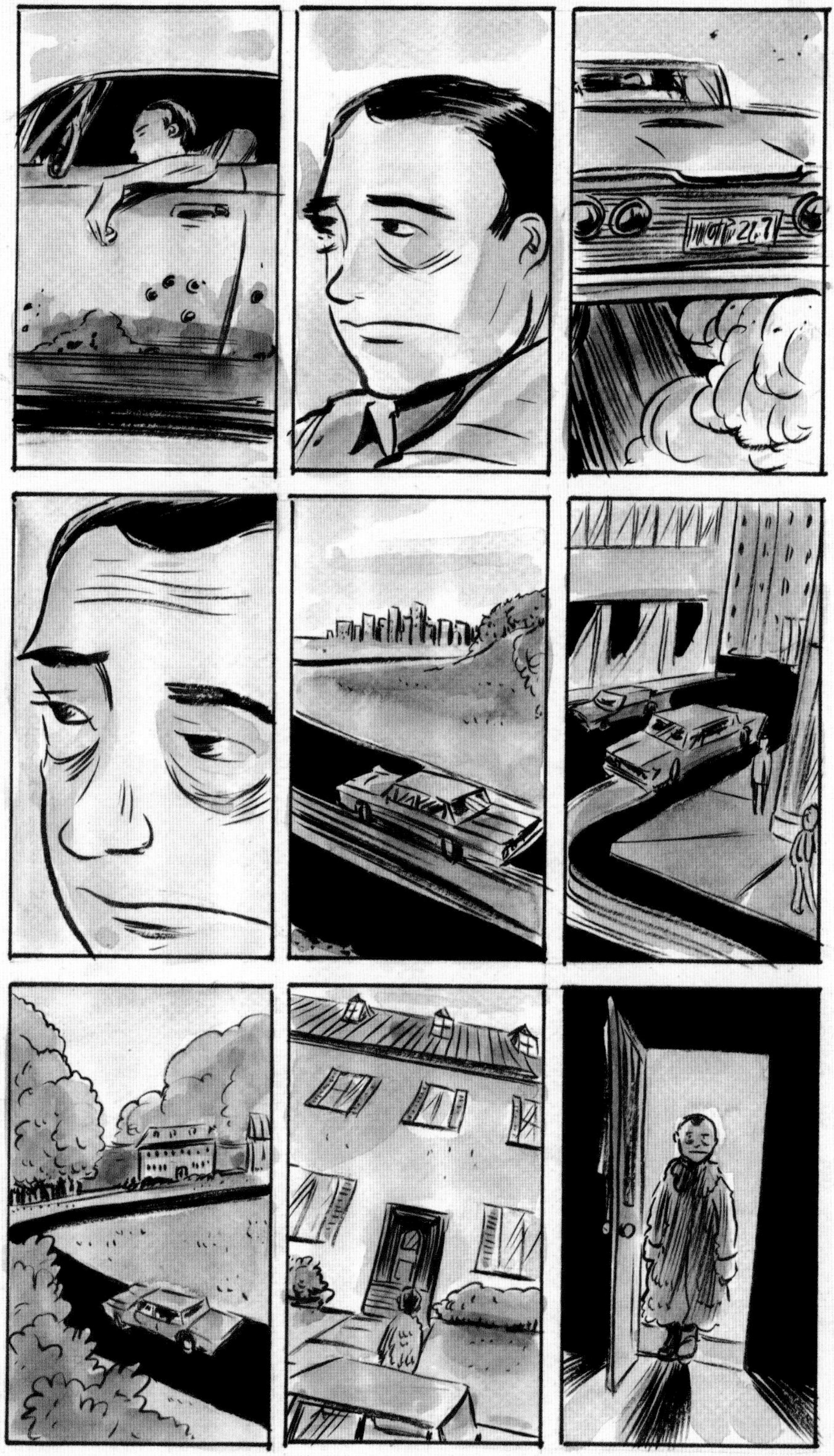

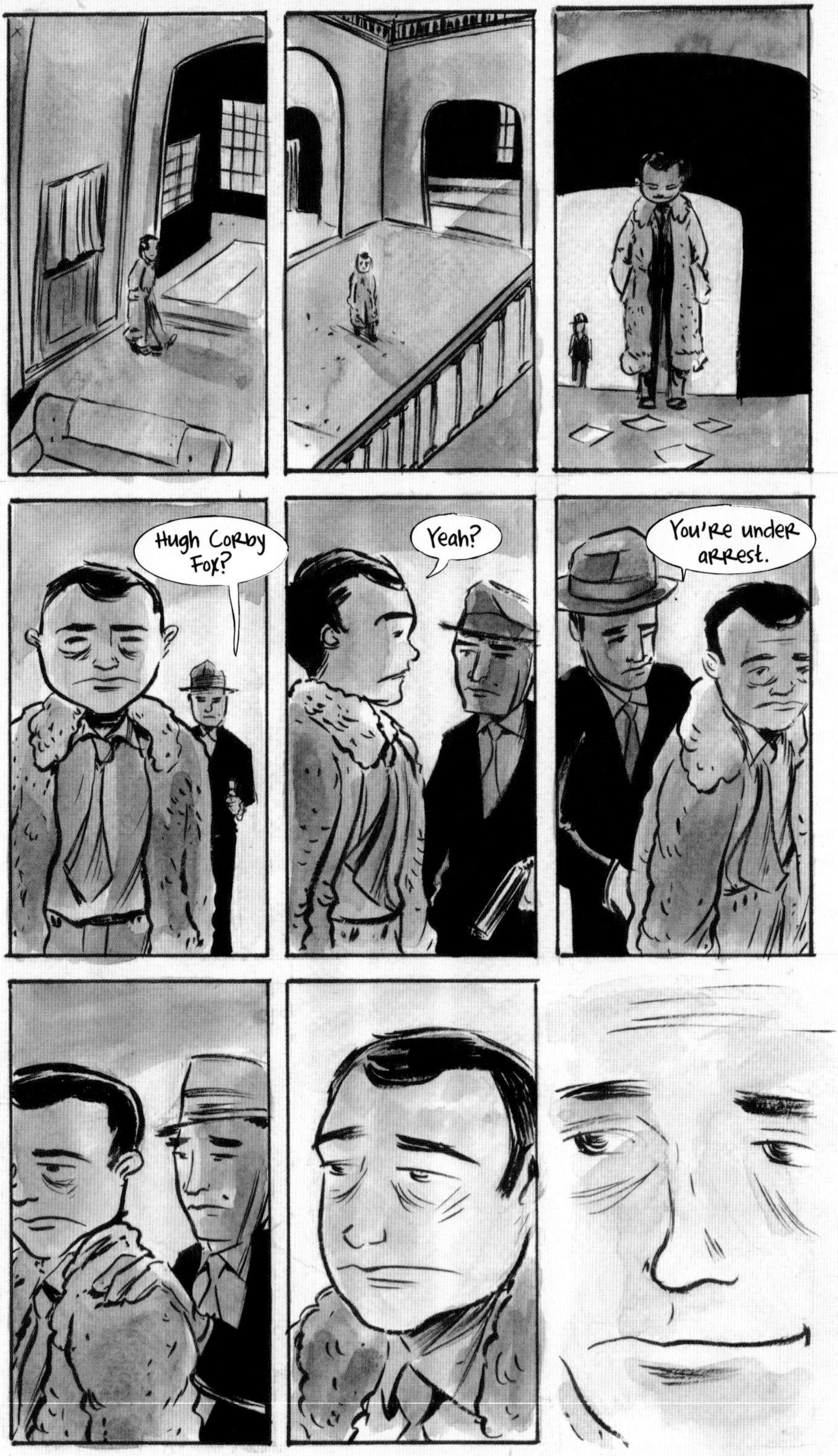
Hugh Corby Fox?
Yeah?
You're under arrest.

GAZ E

trap set at Hugh Corby Fox's house, the elusive Fur Smuggler was finally brought to justice. Fox was a career criminal according to his confession—stealing cars as a teenager in the suburbs of Red Wheel Barrow and gradually working his way into organized crime. Fox allegedly ran gambling, chop shops, and smut rings in addition to the lucrative and illegal fur smuggling that is nearly impossible to stop at the porous northern border. Gould again claims that the latest advances in technology and careful detective work will likely make it impossible for any criminal to escape his detection. Bold words that might seem empty if Gould hadn't backed them up for the last ten years with an impeccable record.

(continued on C12)

Gould (right) apprehends the elusive Fur Smuggler.

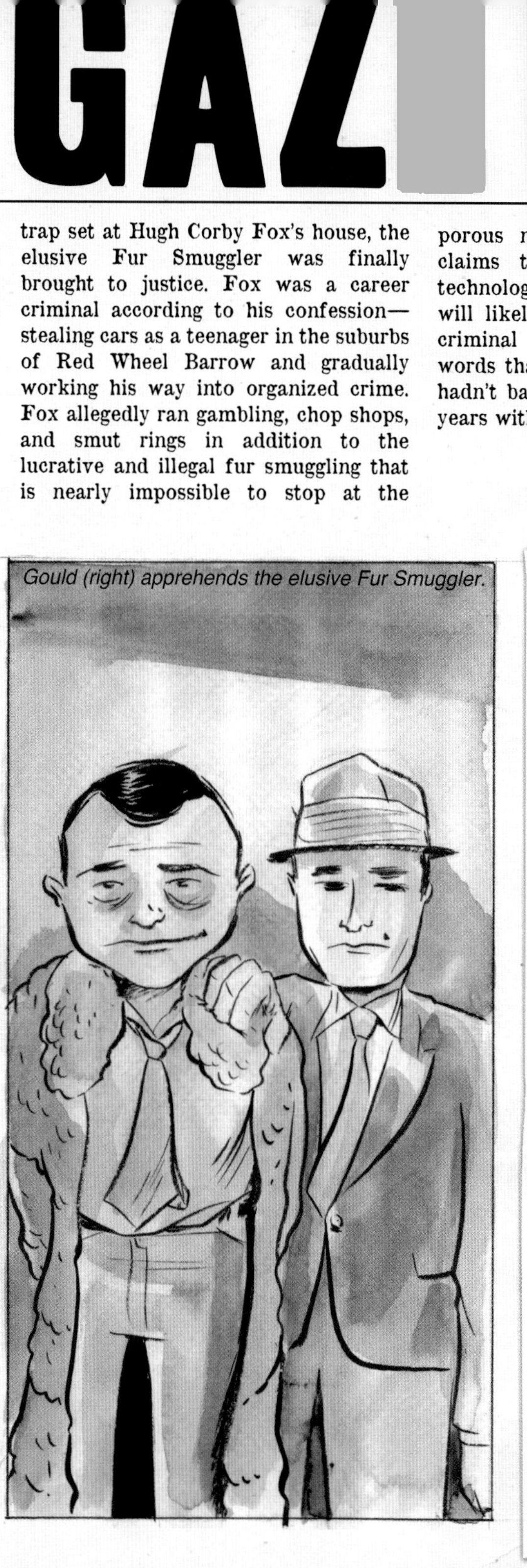

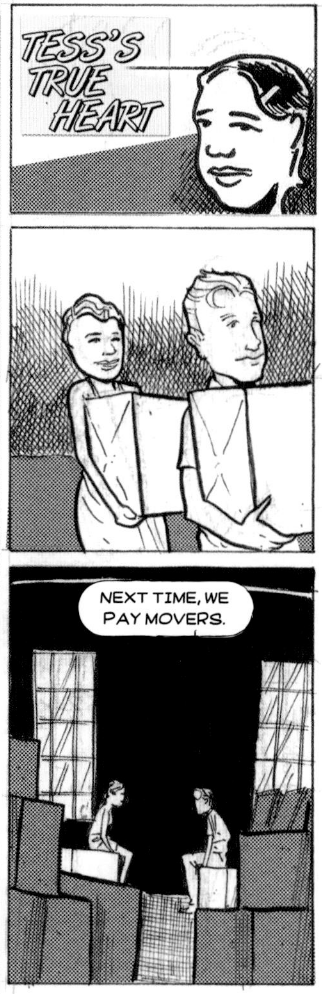
TESS'S TRUE HEART
NEXT TIME, WE PAY MOVERS.

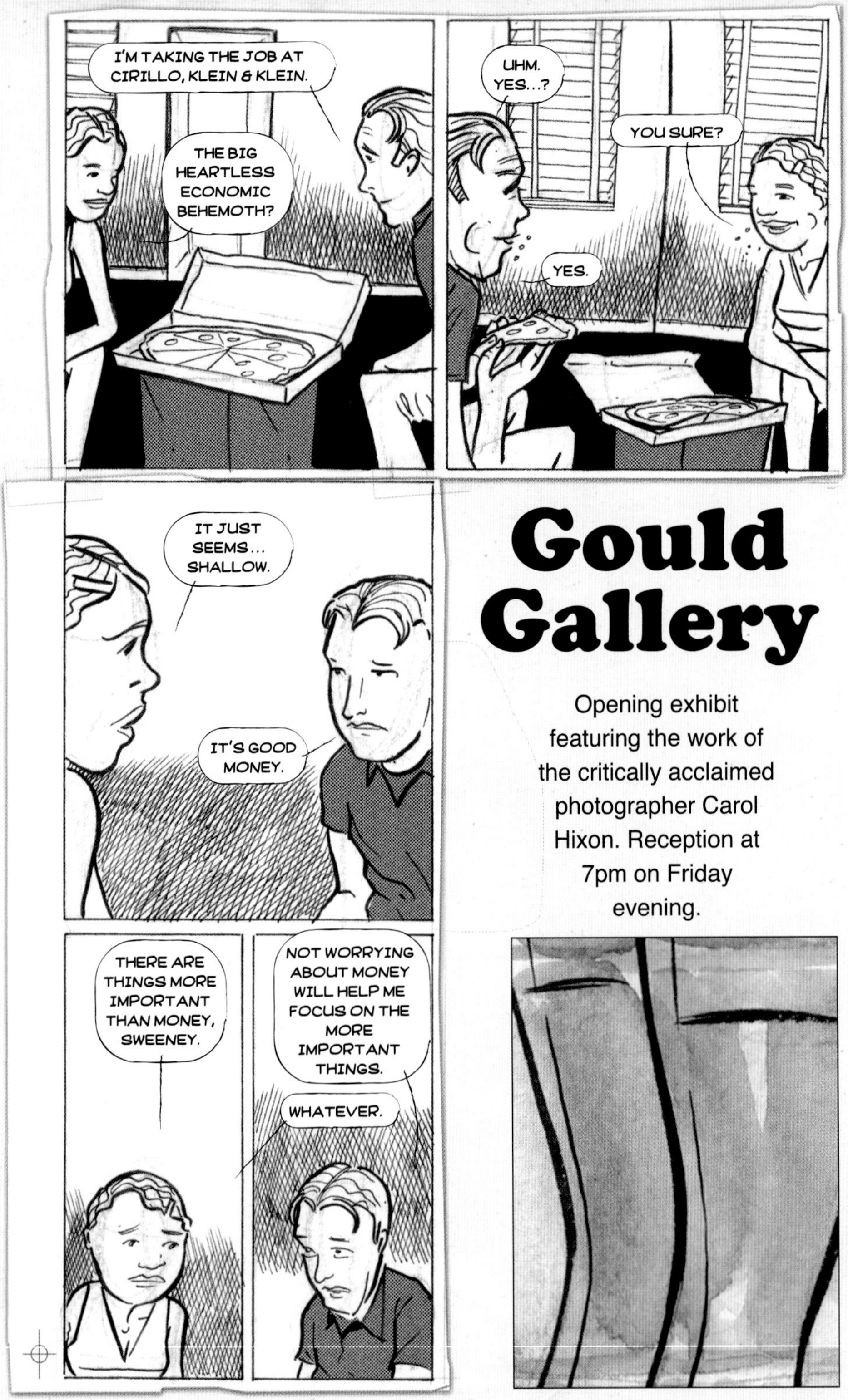
I'M TAKING THE JOB AT CIRILLO, KLEIN & KLEIN.
THE BIG HEARTLESS ECONOMIC BEHEMOTH?
UHM. YES...?
YOU SURE?
YES.
IT JUST SEEMS... SHALLOW.
IT'S GOOD MONEY.
Gould Gallery
Opening exhibit featuring the work of the critically acclaimed photographer Carol Hixon. Reception at 7pm on Friday evening.
THERE ARE THINGS MORE IMPORTANT THAN MONEY, SWEENEY.
NOT WORRYING ABOUT MONEY WILL HELP ME FOCUS ON THE MORE IMPORTANT THINGS.
WHATEVER.

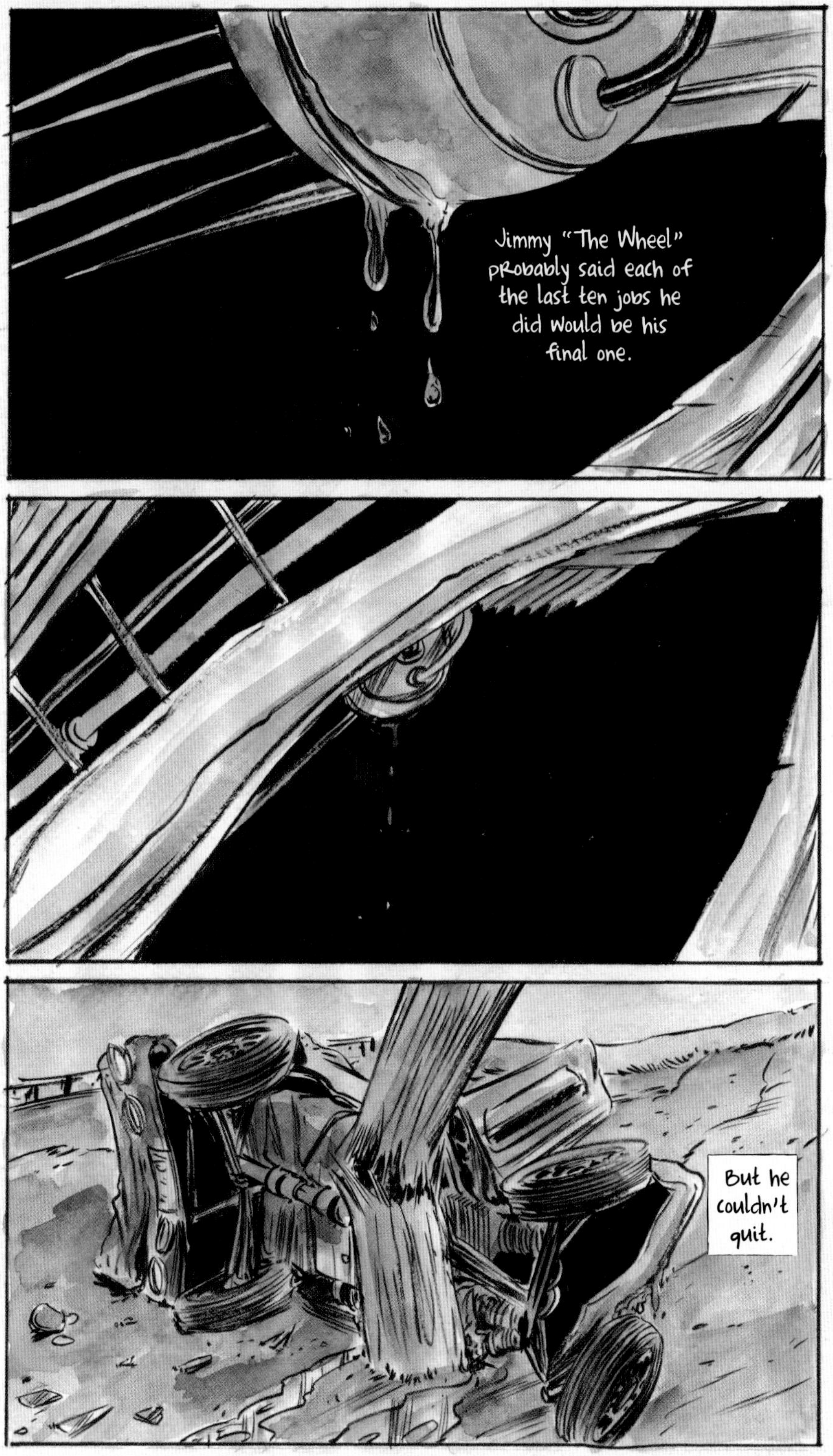
Jimmy "The Wheel" probably said each of the last ten jobs he did would be his final one.
But he couldn't quit.

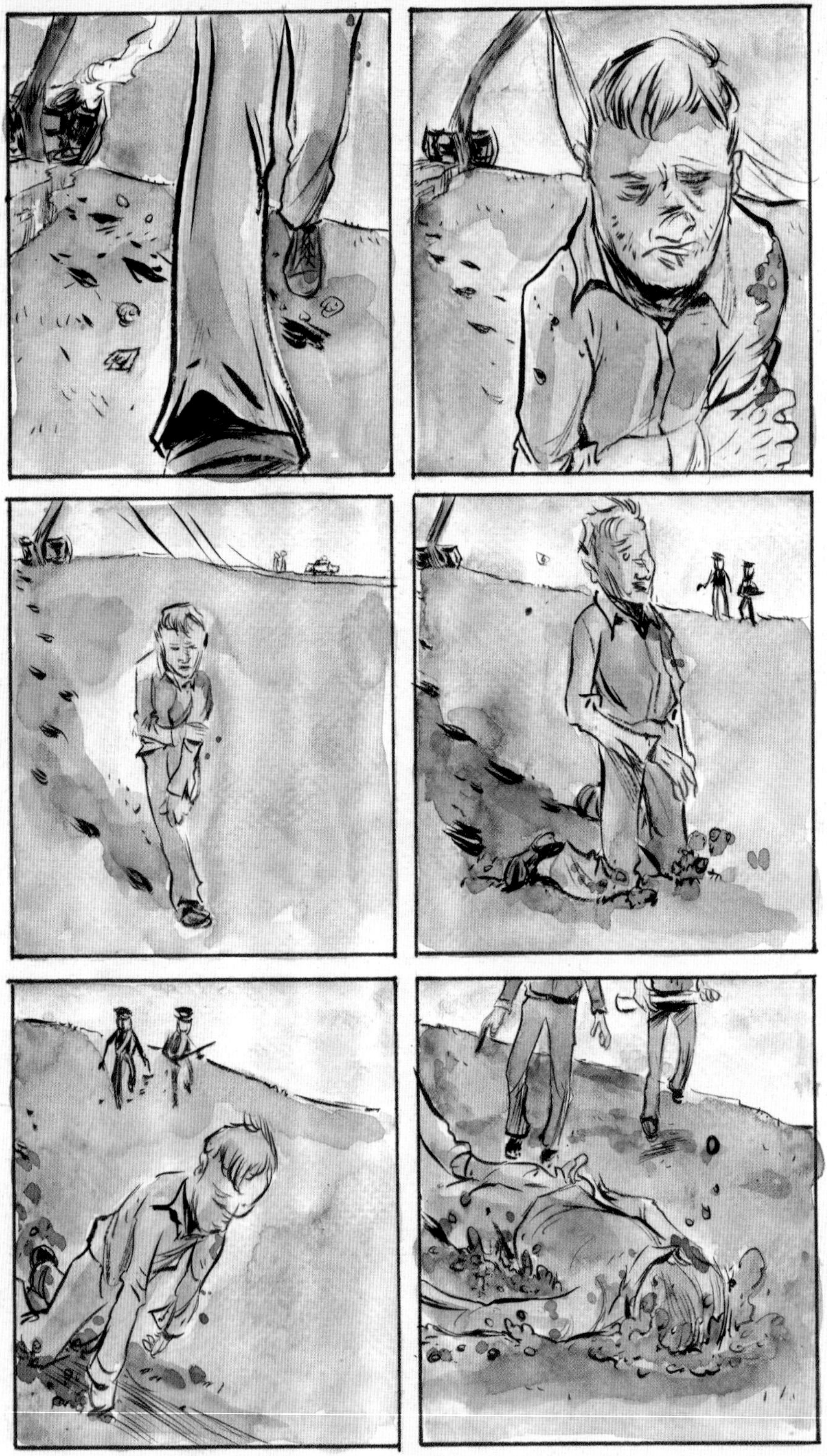

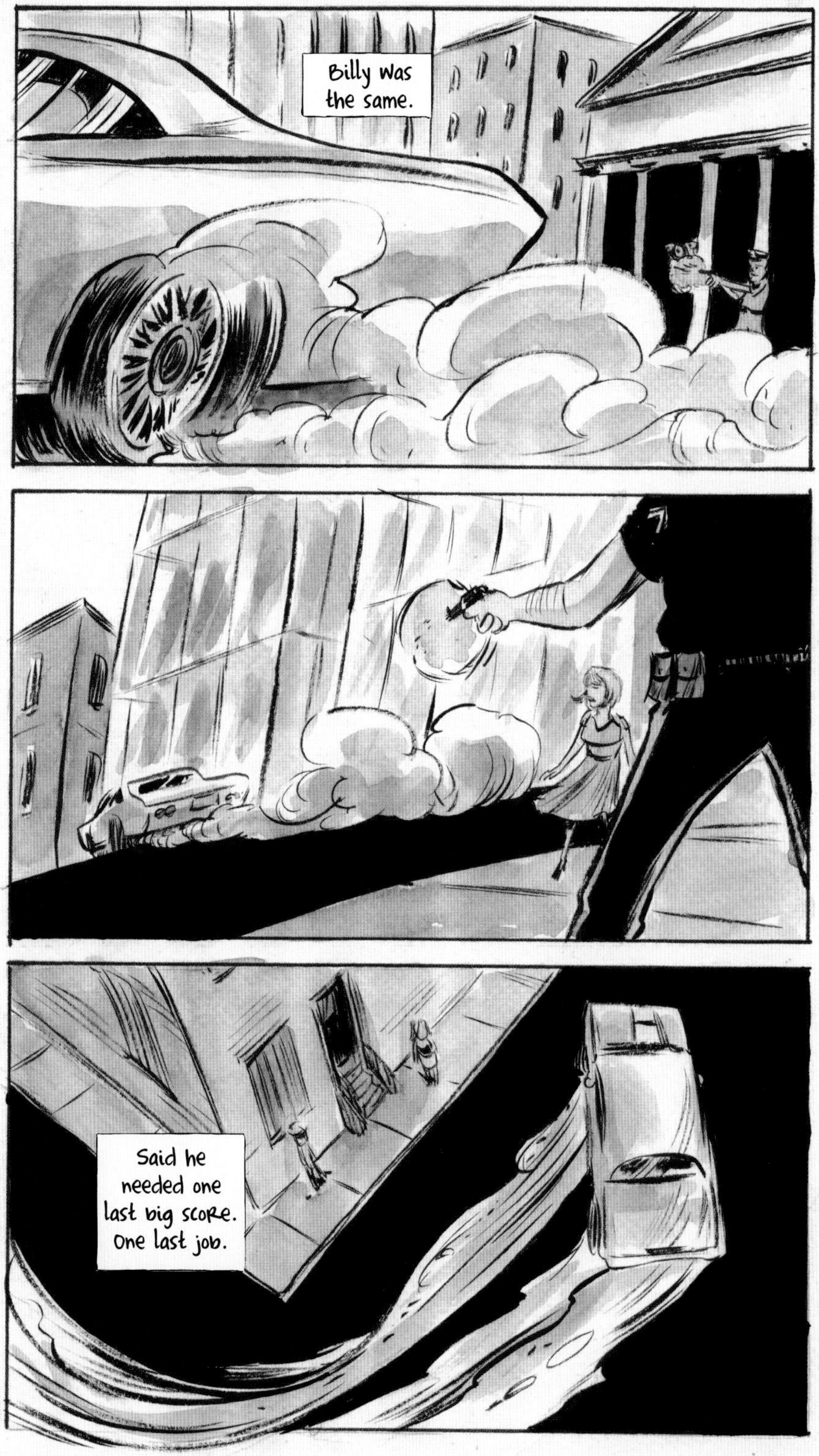
Billy was the same.
Said he needed one last big score. One last job.

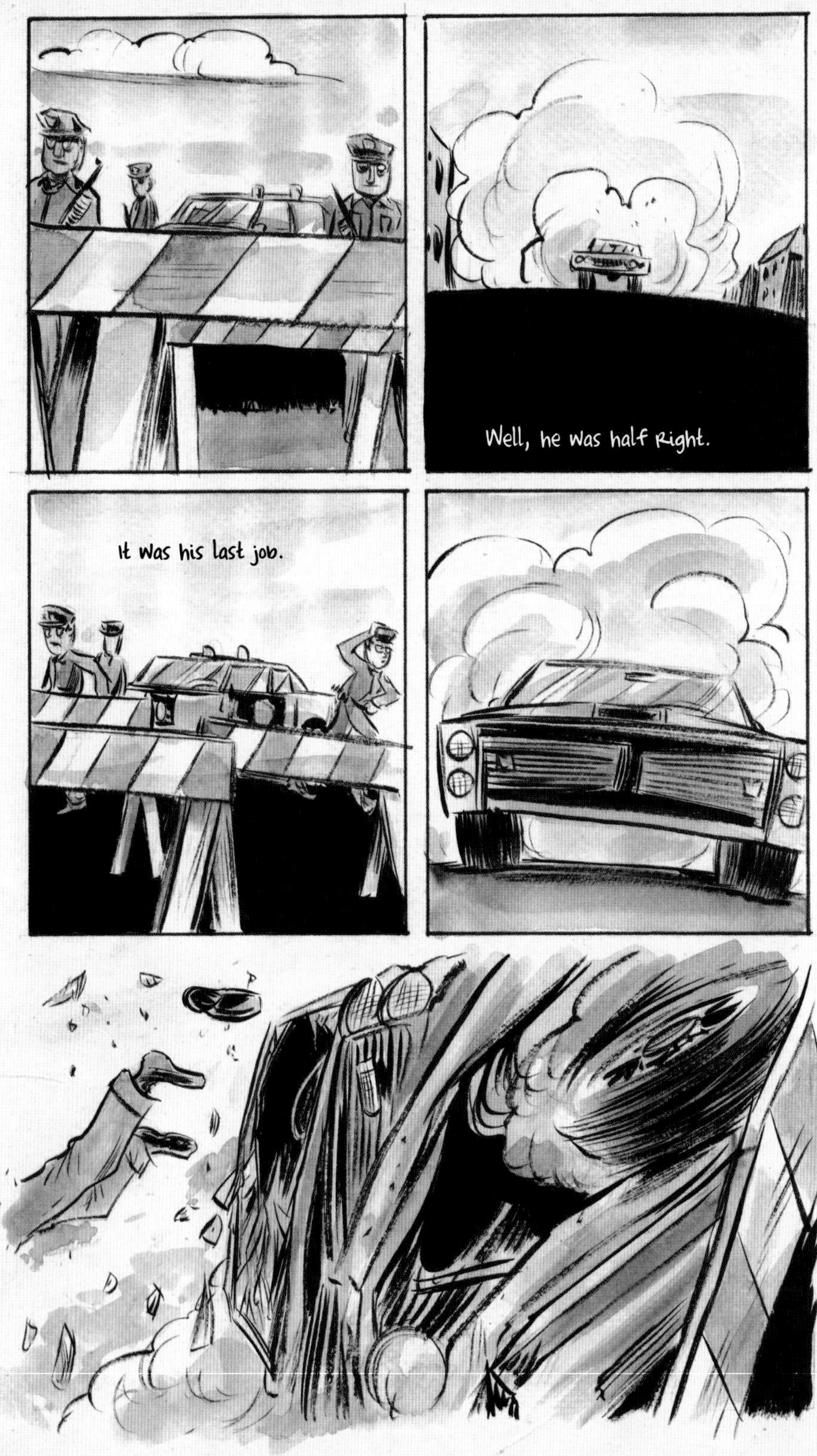
Well, he was half Right.
It was his last job.

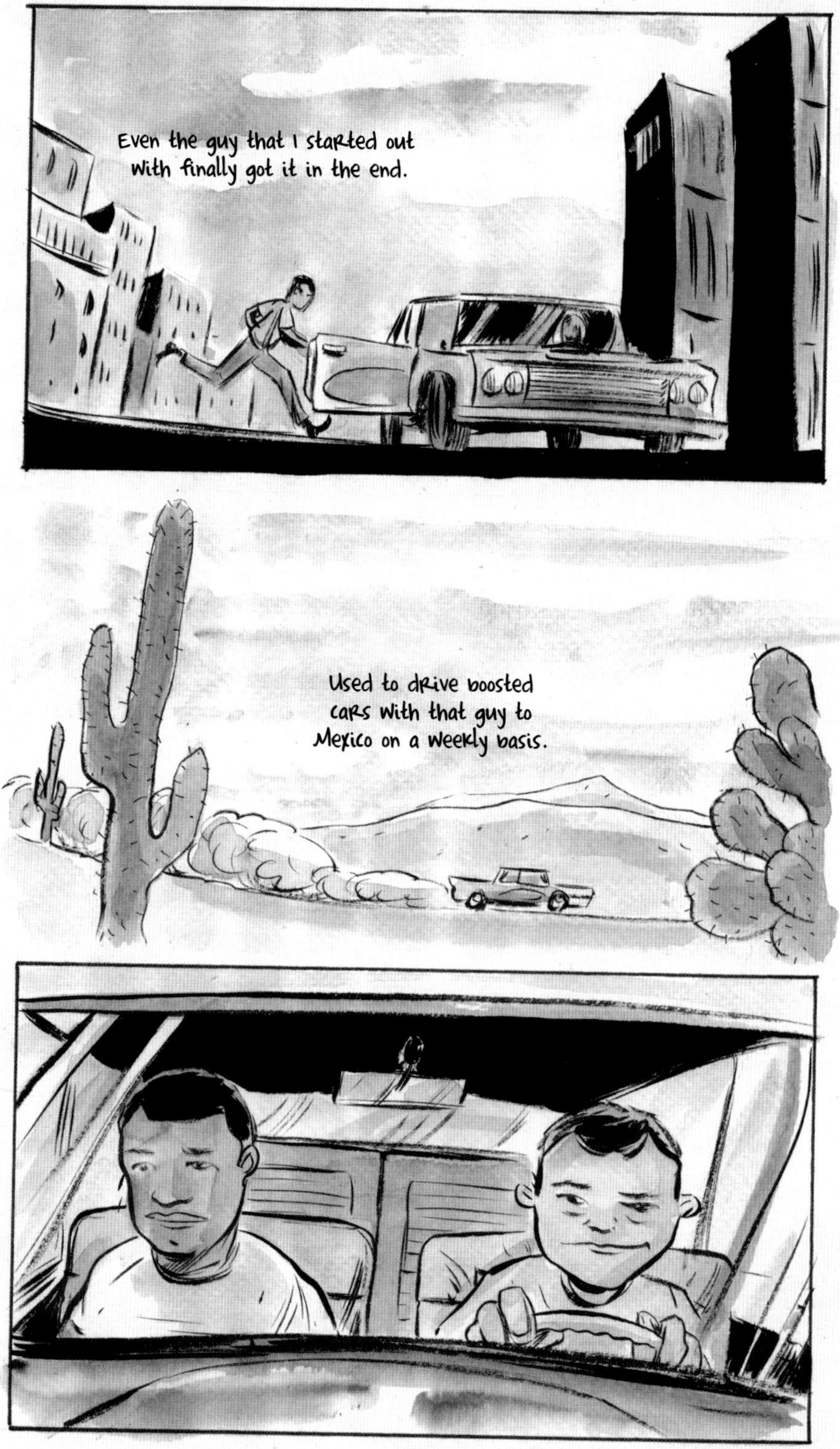
Even the guy that I started out with finally got it in the end.
Used to drive boosted cars with that guy to Mexico on a weekly basis.

THE
ESCAPE
ARTIST

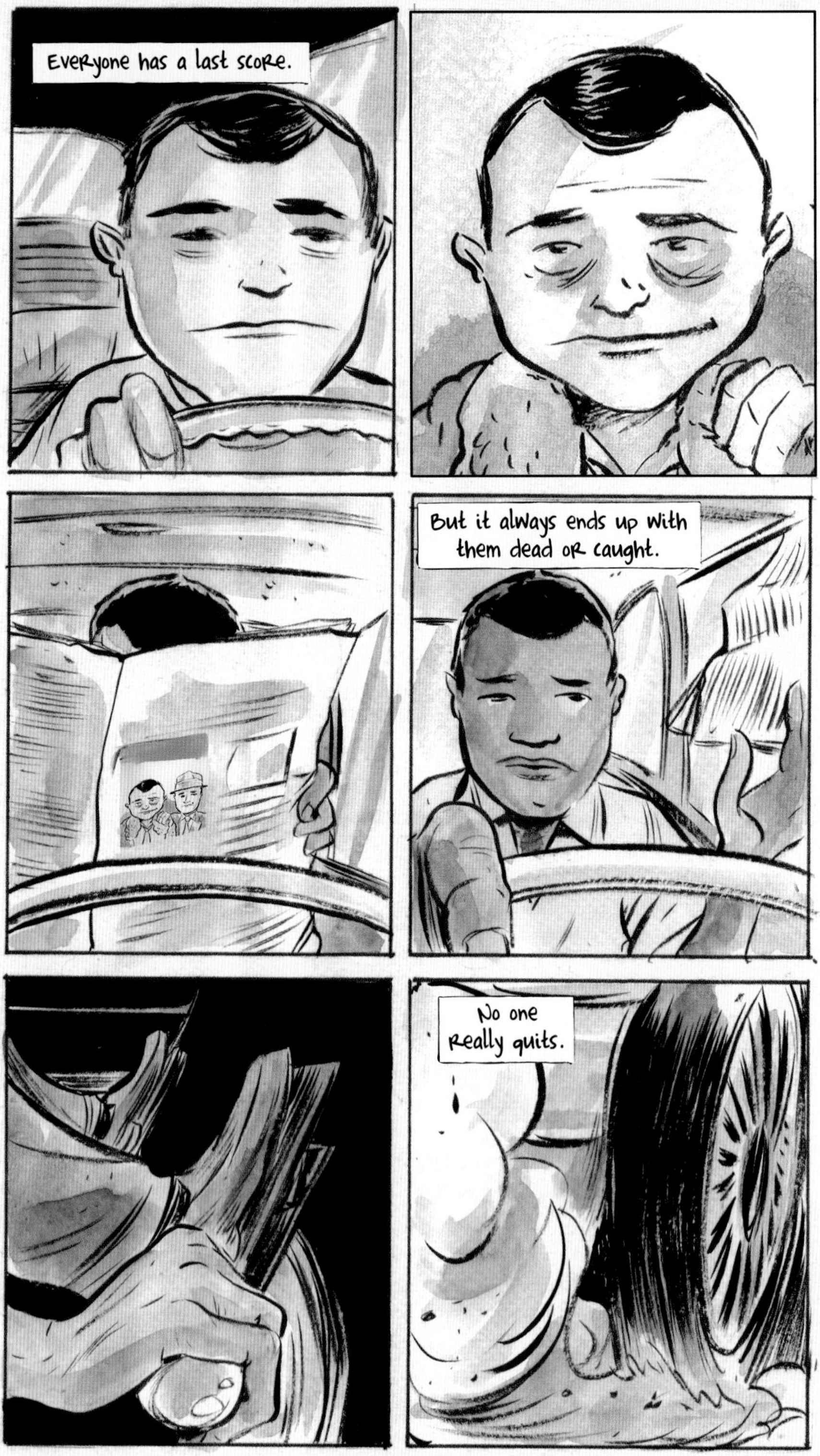
Everyone has a last score.
But it always ends up with them dead or caught.
No one really quits.

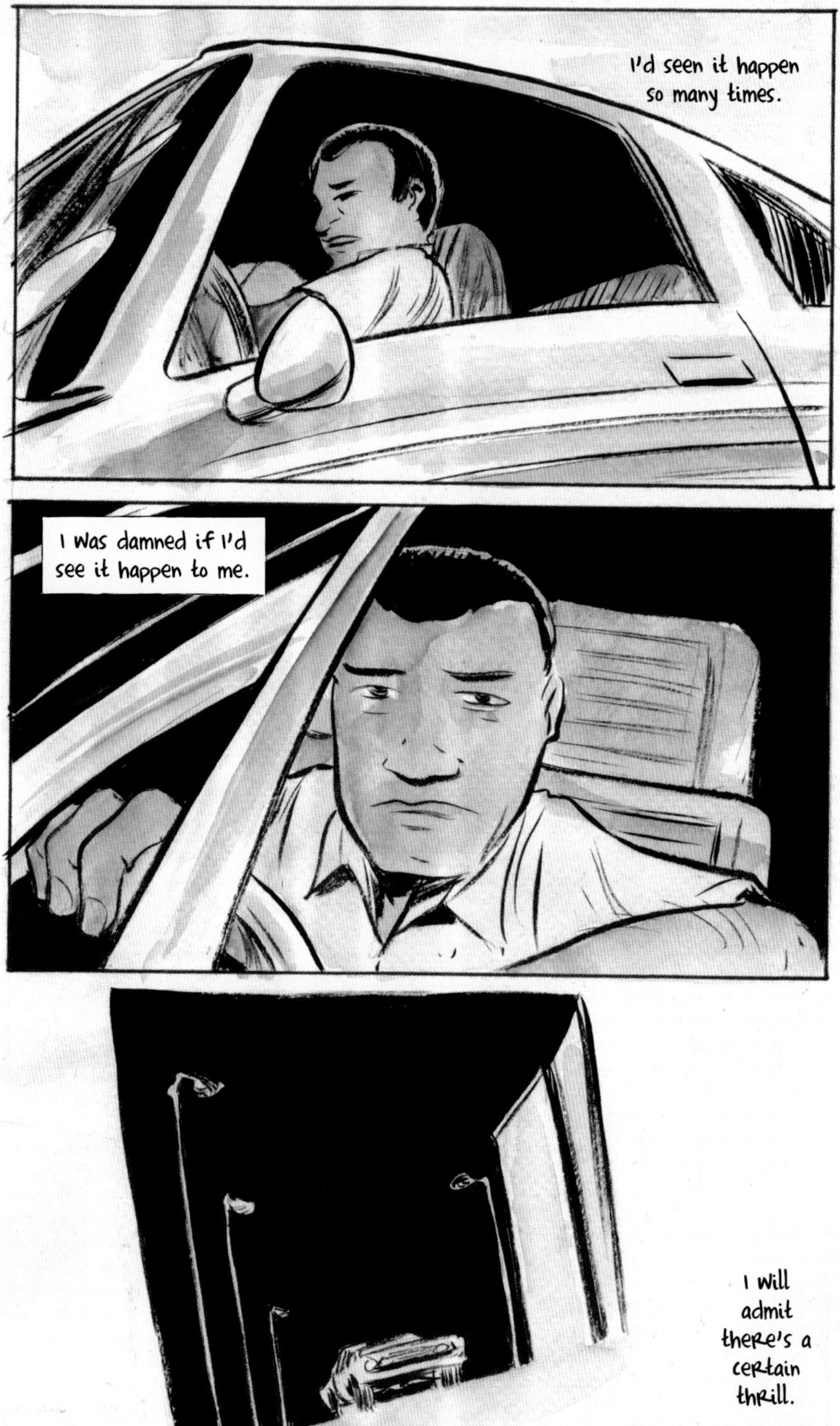
I'd seen it happen so many times.
I was damned if I'd see it happen to me.
I will admit there's a certain thrill.

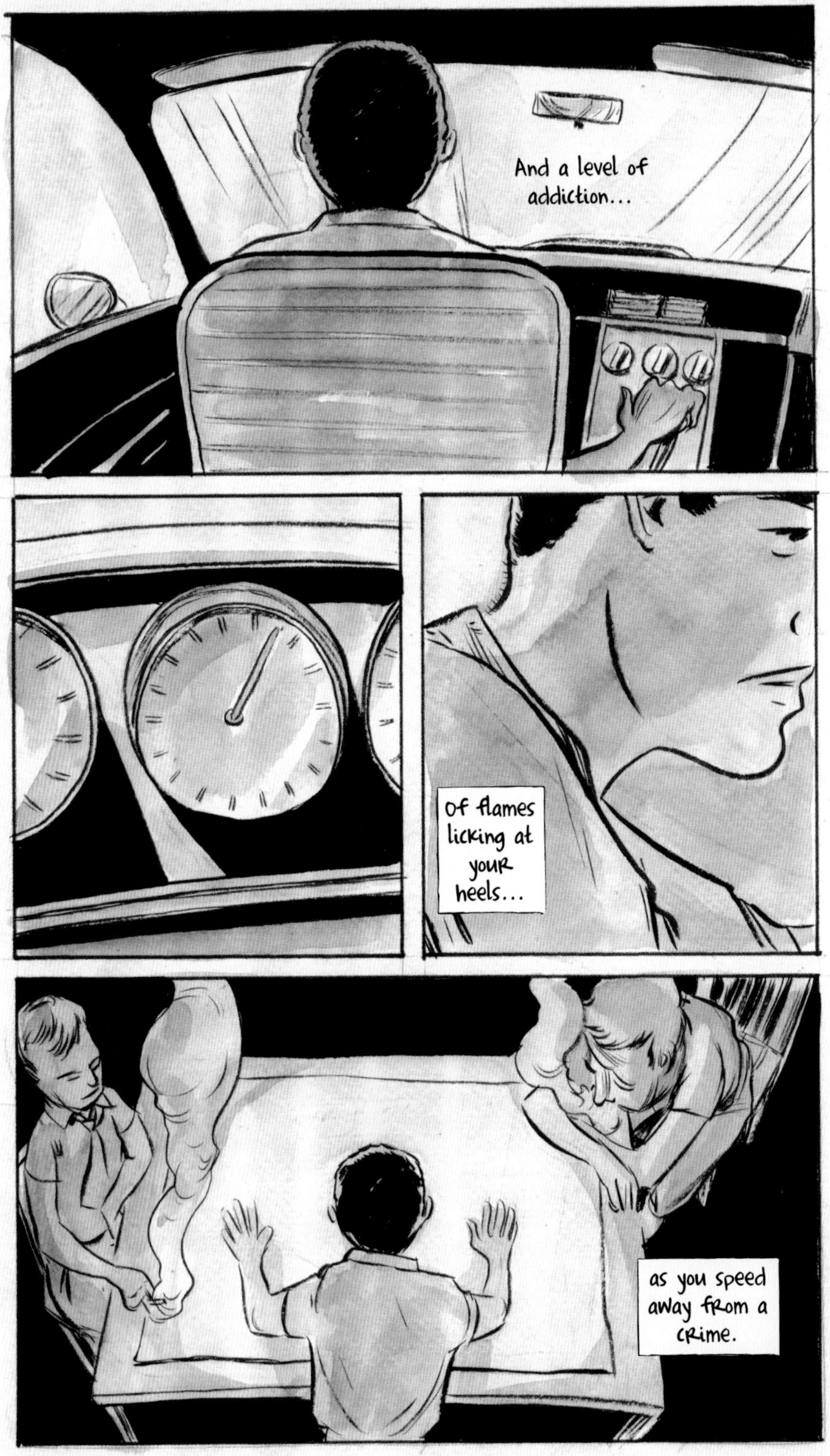
And a level of addiction...
Of flames licking at your heels...
as you speed away from a crime.

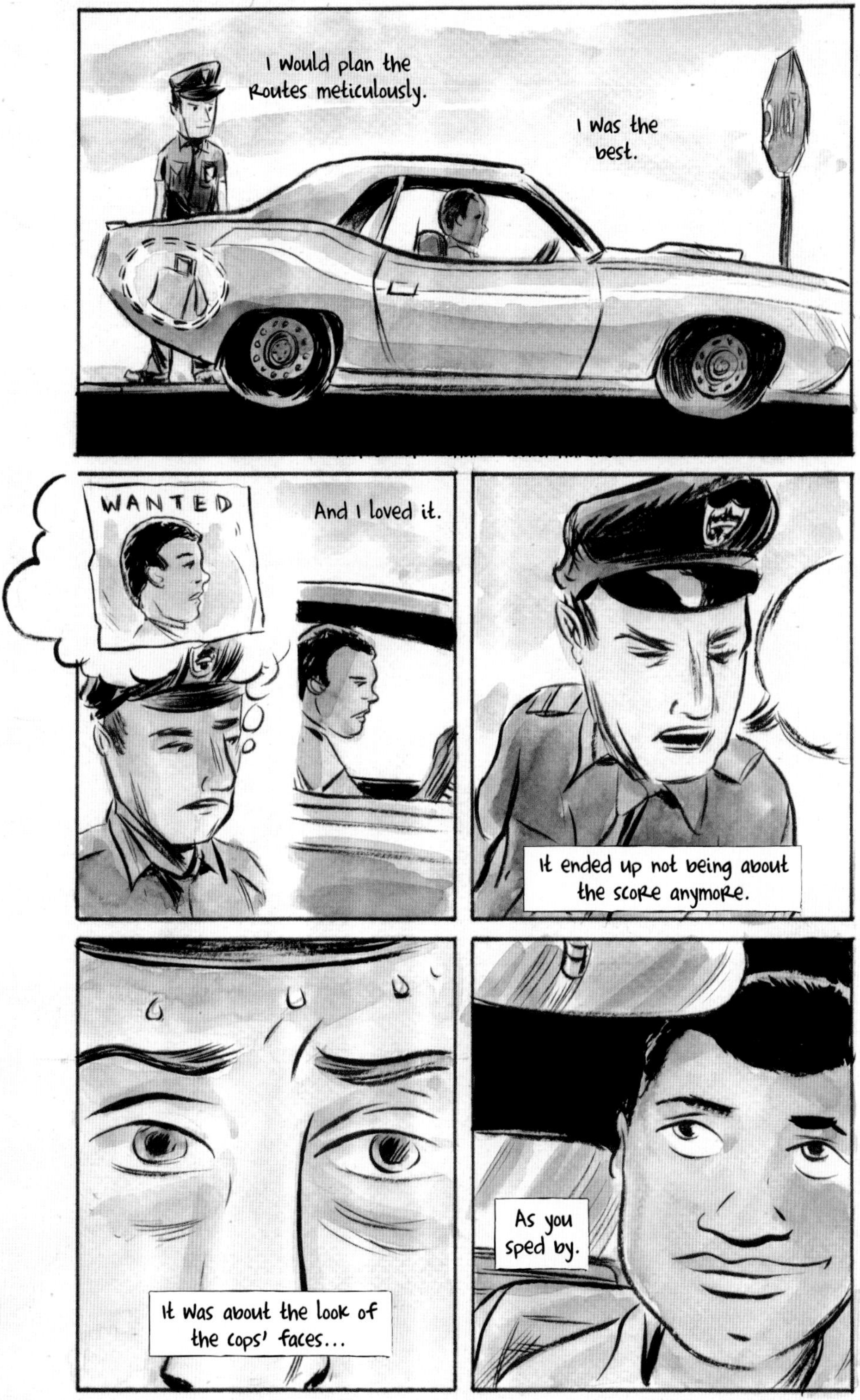
I would plan the Routes meticulously.
I was the best.
WANTED
And I loved it.
It ended up not being about the score anymore.
It was about the look of the cops' faces...
As you sped by.

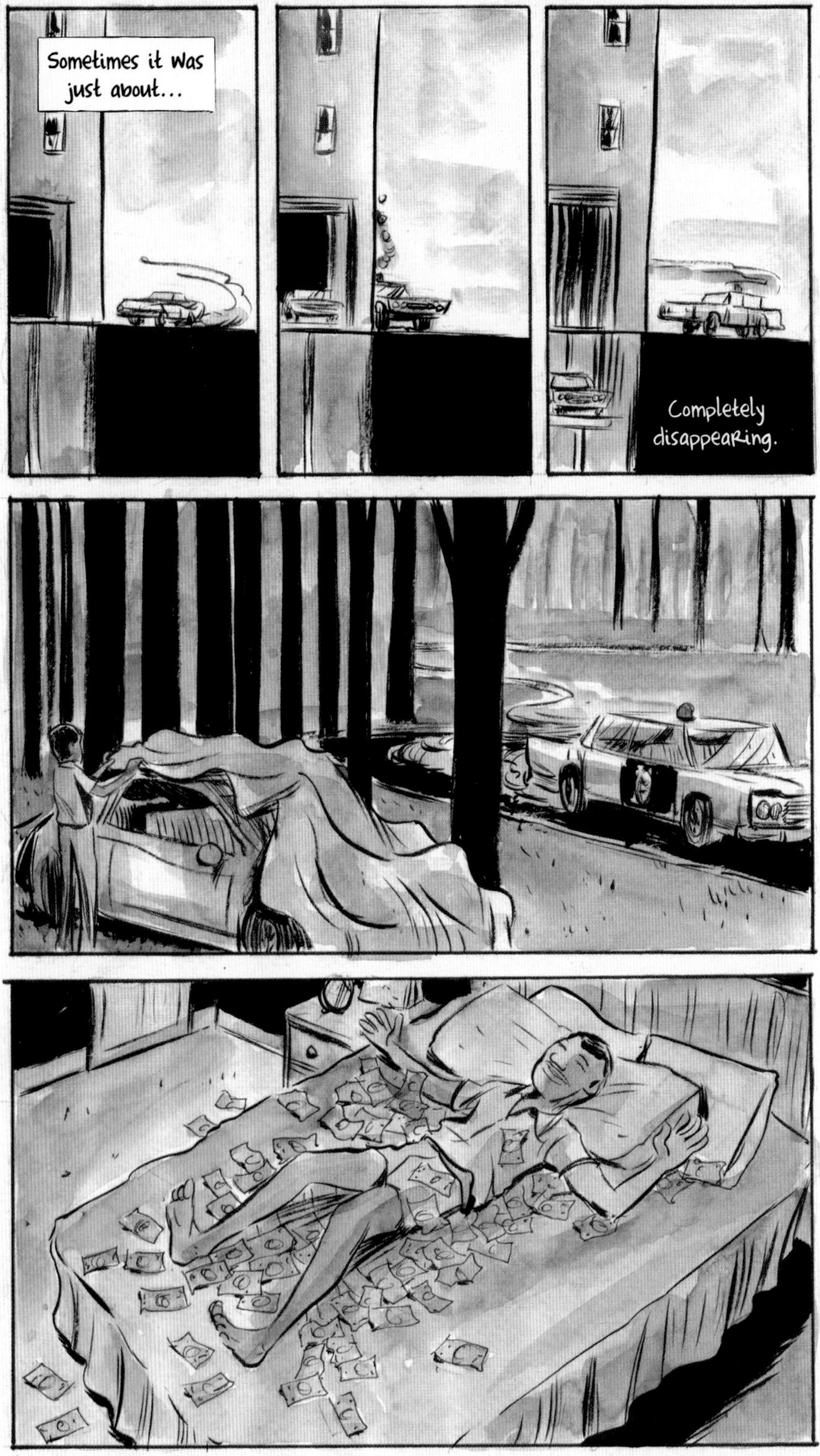
Sometimes it was just about...
Completely disappearing.

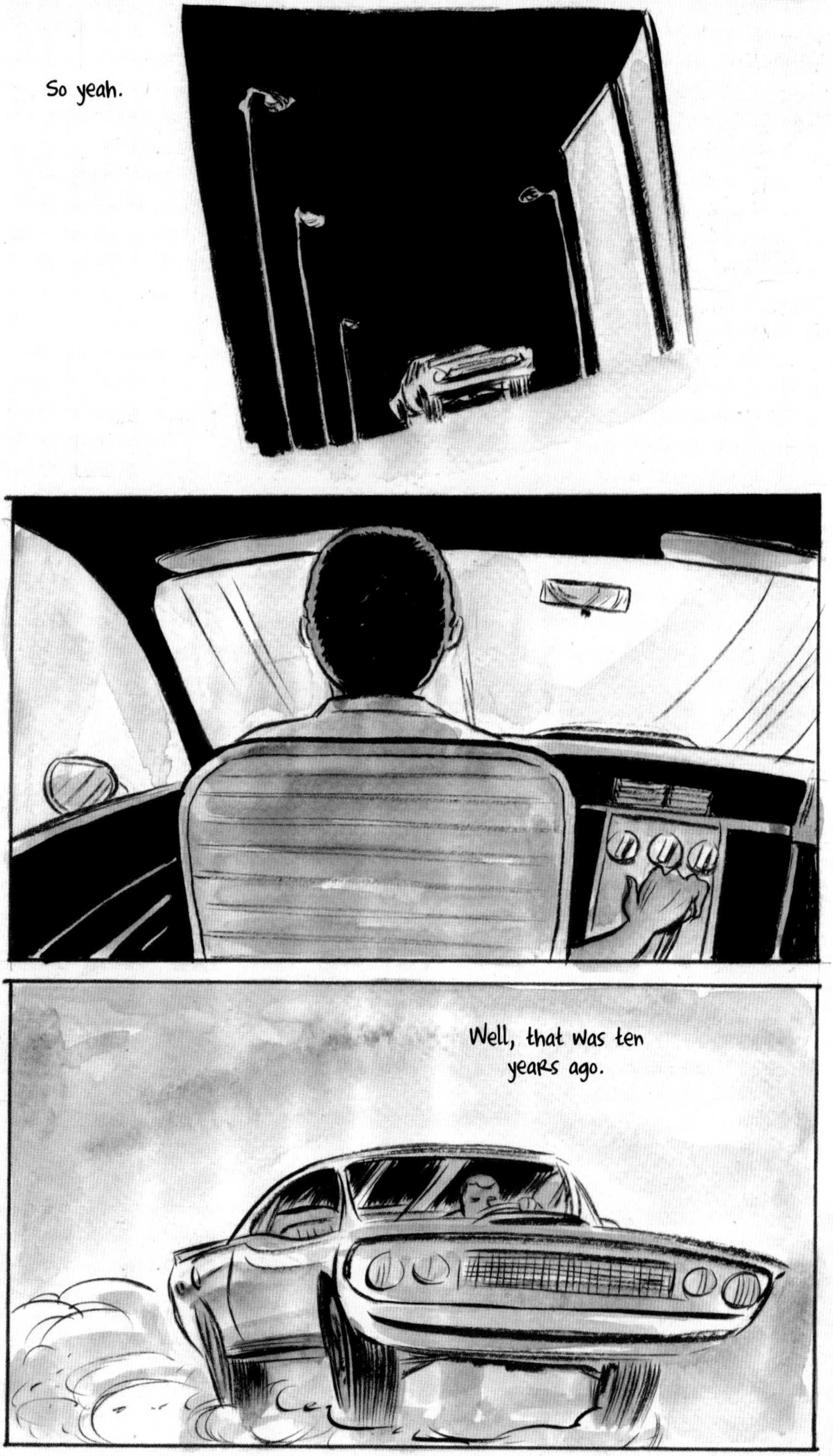
So yeah.
Well, that was ten years ago.

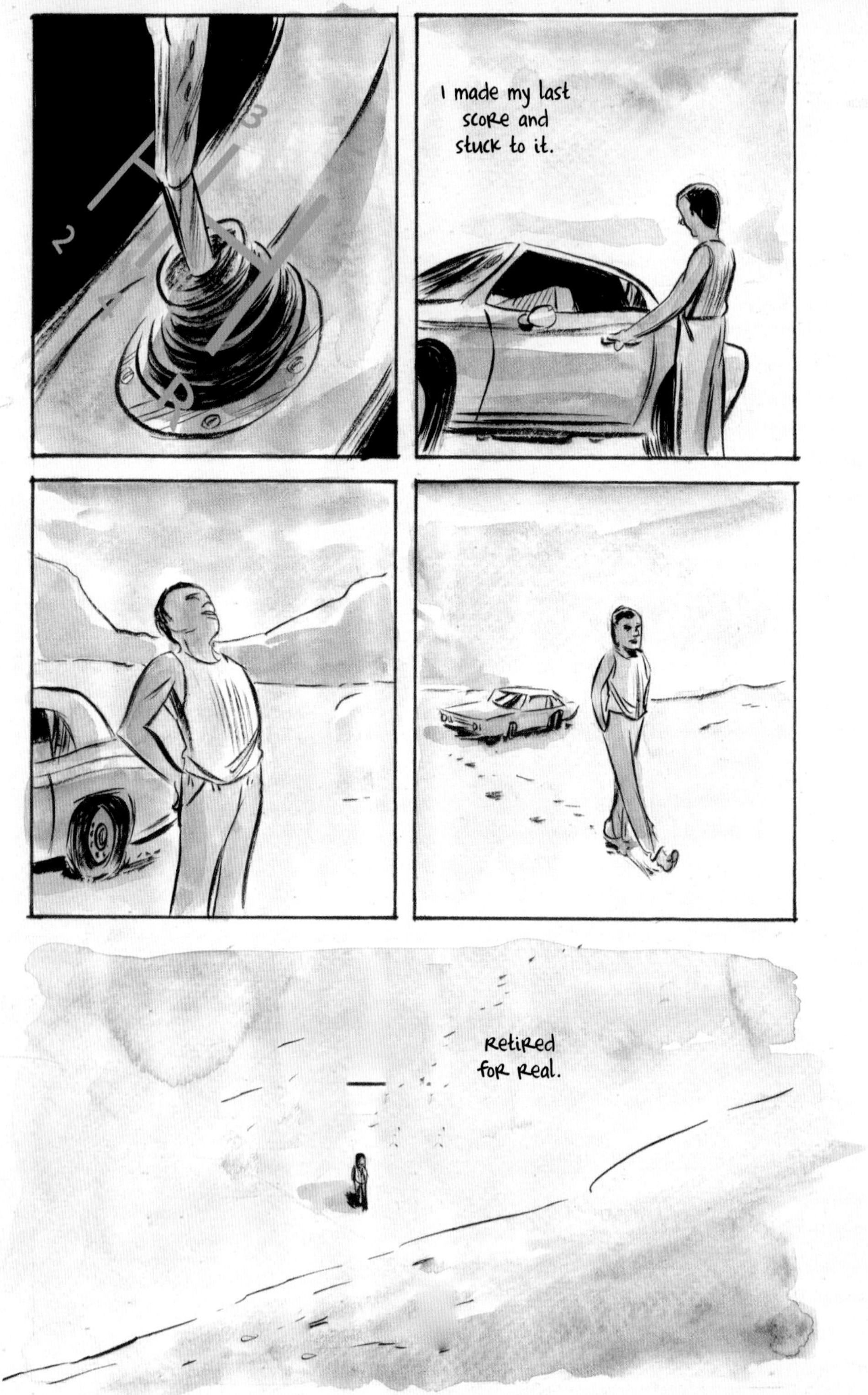
I made my last score and stuck to it.
Retired for real.

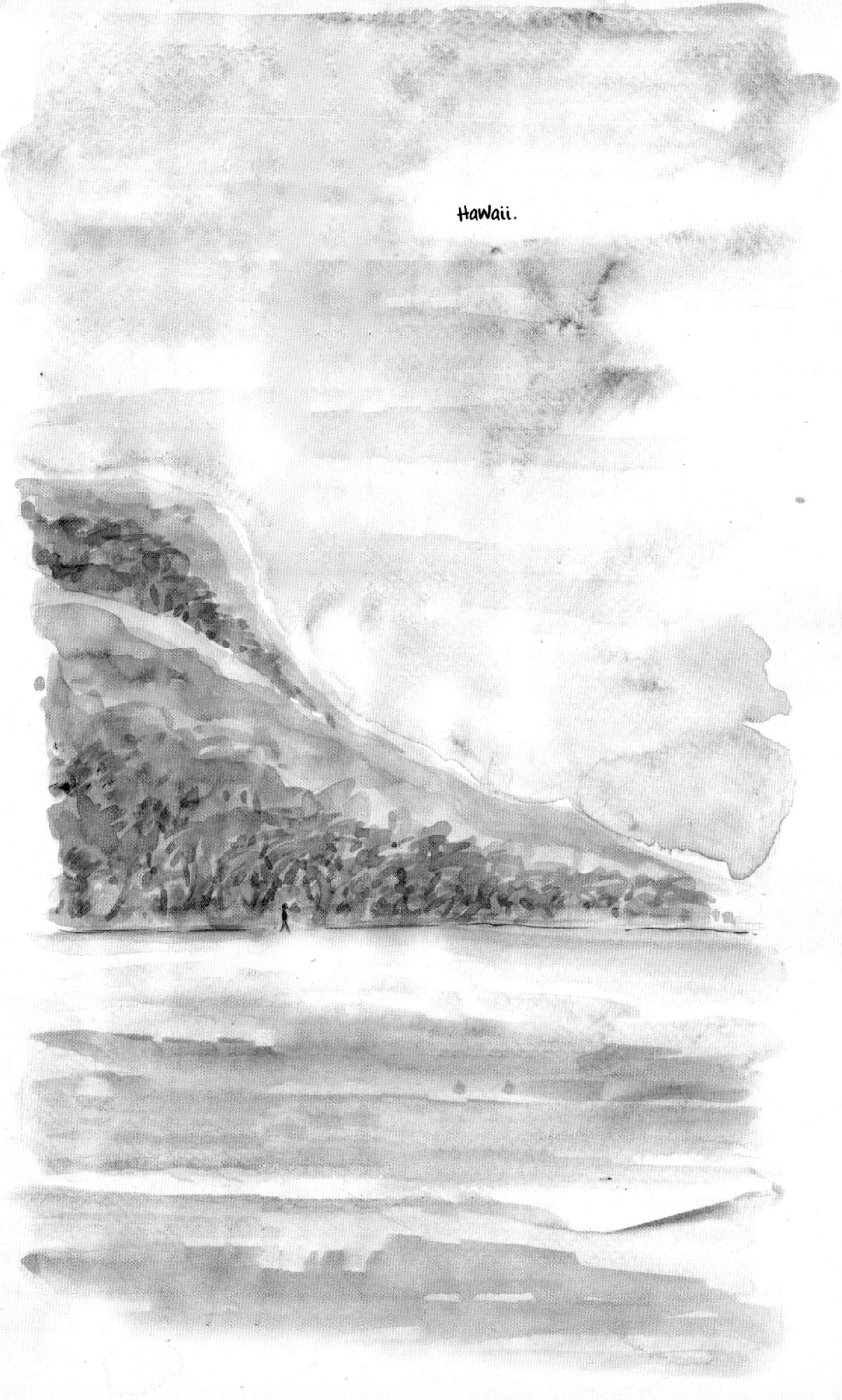
HaWaii.

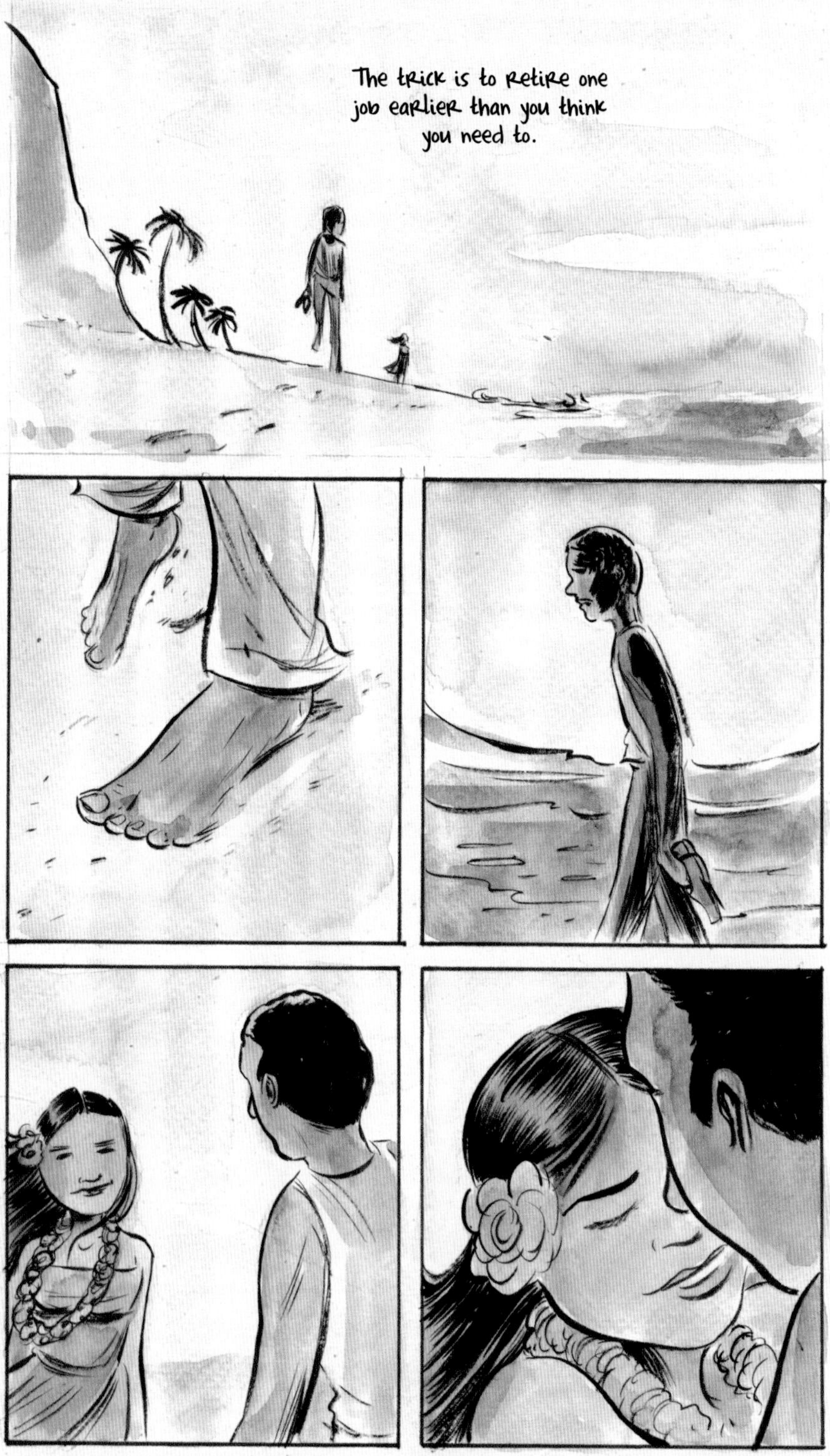
The trick is to retire one job earlier than you think you need to.

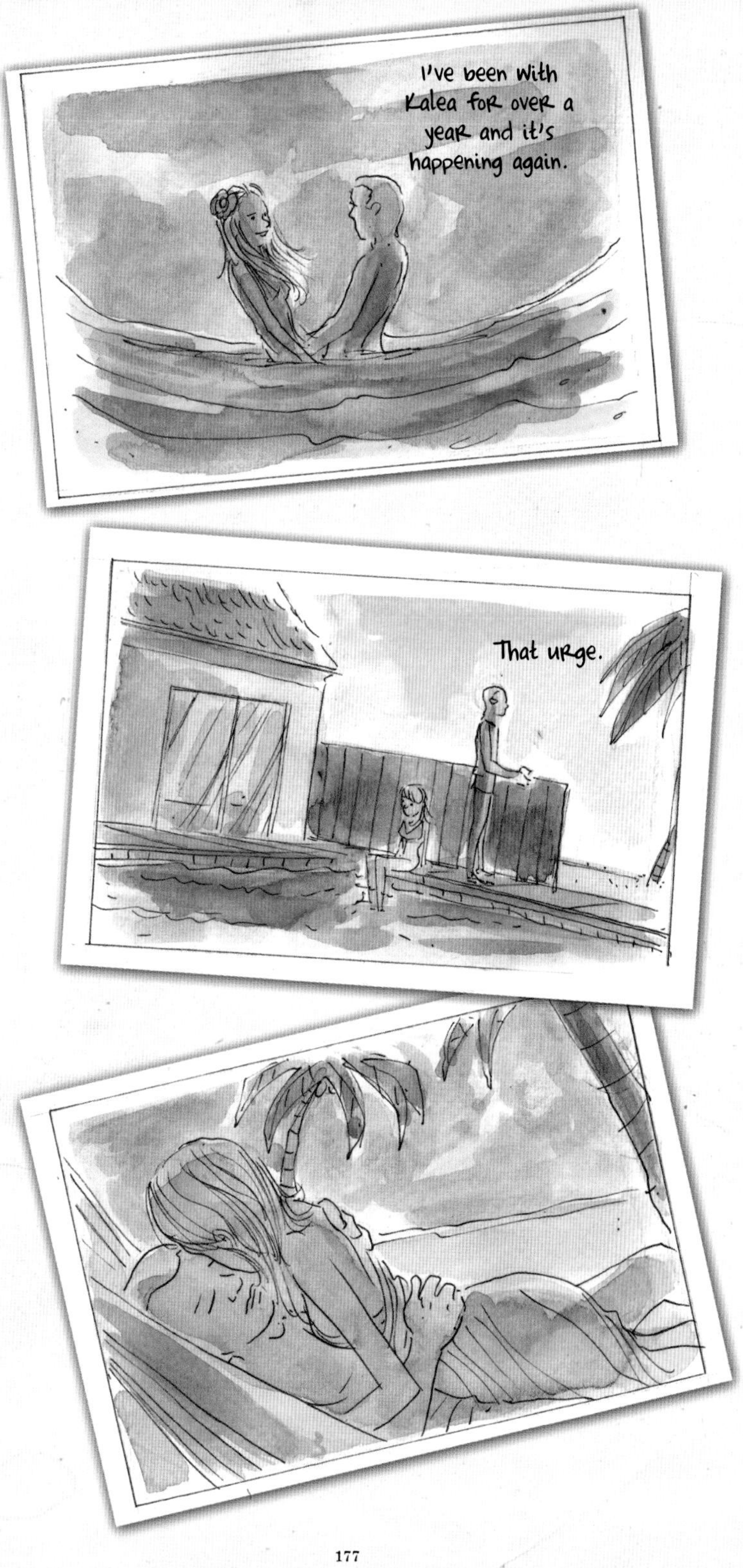
I've been with Kalea for over a year and it's happening again.
That urge.

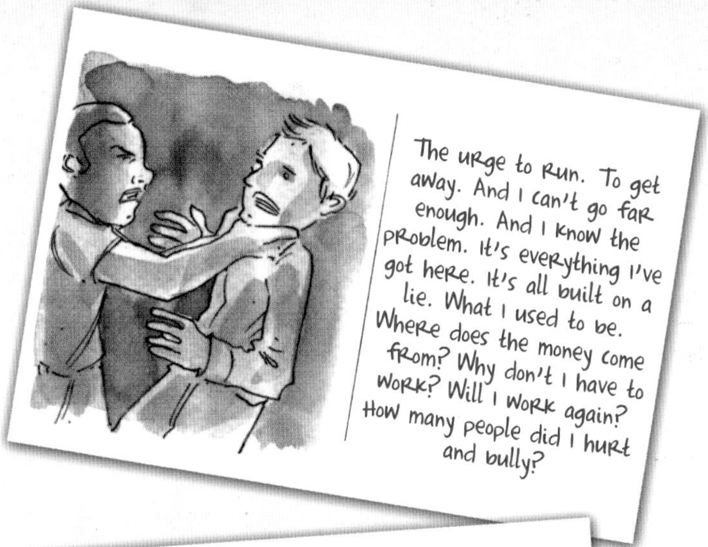
The urge to run. To get away. And I can't go far enough. And I know the problem. It's everything I've got here. It's all built on a lie. What I used to be. Where does the money come from? Why don't I have to work? Will I work again? How many people did I hurt and bully?

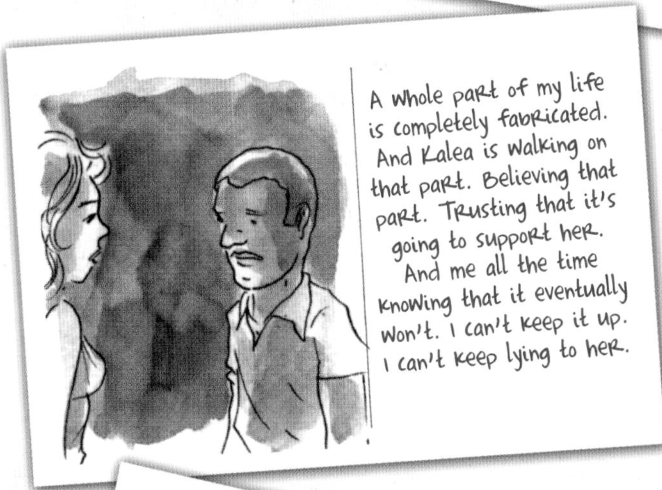
A whole part of my life is completely fabricated. And Kalea is walking on that part. Believing that part. Trusting that it's going to support her. And me all the time knowing that it eventually won't. I can't keep it up. I can't keep lying to her.

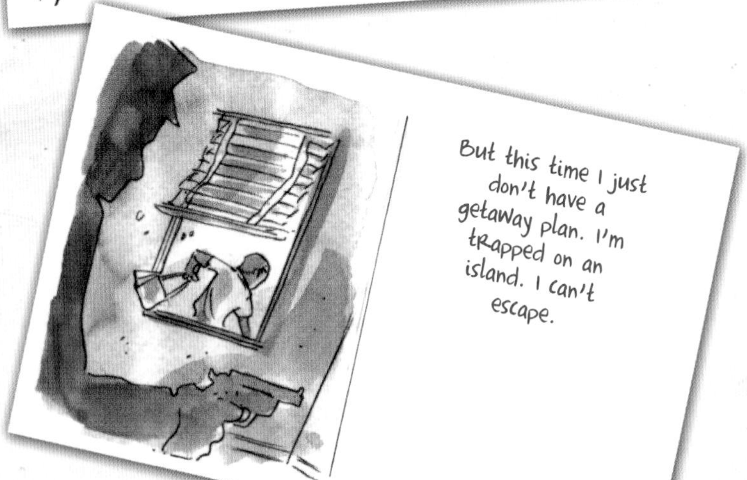
But this time I just don't have a getaway plan. I'm trapped on an island. I can't escape.

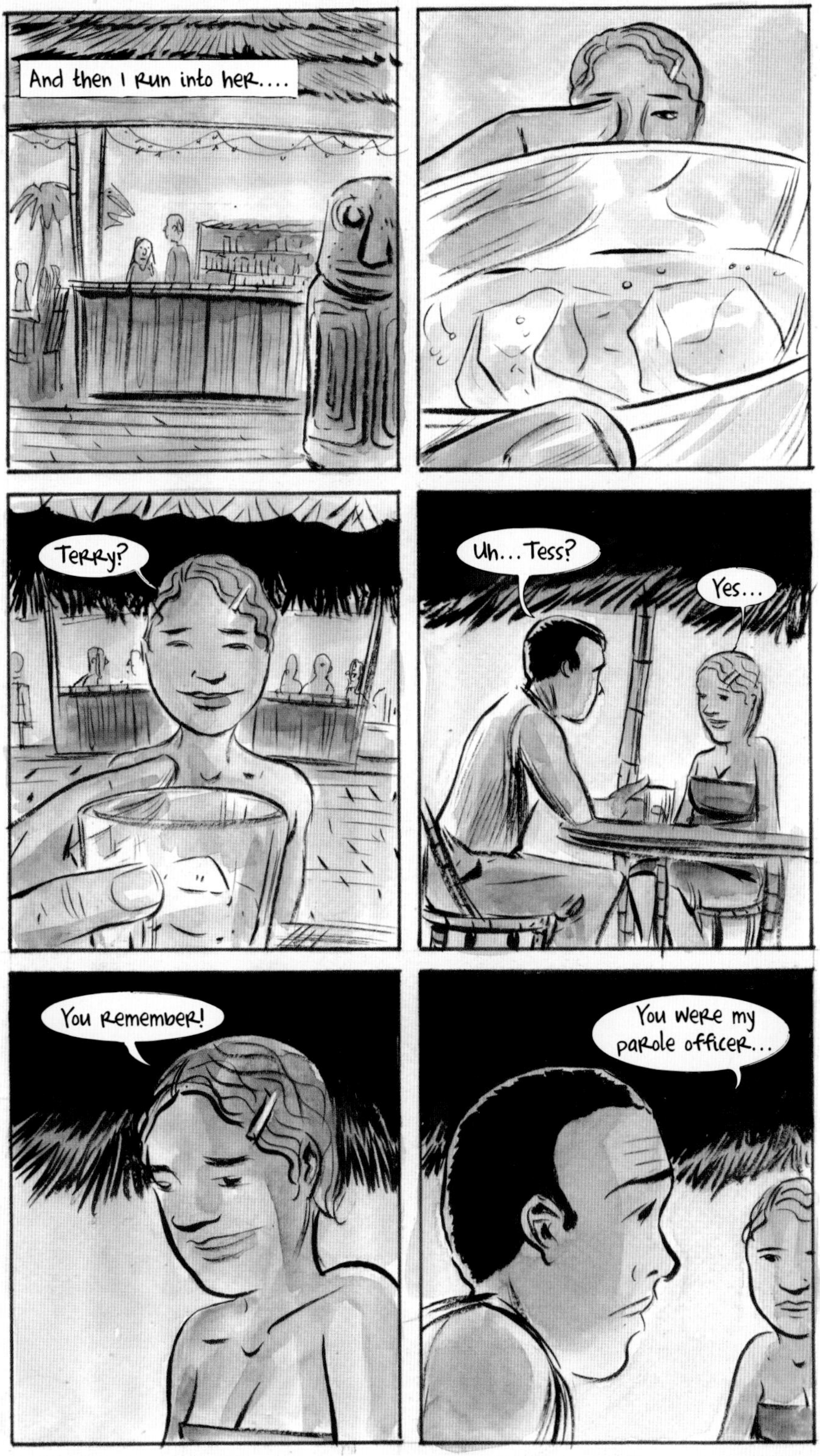
And then I run into her....
Terry?
Uh... Tess?
Yes...
You remember!
You were my parole officer...

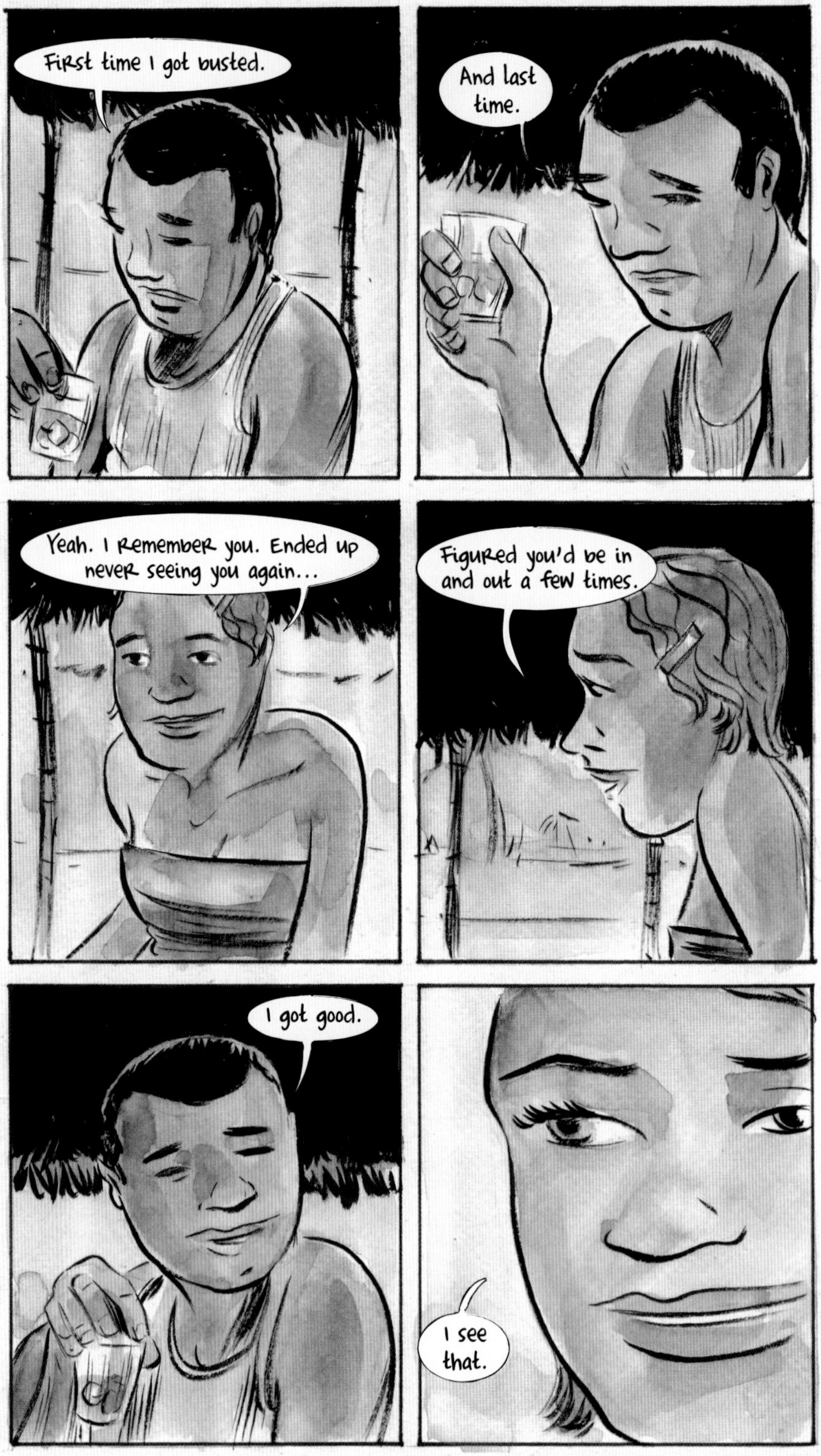
First time I got busted.
And last time.
Yeah. I remember you. Ended up never seeing you again...
Figured you'd be in and out a few times.
I got good.
I see that.

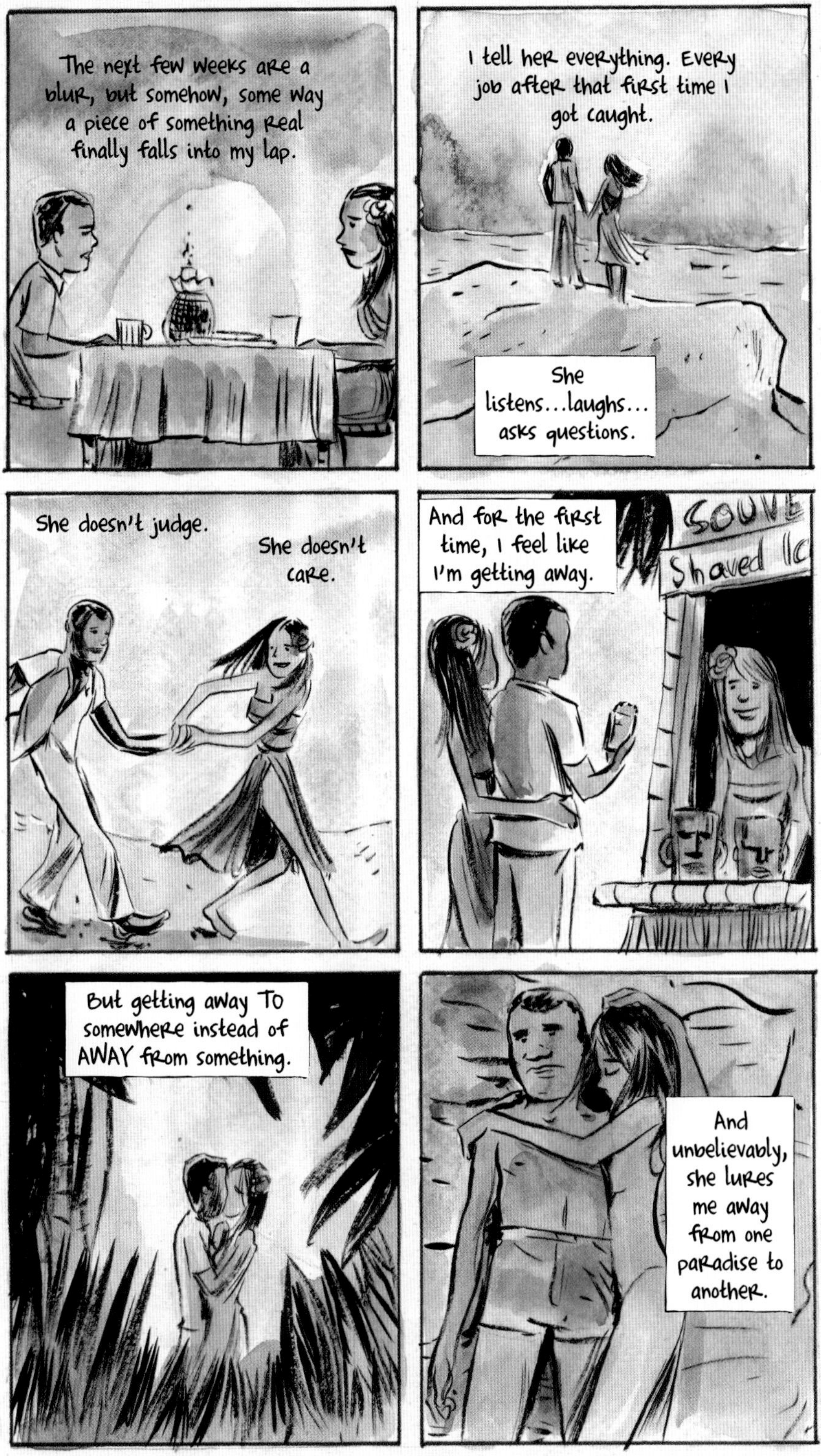
The next few weeks are a blur, but somehow, some way a piece of something real finally falls into my lap.
I tell her everything. Every job after that first time I got caught.
She listens...laughs... asks questions.
She doesn't judge.
She doesn't care.
And for the first time, I feel like I'm getting away.
SOUVE
Shaved Ic
But getting away TO somewhere instead of AWAY from something.
And unbelievably, she lures me away from one paradise to another.

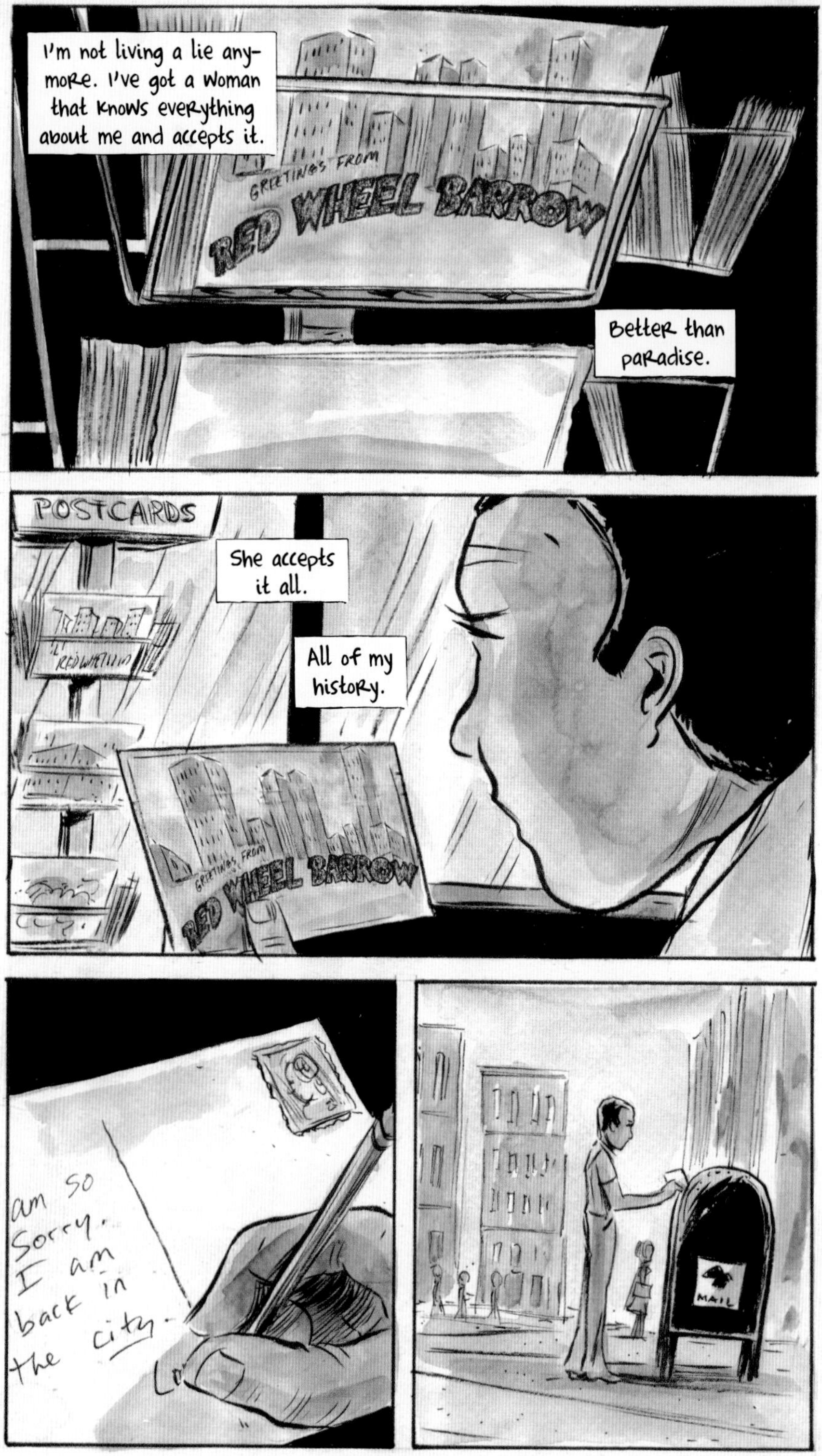
I'm not living a lie anymore. I've got a woman that knows everything about me and accepts it.
GREETINGS FROM
RED WHEEL BARROW
Better than paradise.
POSTCARDS
She accepts it all.
All of my history.
GREETINGS FROM
RED WHEEL BARROW
am so
sorry.
I am
back in
the city.
MAIL

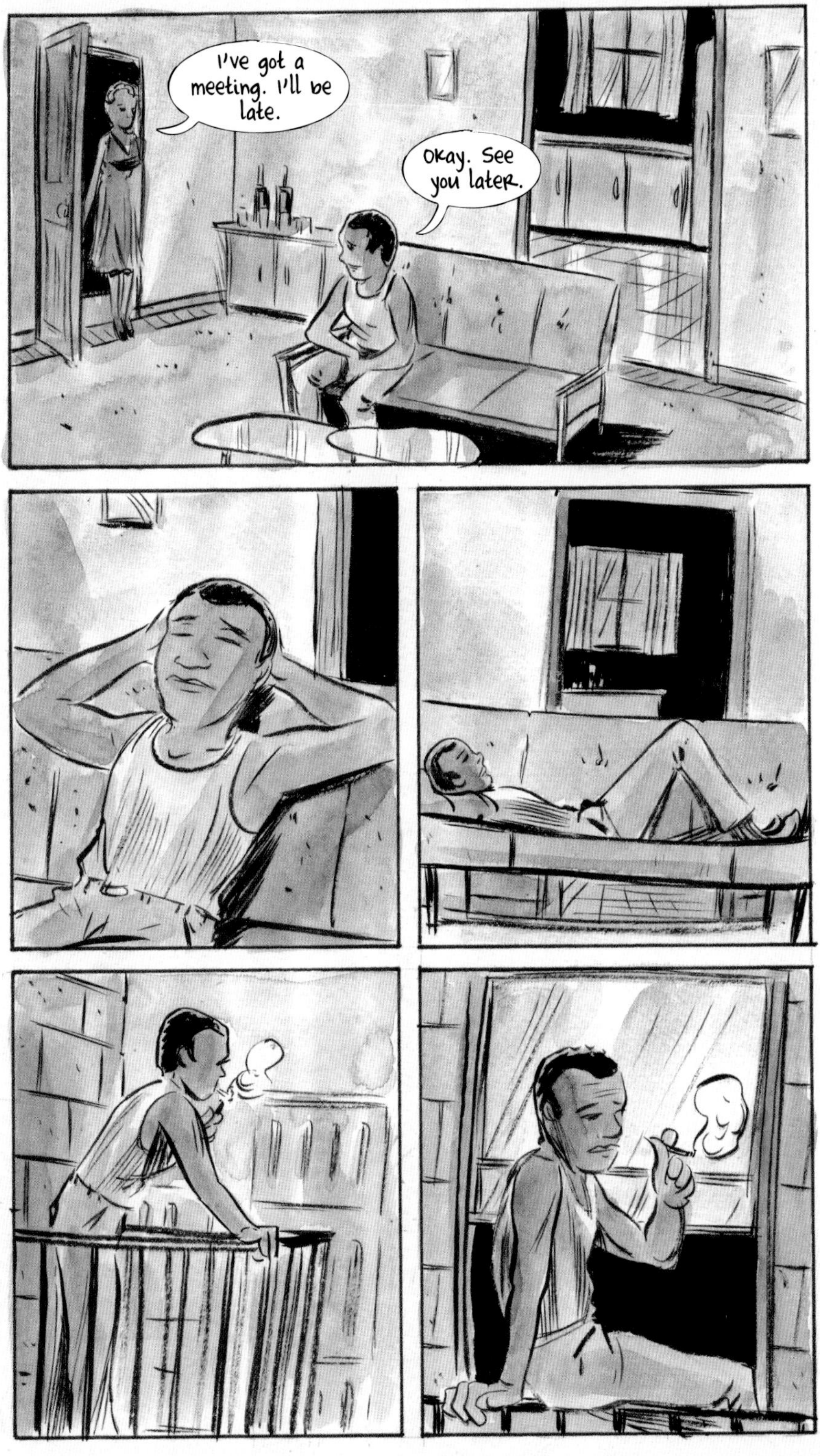
I've got a meeting. I'll be late.
Okay. See you later.

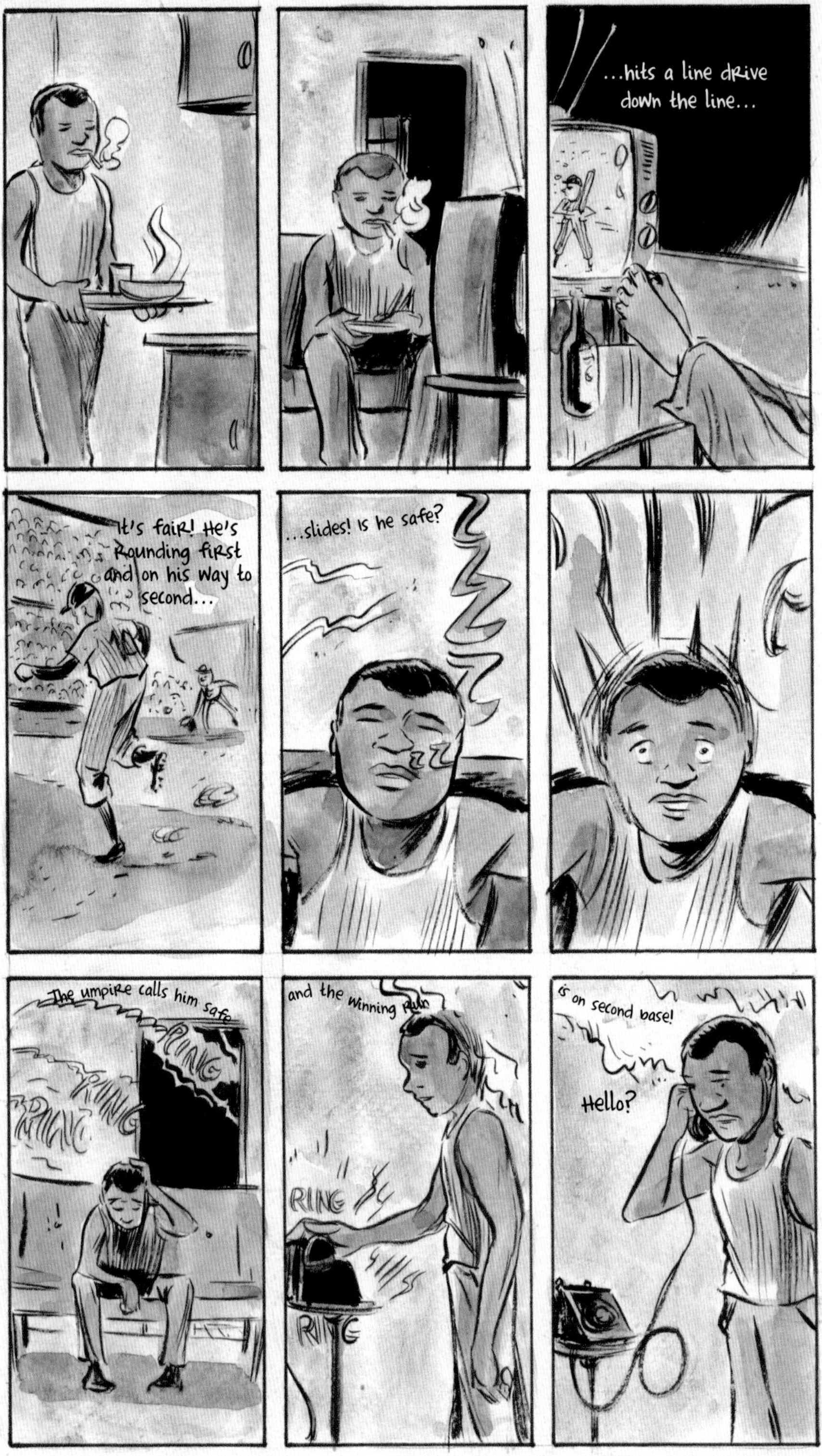
...hits a line drive down the line...
It's fair! He's Rounding first and on his way to second...
...slides! Is he safe?
The umpire calls him safe
RING
RING
and the winning run
RING
RING
is on second base!
Hello?

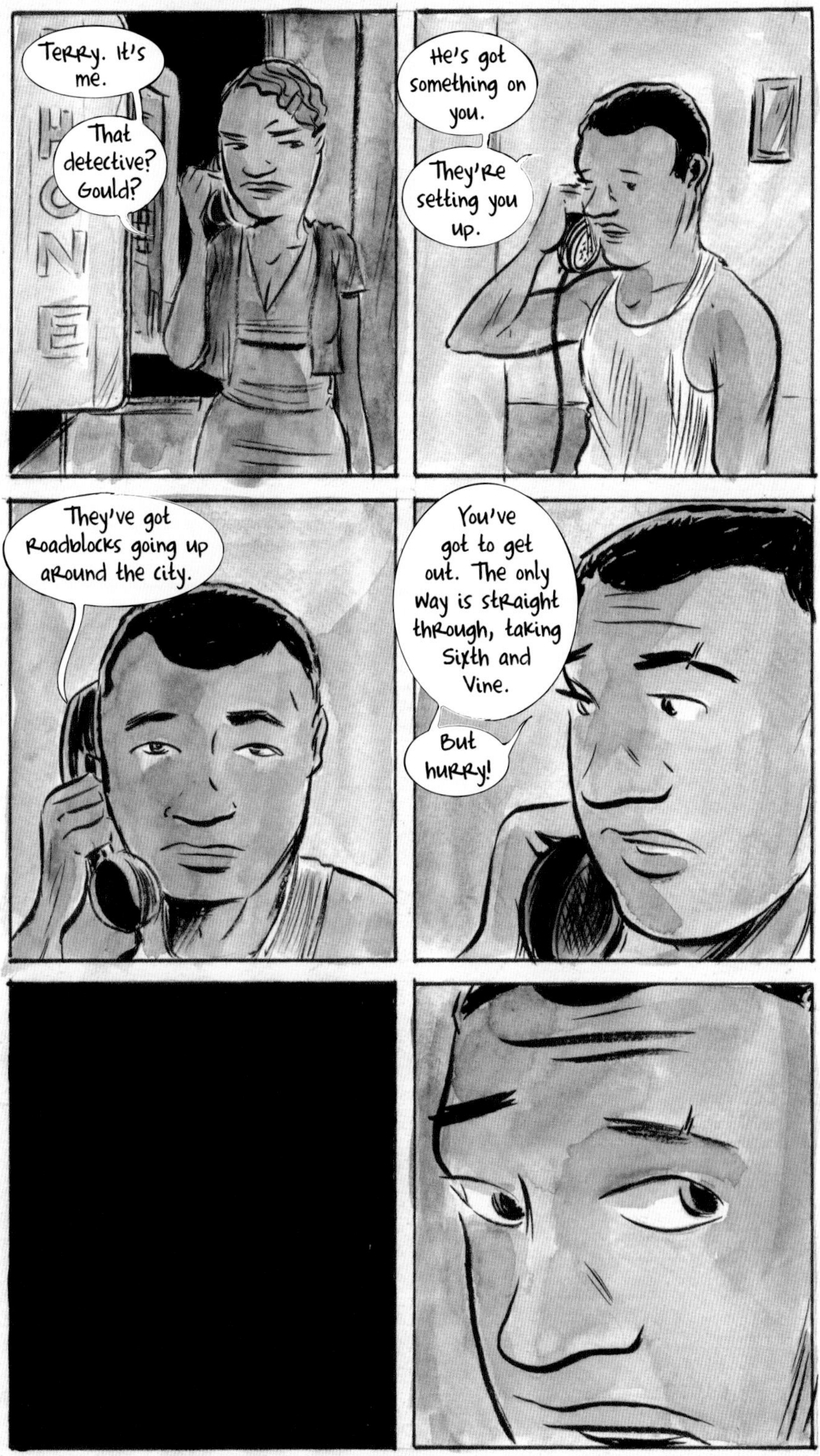
Terry. It's me.
That detective? Gould?
He's got something on you.
They're setting you up.
They've got roadblocks going up around the city.
You've got to get out. The only way is straight through, taking Sixth and Vine.
But hurry!

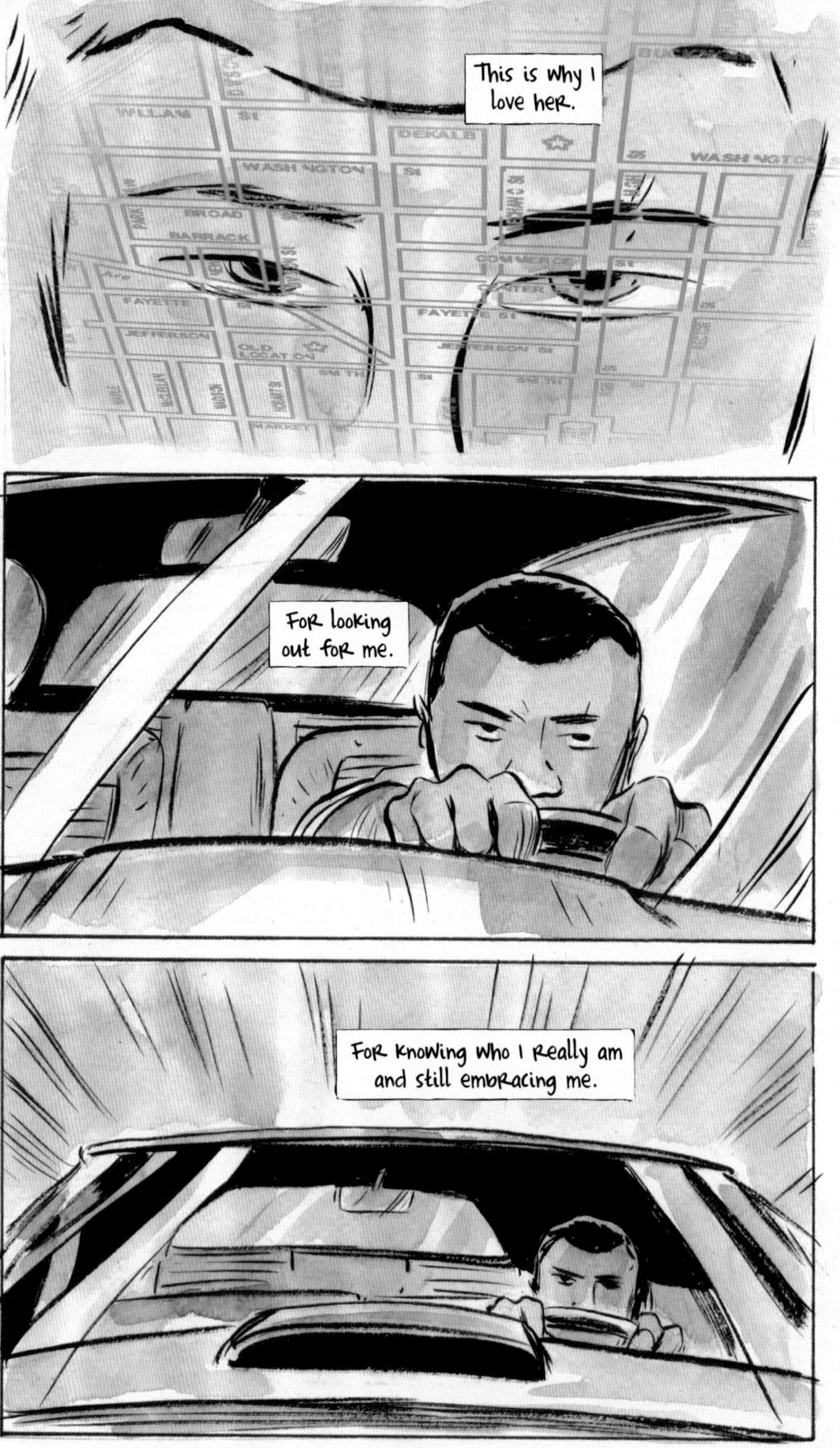
This is why I love her.
For looking out for me.
For knowing who I really am and still embracing me.

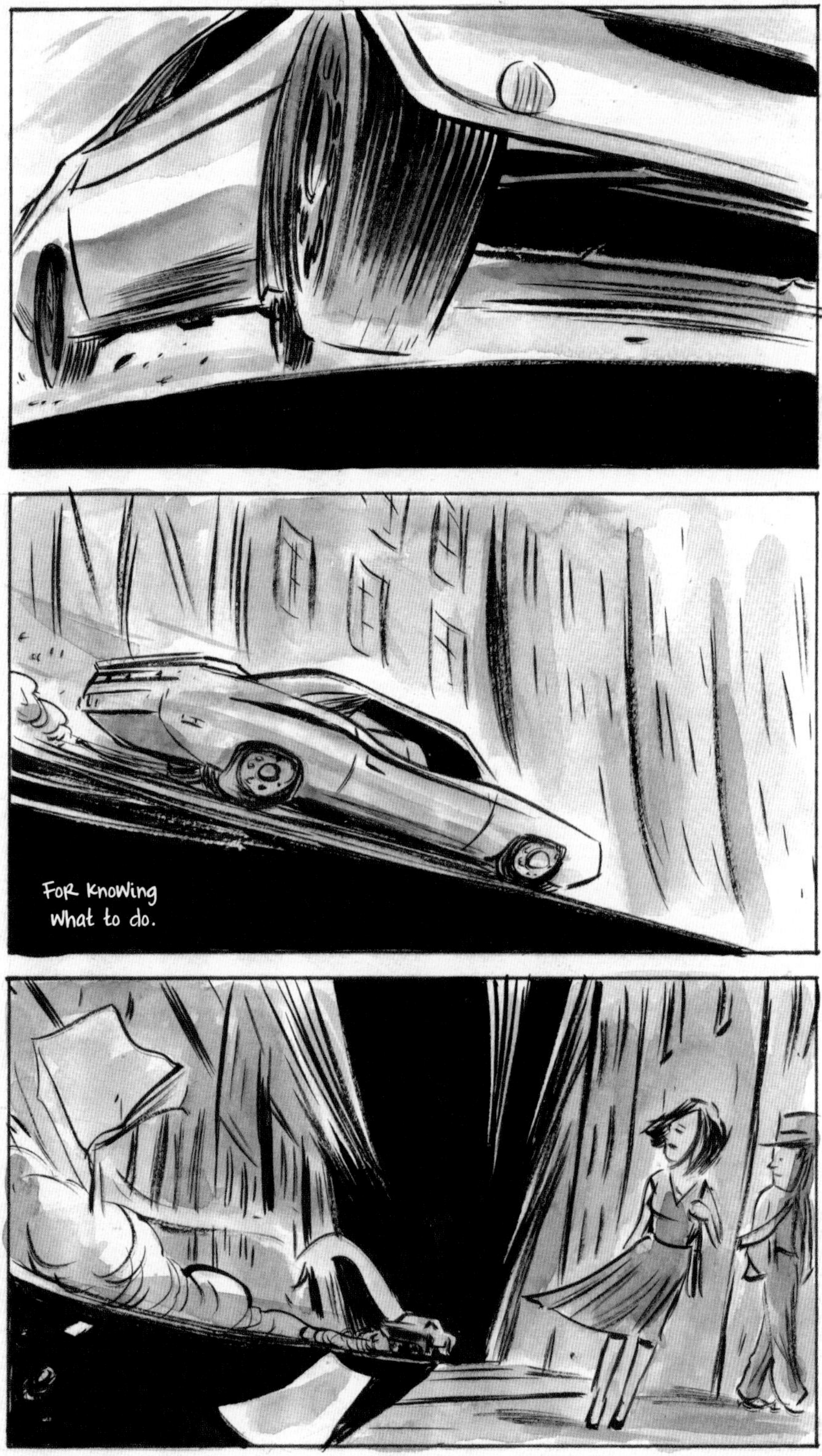
FoR KnoWing
What to do.

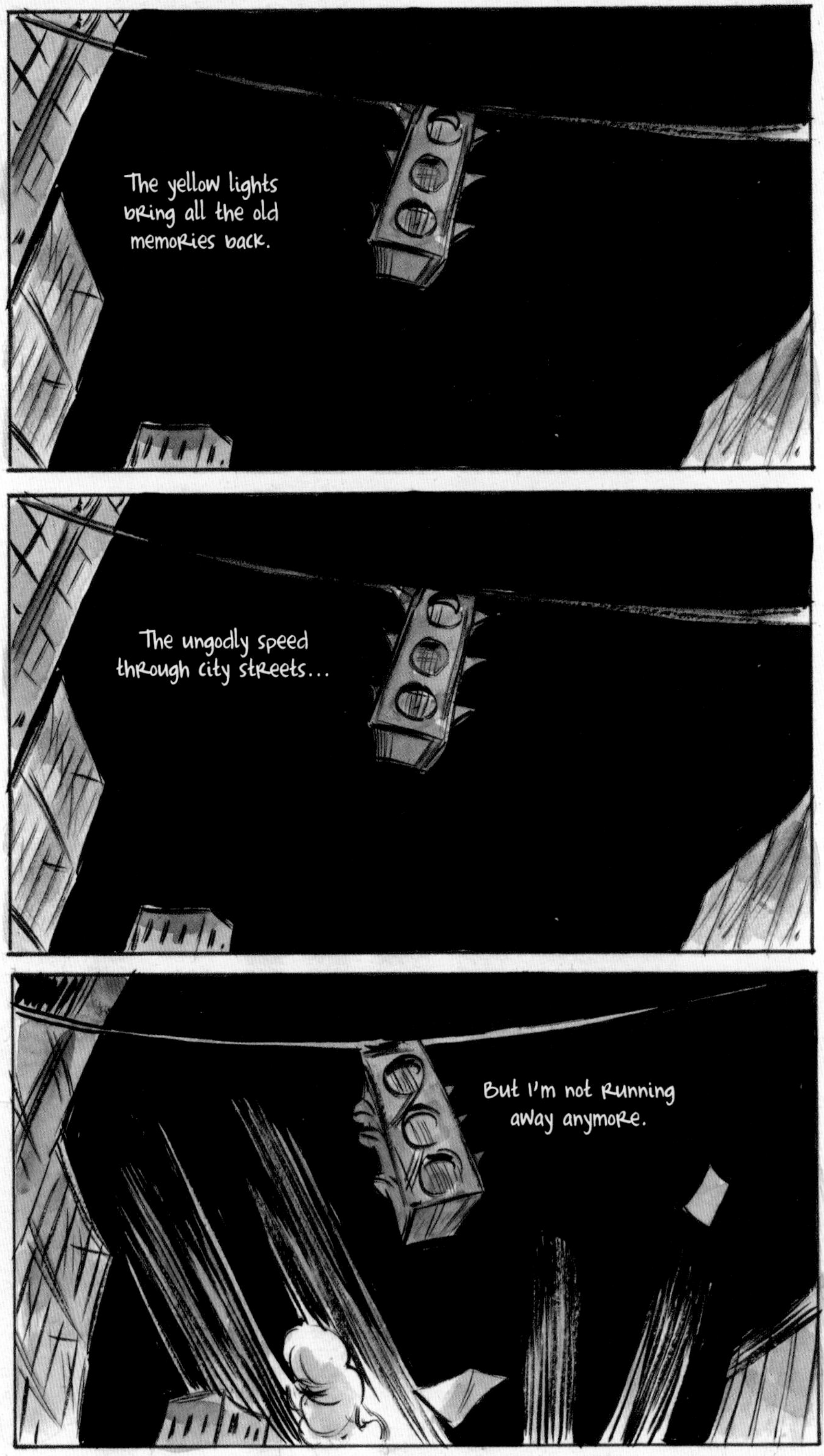
The yellow lights bring all the old memories back.
The ungodly speed through city streets...
But I'm not running away anymore.

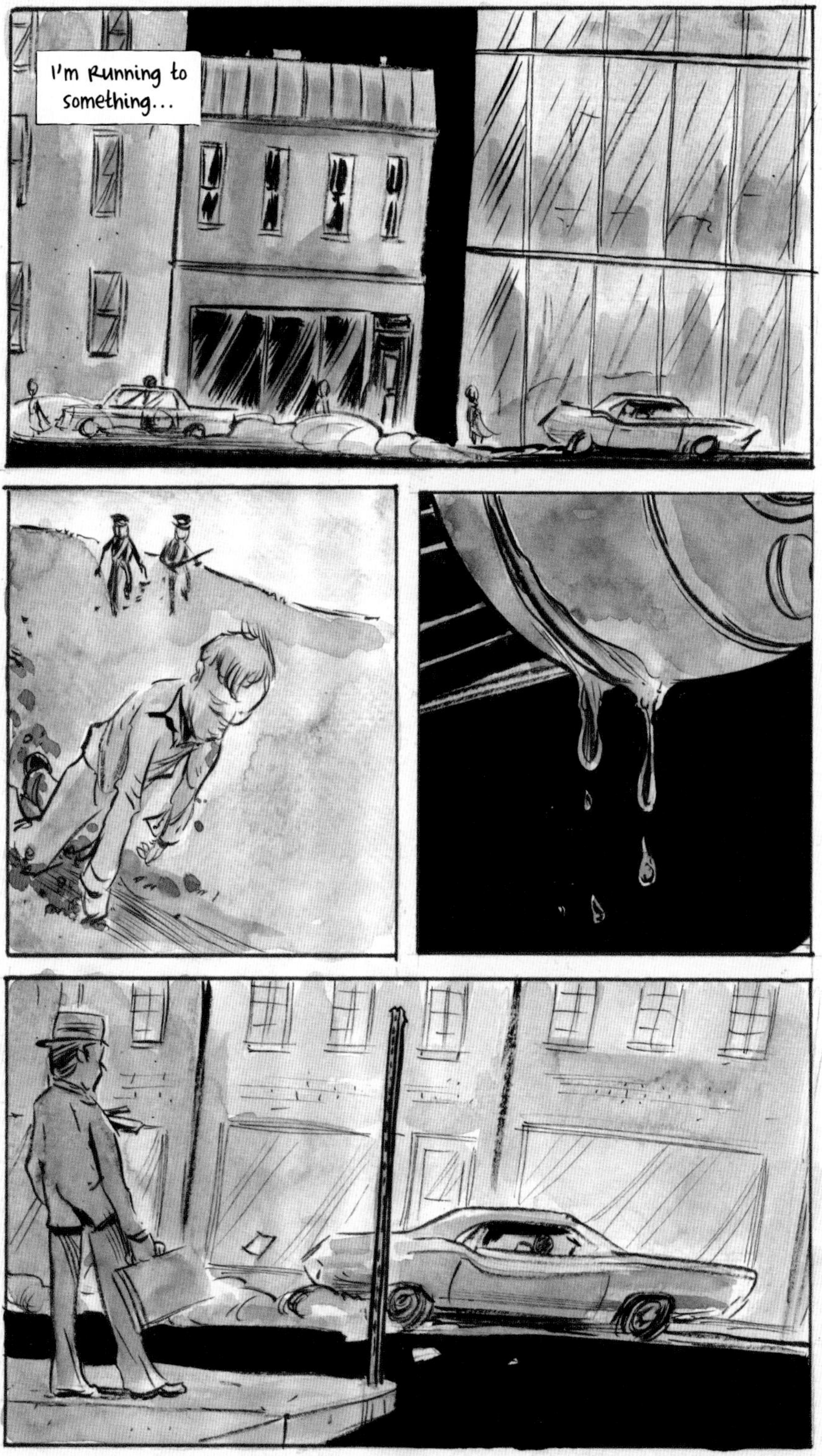
I'm Running to something...

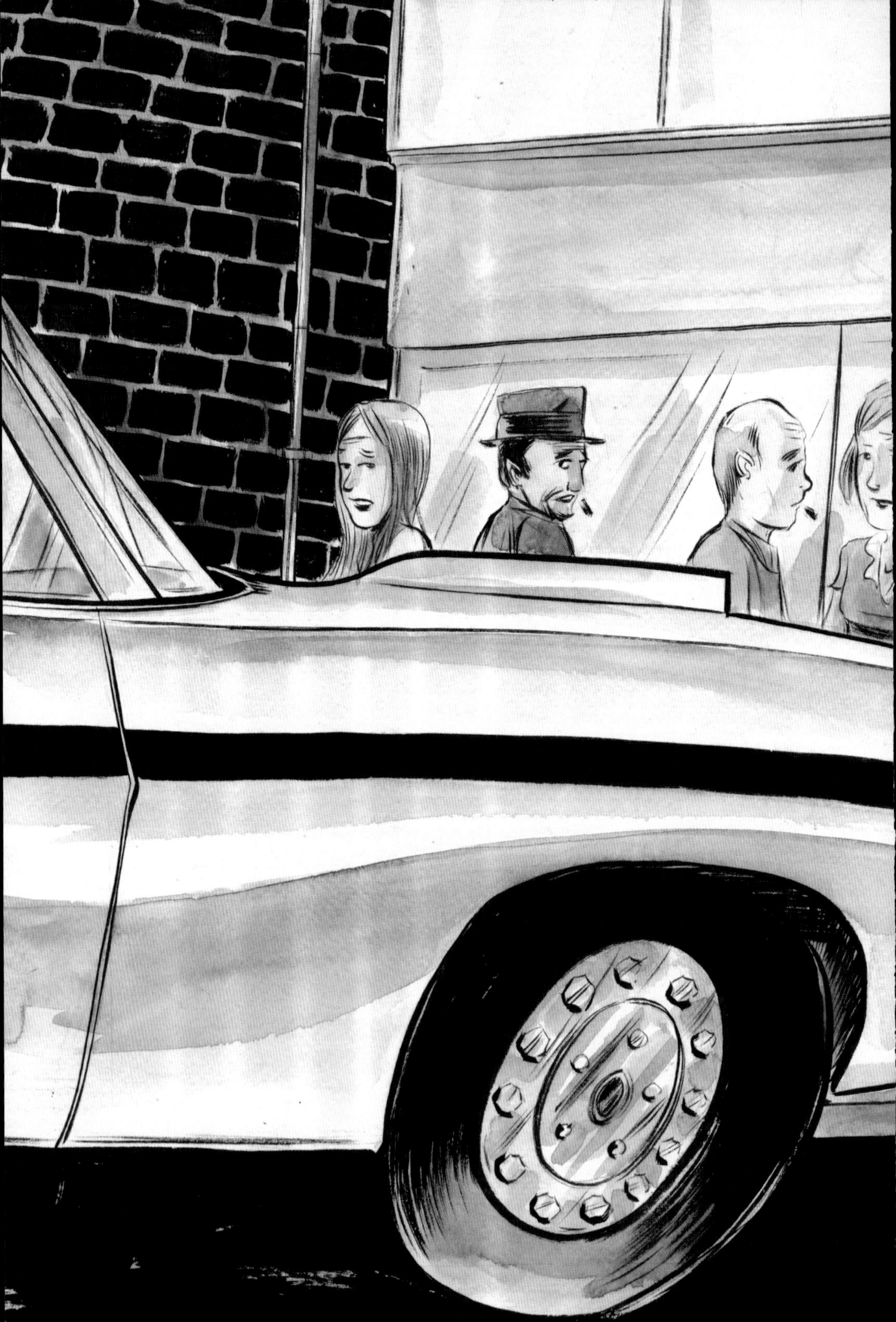

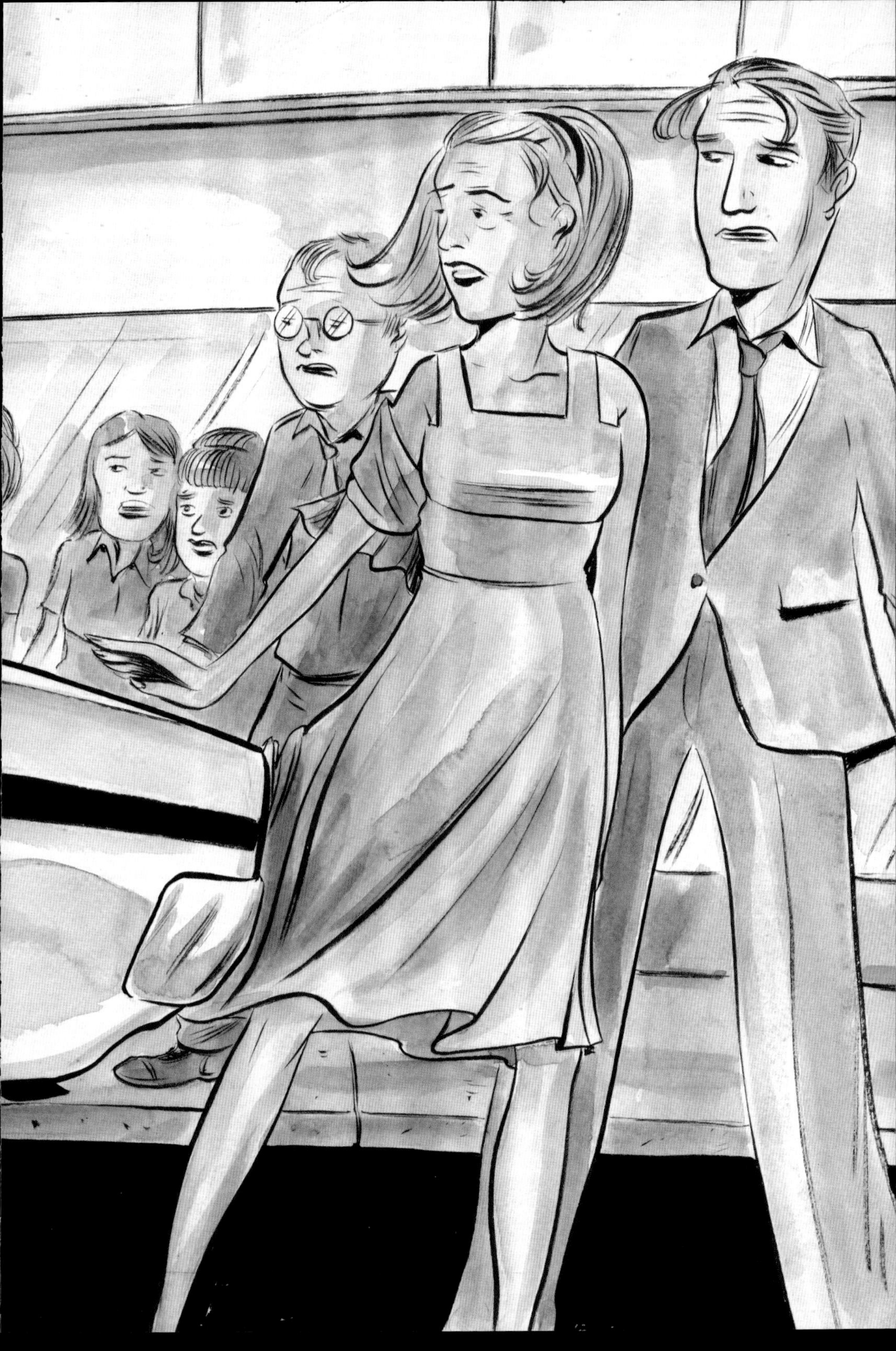

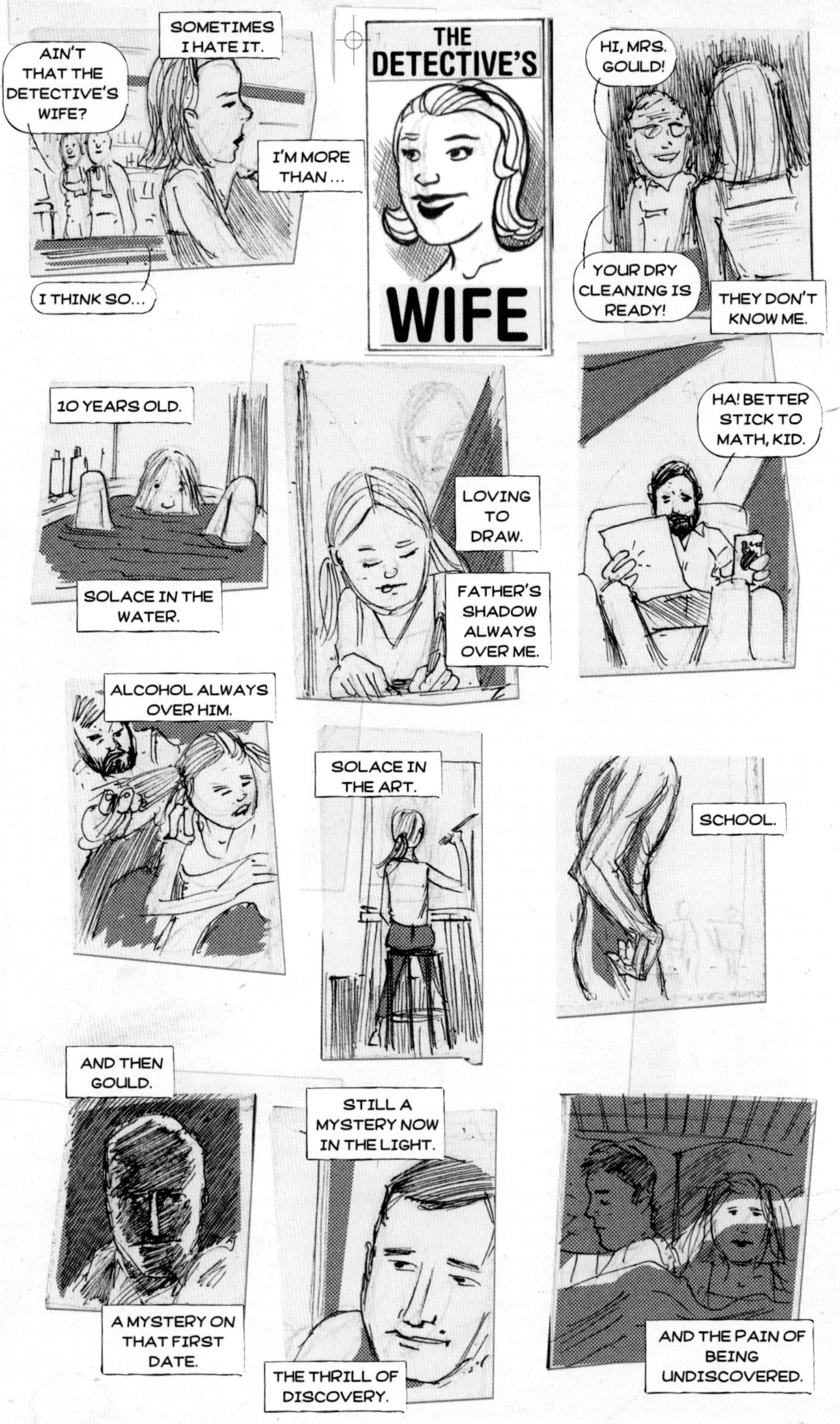
SOMETIMES I HATE IT.
AIN'T THAT THE DETECTIVE'S WIFE?
I'M MORE THAN...
I THINK SO...
THE DETECTIVE'S WIFE
HI, MRS. GOULD!
YOUR DRY CLEANING IS READY!
THEY DON'T KNOW ME.
10 YEARS OLD.
SOLACE IN THE WATER.
LOVING TO DRAW.
FATHER'S SHADOW ALWAYS OVER ME.
HA! BETTER STICK TO MATH, KID.
ALCOHOL ALWAYS OVER HIM.
SOLACE IN THE ART.
SCHOOL.
AND THEN GOULD.
A MYSTERY ON THAT FIRST DATE.
STILL A MYSTERY NOW IN THE LIGHT.
THE THRILL OF DISCOVERY.
AND THE PAIN OF BEING UNDISCOVERED.

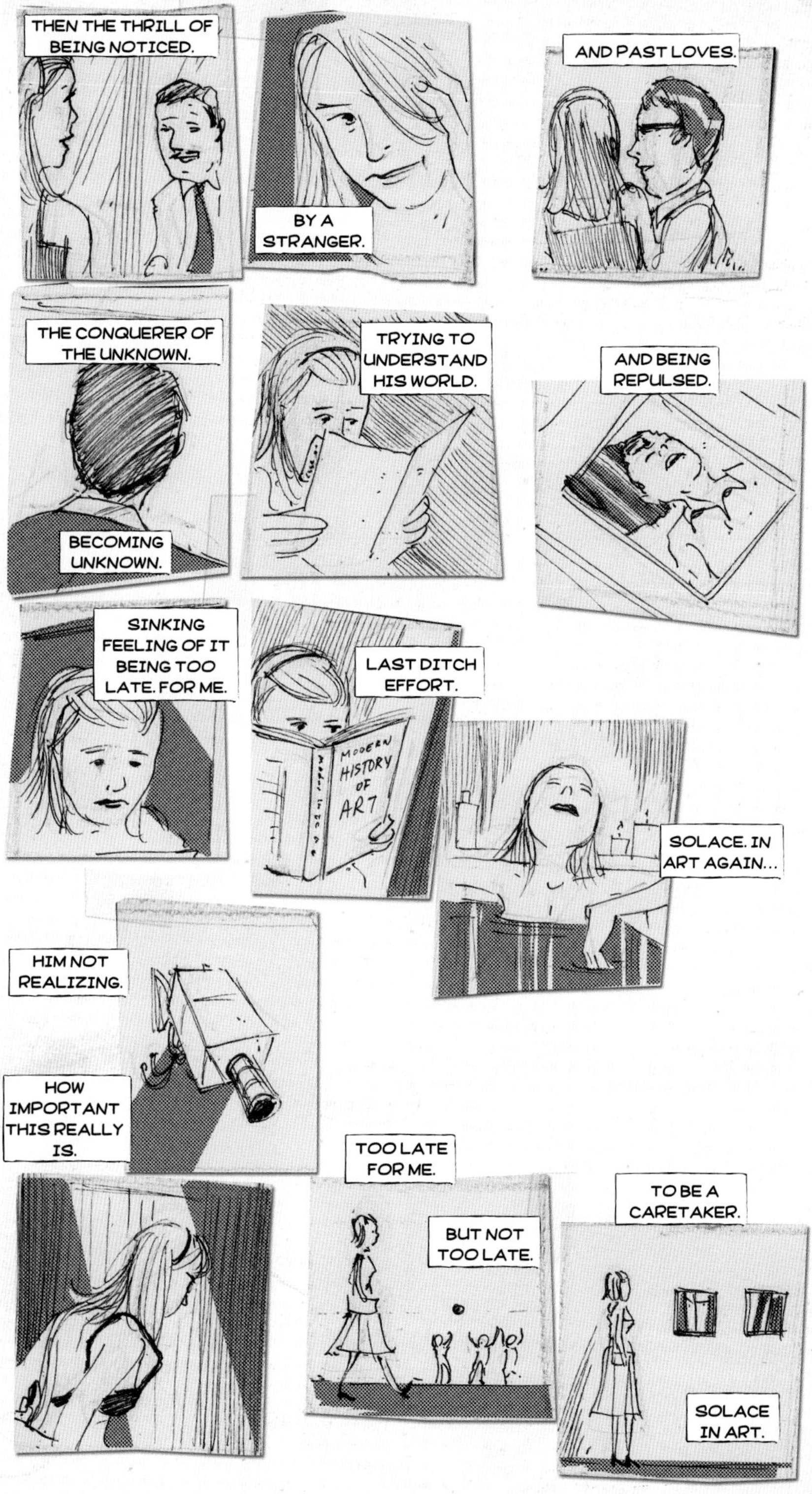
THEN THE THRILL OF BEING NOTICED.
BY A STRANGER.
AND PAST LOVES.
THE CONQUERER OF THE UNKNOWN.
BECOMING UNKNOWN.
TRYING TO UNDERSTAND HIS WORLD.
AND BEING REPULSED.
SINKING FEELING OF IT BEING TOO LATE. FOR ME.
LAST DITCH EFFORT.
MODERN HISTORY OF ART
SOLACE. IN ART AGAIN...
HIM NOT REALIZING.
HOW IMPORTANT THIS REALLY IS.
TOO LATE FOR ME.
BUT NOT TOO LATE.
TO BE A CARETAKER.
SOLACE IN ART.

GAZE TE

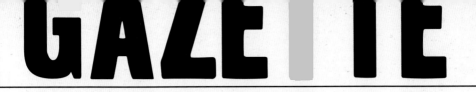

It was a record-breaking week for the city of Red Wheel Barrow as crime reached an all-time high but unsolved crimes were at an all-time low. In fact, the unsolved crimes for this week were nonexistent—due in large part to what the city has known for a while, but the rest of the nation is starting to notice—Detective Gould may be the greatest detective in the history of our nation. In fact, some are saying he rivals the greatest detectives of fiction as well. "Sherlock Holmes has nothing on our Gould," the police chief was quoted as saying at

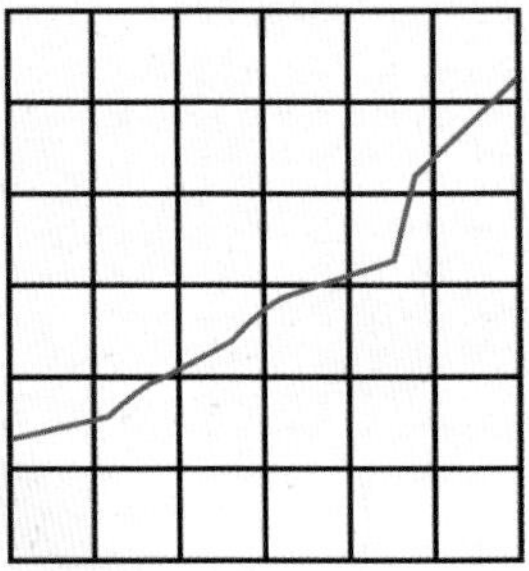

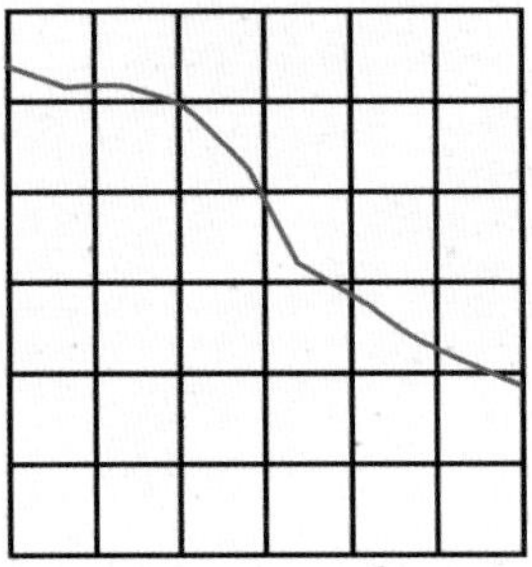

(continued B6)

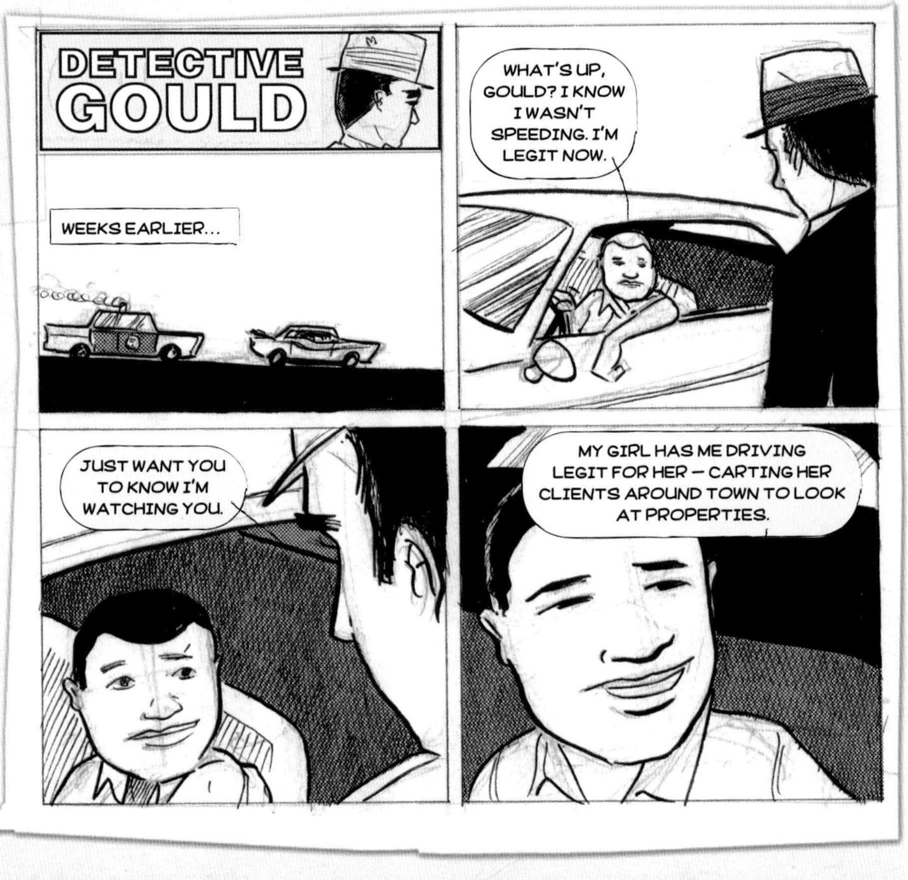
DETECTIVE GOULD
WEEKS EARLIER...
WHAT'S UP, GOULD? I KNOW I WASN'T SPEEDING. I'M LEGIT NOW.
JUST WANT YOU TO KNOW I'M WATCHING YOU.
MY GIRL HAS ME DRIVING LEGIT FOR HER — CARTING HER CLIENTS AROUND TOWN TO LOOK AT PROPERTIES.

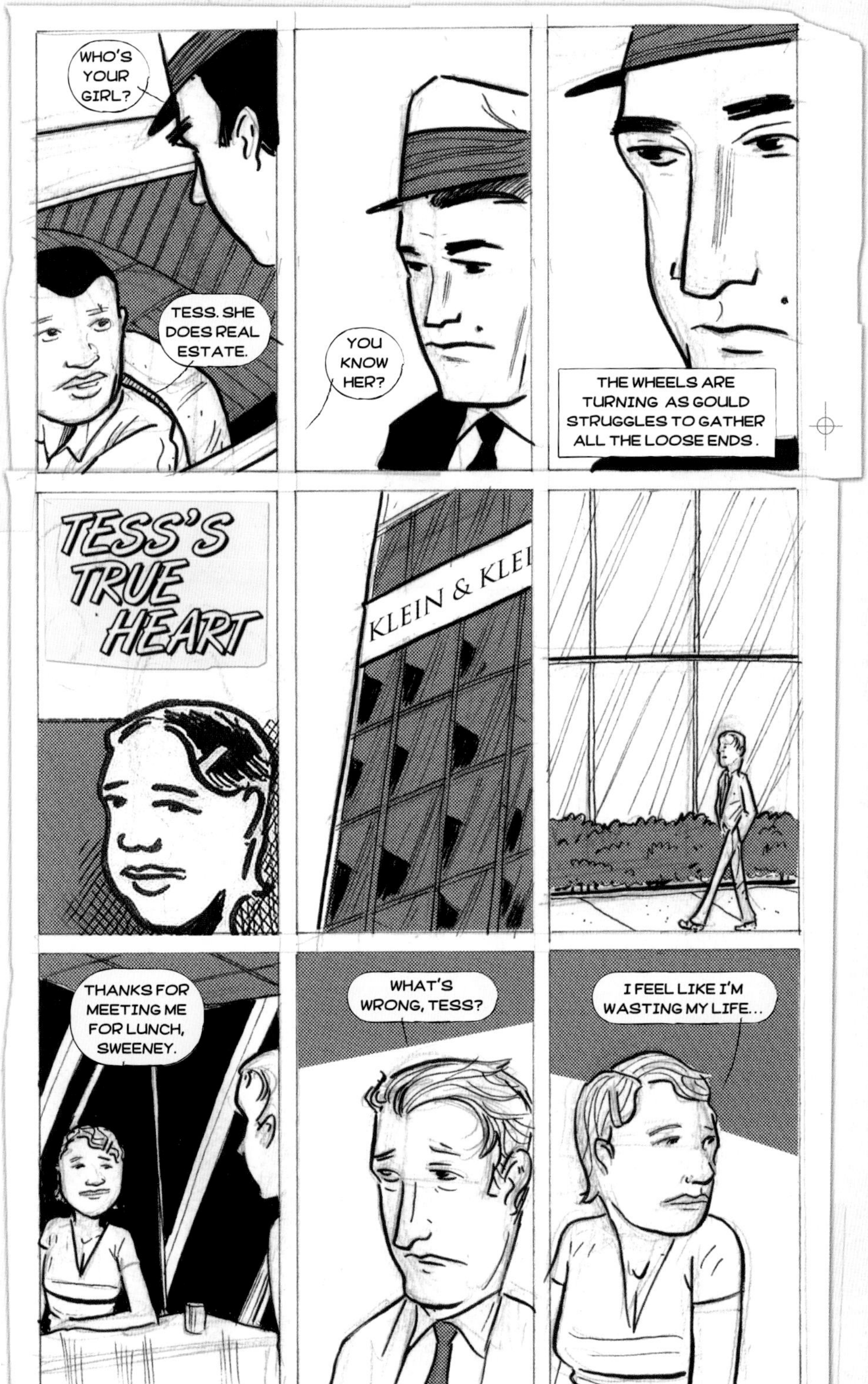
WHO'S YOUR GIRL?
TESS. SHE DOES REAL ESTATE.
YOU KNOW HER?
THE WHEELS ARE TURNING AS GOULD STRUGGLES TO GATHER ALL THE LOOSE ENDS.
TESS'S TRUE HEART
KLEIN & KLEI
THANKS FOR MEETING ME FOR LUNCH, SWEENEY.
WHAT'S WRONG, TESS?
I FEEL LIKE I'M WASTING MY LIFE...

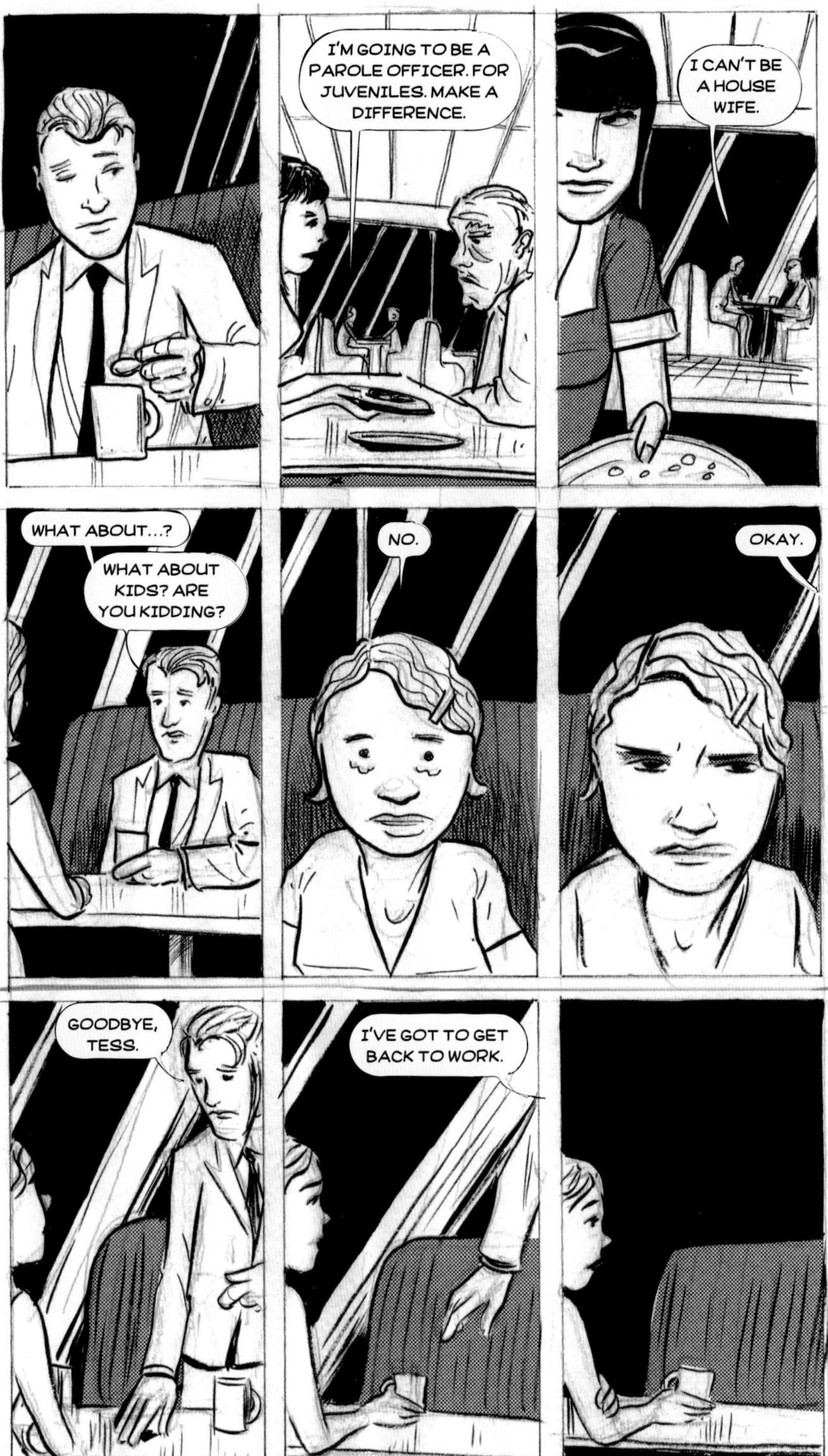
I'M GOING TO BE A PAROLE OFFICER. FOR JUVENILES. MAKE A DIFFERENCE.
I CAN'T BE A HOUSE WIFE.
WHAT ABOUT...?
WHAT ABOUT KIDS? ARE YOU KIDDING?
NO.
OKAY.
GOODBYE, TESS.
I'VE GOT TO GET BACK TO WORK.

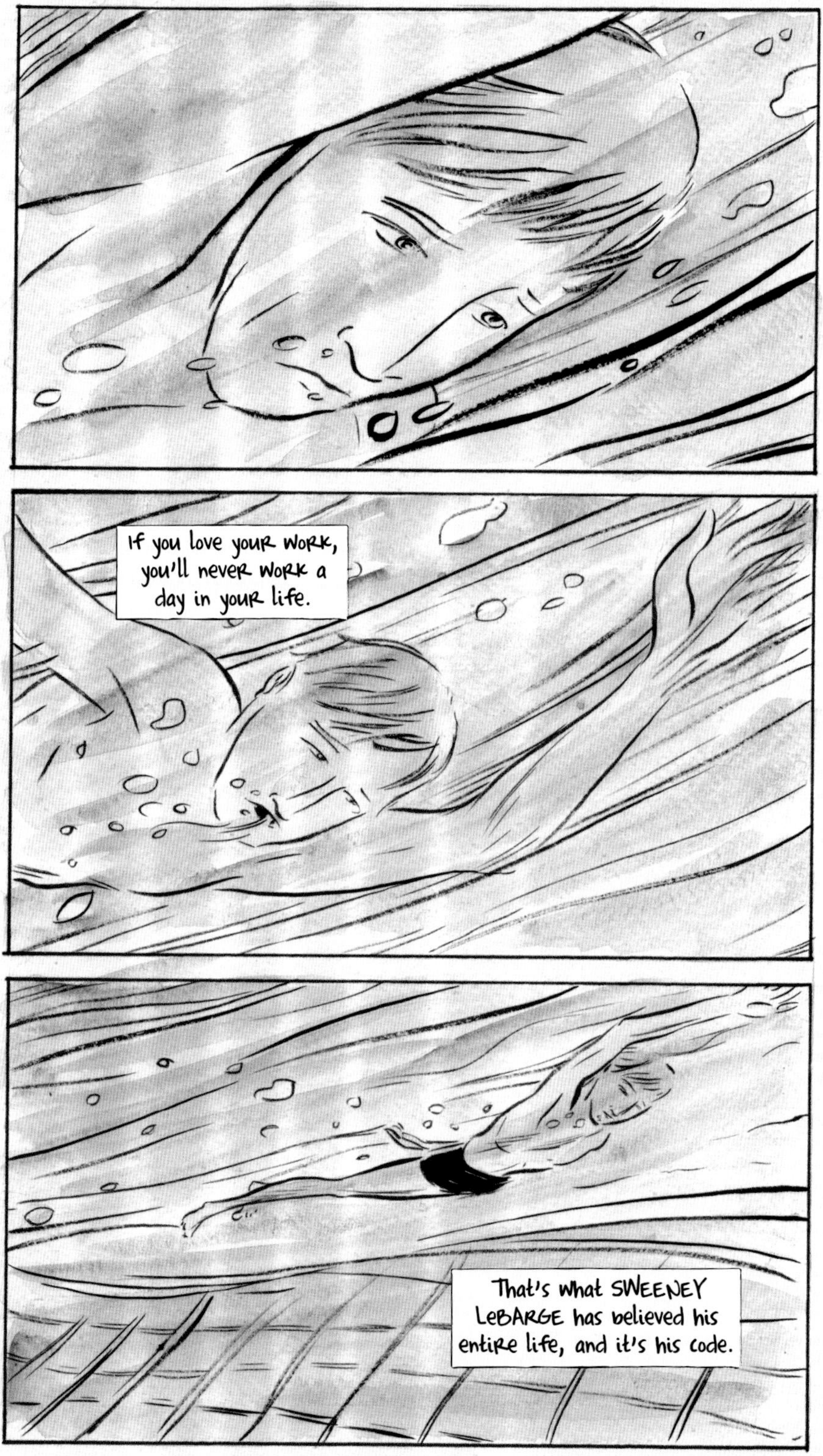
If you love your work, you'll never work a day in your life.
That's what SWEENEY LeBARGE has believed his entire life, and it's his code.

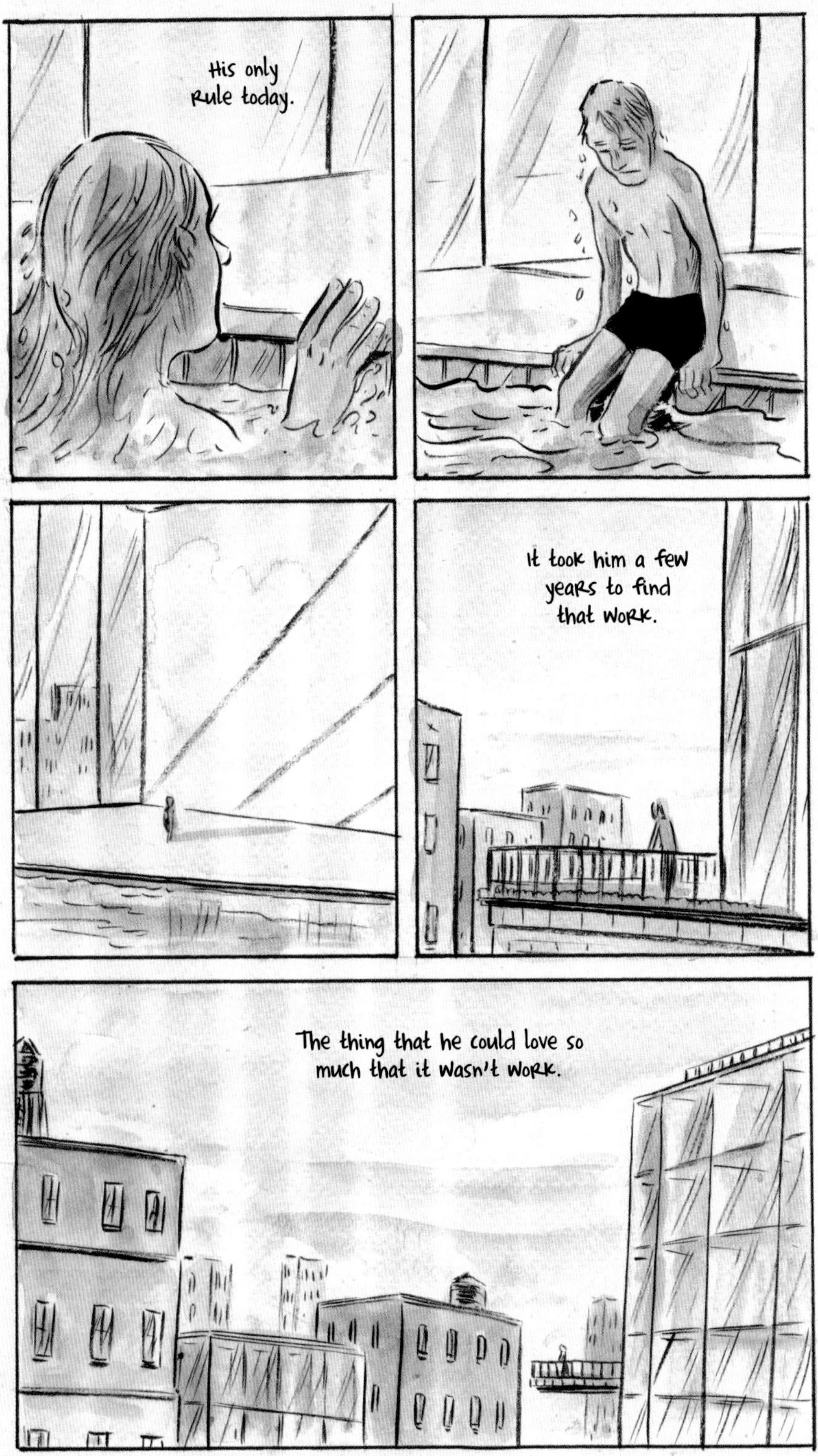
His only rule today.
It took him a few years to find that work.
The thing that he could love so much that it wasn't work.

THE
FIRE
STARTER

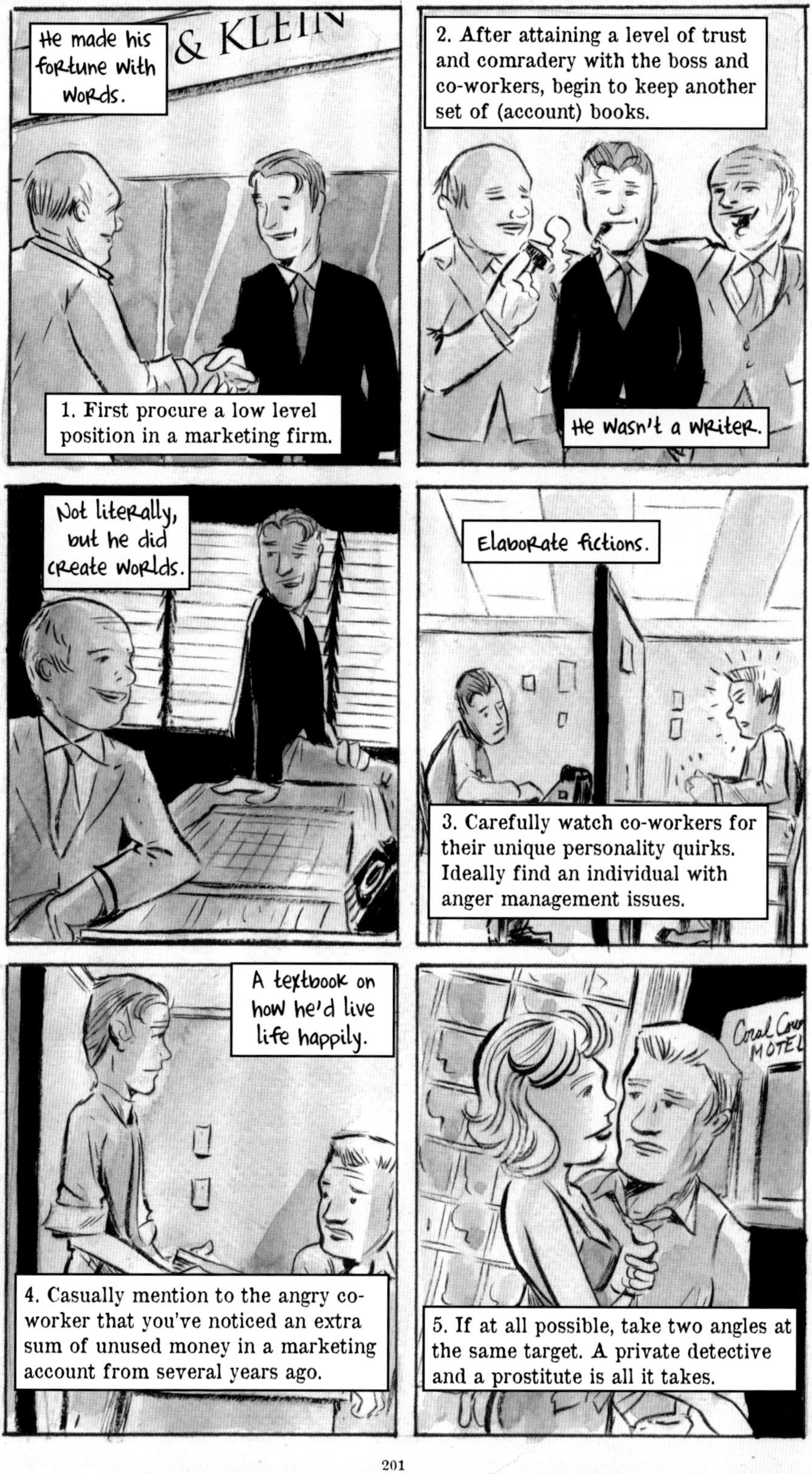
He made his fortune with words.
& KLEIN
1. First procure a low level position in a marketing firm.
2. After attaining a level of trust and comradery with the boss and co-workers, begin to keep another set of (account) books.
He wasn't a writer.
Not literally, but he did create worlds.
Elaborate fictions.
3. Carefully watch co-workers for their unique personality quirks. Ideally find an individual with anger management issues.
A textbook on how he'd live life happily.
4. Casually mention to the angry co-worker that you've noticed an extra sum of unused money in a marketing account from several years ago.
Coral Cou
MOTEL
5. If at all possible, take two angles at the same target. A private detective and a prostitute is all it takes.

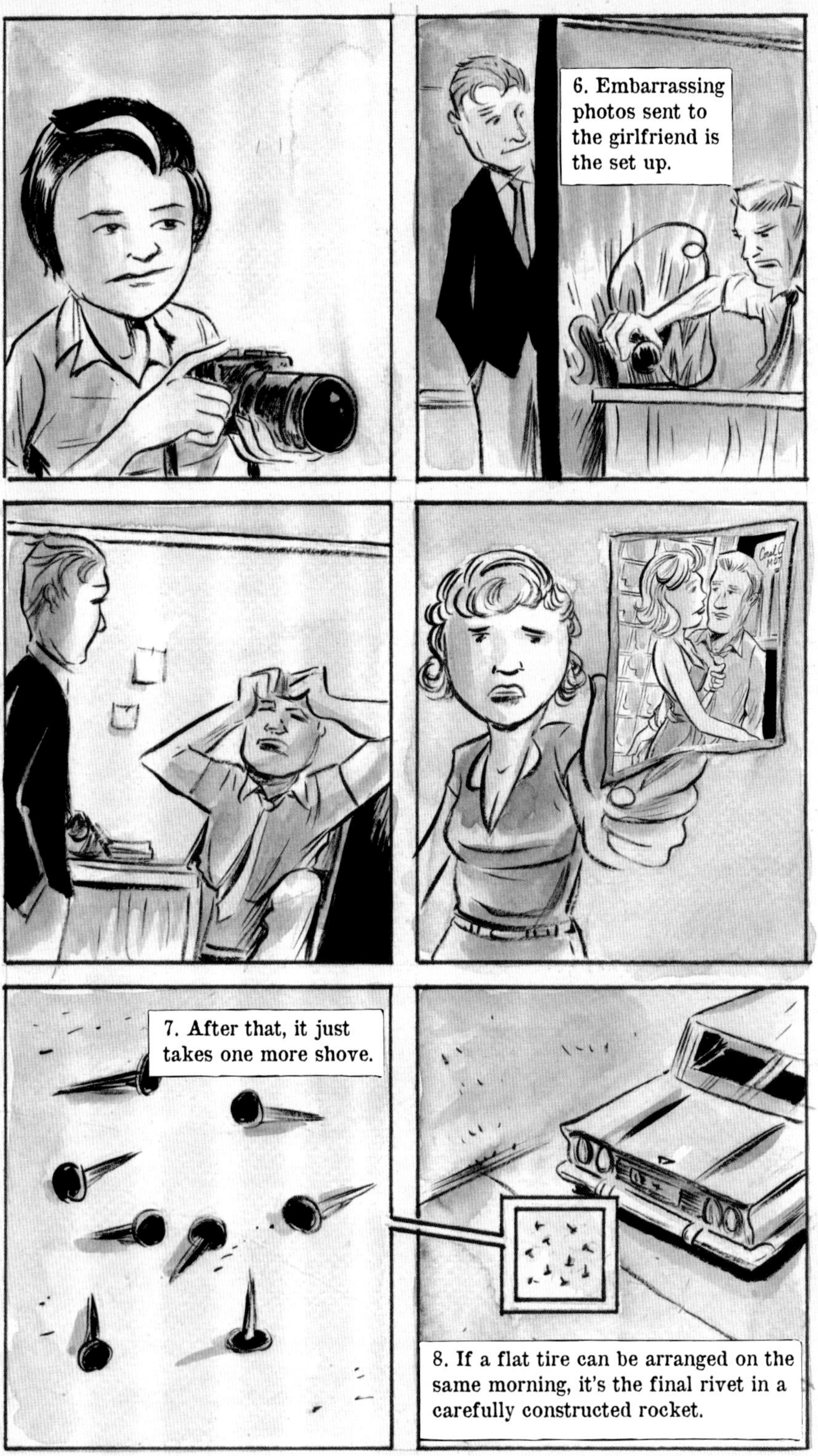
6. Embarrassing photos sent to the girlfriend is the set up.
7. After that, it just takes one more shove.
8. If a flat tire can be arranged on the same morning, it's the final rivet in a carefully constructed rocket.

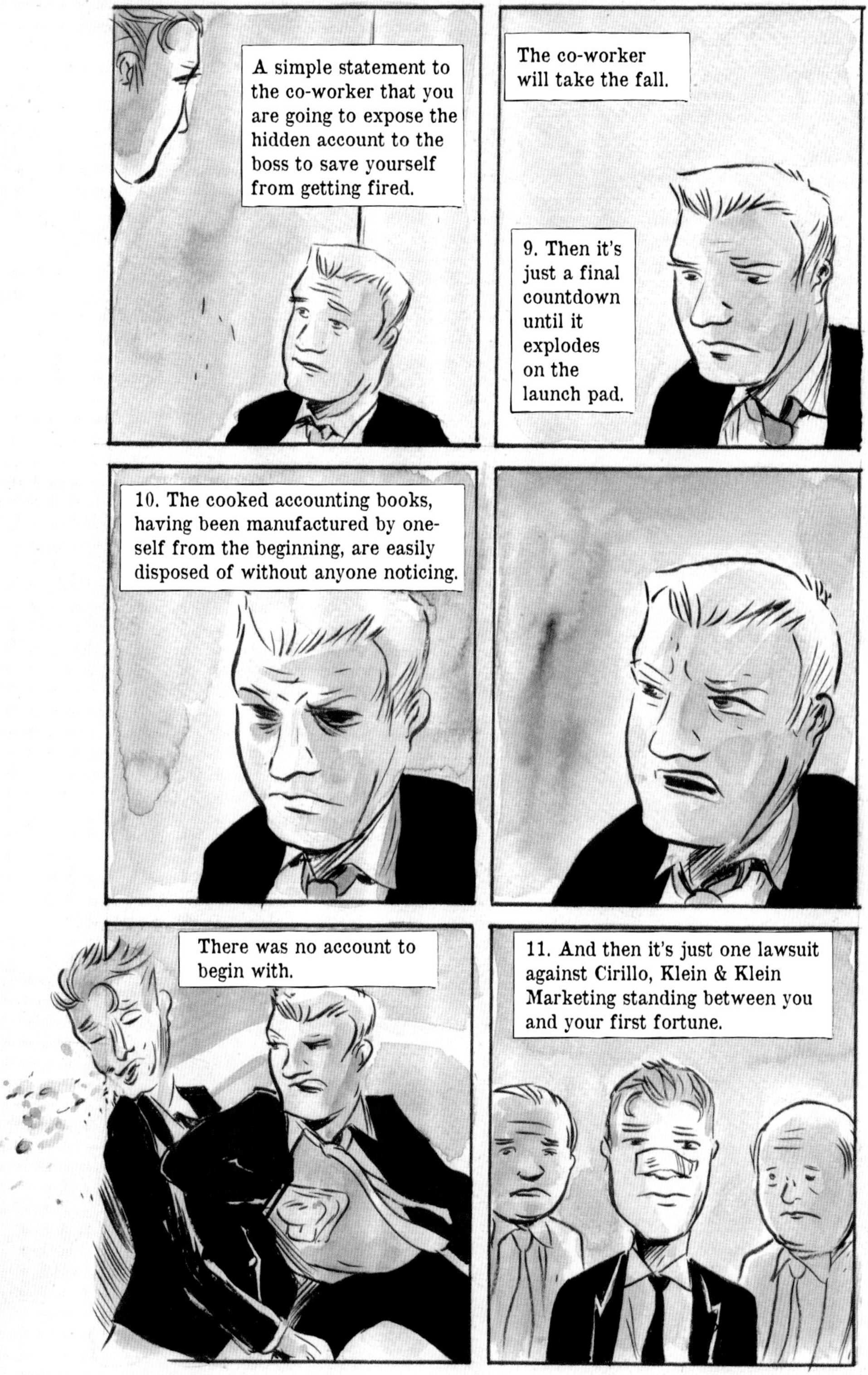
A simple statement to the co-worker that you are going to expose the hidden account to the boss to save yourself from getting fired.
The co-worker will take the fall.
9. Then it's just a final countdown until it explodes on the launch pad.
10. The cooked accounting books, having been manufactured by one-self from the beginning, are easily disposed of without anyone noticing.
There was no account to begin with.
11. And then it's just one lawsuit against Cirillo, Klein & Klein Marketing standing between you and your first fortune.

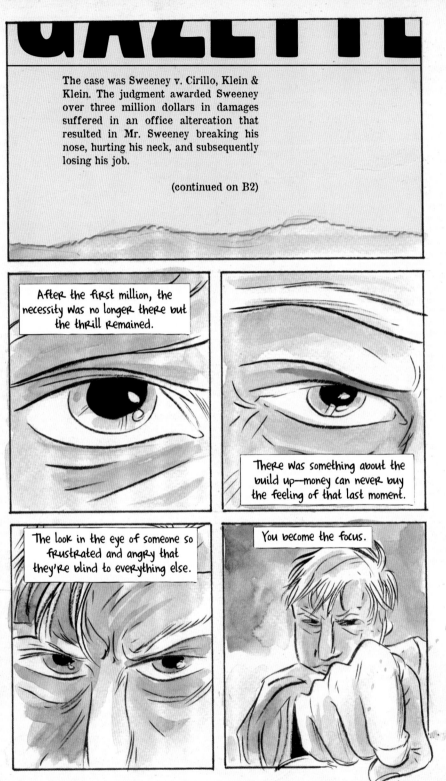

GAZETTE

The case was Sweeney v. Cirillo, Klein & Klein. The judgment awarded Sweeney over three million dollars in damages suffered in an office altercation that resulted in Mr. Sweeney breaking his nose, hurting his neck, and subsequently losing his job.

(continued on B2)

After the first million, the necessity was no longer there but the thrill remained.

There was something about the build up—money can never buy the feeling of that last moment.

The look in the eye of someone so frustrated and angry that they're blind to everything else.

You become the focus.

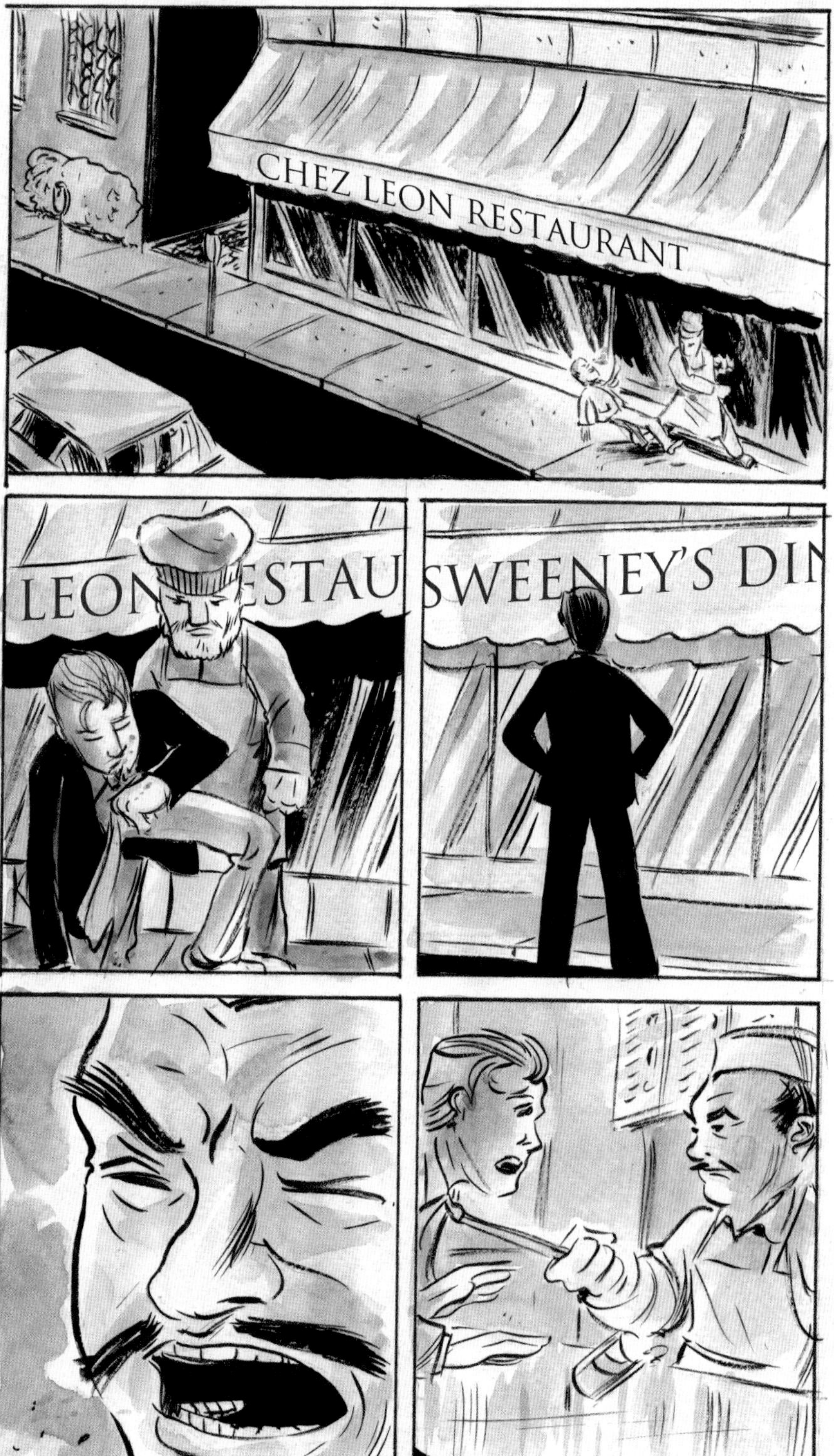
CHEZ LEON RESTAURANT
LEON ESTAU
SWEENEY'S DIN

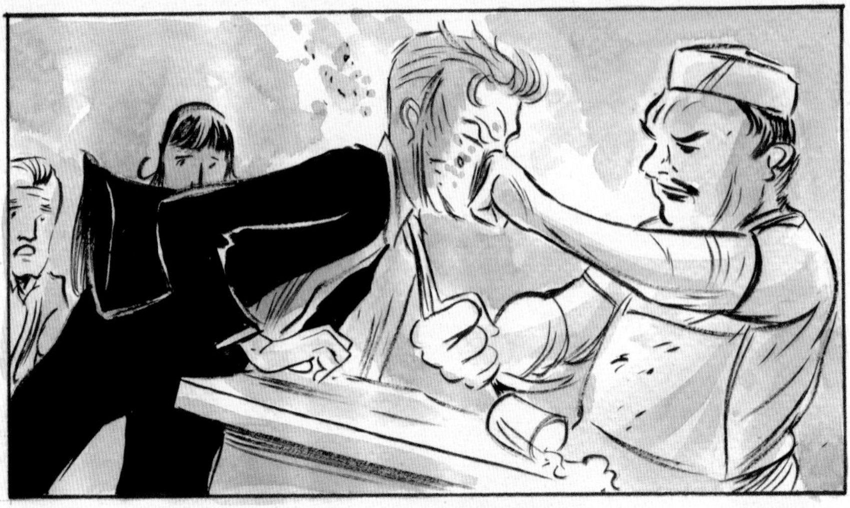

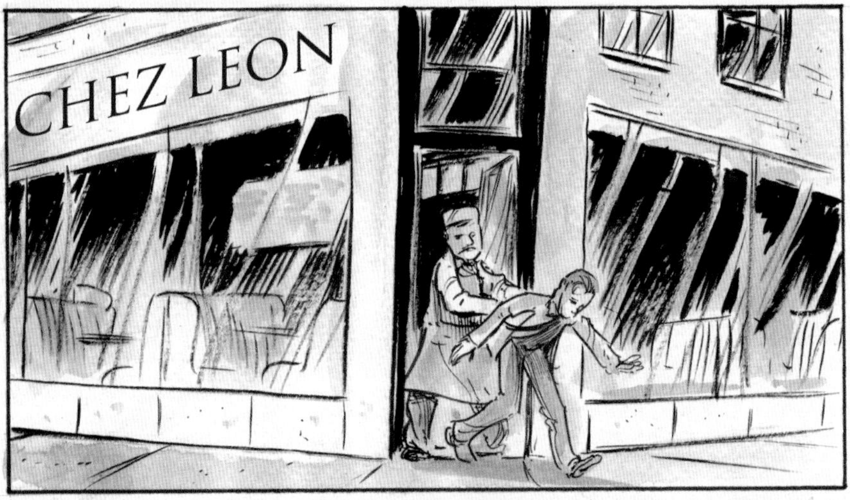
CHEZ LEON

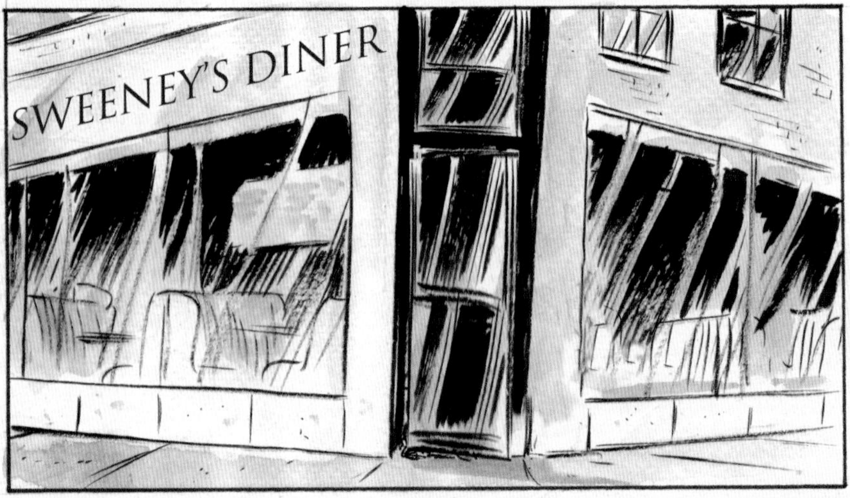
SWEENEY'S DINER

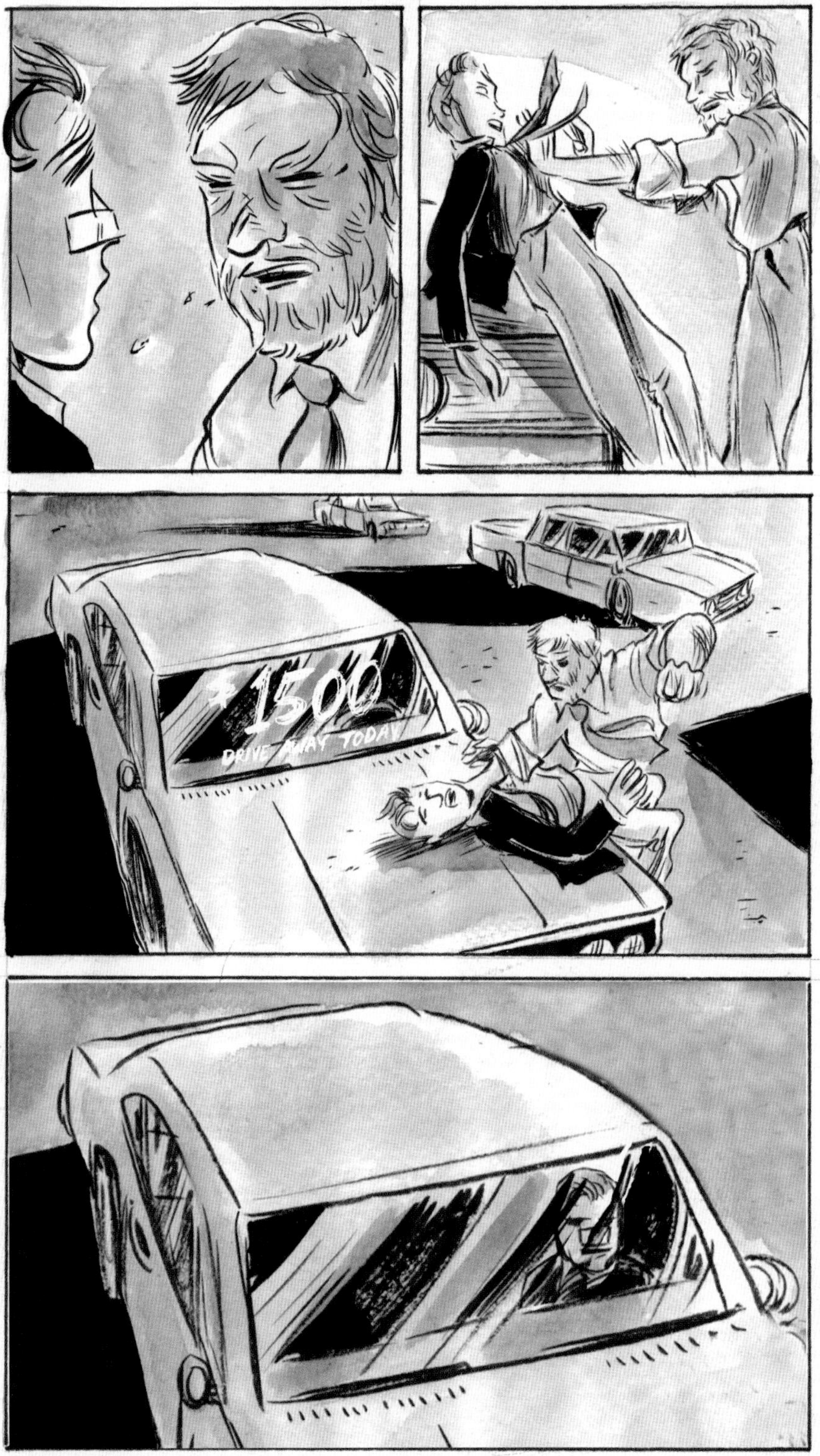
$1500
DRIVE AWAY TODAY

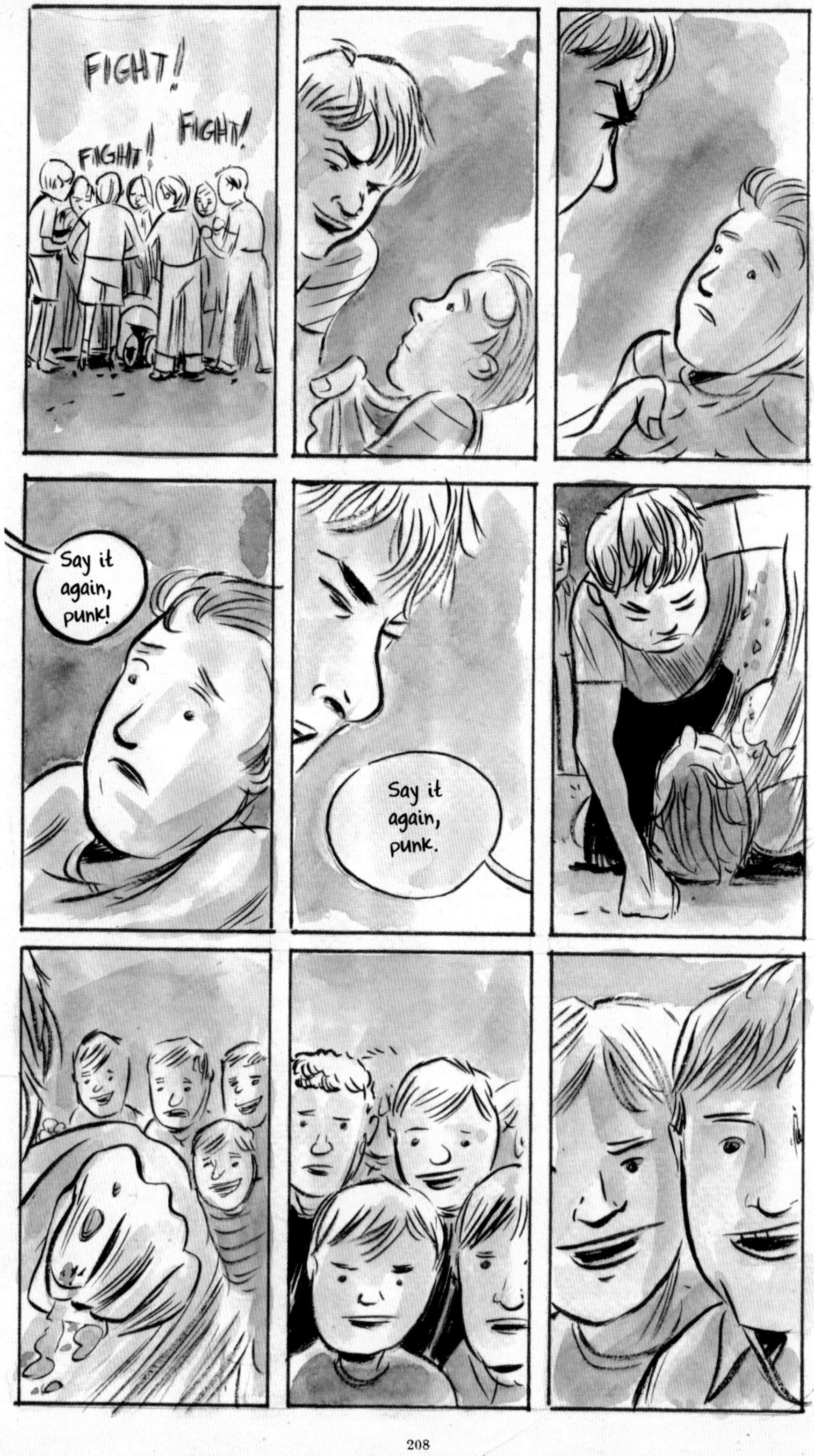
FIGHT!
FIGHT!
FIGHT!
Say it again, punk!
Say it again, punk.

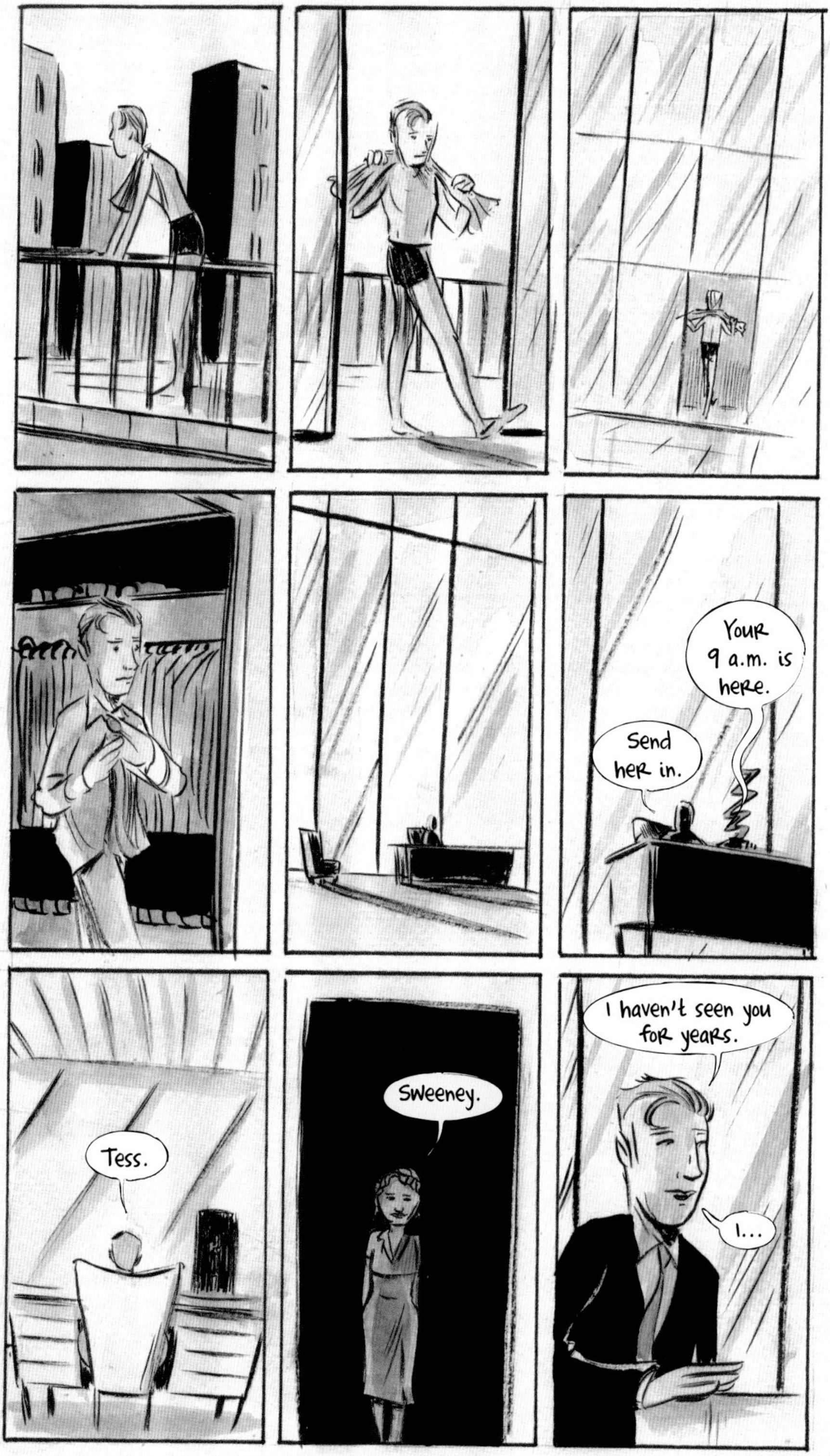
Your 9 a.m. is here.
Send her in.
Tess.
Sweeney.
I haven't seen you for years.
I...

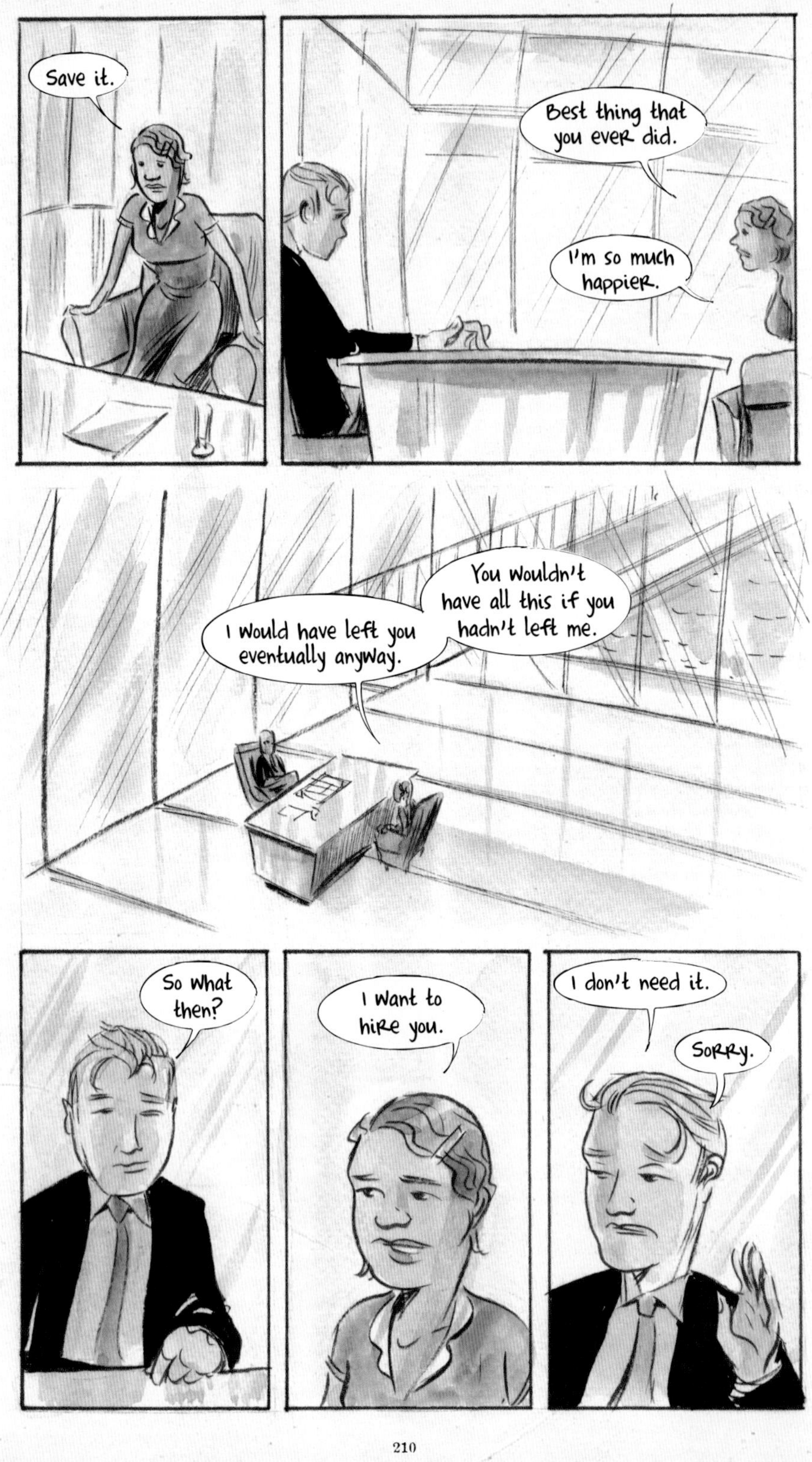
Save it.
Best thing that you ever did.
I'm so much happier.
You wouldn't have all this if you hadn't left me.
I would have left you eventually anyway.
So what then?
I want to hire you.
I don't need it.
Sorry.

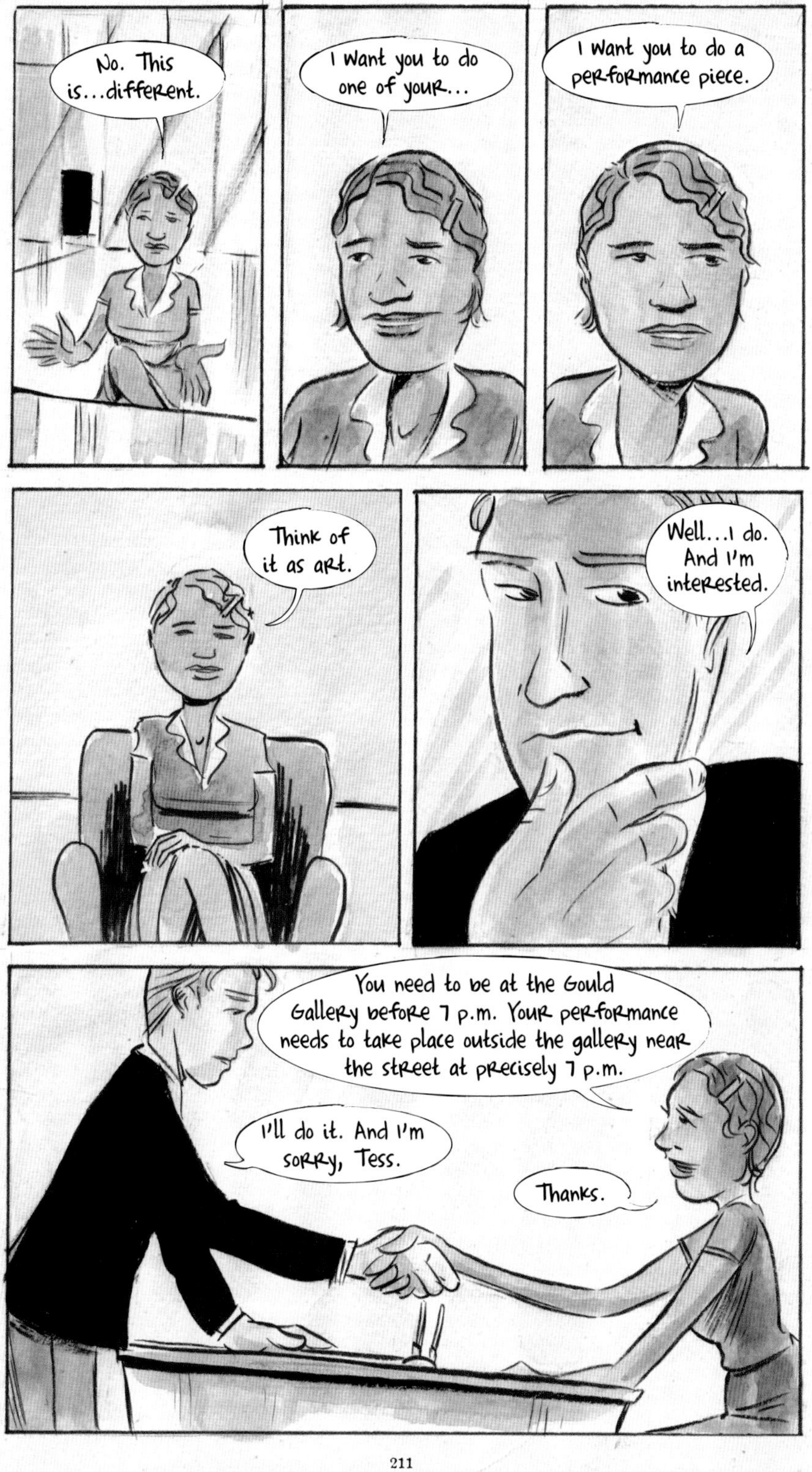
No. This is...different.
I want you to do one of your...
I want you to do a performance piece.
Think of it as art.
Well...I do. And I'm interested.
You need to be at the Gould Gallery before 7 p.m. Your performance needs to take place outside the gallery near the street at precisely 7 p.m.
I'll do it. And I'm sorry, Tess.
Thanks.

AZE E

(Art News Continued)
The Gould Gallery premiere is tonight and if you've read the advance reviews of the show you know you'll be in for a treat. The reception starts at 7 p.m. and artist Carol Hixon will be on hand to talk about her art and upcoming projects.

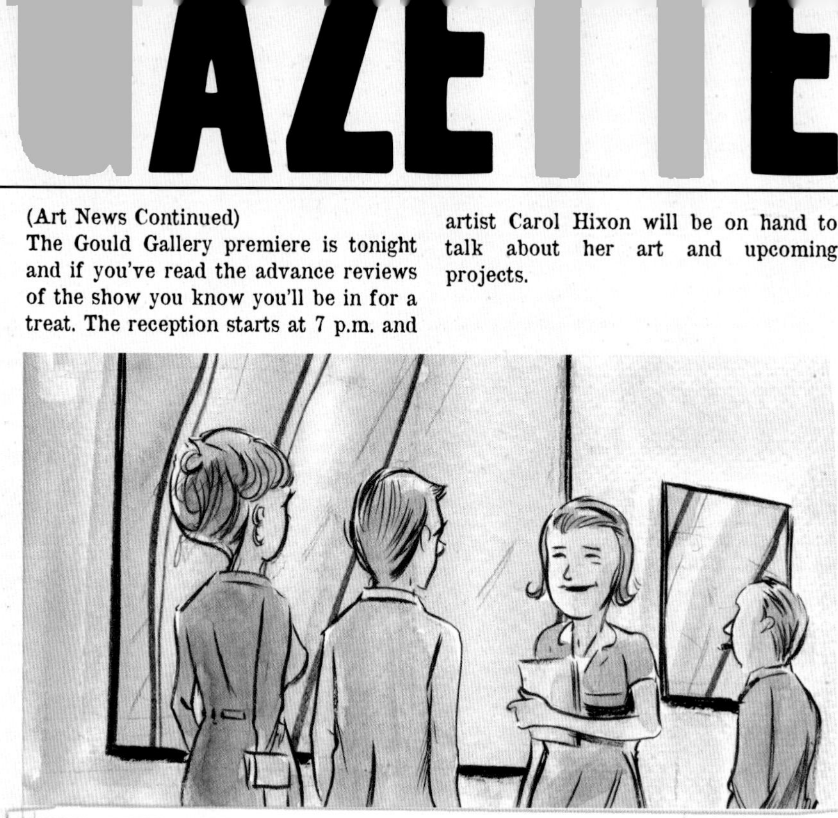

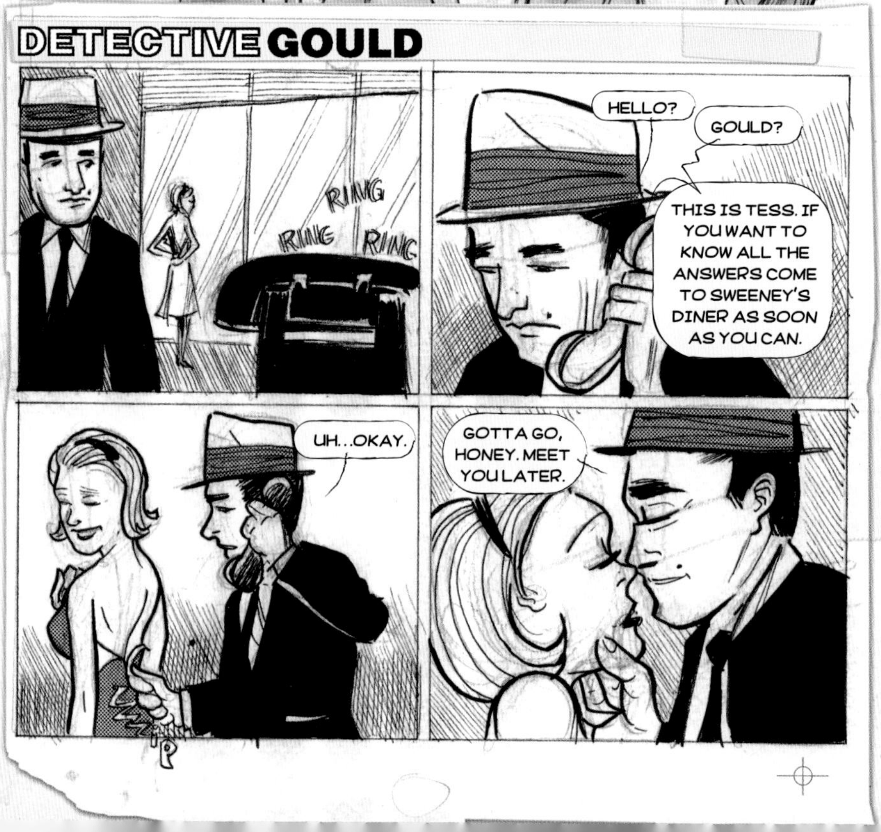
DETECTIVE GOULD
RING
RING RING
HELLO?
GOULD?
THIS IS TESS. IF YOU WANT TO KNOW ALL THE ANSWERS COME TO SWEENEY'S DINER AS SOON AS YOU CAN.
UH...OKAY.
GOTTA GO, HONEY. MEET YOU LATER.

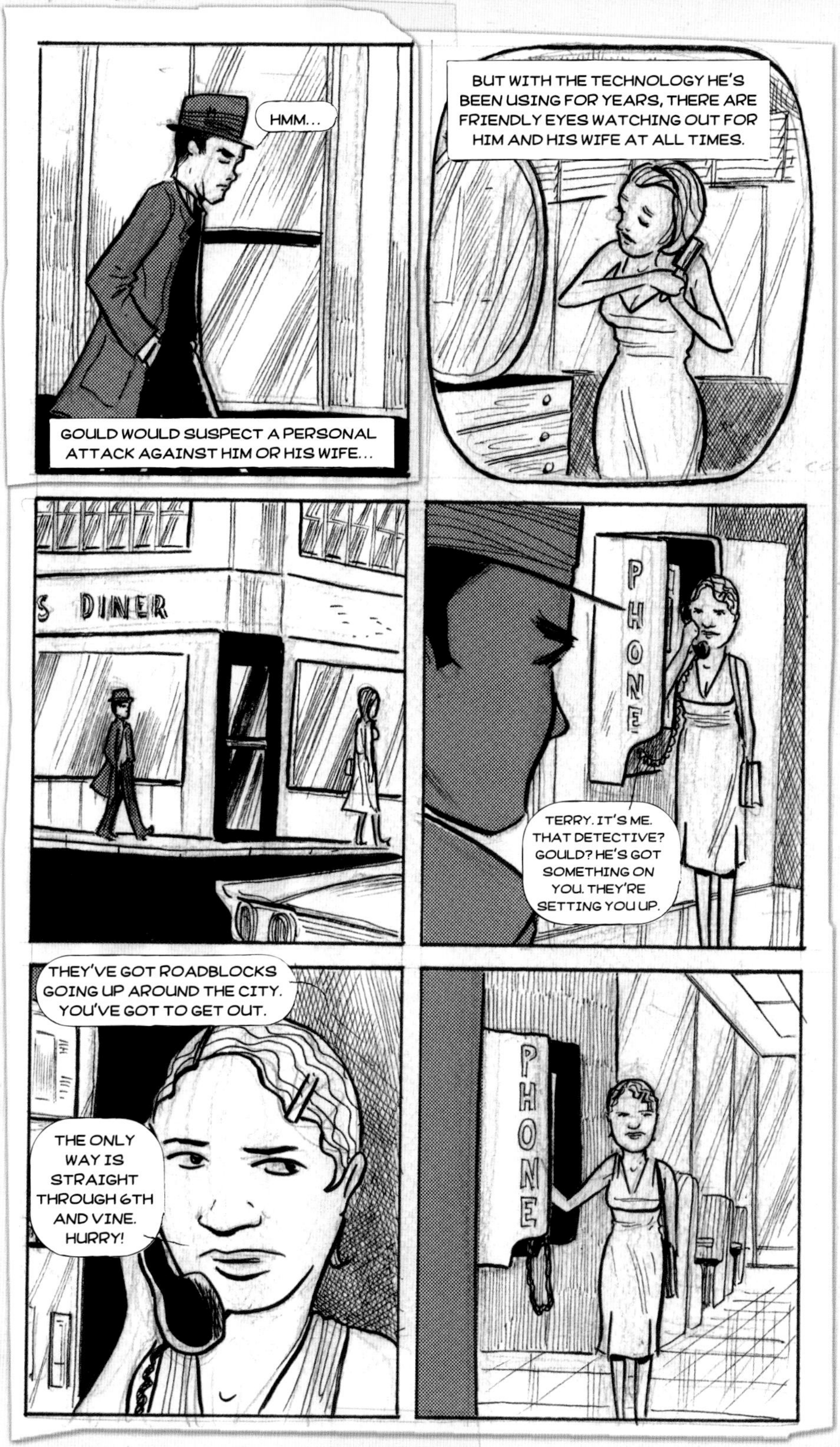
HMM...
GOULD WOULD SUSPECT A PERSONAL ATTACK AGAINST HIM OR HIS WIFE...
BUT WITH THE TECHNOLOGY HE'S BEEN USING FOR YEARS, THERE ARE FRIENDLY EYES WATCHING OUT FOR HIM AND HIS WIFE AT ALL TIMES.
S DINER
PHONE
TERRY. IT'S ME. THAT DETECTIVE? GOULD? HE'S GOT SOMETHING ON YOU. THEY'RE SETTING YOU UP.
THEY'VE GOT ROADBLOCKS GOING UP AROUND THE CITY. YOU'VE GOT TO GET OUT.
THE ONLY WAY IS STRAIGHT THROUGH 6TH AND VINE. HURRY!
PHONE

THE
DETECTIVE

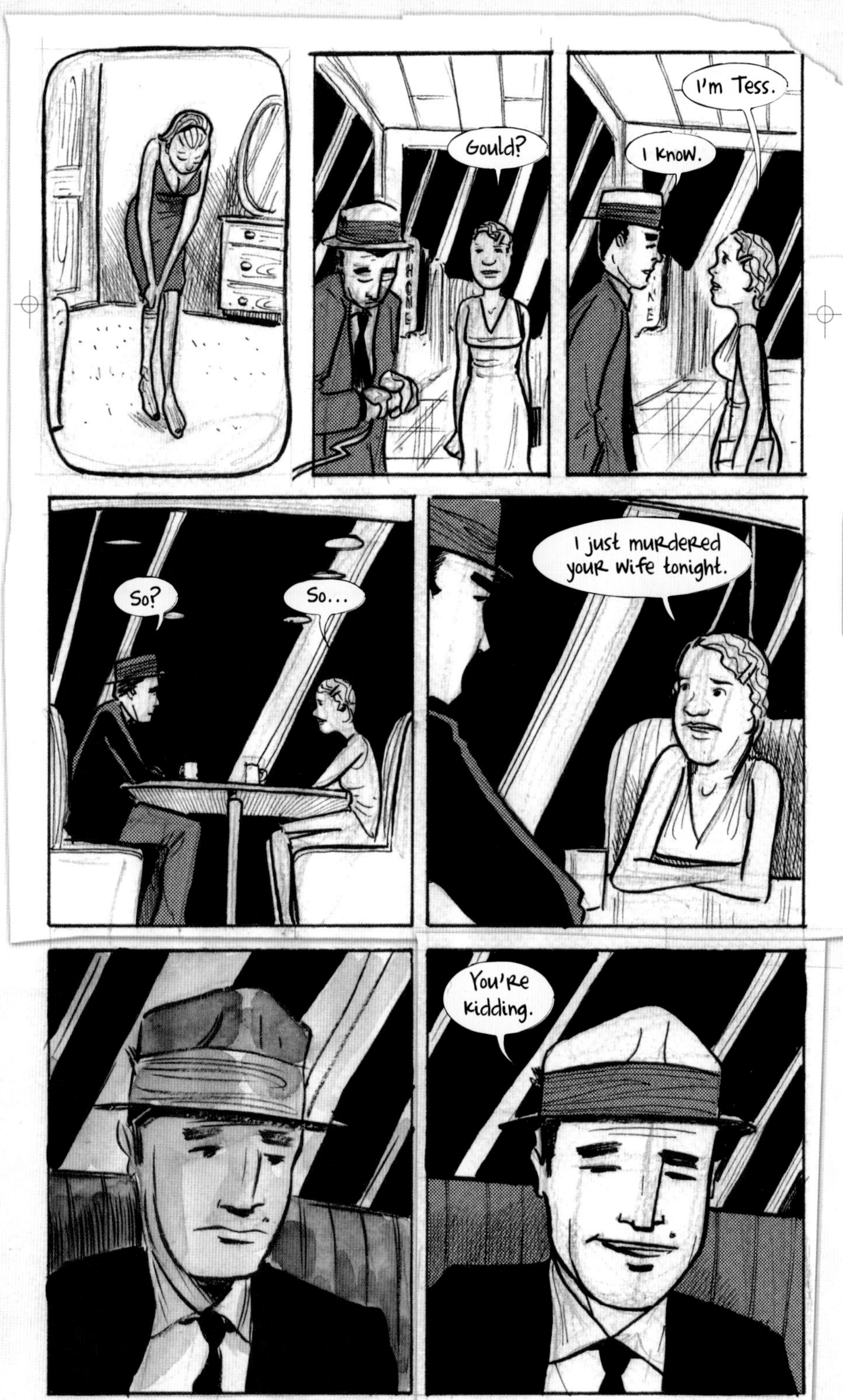
Gould?
I'm Tess.
I know.
So?
So...
I just murdered your wife tonight.
You're kidding.

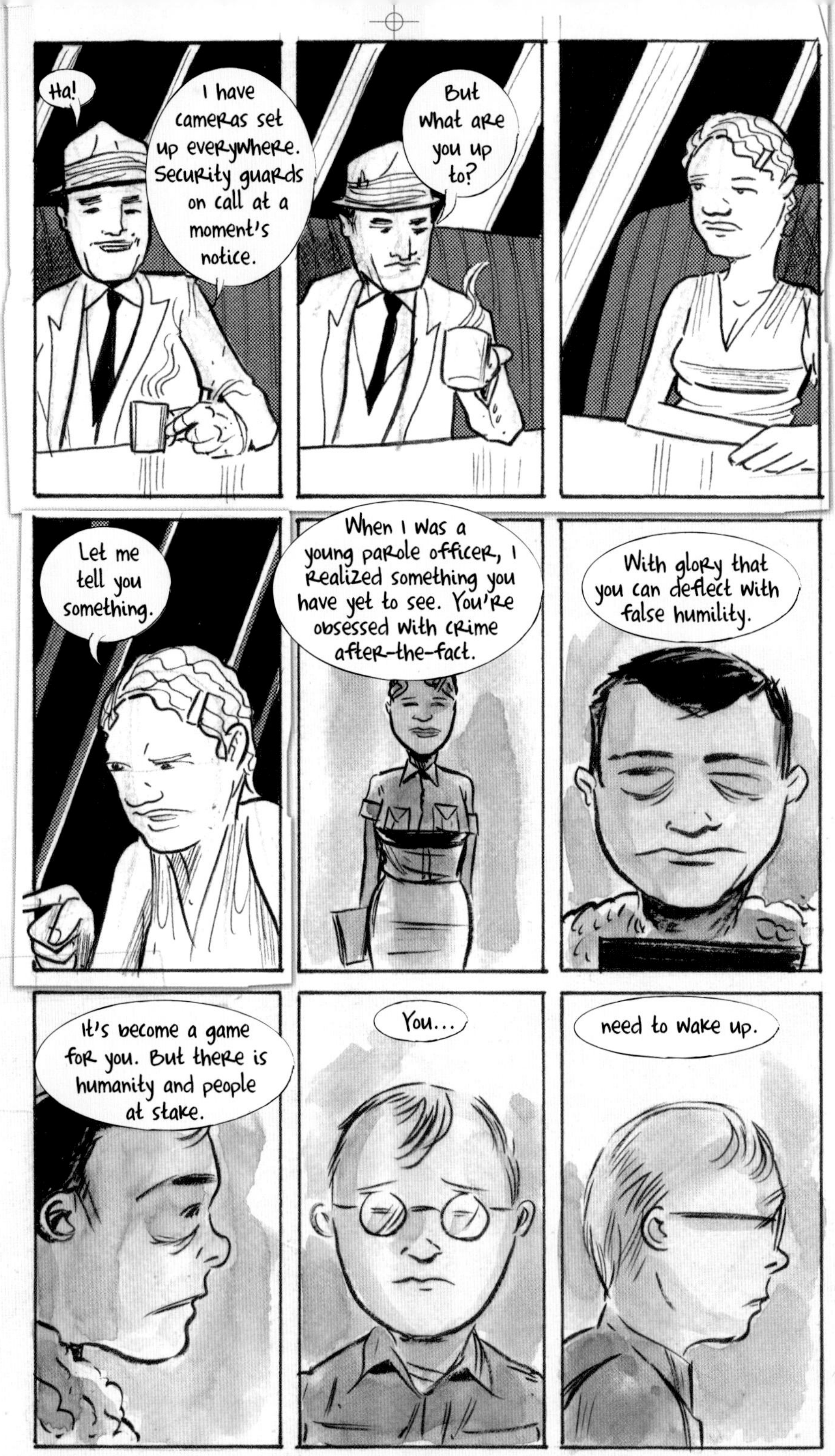
Ha!
I have cameras set up everywhere. Security guards on call at a moment's notice.
But what are you up to?
Let me tell you something.
When I was a young parole officer, I realized something you have yet to see. You're obsessed with crime after-the-fact.
With glory that you can deflect with false humility.
It's become a game for you. But there is humanity and people at stake.
You...
need to wake up.

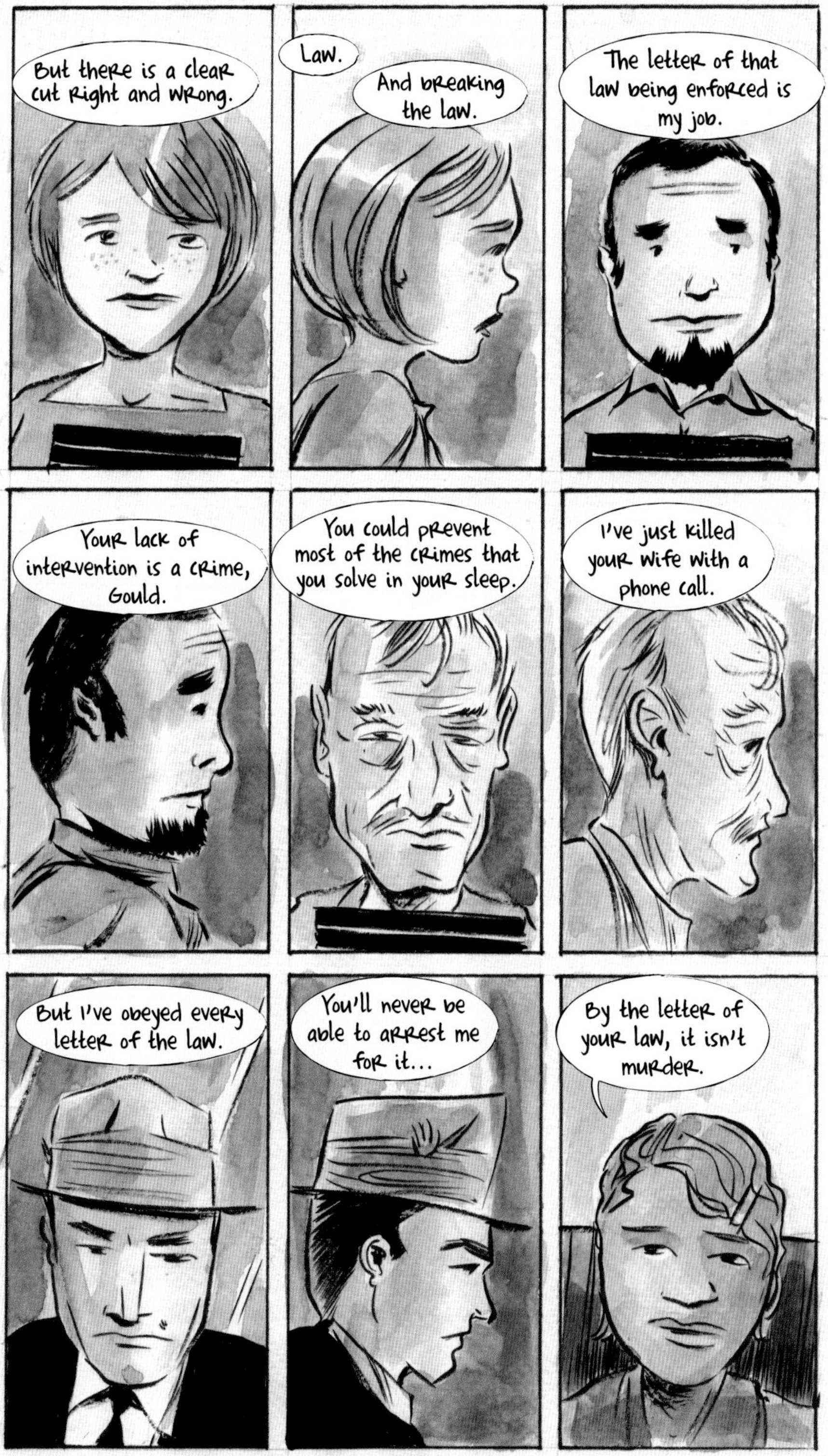
But there is a clear cut right and wrong.
Law.
And breaking the law.
The letter of that law being enforced is my job.
Your lack of intervention is a crime, Gould.
You could prevent most of the crimes that you solve in your sleep.
I've just killed your wife with a phone call.
But I've obeyed every letter of the law.
You'll never be able to arrest me for it...
By the letter of your law, it isn't murder.

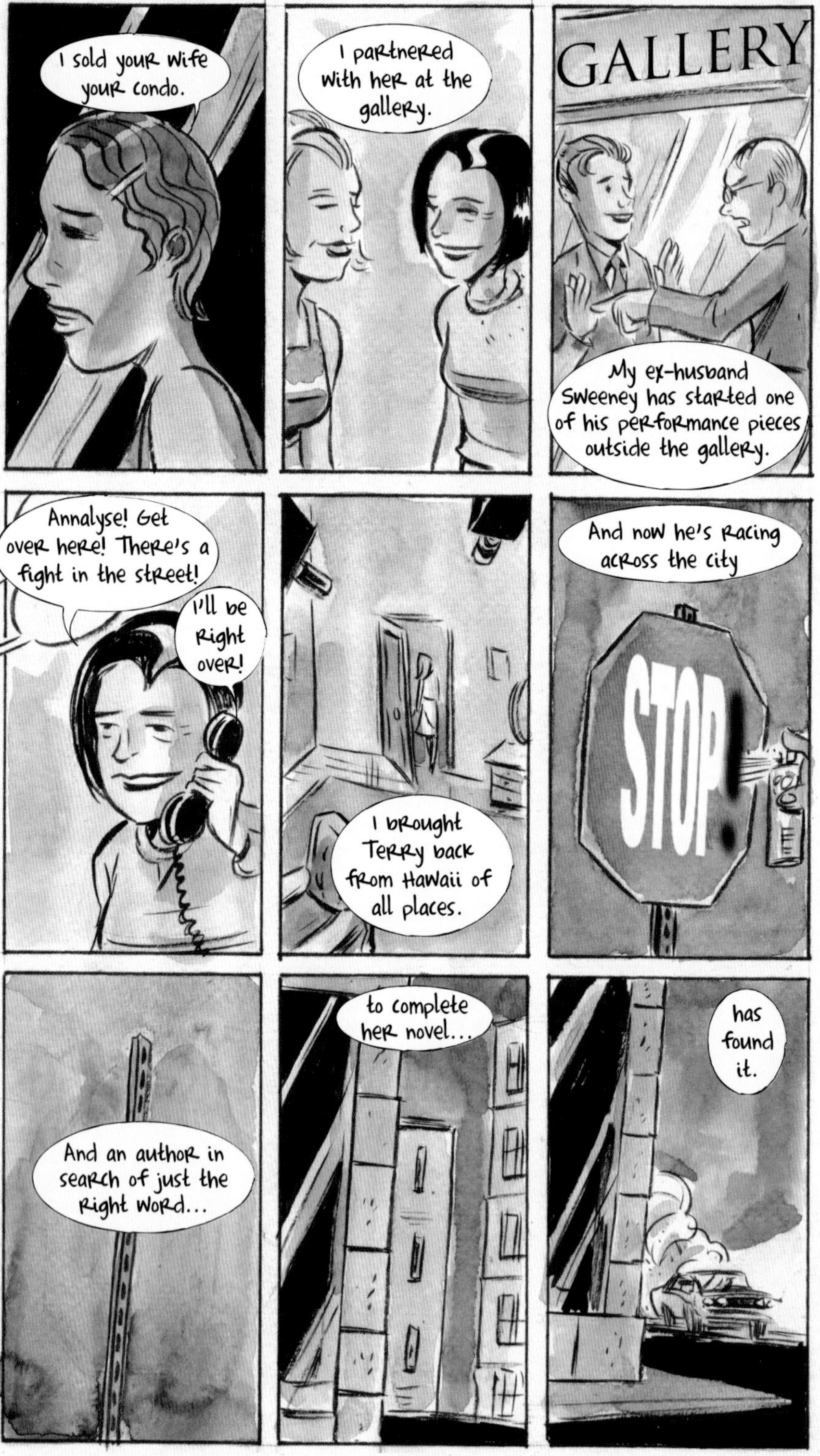
I sold your wife your condo.
I partnered with her at the gallery.
GALLERY
My ex-husband Sweeney has started one of his performance pieces outside the gallery.
Annalyse! Get over here! There's a fight in the street!
I'll be right over!
I brought Terry back from Hawaii of all places.
And now he's racing across the city
STOP
And an author in search of just the right word...
to complete her novel...
has found it.

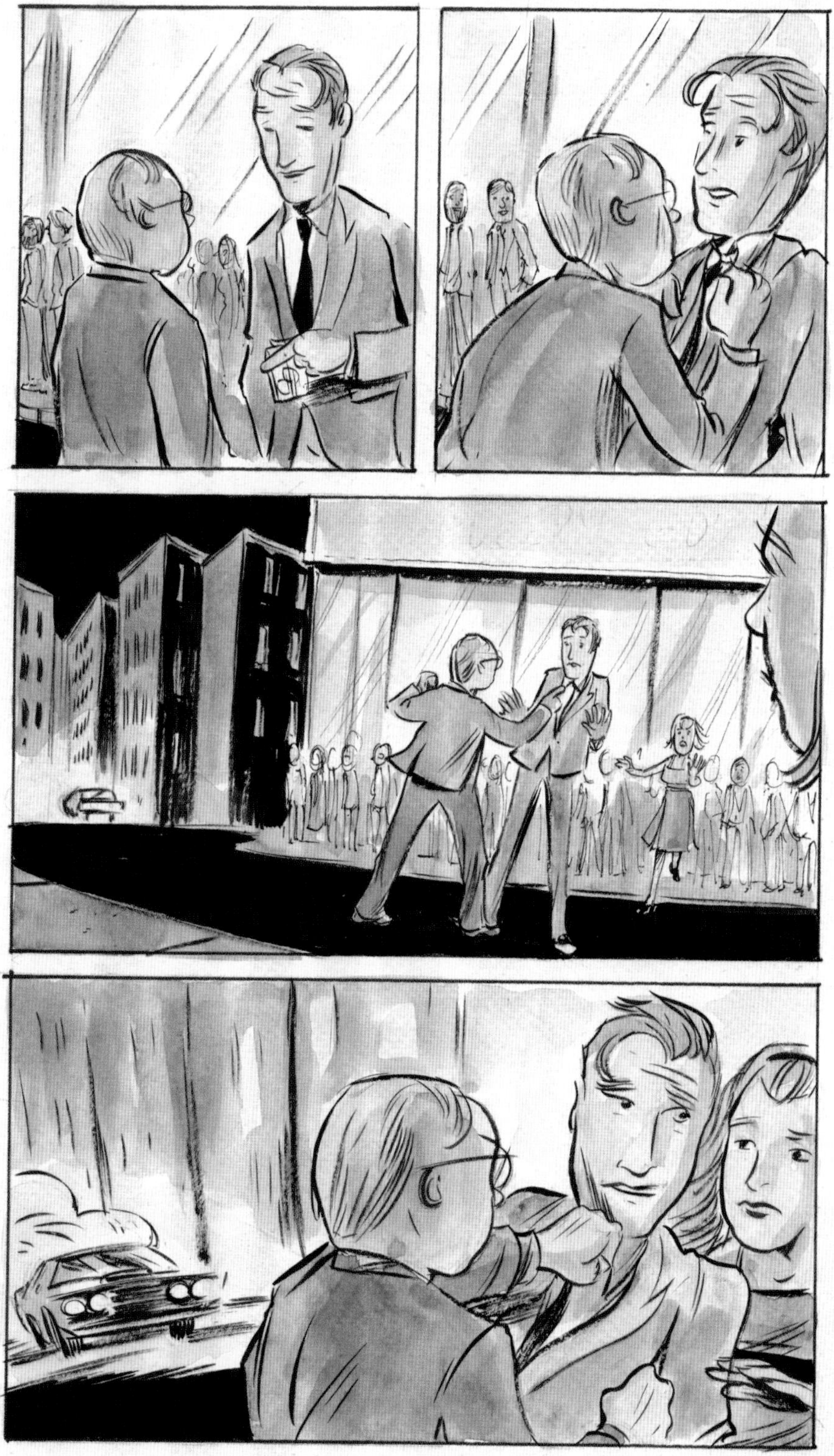

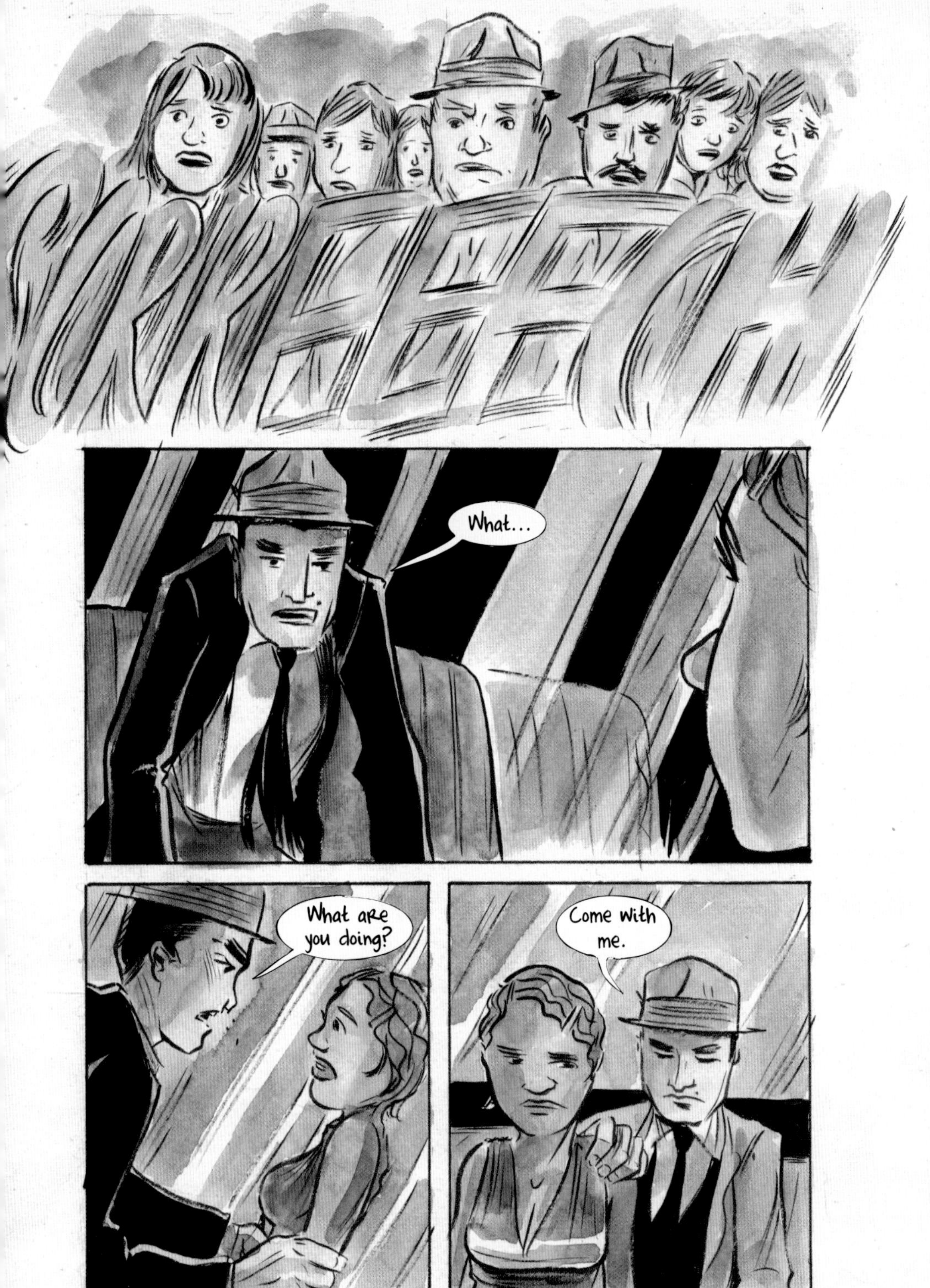
What...
What are you doing?
Come with me.

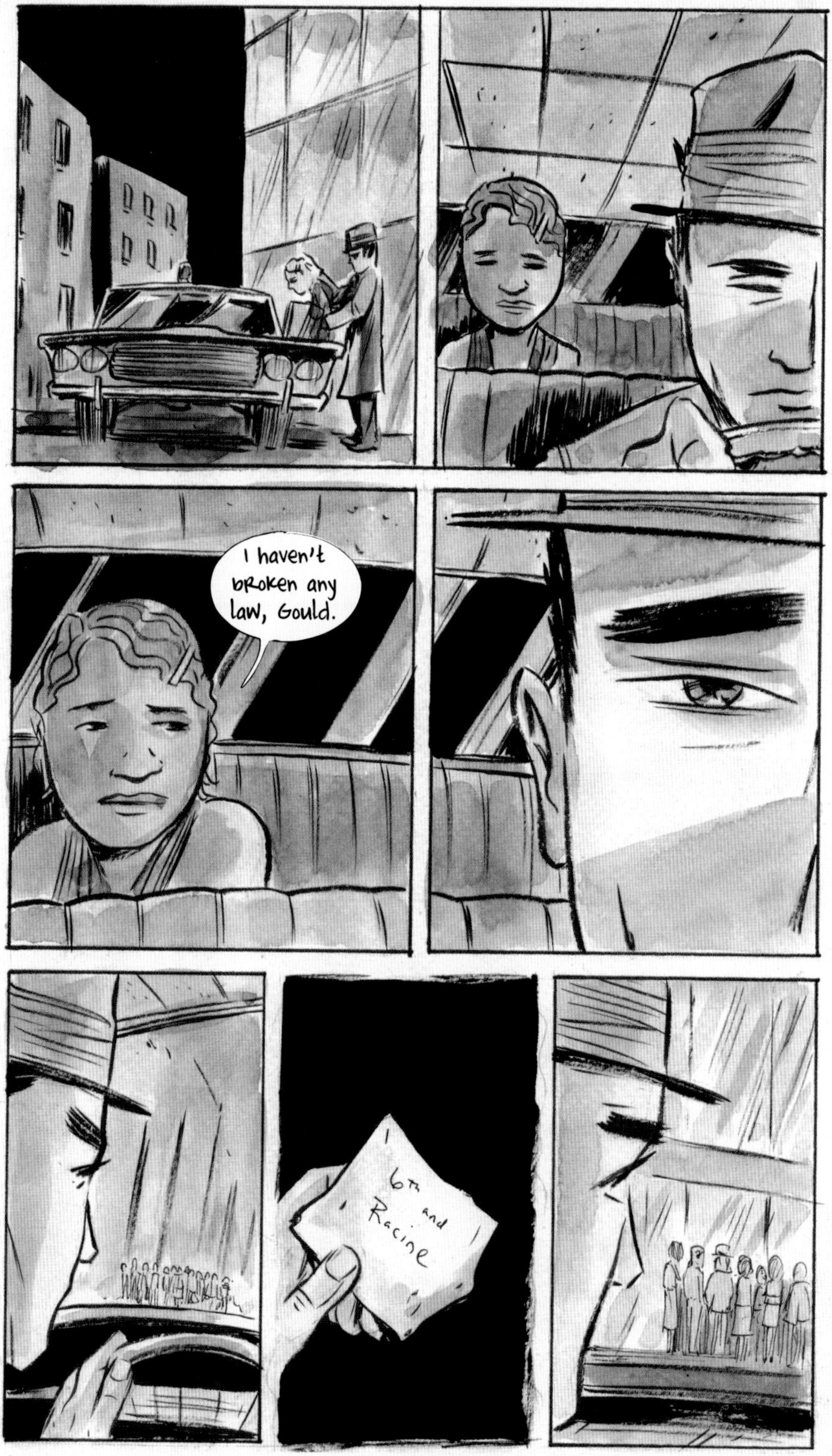
I haven't broken any law, Gould.
6th and Racine

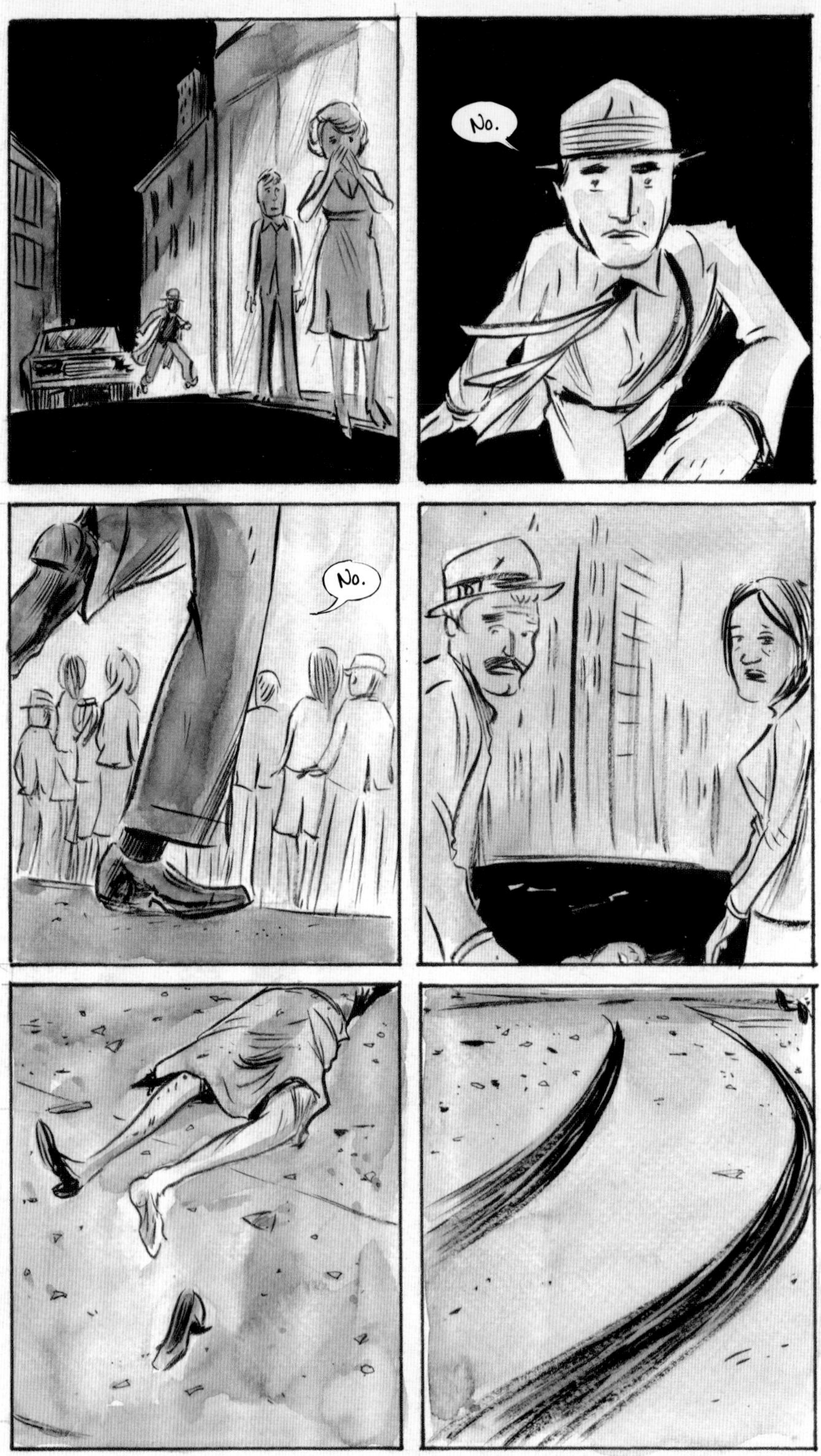
No.
No.

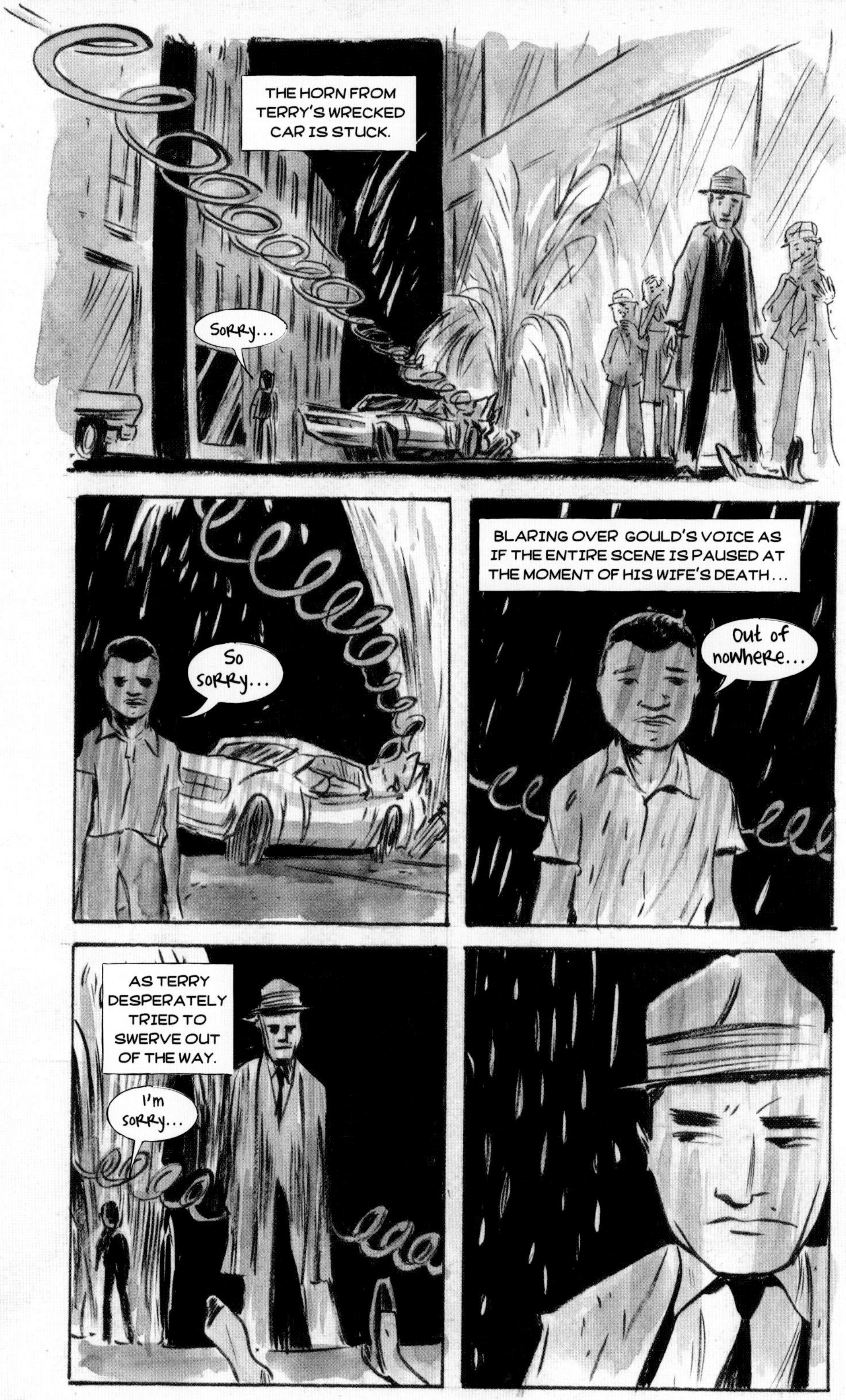
THE HORN FROM TERRY'S WRECKED CAR IS STUCK.
Sorry...
So sorry...
BLARING OVER GOULD'S VOICE AS IF THE ENTIRE SCENE IS PAUSED AT THE MOMENT OF HIS WIFE'S DEATH...
Out of nowhere...
AS TERRY DESPERATELY TRIED TO SWERVE OUT OF THE WAY.
I'm sorry...

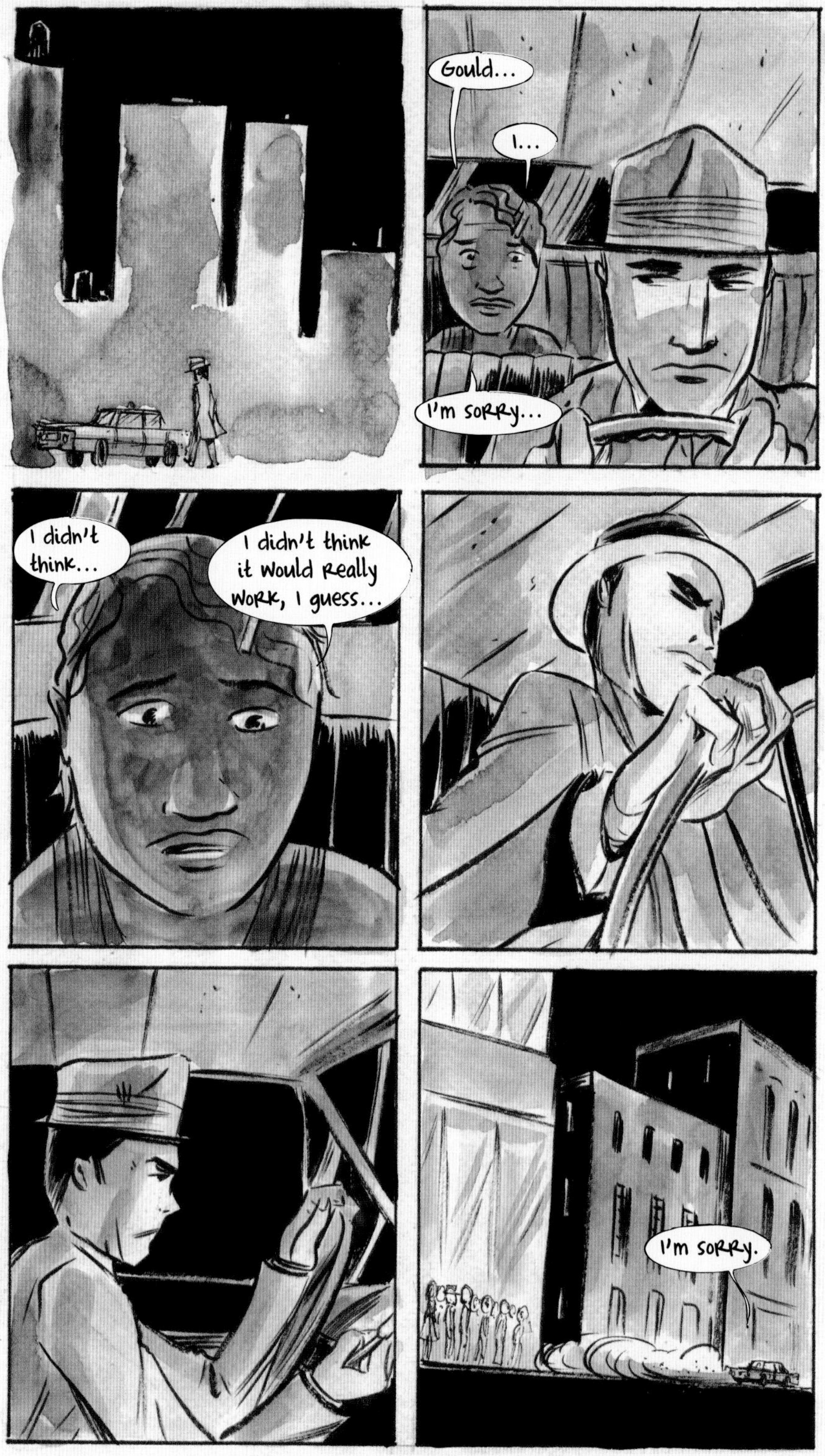
Gould...
I...
I'm sorry...
I didn't think...
I didn't think it would really work, I guess...
I'm sorry.

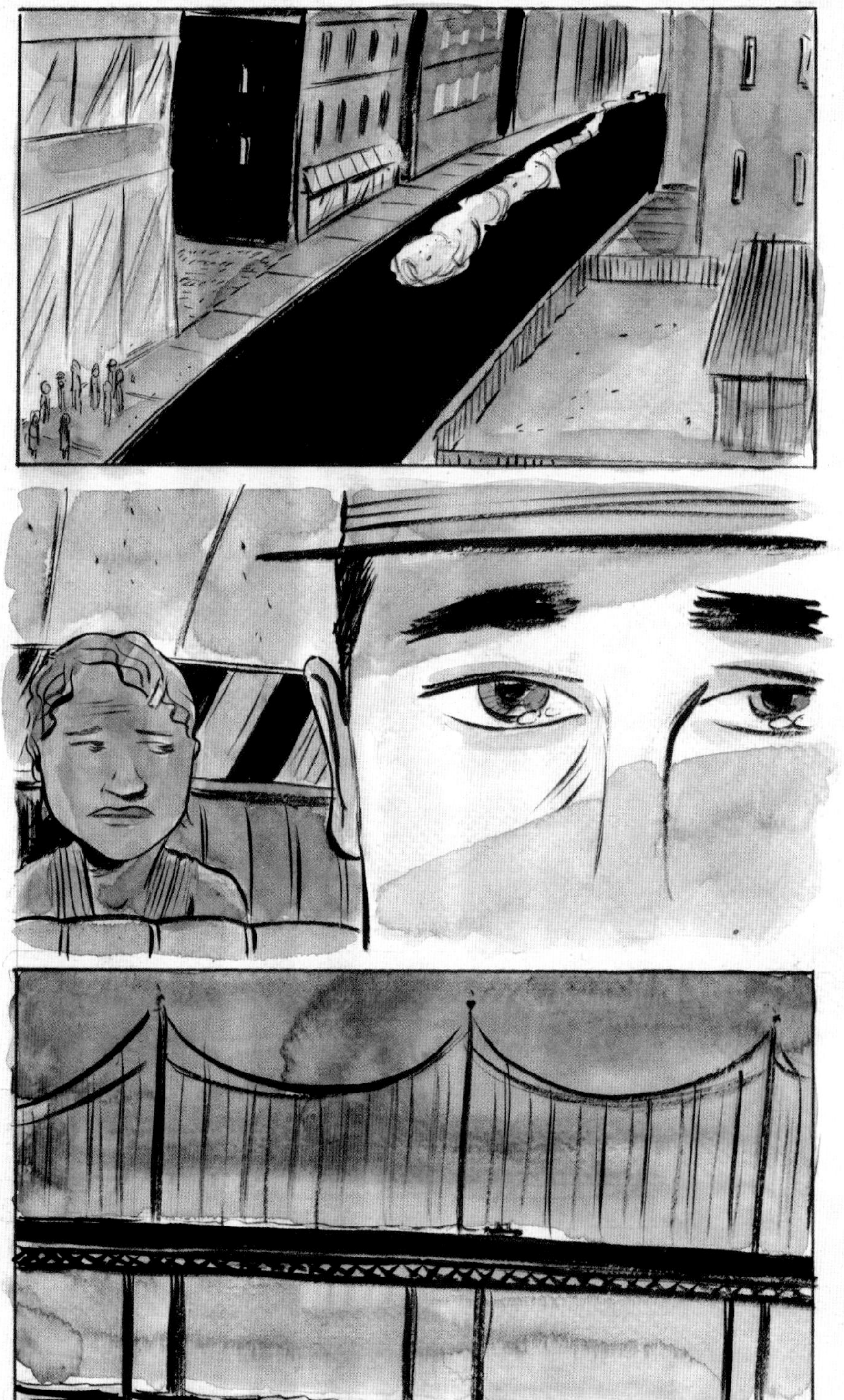

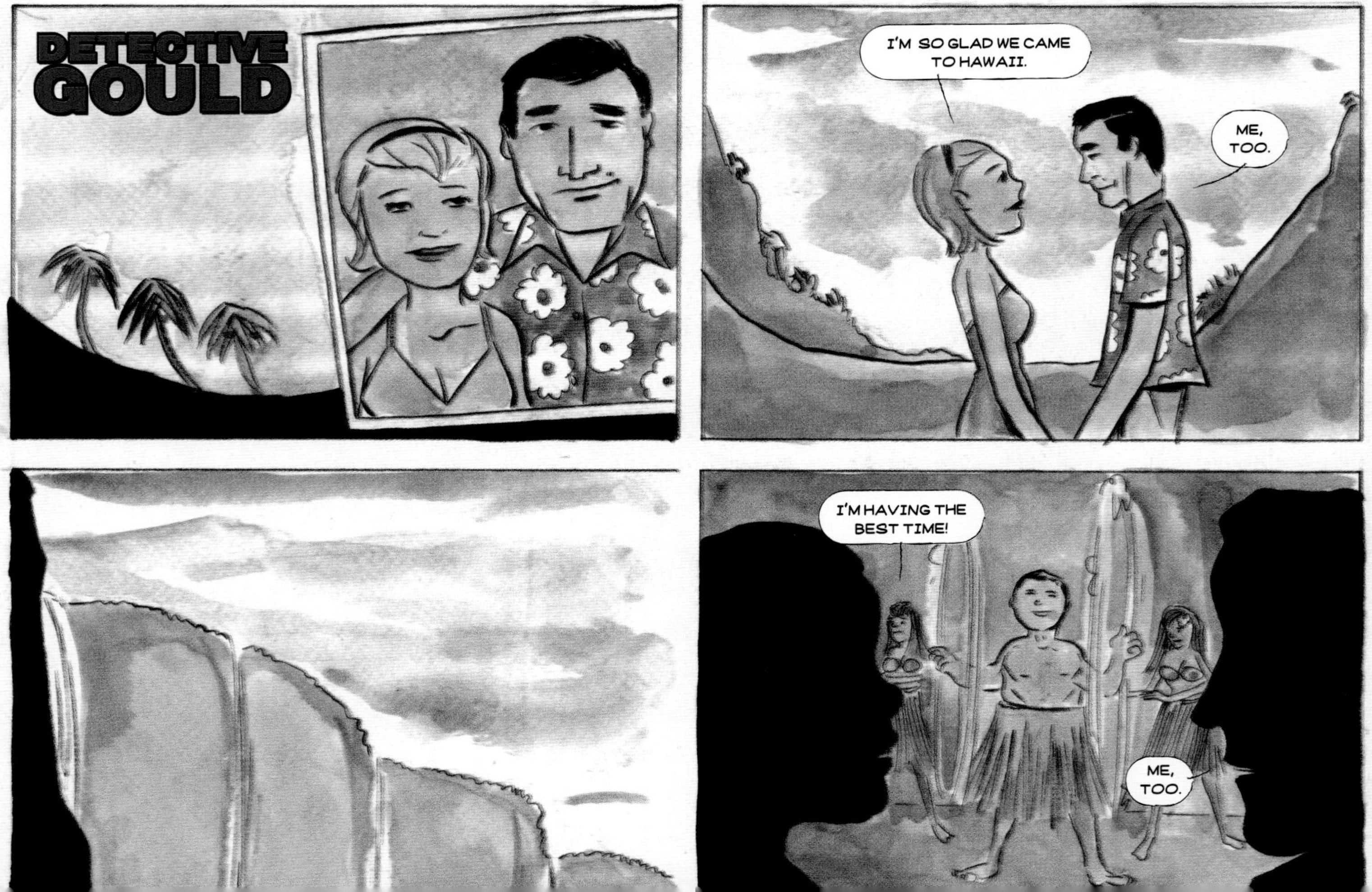
DETECTIVE GOULD
I'M SO GLAD WE CAME TO HAWAII.
ME, TOO.
I'M HAVING THE BEST TIME!
ME, TOO.

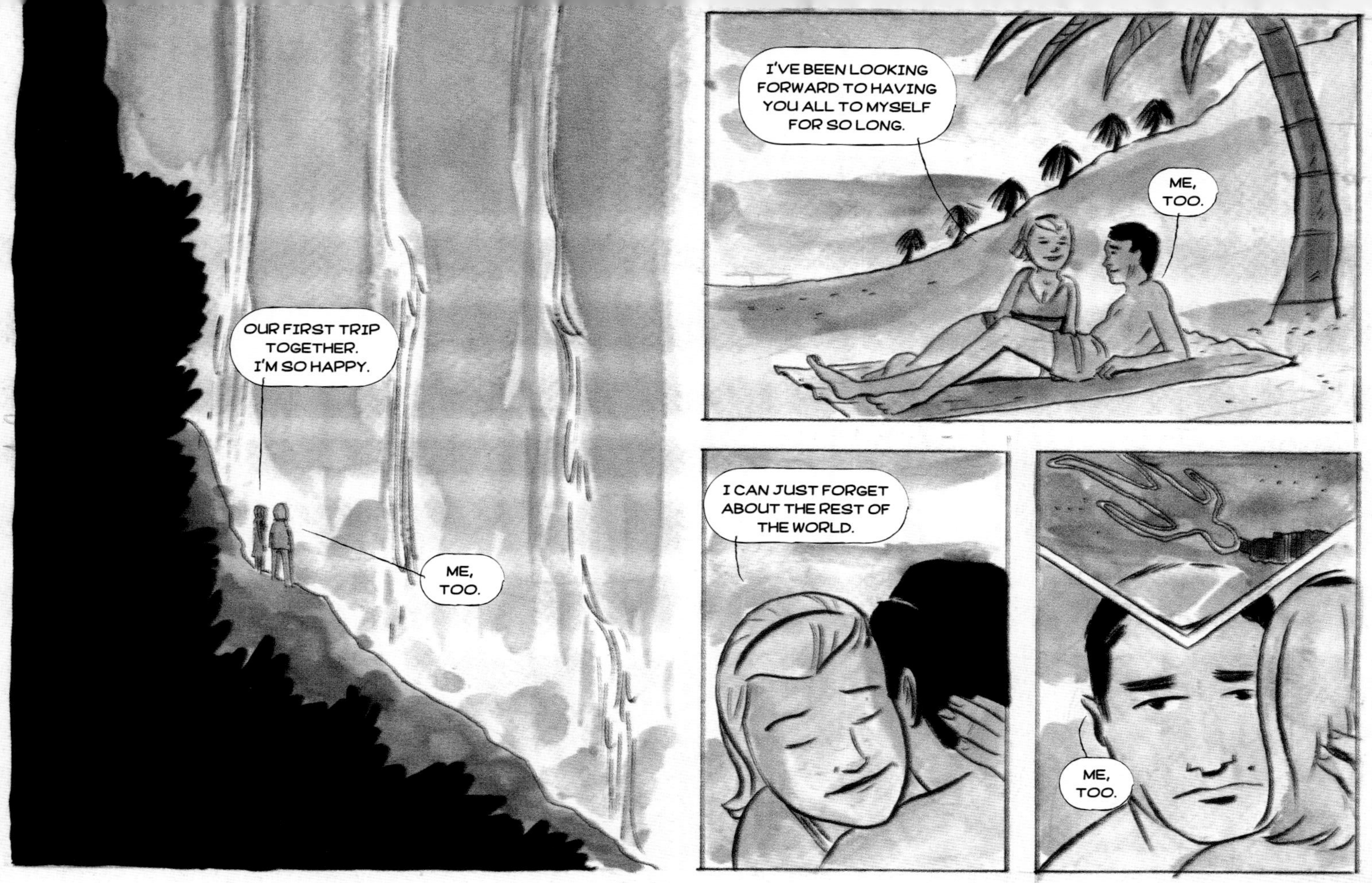
OUR FIRST TRIP TOGETHER. I'M SO HAPPY.
ME, TOO.
I'VE BEEN LOOKING FORWARD TO HAVING YOU ALL TO MYSELF FOR SO LONG.
ME, TOO.
I CAN JUST FORGET ABOUT THE REST OF THE WORLD.
ME, TOO.

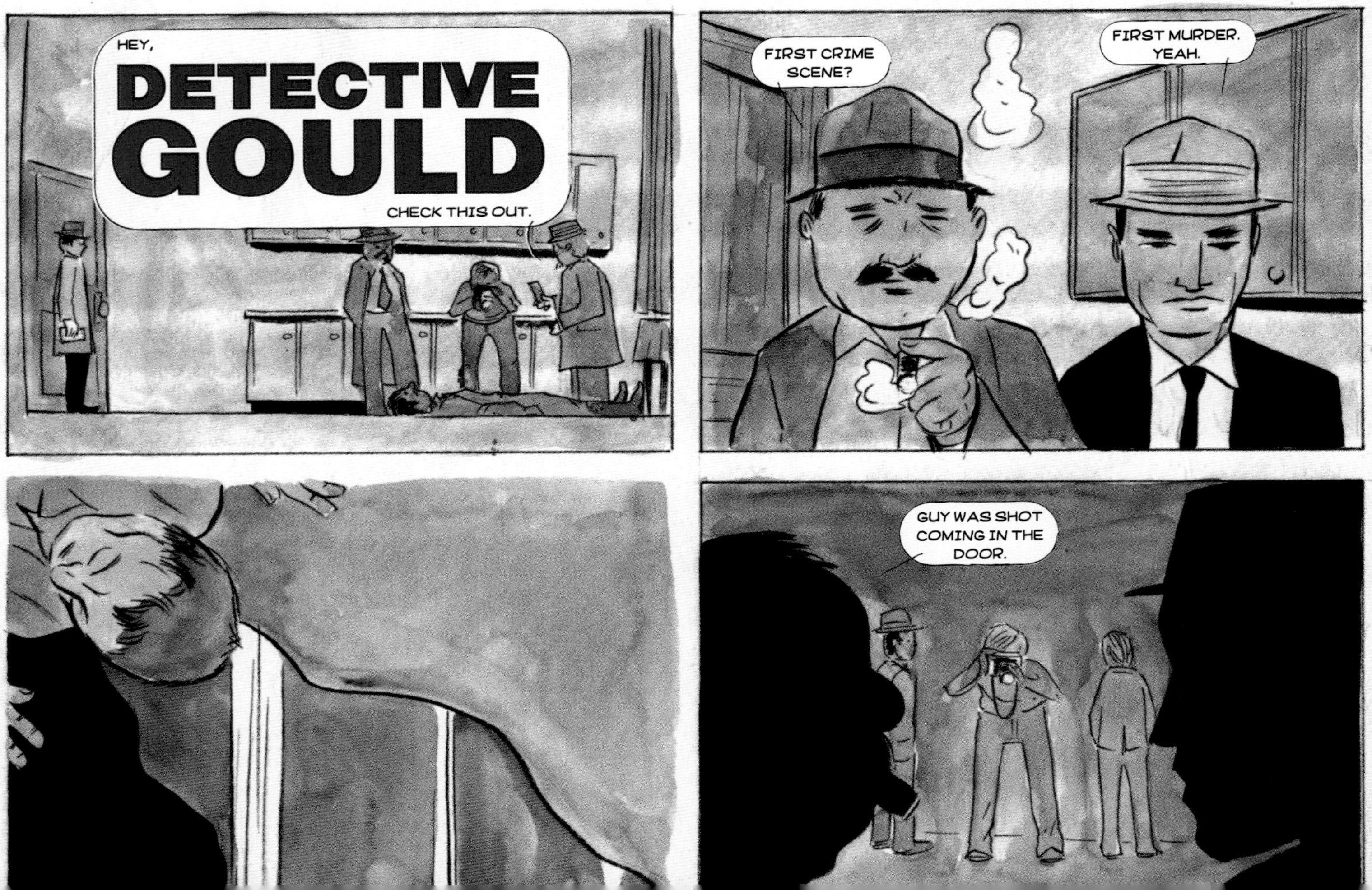
HEY, DETECTIVE GOULD CHECK THIS OUT.
FIRST CRIME SCENE?
FIRST MURDER. YEAH.
GUY WAS SHOT COMING IN THE DOOR.

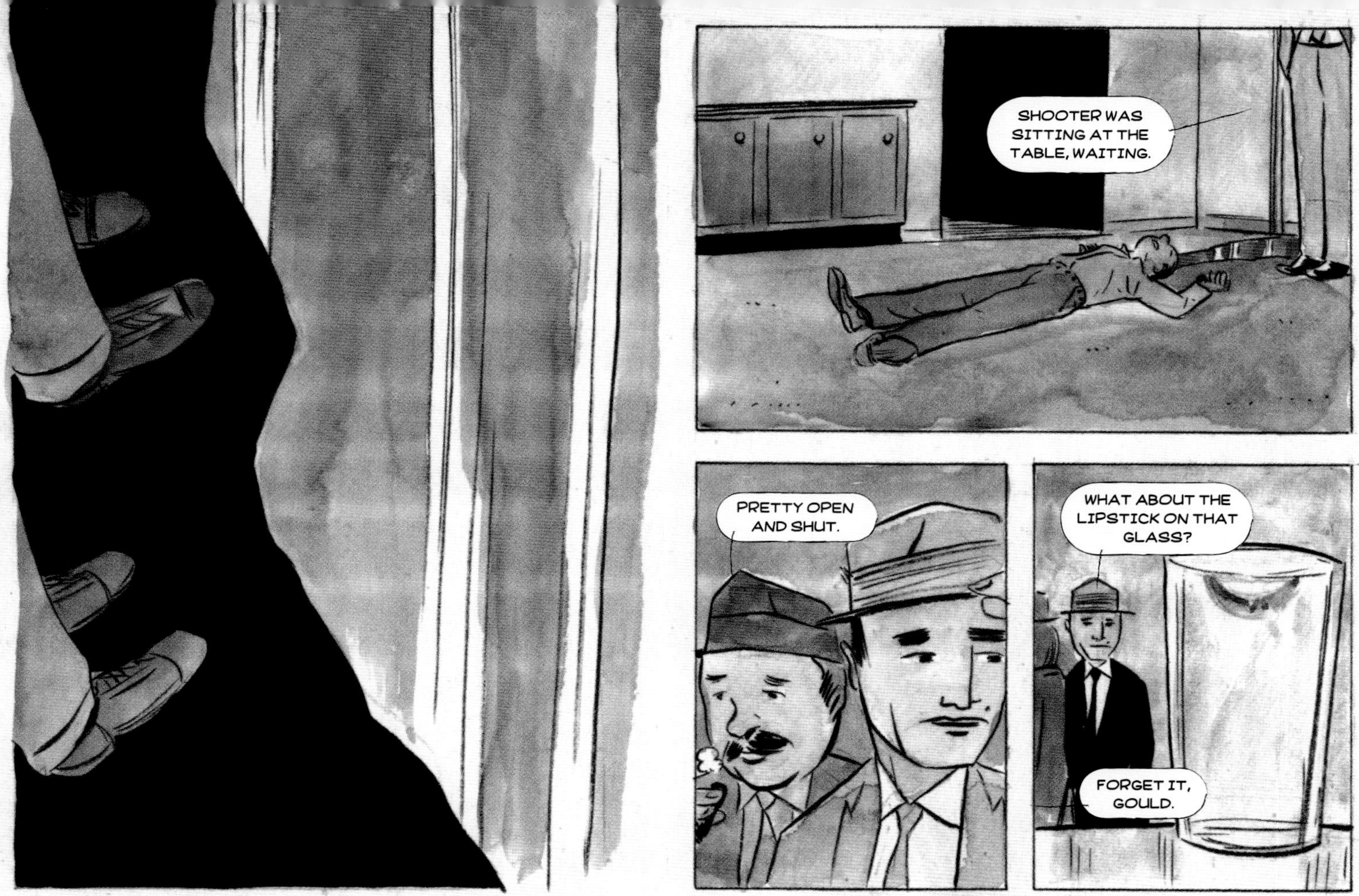
SHOOTER WAS SITTING AT THE TABLE, WAITING.
PRETTY OPEN AND SHUT.
WHAT ABOUT THE LIPSTICK ON THAT GLASS?
FORGET IT, GOULD.

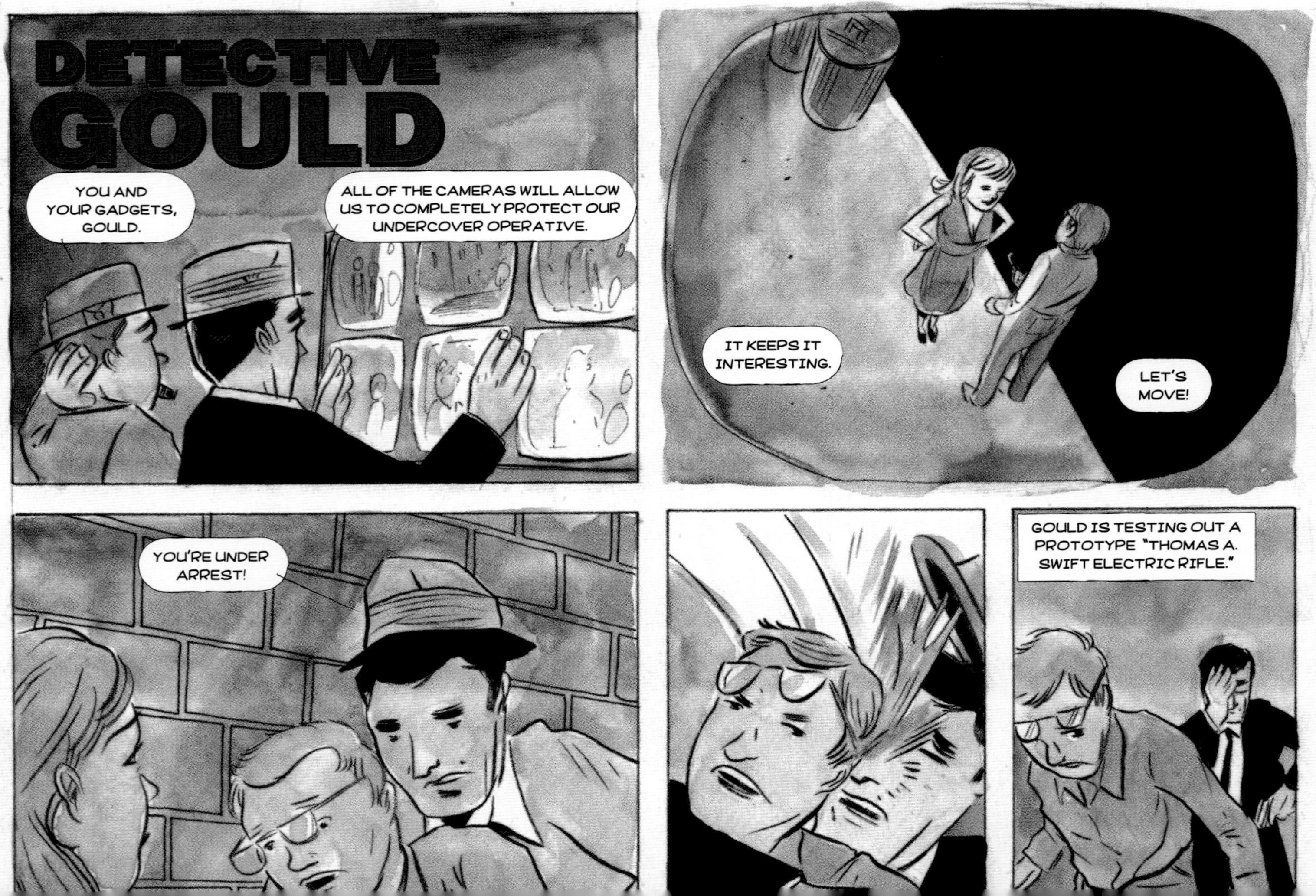
DETECTIVE GOULD
YOU AND YOUR GADGETS, GOULD.
ALL OF THE CAMERAS WILL ALLOW US TO COMPLETELY PROTECT OUR UNDERCOVER OPERATIVE.
IT KEEPS IT INTERESTING.
LET'S MOVE!
YOU'RE UNDER ARREST!
GOULD IS TESTING OUT A PROTOTYPE "THOMAS A. SWIFT ELECTRIC RIFLE."

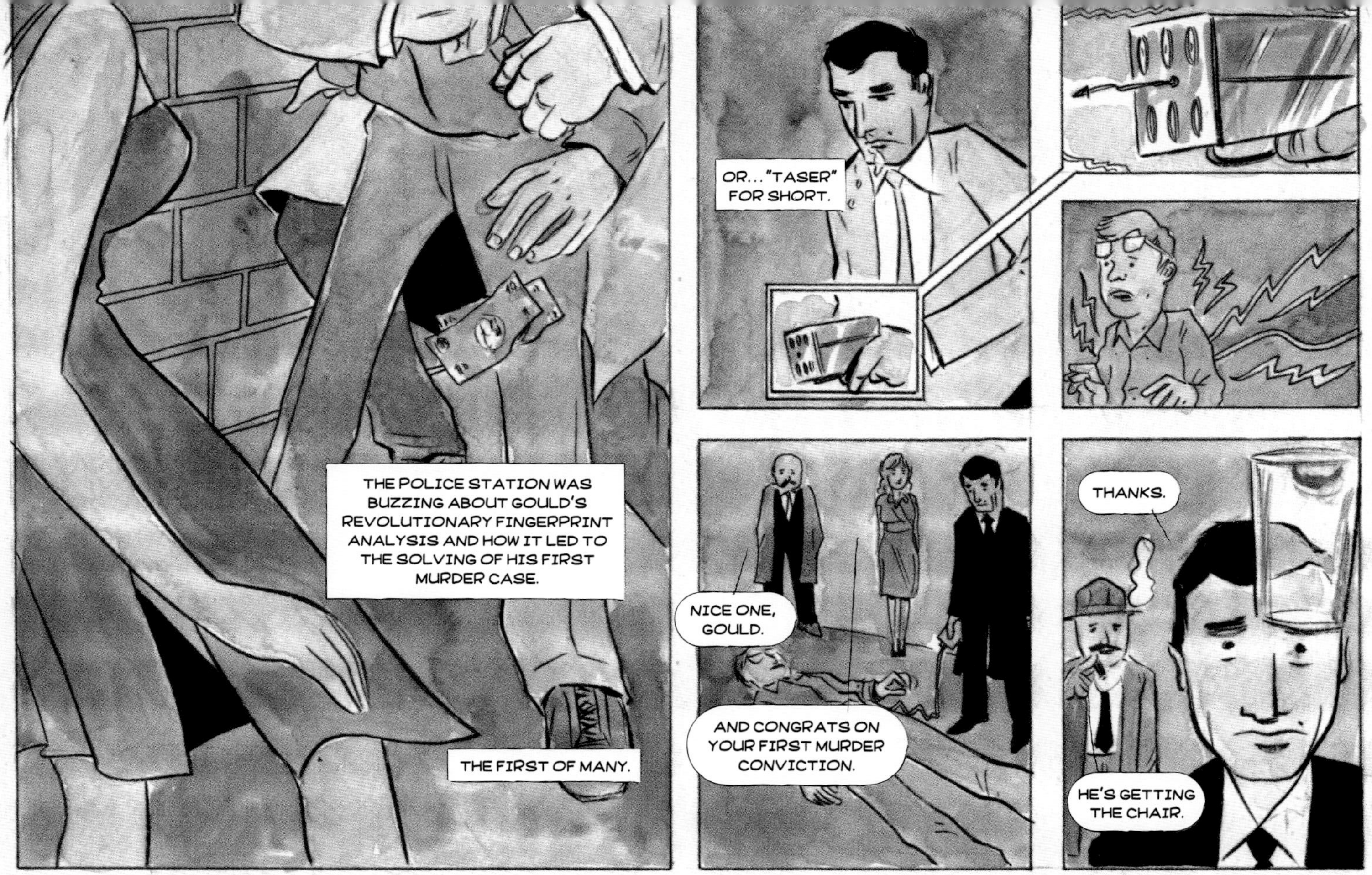
THE POLICE STATION WAS BUZZING ABOUT GOULD'S REVOLUTIONARY FINGERPRINT ANALYSIS AND HOW IT LED TO THE SOLVING OF HIS FIRST MURDER CASE.
THE FIRST OF MANY.
OR... "TASER" FOR SHORT.
NICE ONE, GOULD.
AND CONGRATS ON YOUR FIRST MURDER CONVICTION.
THANKS.
HE'S GETTING THE CHAIR.

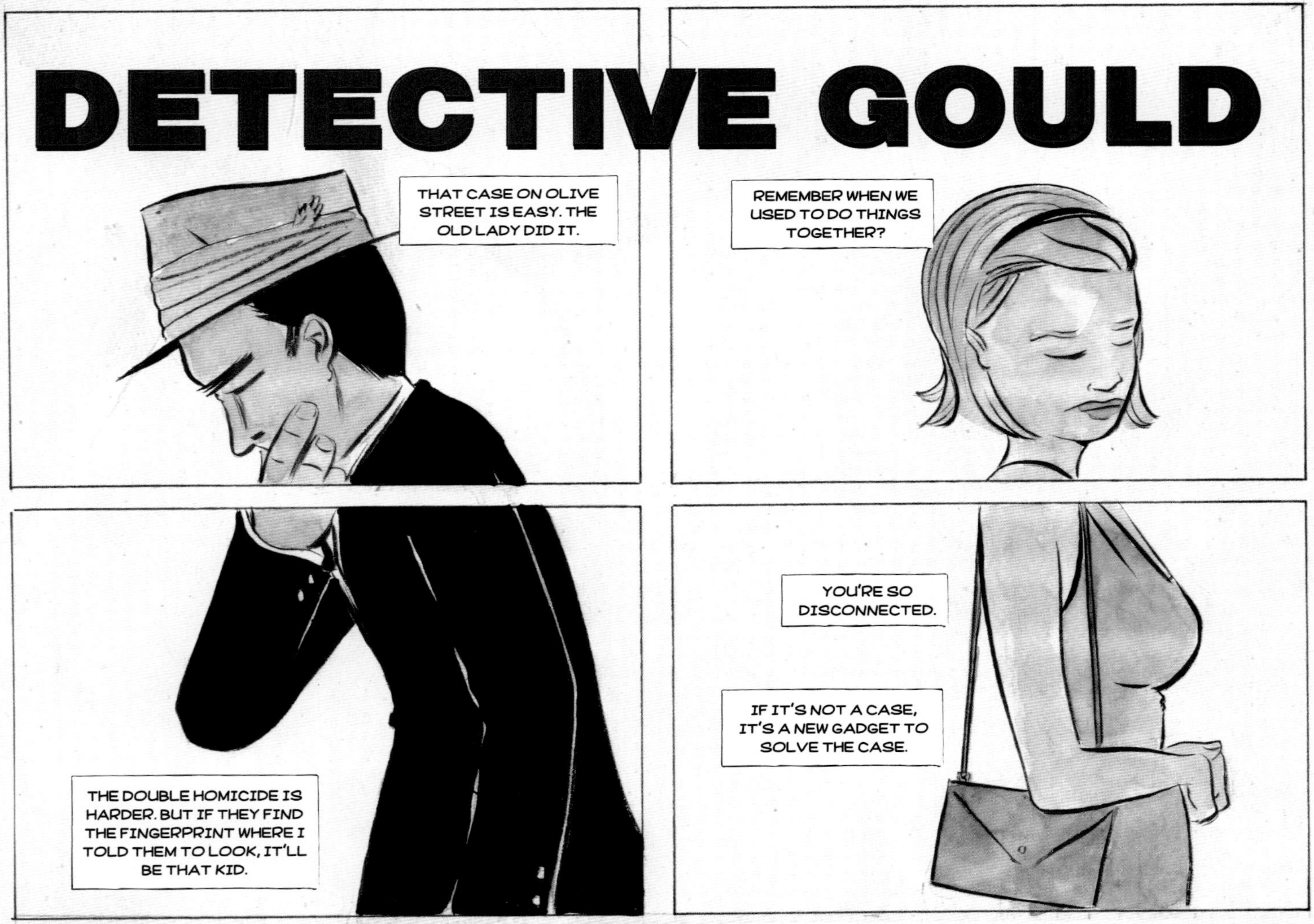
DETECTIVE GOULD
THAT CASE ON OLIVE STREET IS EASY. THE OLD LADY DID IT.
REMEMBER WHEN WE USED TO DO THINGS TOGETHER?
THE DOUBLE HOMICIDE IS HARDER. BUT IF THEY FIND THE FINGERPRINT WHERE I TOLD THEM TO LOOK, IT'LL BE THAT KID.
YOU'RE SO DISCONNECTED.
IF IT'S NOT A CASE, IT'S A NEW GADGET TO SOLVE THE CASE.

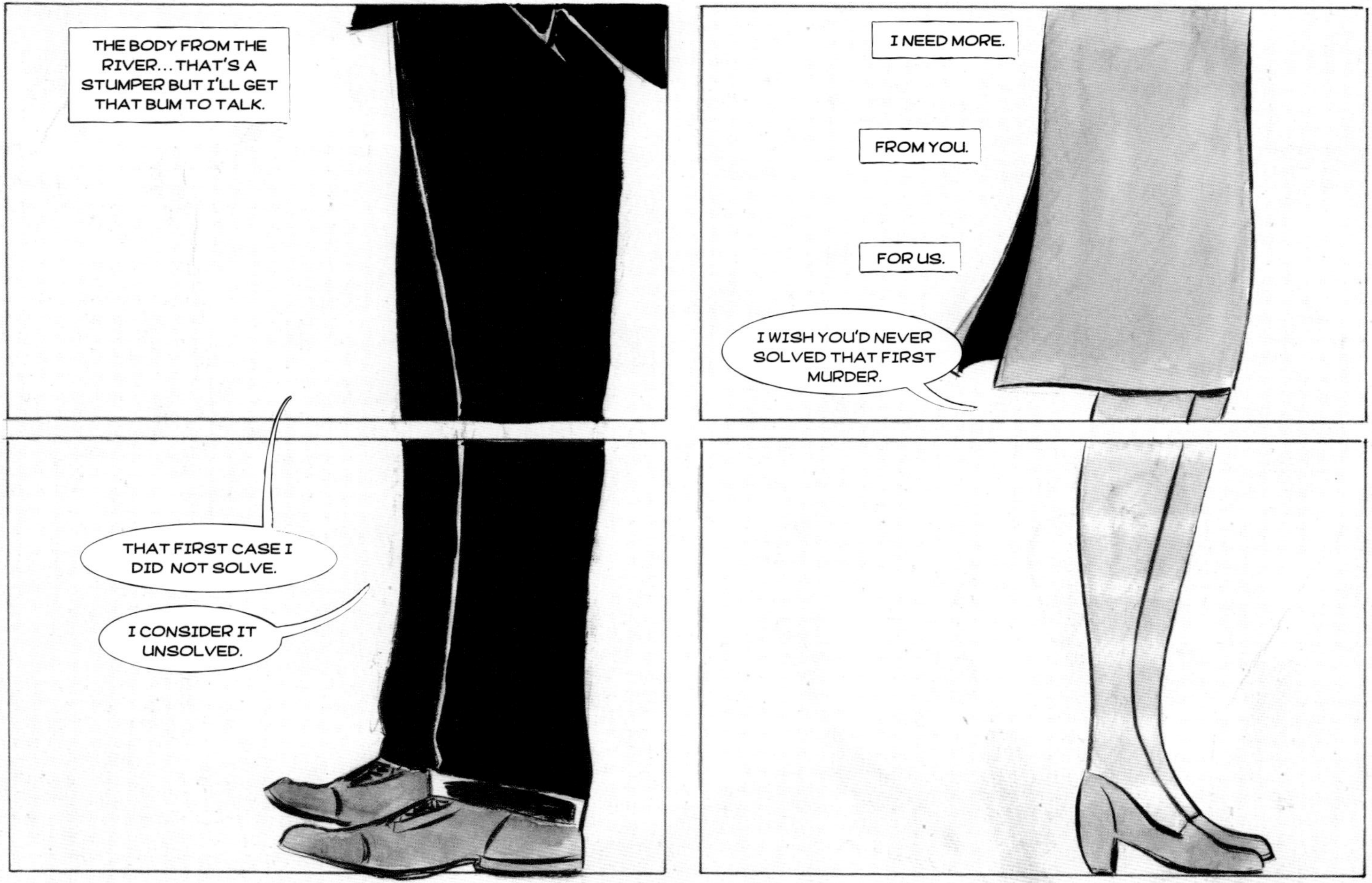
THE BODY FROM THE RIVER... THAT'S A STUMPER BUT I'LL GET THAT BUM TO TALK.
THAT FIRST CASE I DID NOT SOLVE.
I CONSIDER IT UNSOLVED.
I NEED MORE.
FROM YOU.
FOR US.
I WISH YOU'D NEVER SOLVED THAT FIRST MURDER.

COMIC ★ STRIPS

Are you asking me out?

CAPTAIN CRANE

GIRL ADVENTURER

CAPTAIN CRANE, EXHAUSTED FROM HER ADVENTURE IN TIBET, IS EAGER TO SEE THE LOVE OF HER LIFE, LIEUTENANT JAMES.

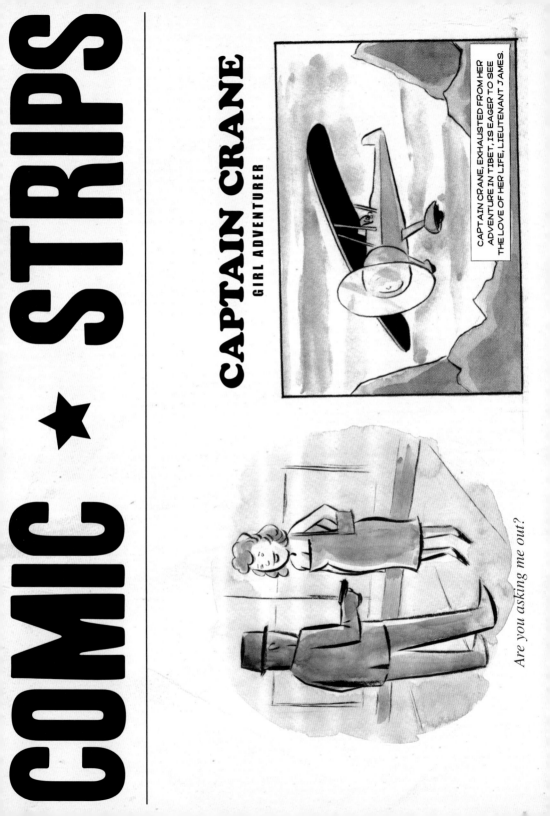

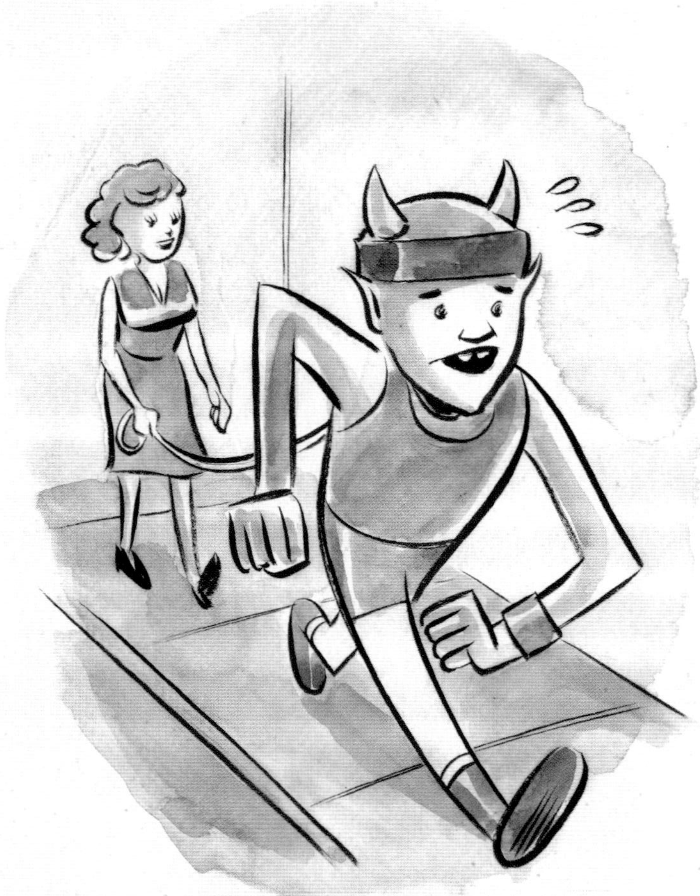

Exercise your demons.

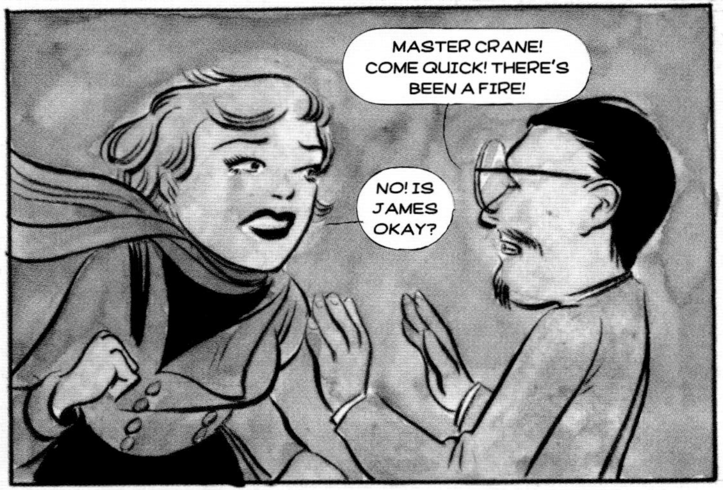
MASTER CRANE! COME QUICK! THERE'S BEEN A FIRE!
NO! IS JAMES OKAY?

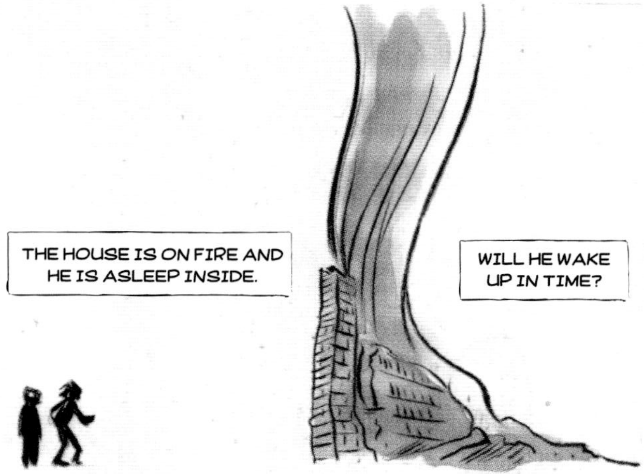
THE HOUSE IS ON FIRE AND HE IS ASLEEP INSIDE.
WILL HE WAKE UP IN TIME?

GAZETTE

CONTINUED FROM A1

in a unanimous decision, the jury sentenced Karl House to death for the cold-blooded shooting death of what many believe was his partner-in-crime.

The sentence is to be carried out at 12:01 a.m. tomorrow morning. The last of House's appeals were unsuccessful, and many thought he might actually escape the death sentence. Detective Gould was reportedly questioning House up until the last minute. Gould remained convinced that someone else in addition to House was involved in the killing.

In House's testimony during the murder trial, he claimed that he acted alone and seemed to contradict himself when announcing that if he, quote: "Said any more, I would betray the woman I love. I would gladly die for her."

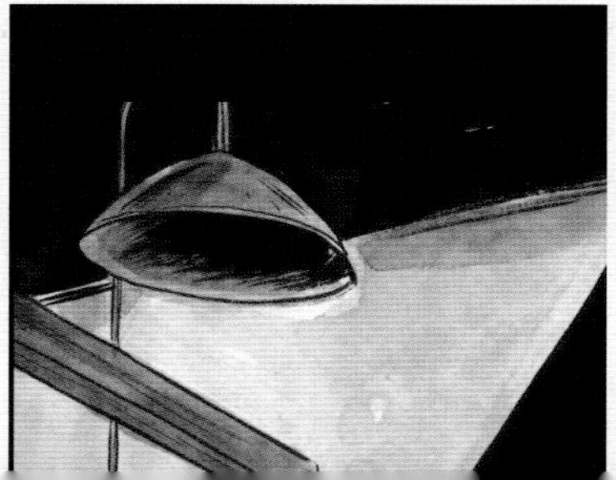

House's attorney pleaded with the jury to show mercy and called into question his client's sanity on more than one occasion.

House's story has been dragging on for years.

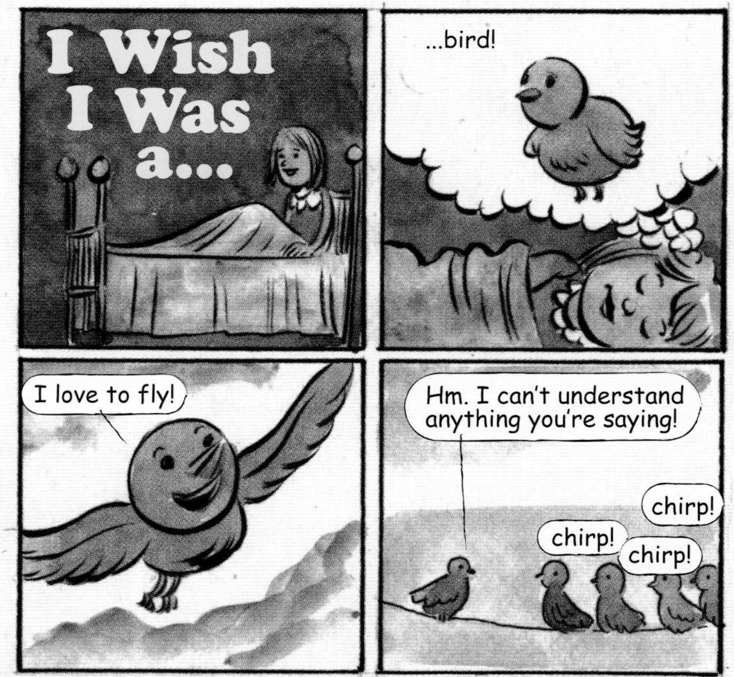
I Wish I Was a...
...bird!
I love to fly!
Hm. I can't understand anything you're saying!
chirp!
chirp!
chirp!

case assigned to Detective Gould and became the first of many successfully solved cases.

In a shocking twist to this convoluted story, the electric chair at the prison has actually gone missing. When questioned about the disapperance, the Warden declined to comment. The absence of an electric chair may actually postpone the execution indefinitely.

House's attorney is already calling for the Governor to issue a pardon and claims that it is cruel and unusual punishment to reschedule an execution. Experts say that if the chair isn't recovered in time for the early morning execution, House may escape with his life after all.

BE AN ARTIST!

You can do anything if you practice hard enough! Try your hand! Use the try-out panel and earn an art scholarship today!

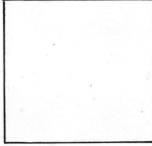

Name & Address:

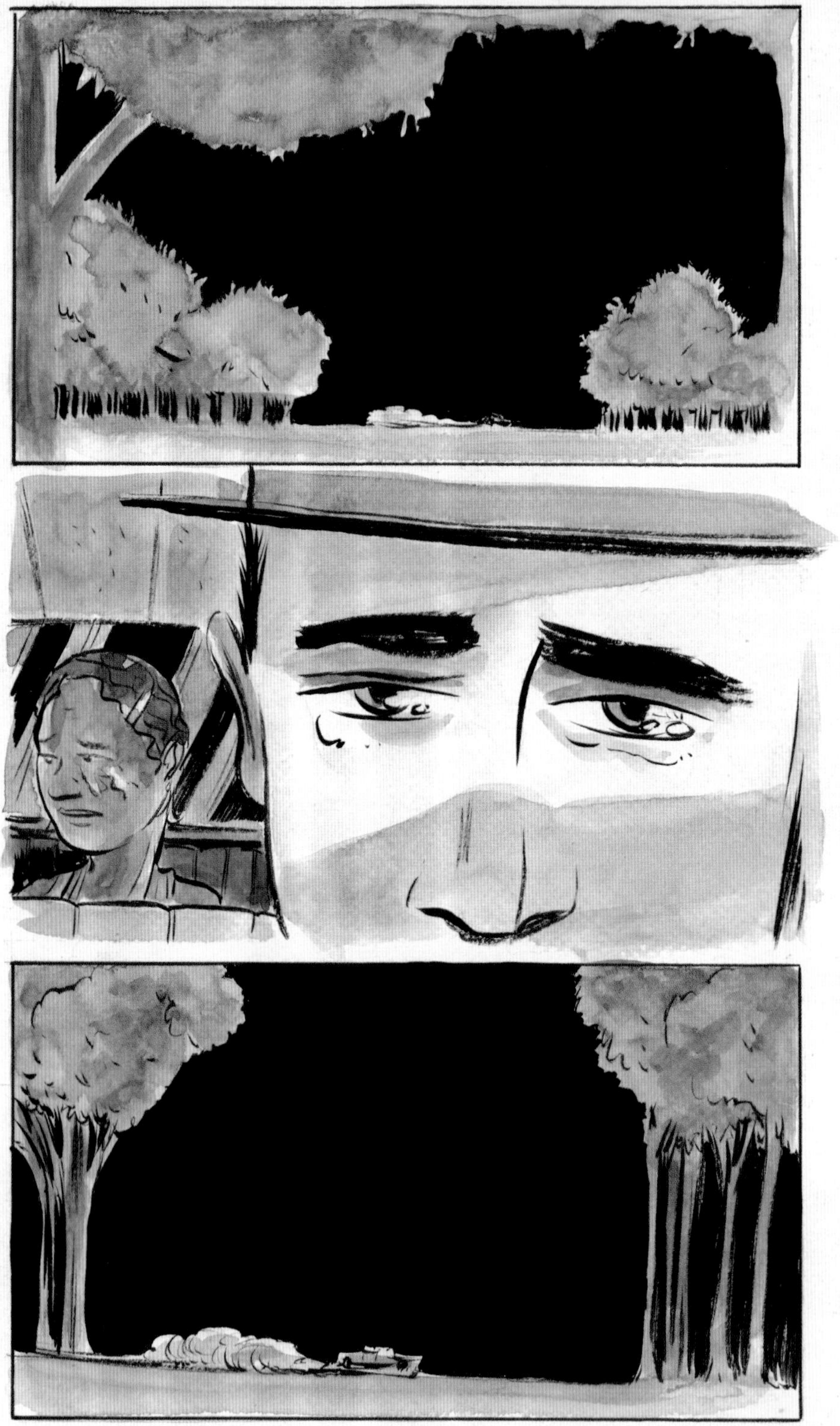

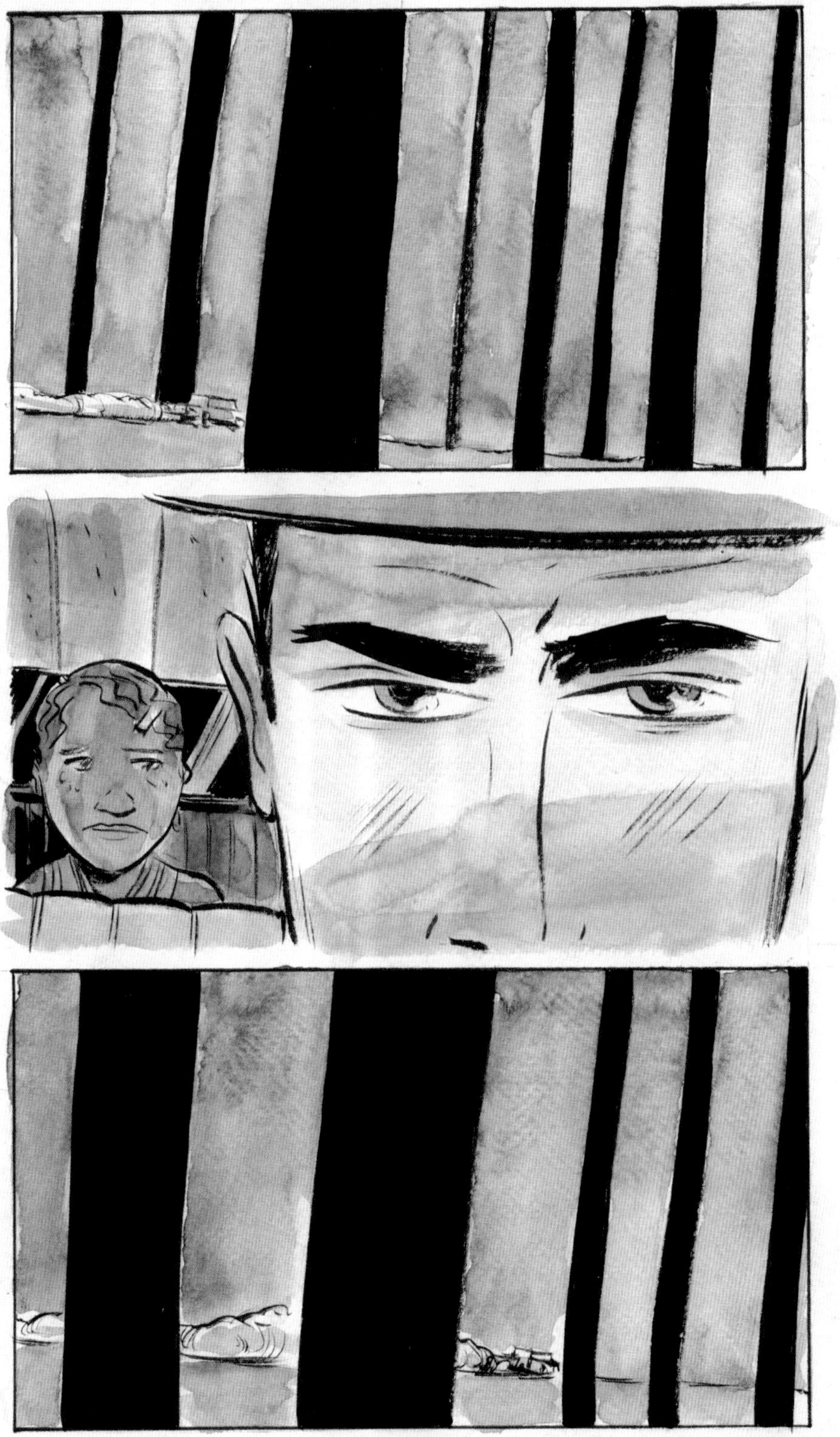

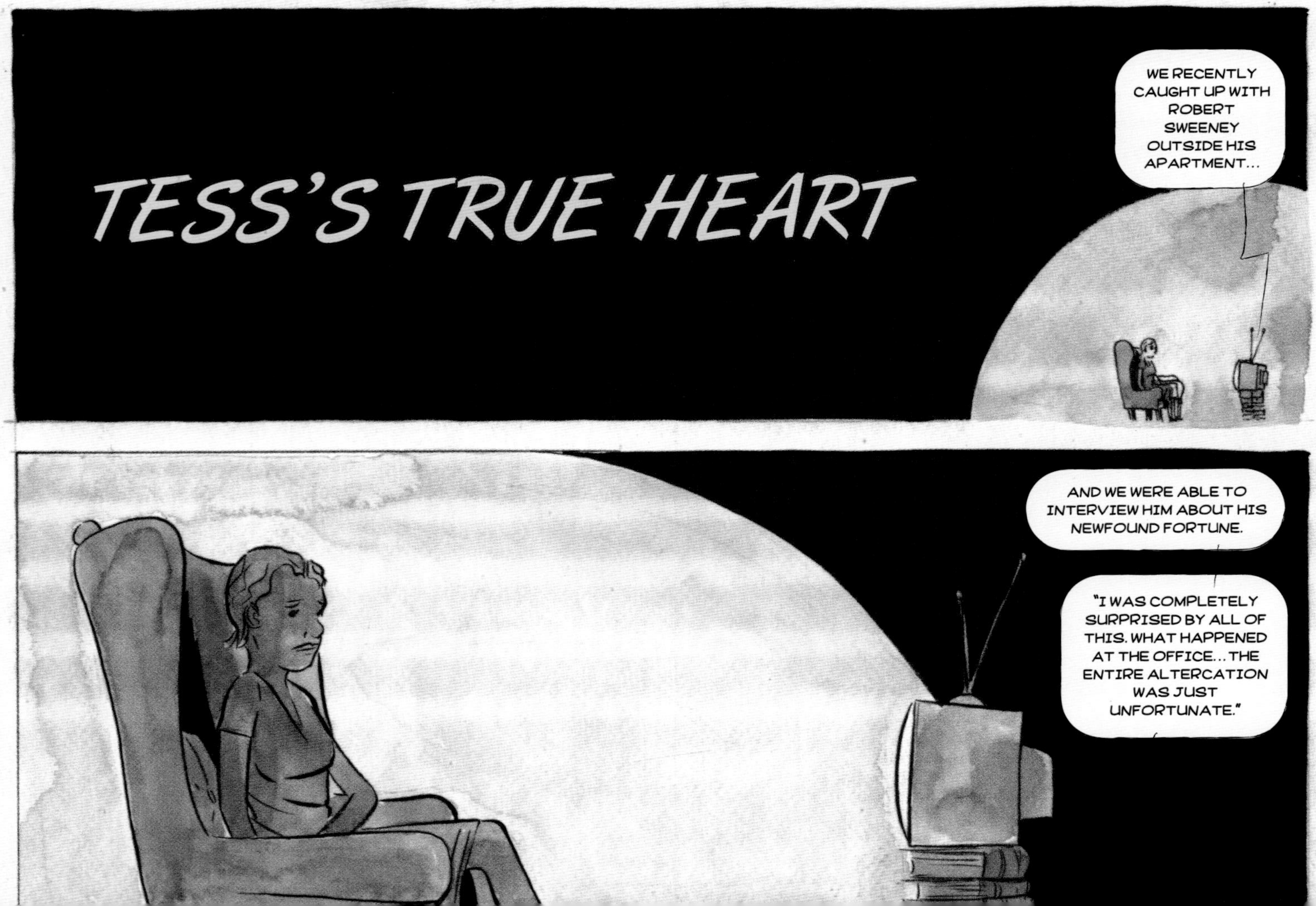
TESS'S TRUE HEART
WE RECENTLY CAUGHT UP WITH ROBERT SWEENEY OUTSIDE HIS APARTMENT...
AND WE WERE ABLE TO INTERVIEW HIM ABOUT HIS NEWFOUND FORTUNE.
"I WAS COMPLETELY SURPRISED BY ALL OF THIS. WHAT HAPPENED AT THE OFFICE... THE ENTIRE ALTERCATION WAS JUST UNFORTUNATE."

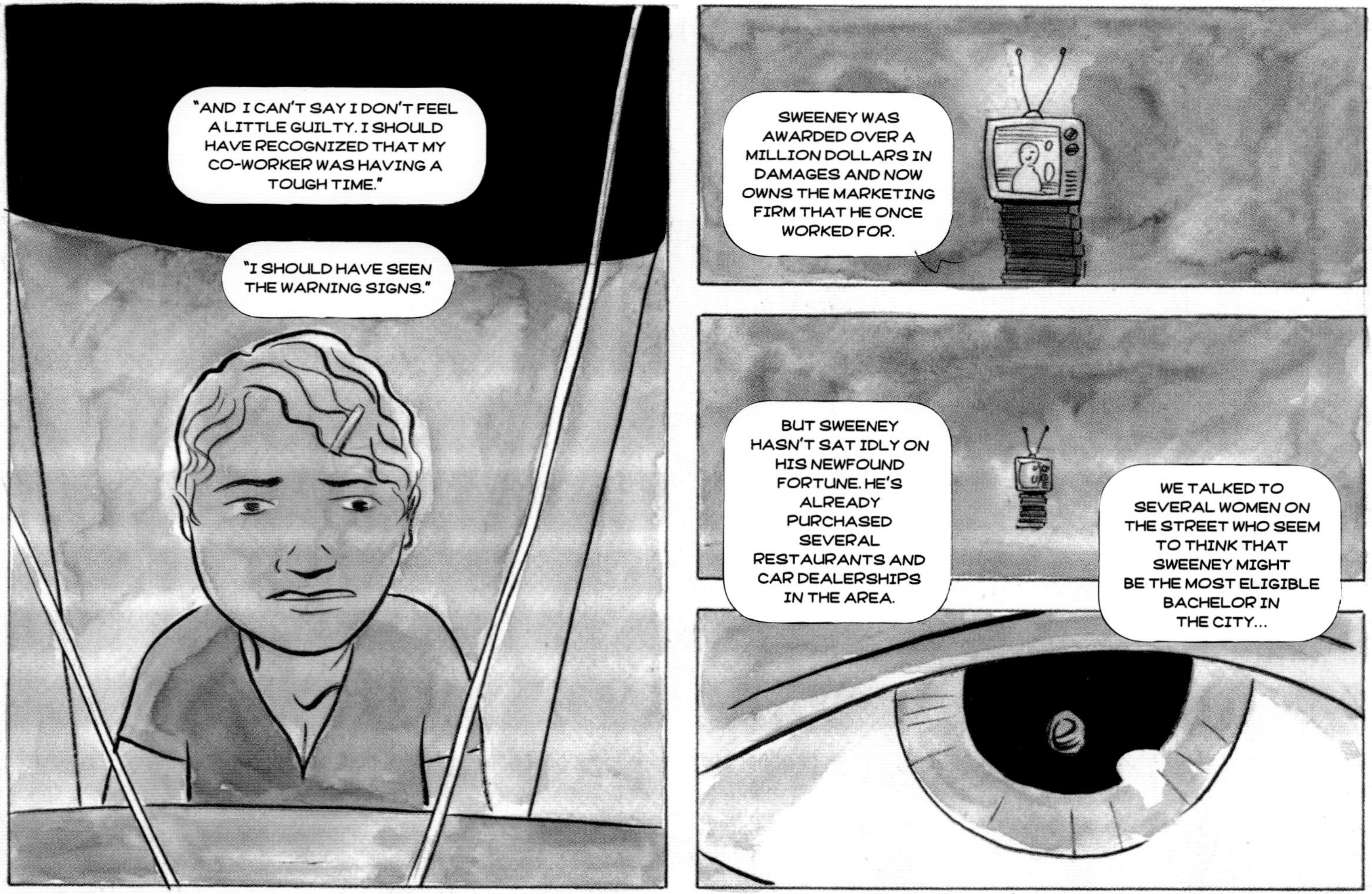
"AND I CAN'T SAY I DON'T FEEL A LITTLE GUILTY. I SHOULD HAVE RECOGNIZED THAT MY CO-WORKER WAS HAVING A TOUGH TIME."
"I SHOULD HAVE SEEN THE WARNING SIGNS."
SWEENEY WAS AWARDED OVER A MILLION DOLLARS IN DAMAGES AND NOW OWNS THE MARKETING FIRM THAT HE ONCE WORKED FOR.
BUT SWEENEY HASN'T SAT IDLY ON HIS NEWFOUND FORTUNE. HE'S ALREADY PURCHASED SEVERAL RESTAURANTS AND CAR DEALERSHIPS IN THE AREA.
WE TALKED TO SEVERAL WOMEN ON THE STREET WHO SEEM TO THINK THAT SWEENEY MIGHT BE THE MOST ELIGIBLE BACHELOR IN THE CITY...

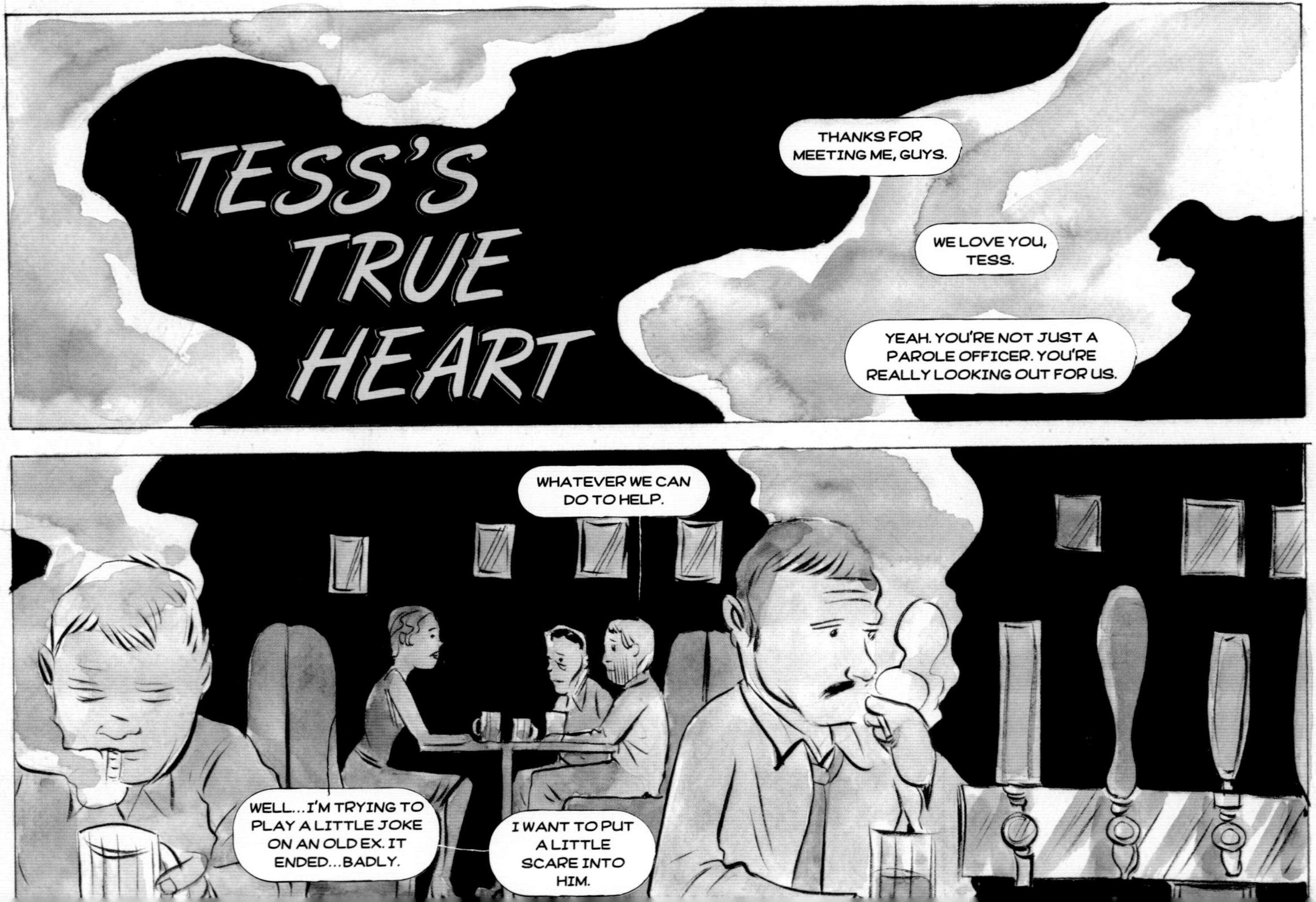
TESS'S TRUE HEART
THANKS FOR MEETING ME, GUYS.
WE LOVE YOU, TESS.
YEAH. YOU'RE NOT JUST A PAROLE OFFICER. YOU'RE REALLY LOOKING OUT FOR US.
WHATEVER WE CAN DO TO HELP.
WELL...I'M TRYING TO PLAY A LITTLE JOKE ON AN OLD EX. IT ENDED...BADLY.
I WANT TO PUT A LITTLE SCARE INTO HIM.

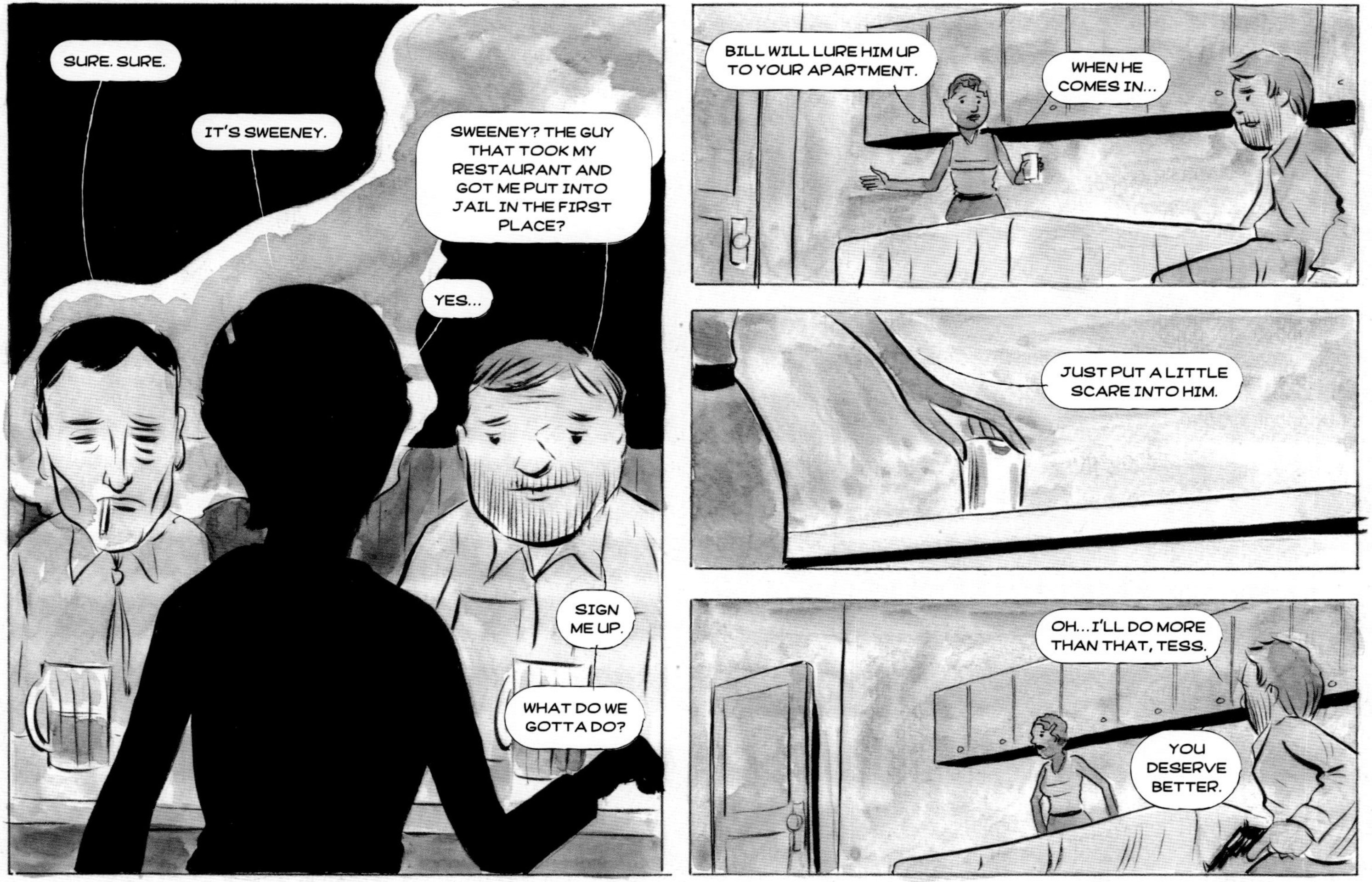
SURE. SURE.
IT'S SWEENEY.
SWEENEY? THE GUY THAT TOOK MY RESTAURANT AND GOT ME PUT INTO JAIL IN THE FIRST PLACE?
YES...
SIGN ME UP.
WHAT DO WE GOTTA DO?
BILL WILL LURE HIM UP TO YOUR APARTMENT.
WHEN HE COMES IN...
JUST PUT A LITTLE SCARE INTO HIM.
OH...I'LL DO MORE THAN THAT, TESS.
YOU DESERVE BETTER.

TESS'S TRUE HEART

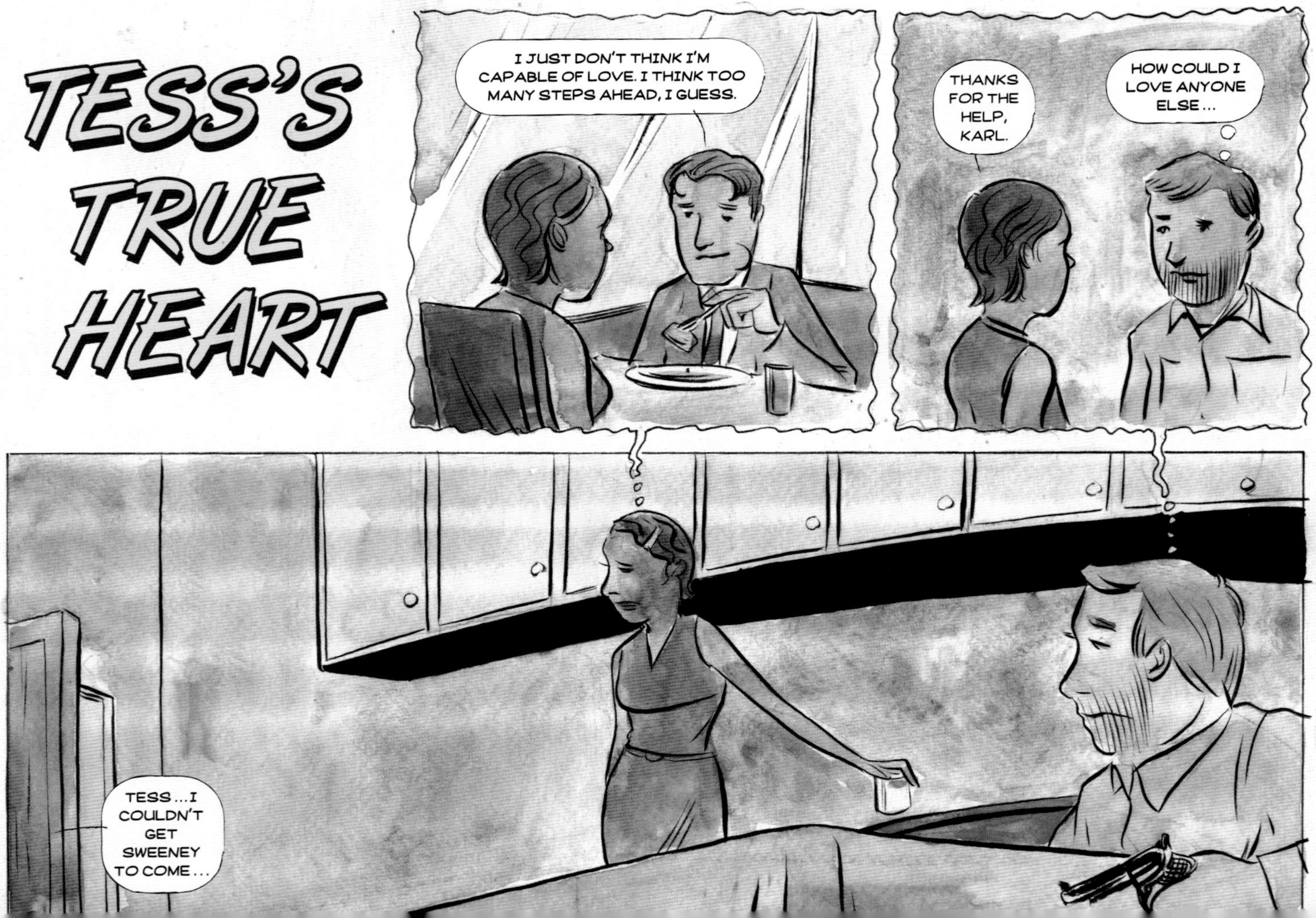
I JUST DON'T THINK I'M CAPABLE OF LOVE. I THINK TOO MANY STEPS AHEAD, I GUESS.
THANKS FOR THE HELP, KARL.
HOW COULD I LOVE ANYONE ELSE...
TESS...I COULDN'T GET SWEENEY TO COME...

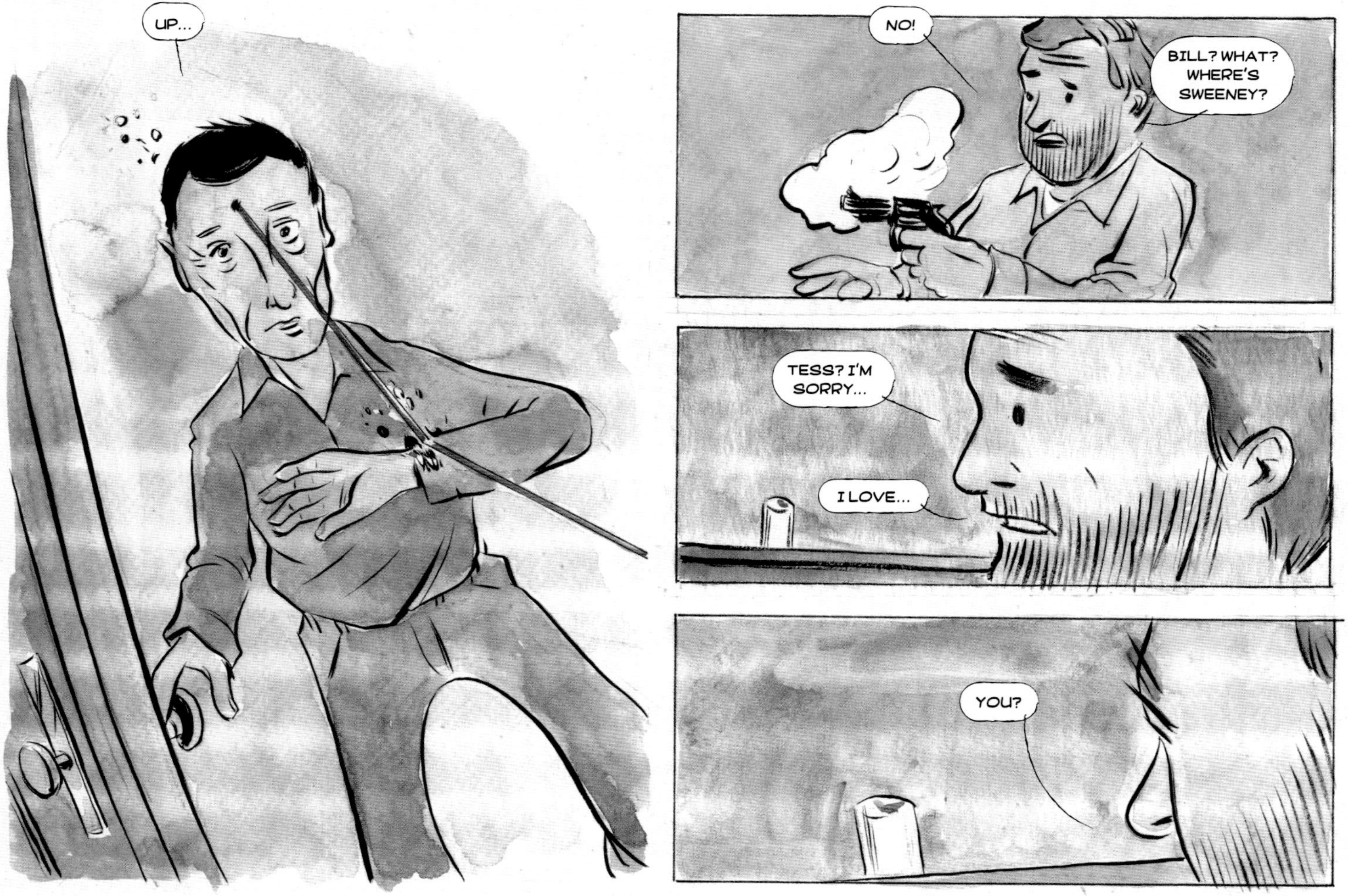
UP...
NO!
BILL? WHAT? WHERE'S SWEENEY?
TESS? I'M SORRY...
I LOVE...
YOU?

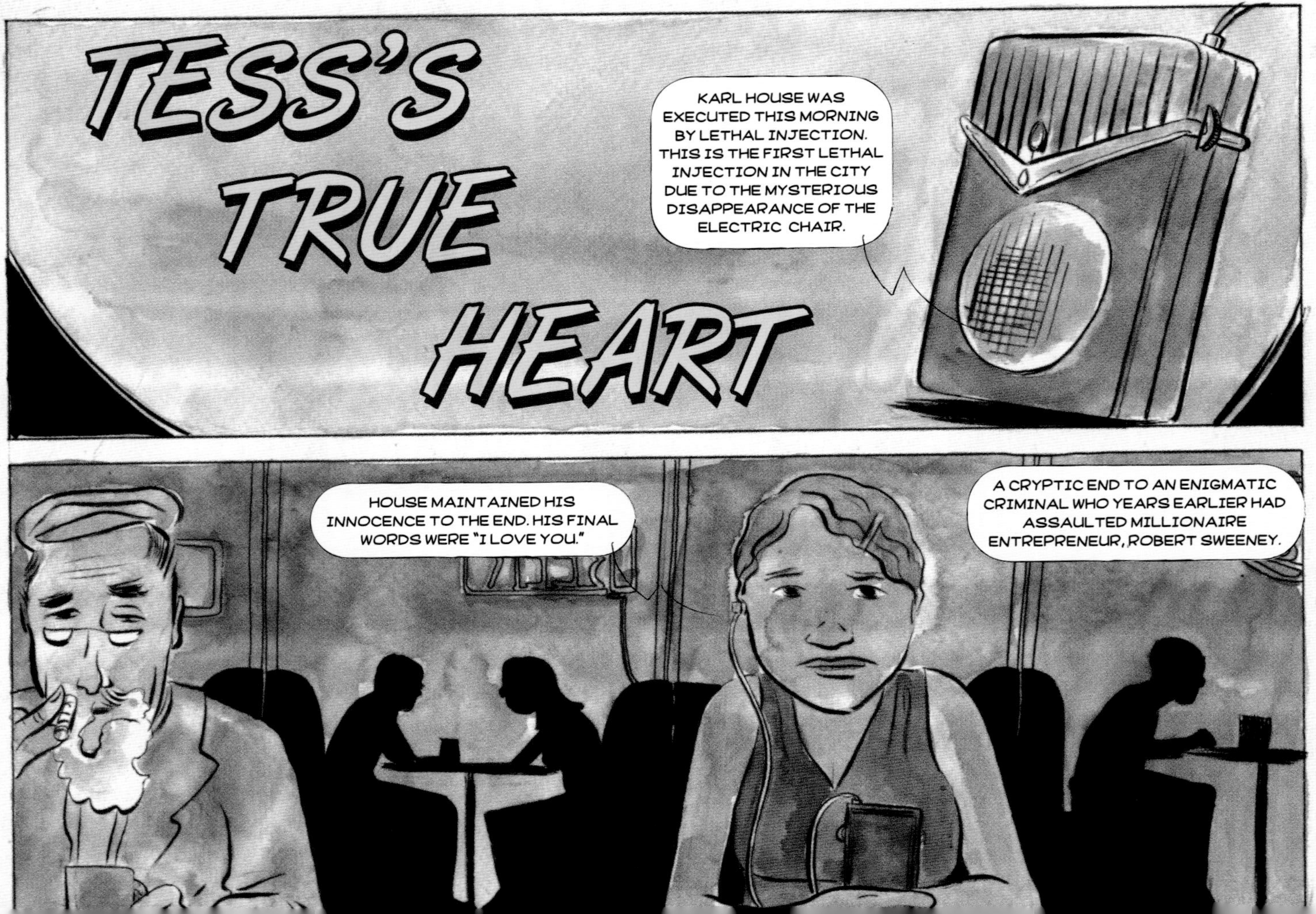
TESS'S TRUE HEART
KARL HOUSE WAS EXECUTED THIS MORNING BY LETHAL INJECTION. THIS IS THE FIRST LETHAL INJECTION IN THE CITY DUE TO THE MYSTERIOUS DISAPPEARANCE OF THE ELECTRIC CHAIR.
HOUSE MAINTAINED HIS INNOCENCE TO THE END. HIS FINAL WORDS WERE "I LOVE YOU."
A CRYPTIC END TO AN ENIGMATIC CRIMINAL WHO YEARS EARLIER HAD ASSAULTED MILLIONAIRE ENTREPRENEUR, ROBERT SWEENEY.

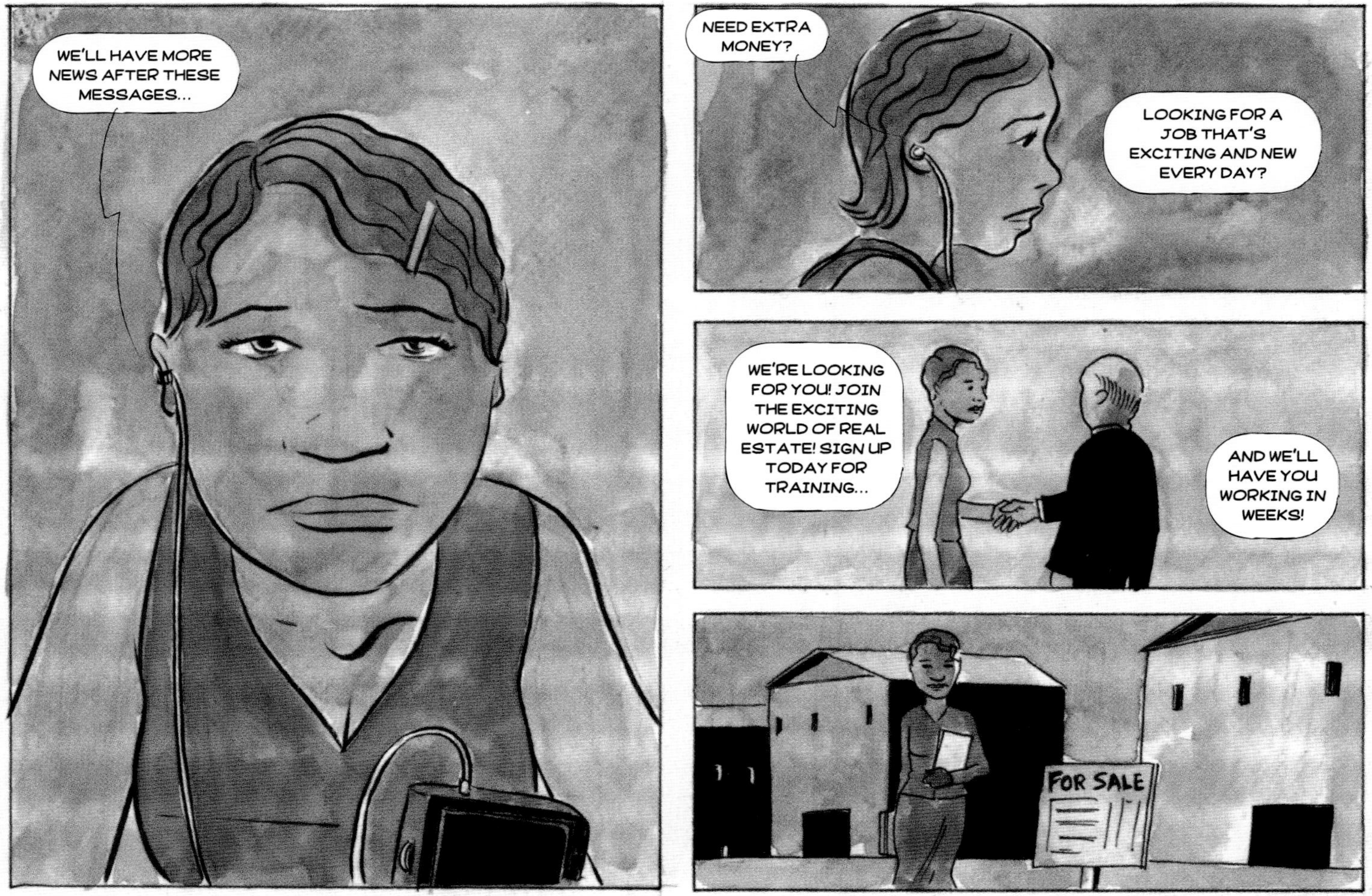
WE'LL HAVE MORE NEWS AFTER THESE MESSAGES...
NEED EXTRA MONEY?
LOOKING FOR A JOB THAT'S EXCITING AND NEW EVERY DAY?
WE'RE LOOKING FOR YOU! JOIN THE EXCITING WORLD OF REAL ESTATE! SIGN UP TODAY FOR TRAINING...
AND WE'LL HAVE YOU WORKING IN WEEKS!
FOR SALE

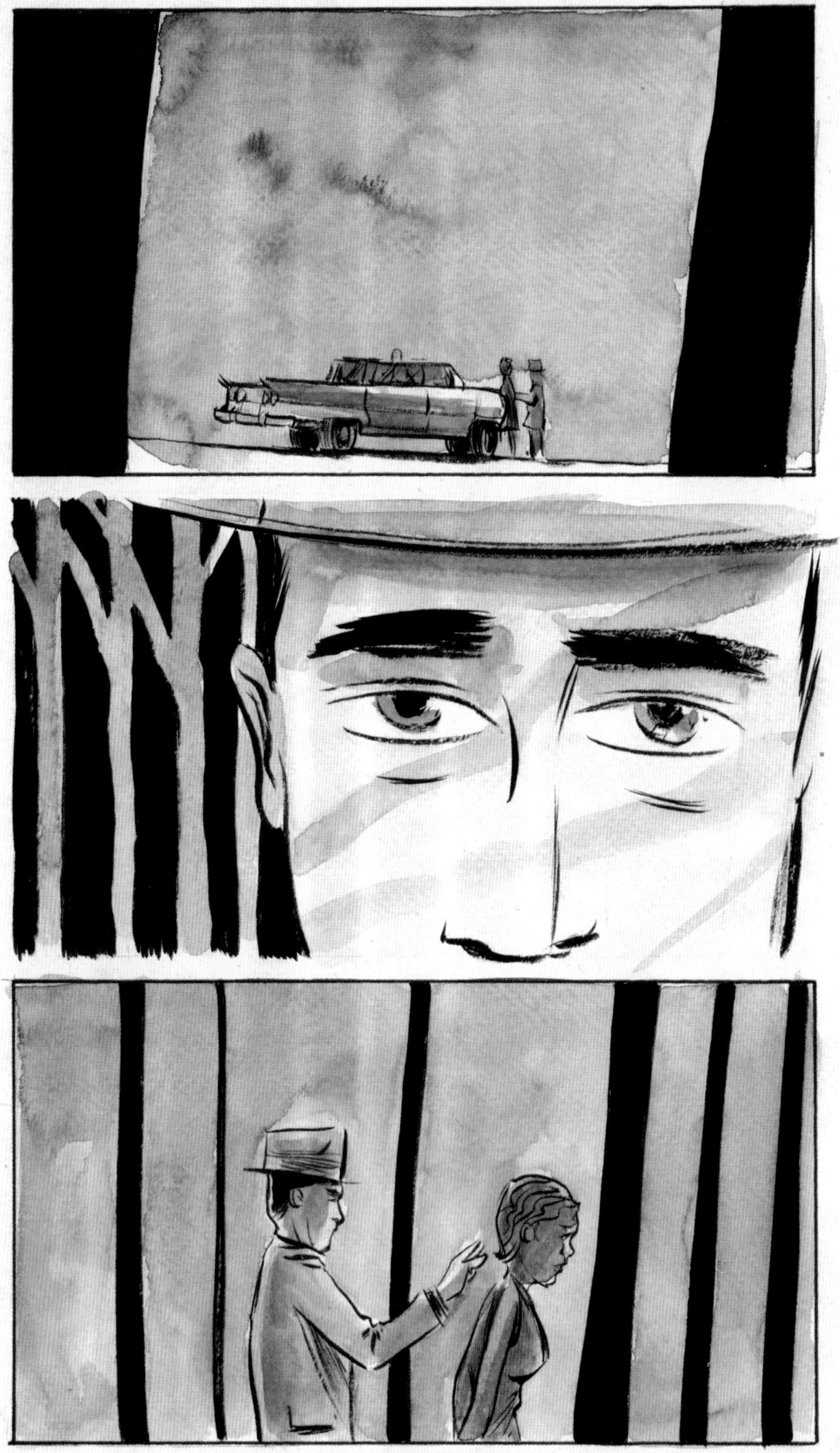

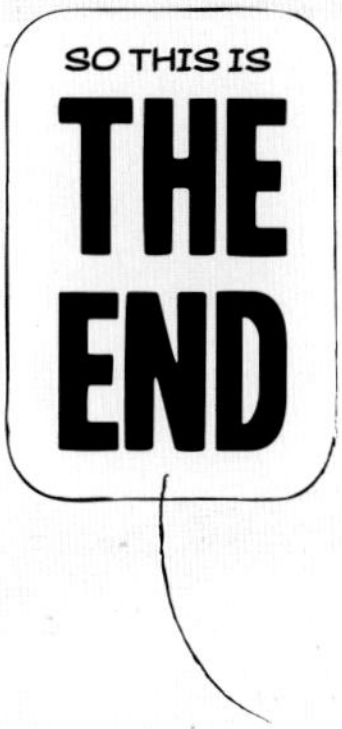
SO THIS IS
THE END

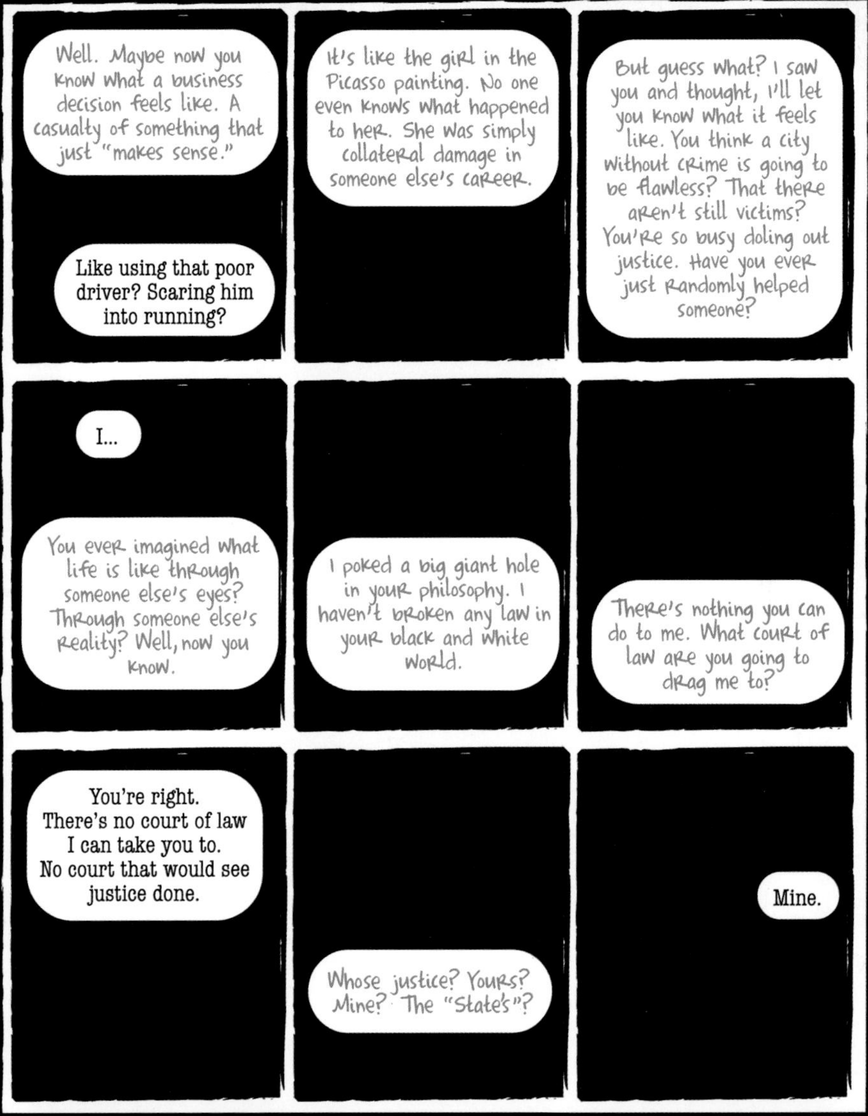
Well. Maybe now you know what a business decision feels like. A casualty of something that just "makes sense."
Like using that poor driver? Scaring him into running?
It's like the girl in the Picasso painting. No one even knows what happened to her. She was simply collateral damage in someone else's career.
But guess what? I saw you and thought, I'll let you know what it feels like. You think a city without crime is going to be flawless? That there aren't still victims? You're so busy doling out justice. Have you ever just randomly helped someone?
I...
You ever imagined what life is like through someone else's eyes? Through someone else's reality? Well, now you know.
I poked a big giant hole in your philosophy. I haven't broken any law in your black and white world.
There's nothing you can do to me. What court of law are you going to drag me to?
You're right. There's no court of law I can take you to. No court that would see justice done.
Whose justice? Yours? Mine? The "State's"?
Mine.
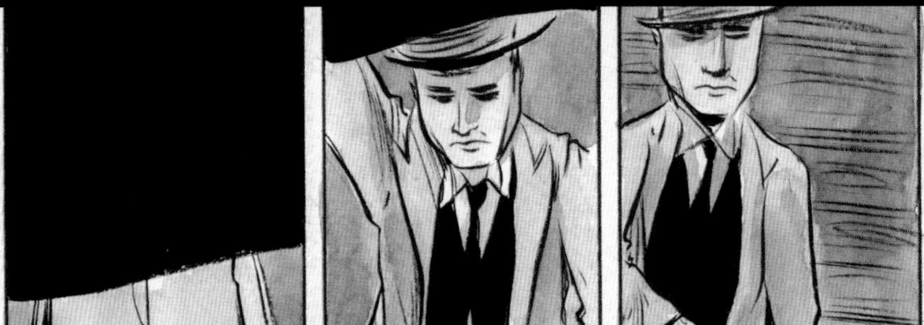

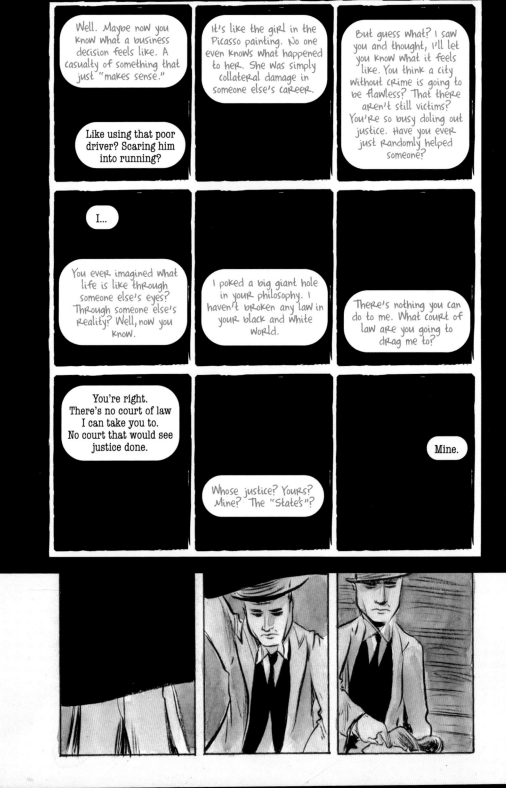

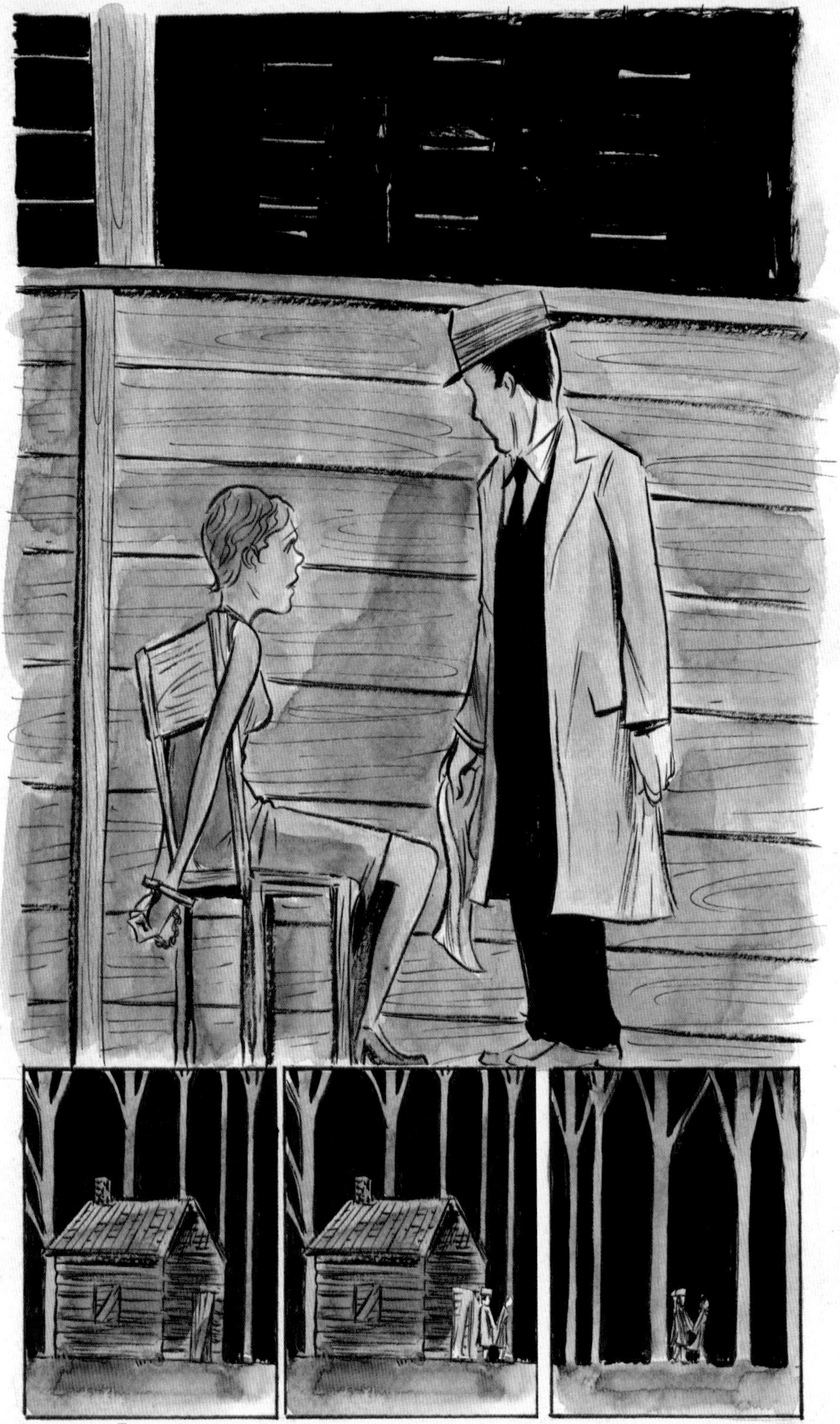

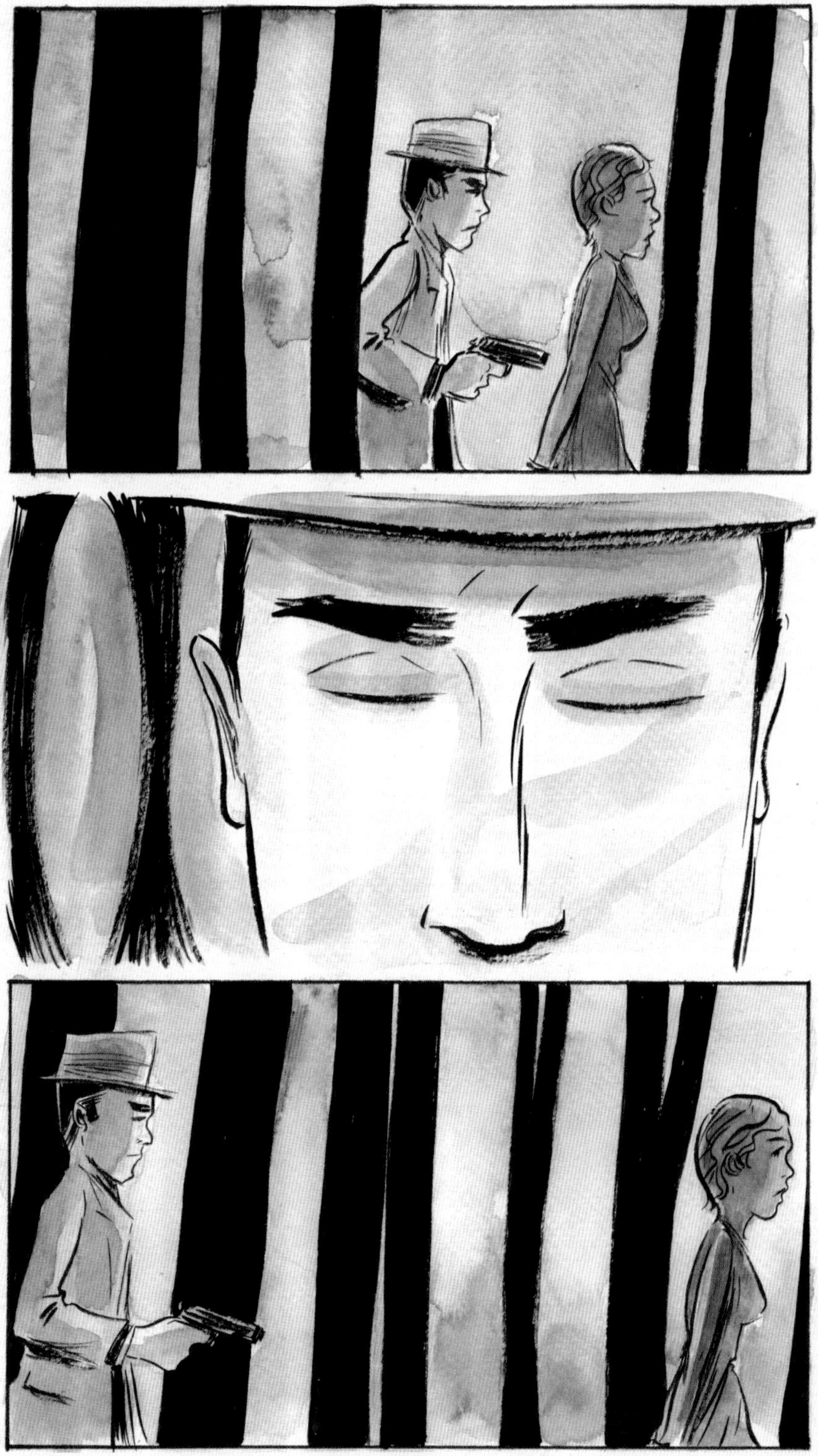

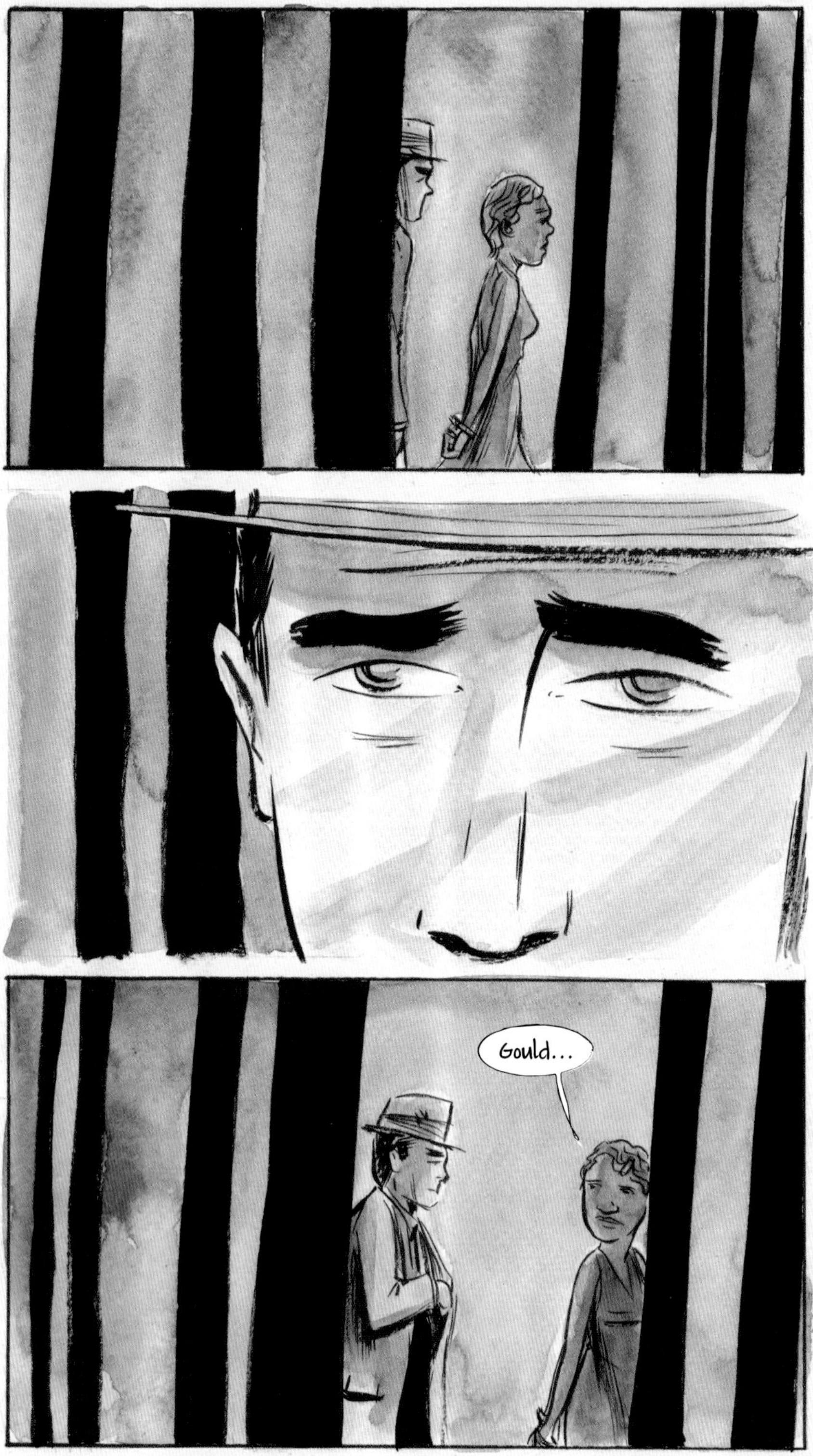
Gould...

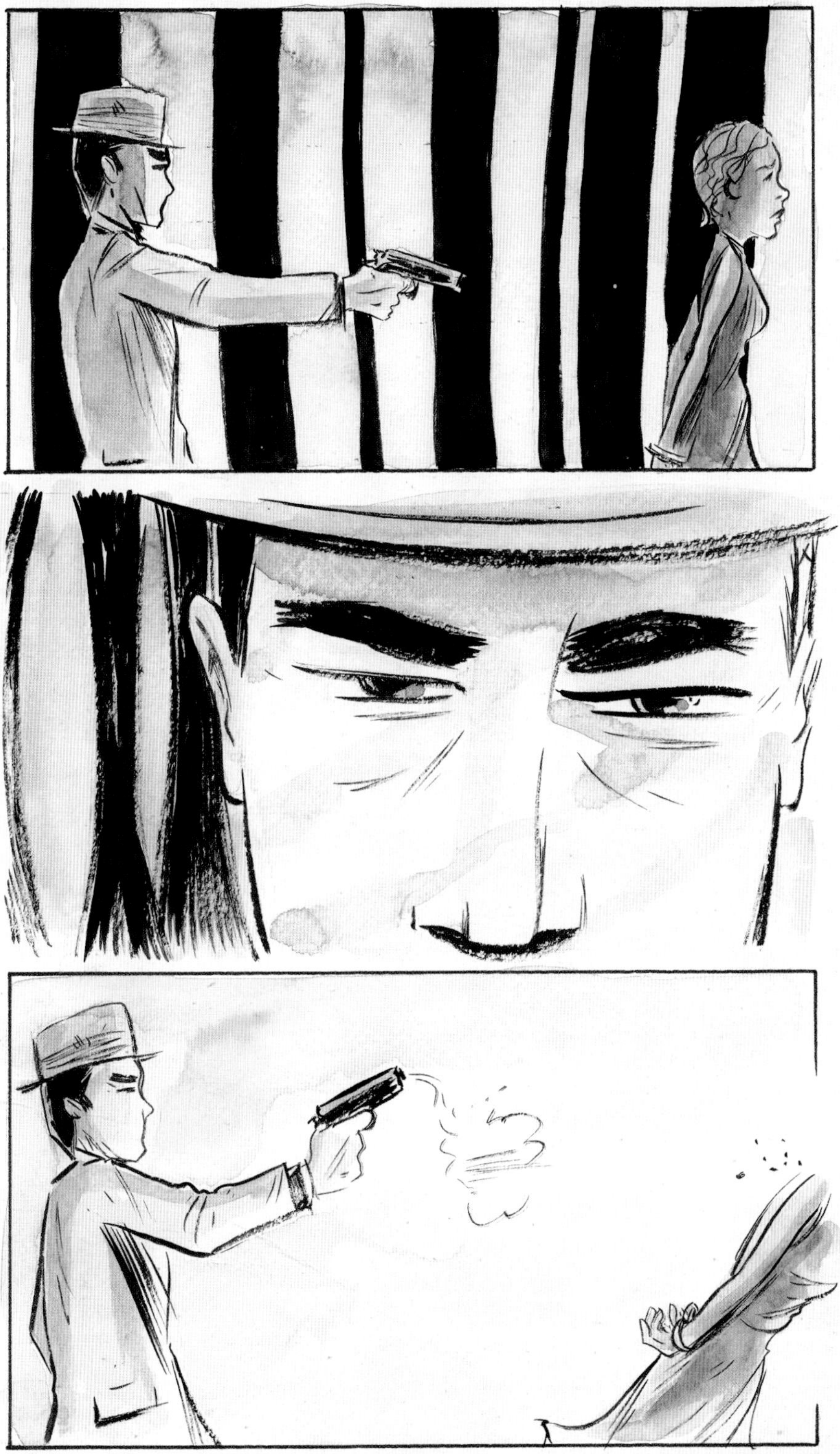

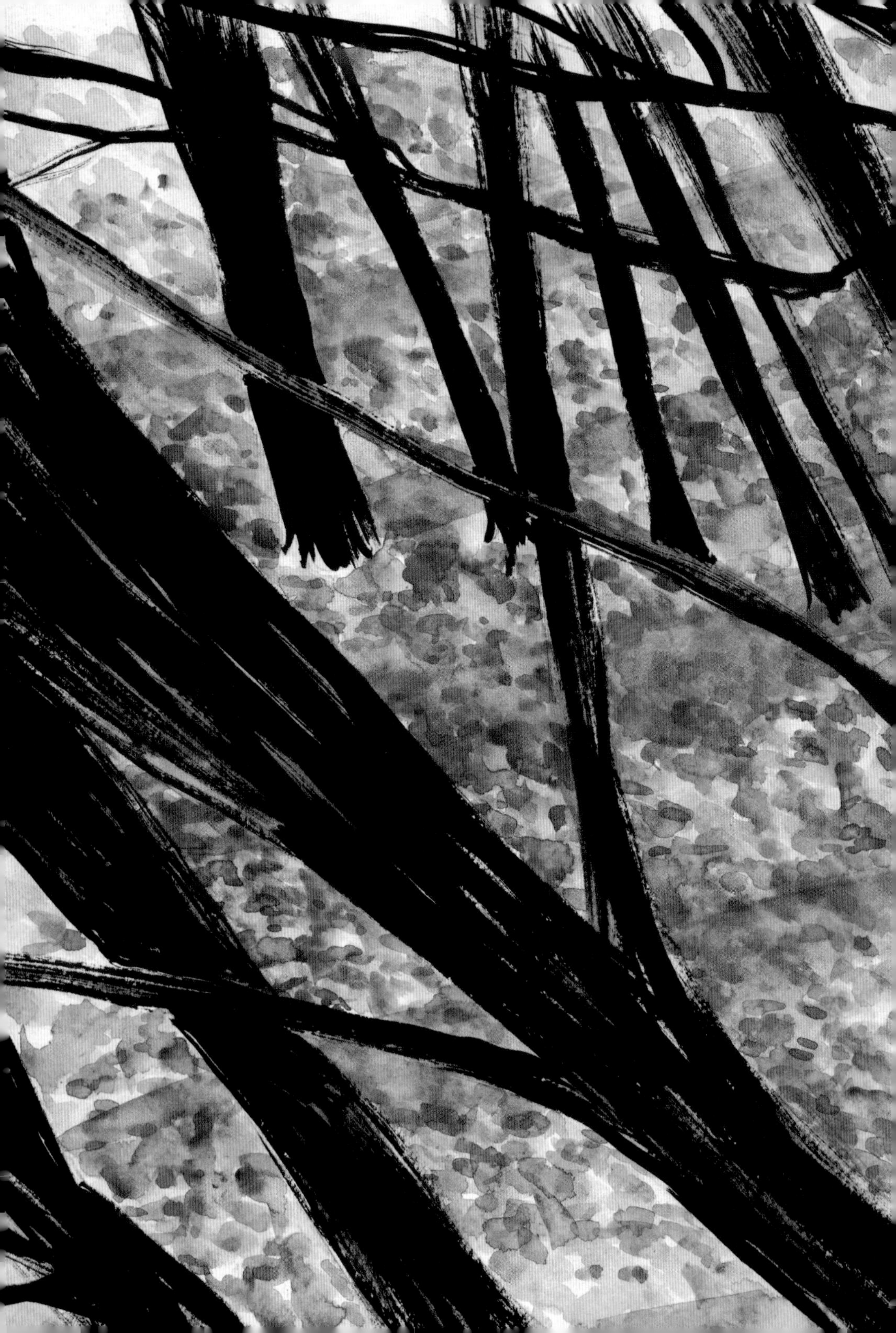

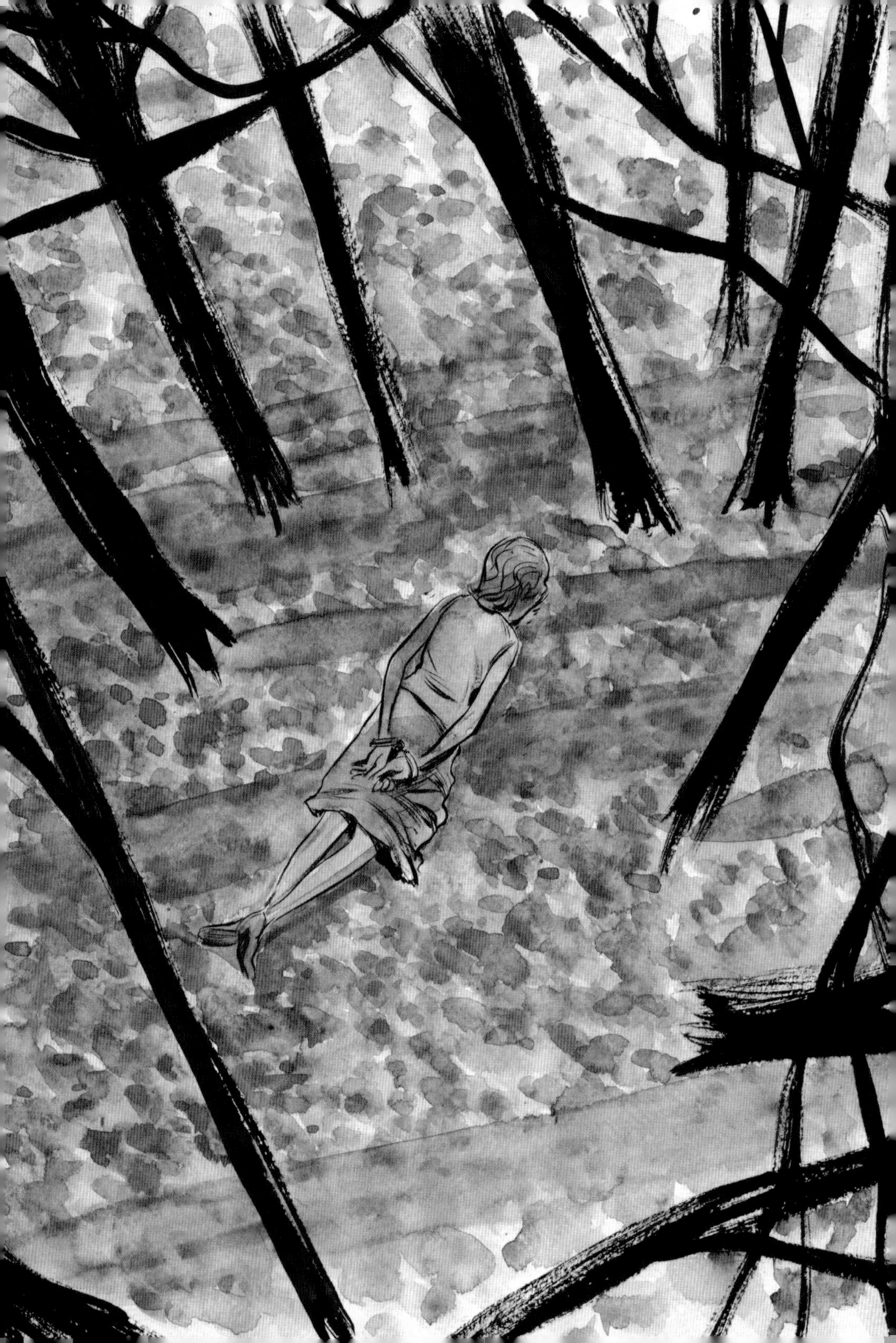

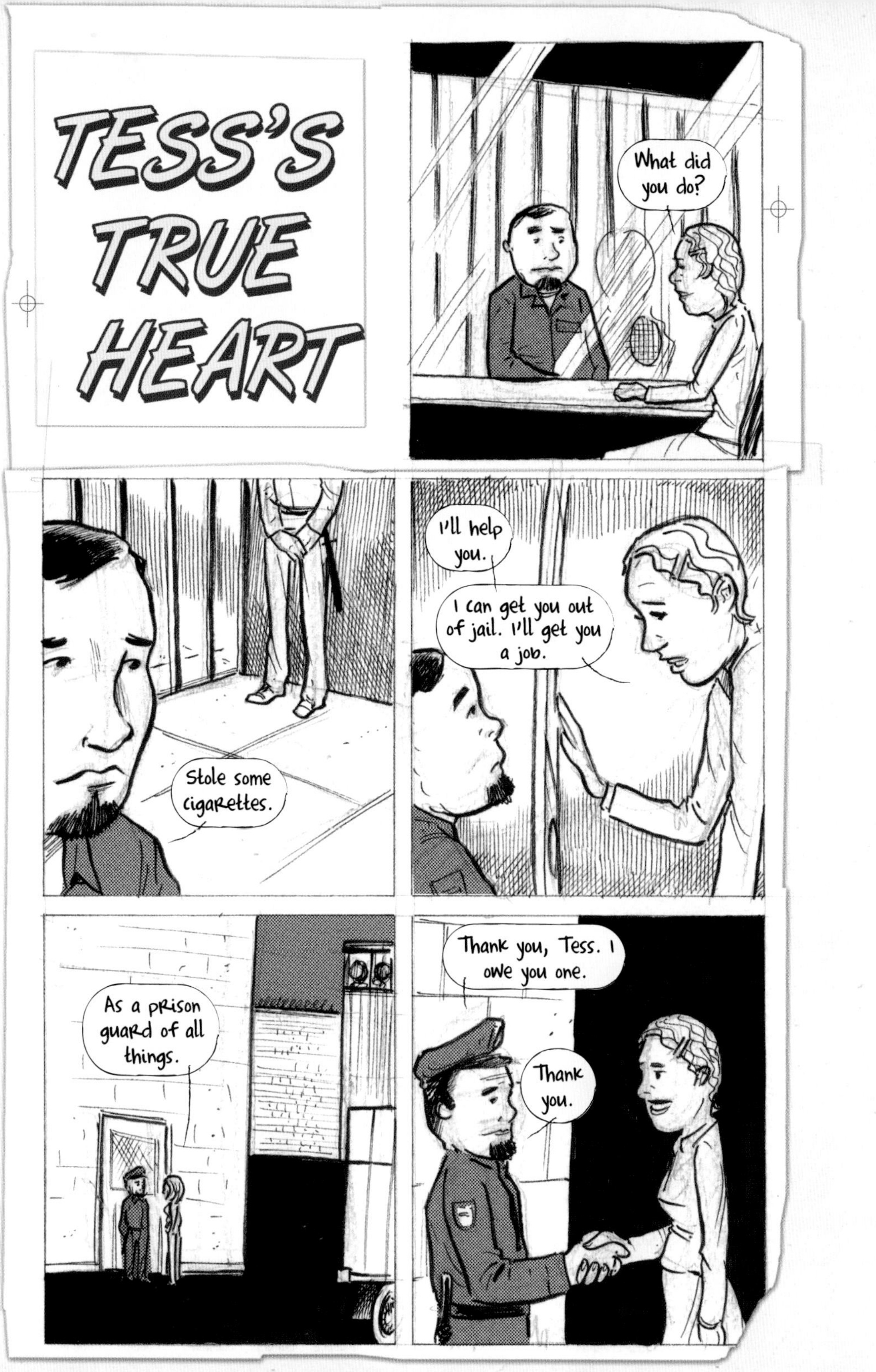
TESS'S TRUE HEART
What did you do?
Stole some cigarettes.
I'll help you.
I can get you out of jail. I'll get you a job.
As a prison guard of all things.
Thank you, Tess. I owe you one.
Thank you.

GAZETTE

FIRST UNSOLVED MURDER IN 10 YEARS

the body of local real estate agent Tess Riley was found in the woods outside the city earlier in the week. The woman was found shot in the back. No suspects have yet been named but police are hopeful that they will find the suspect soon. This murder comes on the heels of the surprise resignation of Detective Gould from the force. Gould could not be reached for comment and has virtually disappeared after the death of his wife in a traffic accident earlier in the week. Many are fearful that Gould's resignation could lead to an increase in crime but it will certainly lead to an increase in unsolved cases. However the Police Chief...

(continued B2)

STAR DETECTIVE'S WIFE KILLED

Detective Gould's wife was struck and killed by a speeding car outside of her newly opened art gallery earlier in the week. The tragic accident happened in front of a crowd of hundreds. According to eyewitness reports, a scuffle involving millionaire Robert Sweeney had brought a large crowd out into the street. The sedan that struck Mrs. Gould was estimated to be going over 60 miles an hour when it struck the victim. She was pronounced dead on the scene. Other reports are saying that . . .

(continued)

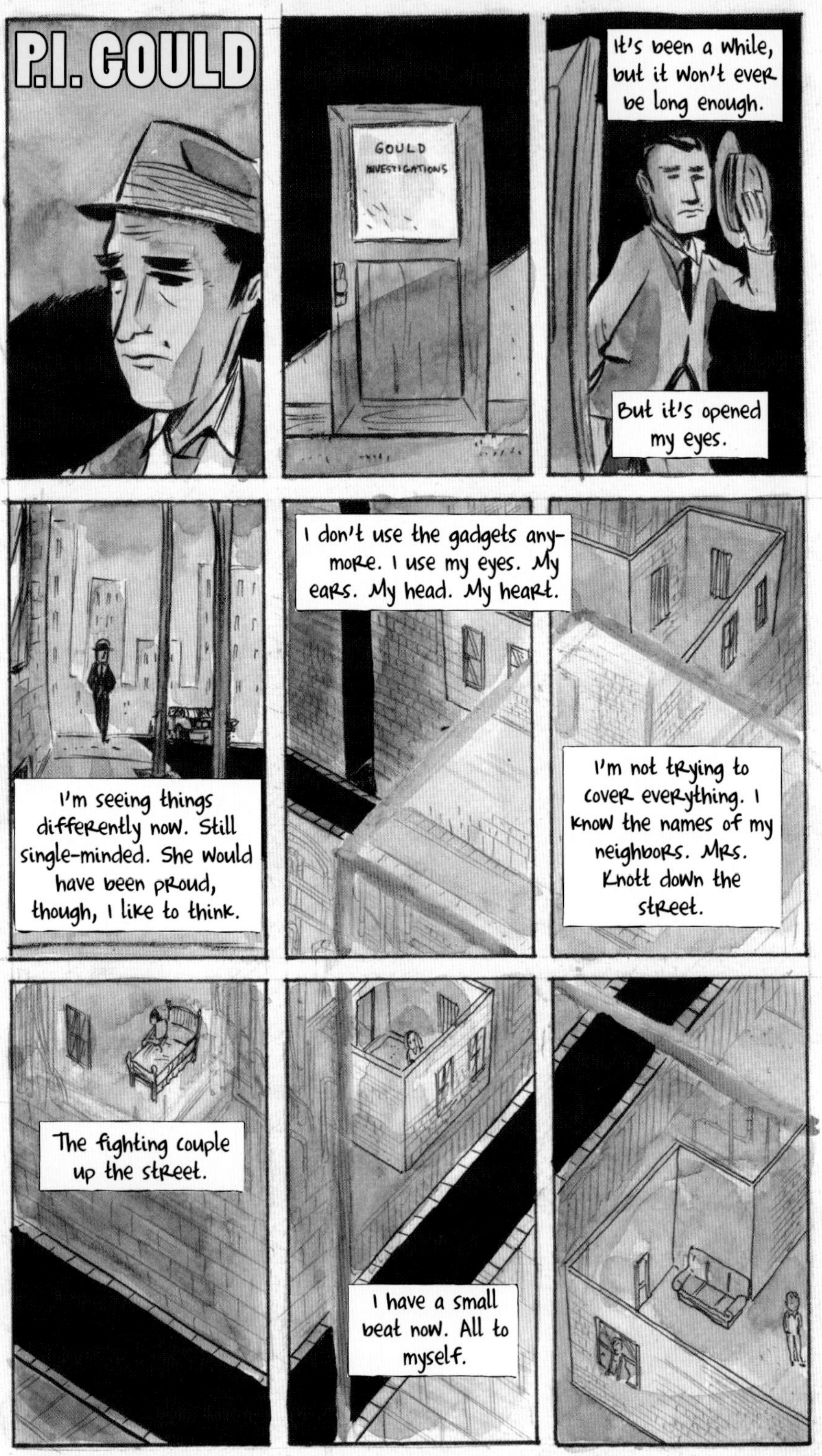
P.I. GOULD
GOULD INVESTIGATIONS
It's been a while, but it won't ever be long enough.
But it's opened my eyes.
I'm seeing things differently now. Still single-minded. She would have been proud, though, I like to think.
I don't use the gadgets anymore. I use my eyes. My ears. My head. My heart.
I'm not trying to cover everything. I know the names of my neighbors. Mrs. Knott down the street.
The fighting couple up the street.
I have a small beat now. All to myself.

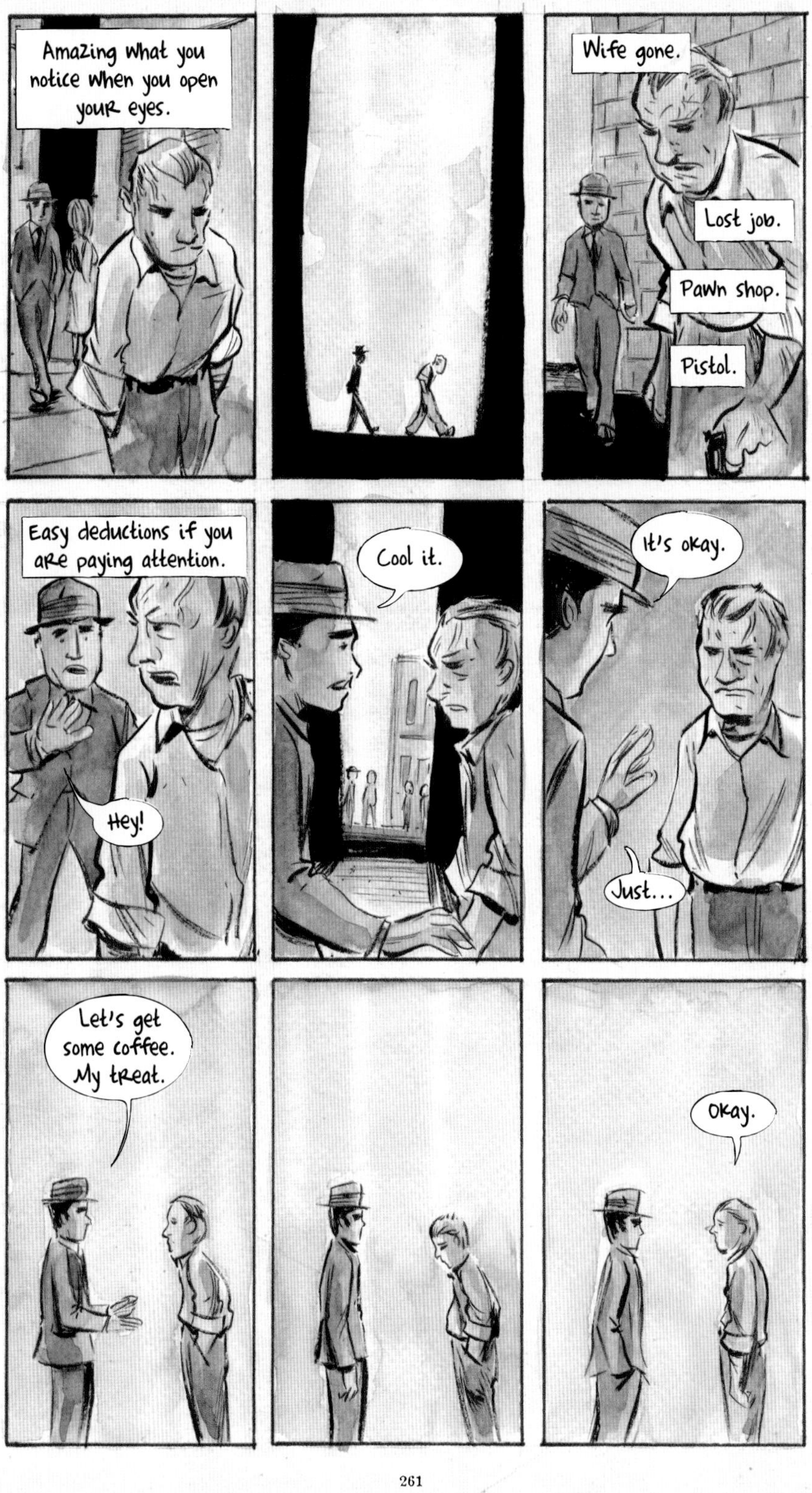
Amazing what you notice when you open your eyes.
Wife gone.
Lost job.
Pawn shop.
Pistol.
Easy deductions if you are paying attention.
Hey!
Cool it.
It's okay.
Just...
Let's get some coffee. My treat.
Okay.

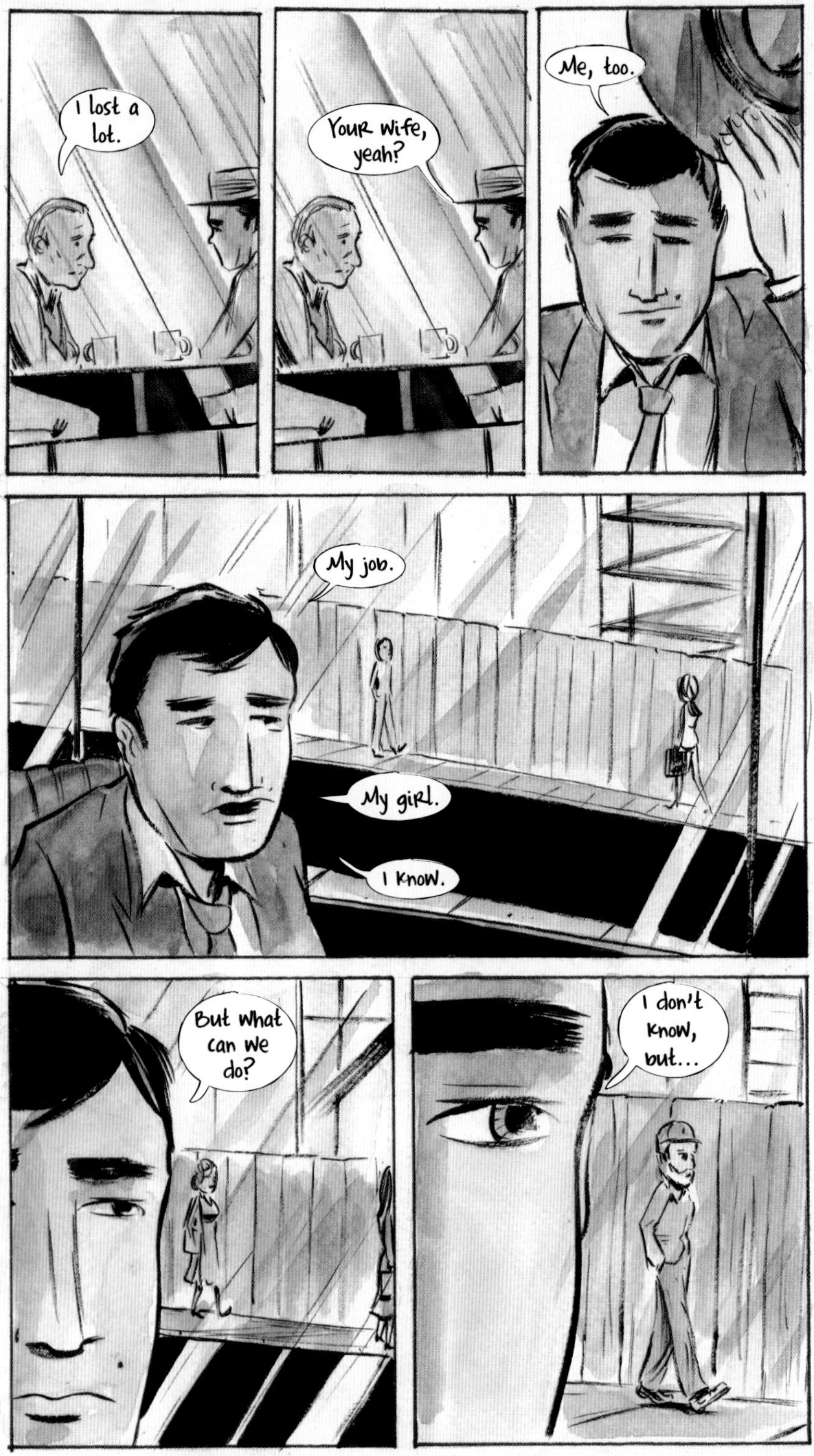
I lost a lot.
Your wife, yeah?
Me, too.
My job.
My girl.
I know.
But what can we do?
I don't know, but...

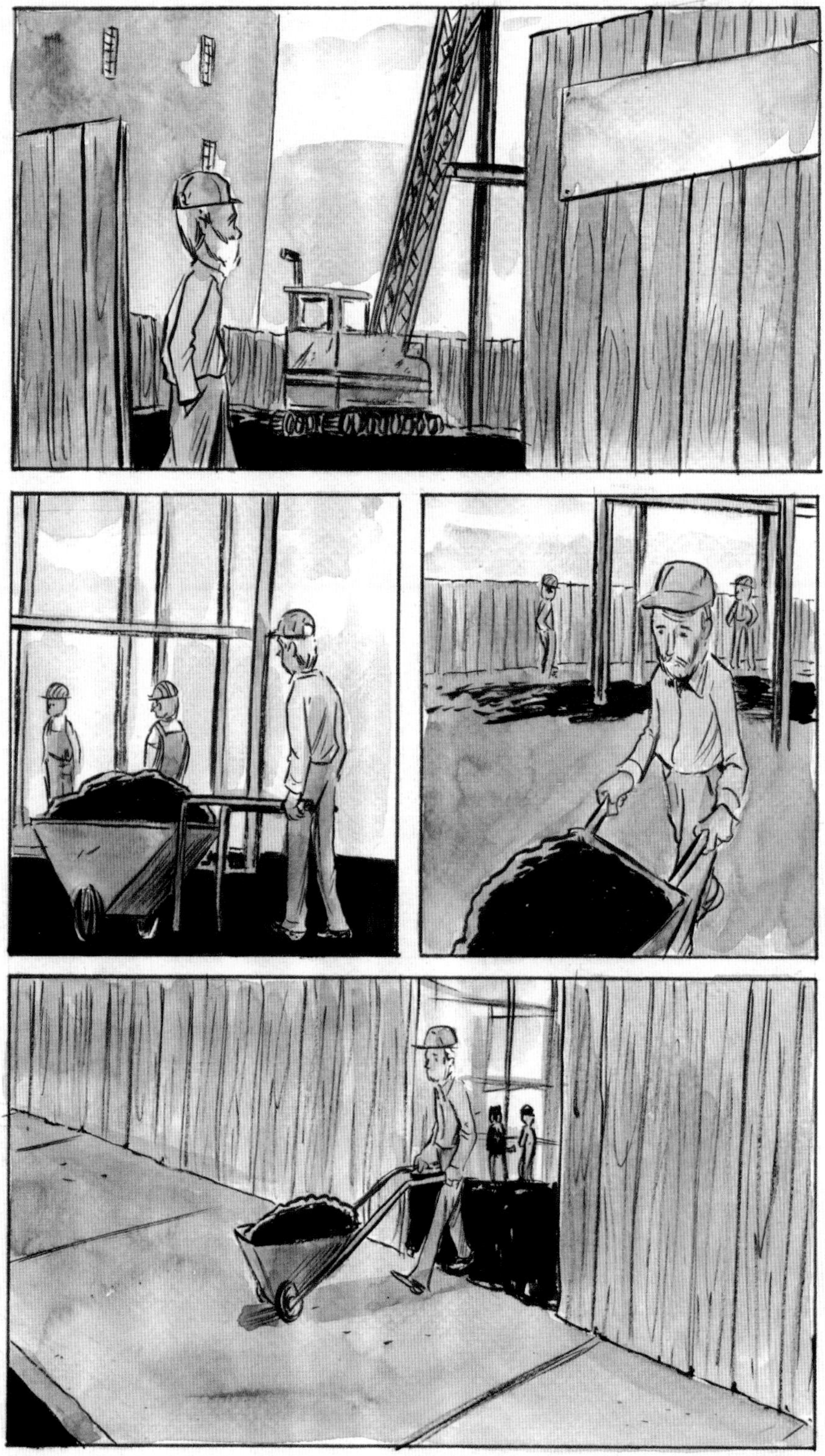

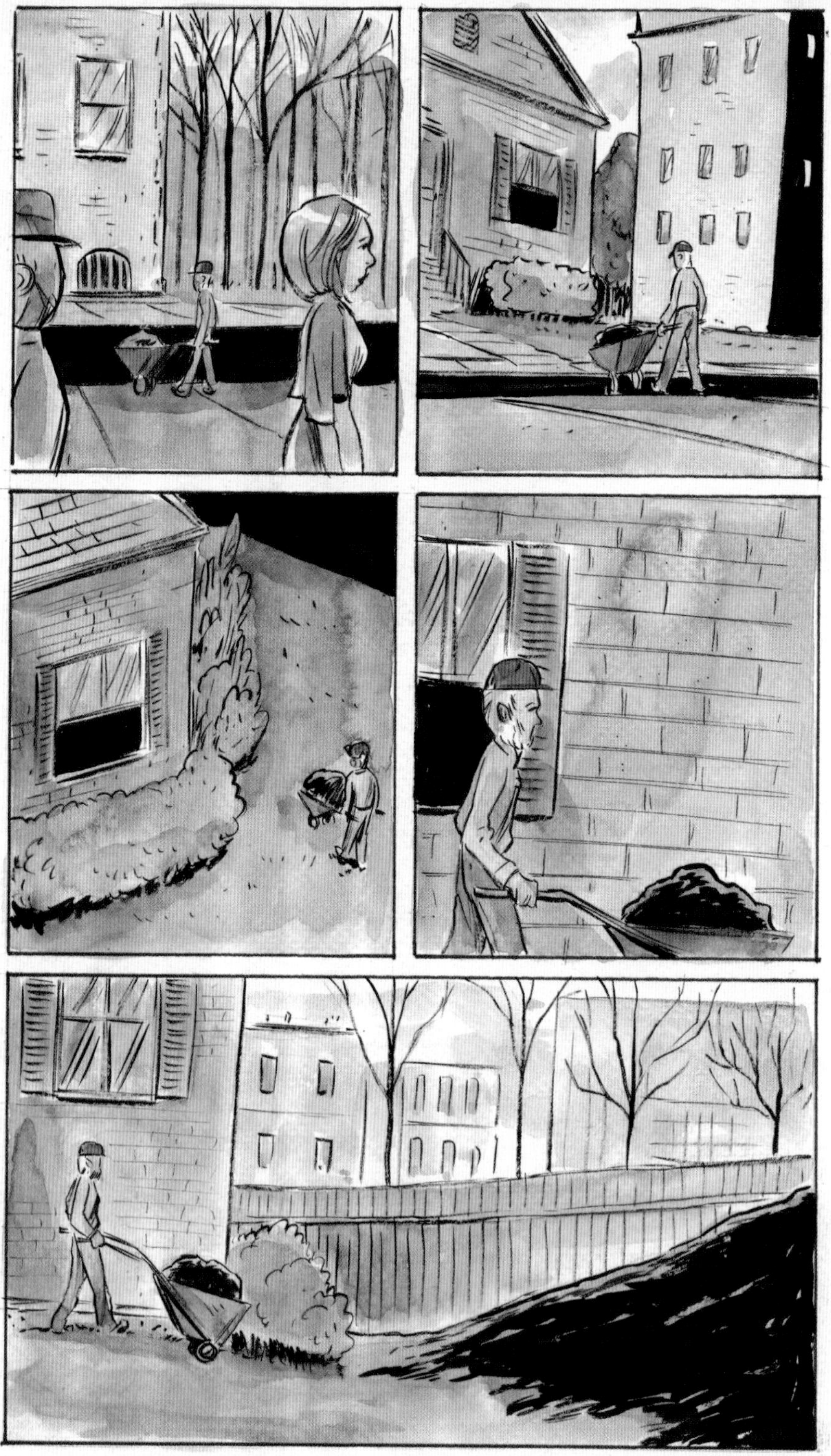

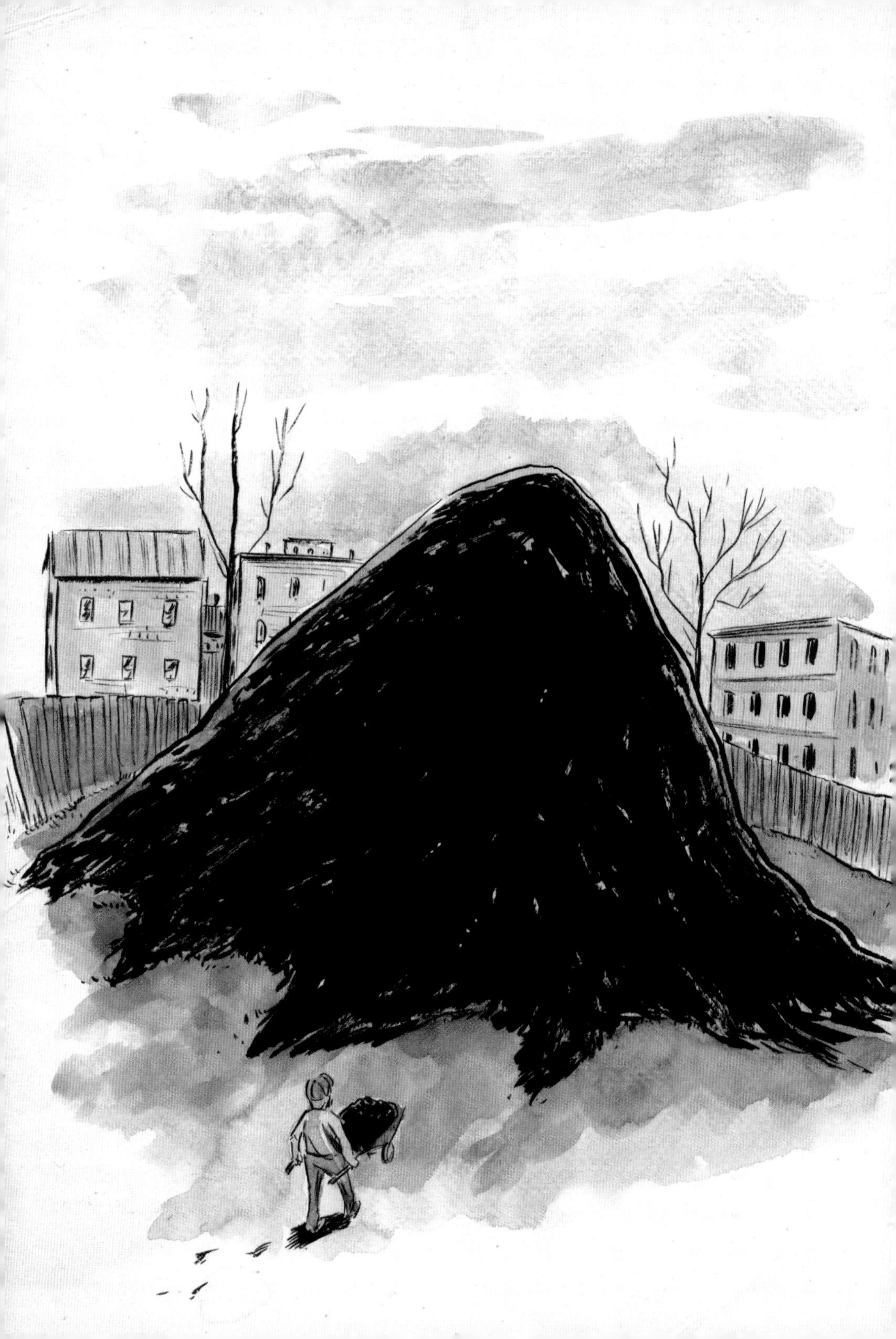

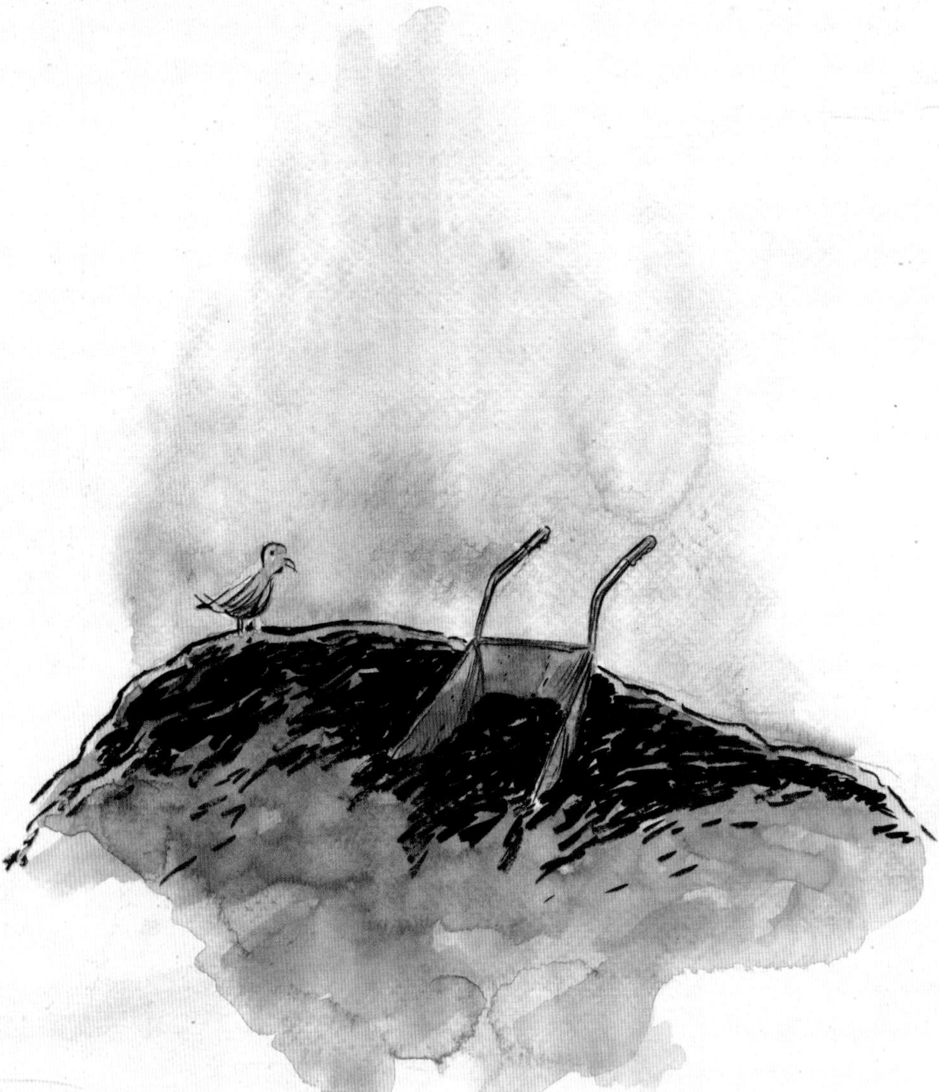

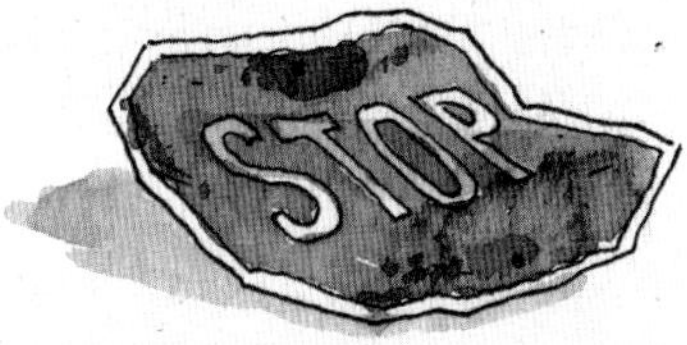
STOP

THANK YOU:

Sharlene Kindt (for listening to every idea I've ever had)
Ella Kindt (for painting all the skin color in this book)
Charlie Olsen (for making it happen)
Karl Kindt IV (for making it make sense)
David Cirillo (for telling me to add more words)
Brian Hurtt (for inking one mystery panel in this book)
Jeff Lemire (for saving me that one time)
My adopted parents, Dave & Gloria Vowels (for the cabin)
and my parents, Karl & Margie Kindt
(for buying me every book I ever wanted)

:01

First Second

Copyright © 2013 by Matt Kindt

Published by First Second
First Second is an imprint of Roaring Brook Press, a division of
Holtzbrinck Publishing Holdings Limited Partnership
175 Fifth Avenue, New York, New York 10010
All rights reserved

Cataloging-in-Publication Data is on file at the Library of Congress

978-1-59643-662-6

First Second books are available for special promotions and premiums.
For details, contact: Director of Special Markets, Holtzbrinck Publishers.

First edition 2013
Book design by Matt Kindt and Colleen AF Venable
Printed in China

10 9 8 7 6 5 4 3 2 1